THE SOLUTION

BCOM

Every 4LTR Press solution includes:

Heading Numbers Connect Print & eBook

Visually Engaging Textbook

Online Study Tools

Tear-out Review Cards

Interactive eBook

STUDENT RESOURCES:

- Interactive eBook
- Auto-Graded Quizzes
- Flashcards
- NEW Trackable Activities
- Games: Crossword & Puzzles
- PowerPoint® Slides
- Videos
- Audio Chapter Summaries
- Cases & Assignments
- Language Review
- Career Transitions
- KnowNOW! Blog
- Review Cards
- Style Cards

Students sign in at
www.cengagebrain.com

INSTRUCTOR RESOURCES:

- All Student Resources
- Engagement Tracker
- First Day of Class Instructions
- LMS Integration
- Instructor's Manual
- Test Bank
- PowerPoint® Slides
- Instructor Prep Cards

Instructors sign in at
www.cengage.com/login

"I really like this book. It is so easy to read and understand. Plus, the format makes it easy to quickly find what I am looking for."

— **Tina Iannone**, Student, *Tri County Technical College*

CENGAGE
Learning®

BCOM6
Carol Lehman, Debbie DuFrene, Robyn Walker

Vice President, General Manager:
   Erin Joyner

Product Director: Mike Schenk

Product Director, 4LTR Press: Steven Joos

Sr. Product Manager: Michele Rhoades

Managing Developer:
   Joanne Dauksewicz

Content Developer: Sarah Blasco

Sr. Brand Manager: Kristen Hurd

Sr. Content Project Manager: Martha Conway

Sr. Media Developer: John Rich

Manufacturing Planner: Ron Montgomery

Production Service: PreMediaGlobal

Sr. Art Director: Stacy Jenkins Shirley

Internal and Cover Designer: Craig Ramsdell

Sr. Rights Acquisitions Specialist:
   John Hill

Cover Images: © ostill /Shutterstock.com;
   © Pavel L. Photo and Video /
   Shutterstock.com; © LFor /
   Shutterstock.com

Inside Front Cover Images: woman with
   magazine © iStockphoto.com/sdominick;
   money © iStockphoto.com/alexsl; college
   hangout © iStockphoto.com/A-Digit

Title Page Images: laptop © iStockphoto.
   com/CostinT; A+ © iStockphoto.com/
   photovideostock; crowd © iStockphoto.
   com/Leontura

Back Cover Image: © iStockphoto.com/René
   Mansi

Front and Back Matter Keyboard Image:
   © iStockphoto.com/Jimmy Anderson

Microsoft product screenshots used with
   permission from Microsoft Corporation.

Unless otherwise noted, all items
   © Cengage Learning.

For product information and technology assistance, contact us at
Cengage Learning Customer & Sales Support, 1-800-354-9706

For permission to use material from this text or product,
submit all requests online at **www.cengage.com/permissions**
Further permissions questions can be emailed to
permissionrequest@cengage.com

Cengage Learning WebTutor™ is a trademark of Cengage Learning.

Library of Congress Control Number: 2013953893

Student Edition package ISBN-13: 978-1-285-43164-2
Student Edition package ISBN-10: 1-285-43164-2

Student Edition ISBN-13: 978-1-285-43271-7
Student Edition ISBN-10: 1-285-43271-1

Cengage Learning
200 First Stamford Place
Stamford, CT 06902
USA

Cengage Learning is a leading provider of customized learning solutions with office locations around the globe, including Singapore, the United Kingdom, Australia, Mexico, Brazil, and Japan. Locate your local office at: **www.cengage.com/global**

Cengage Learning products are represented in Canada by Nelson Education, Ltd.

To learn more about Cengage Learning Solutions, visit **www.cengage.com**

Purchase any of our products at your local college store or at our preferred online store **www.cengagebrain.com**

Printed in the United States of America
1 2 3 4 5 6 7 17 16 15 14 13

Arrow/Fotolia LLC

Thank you

© iStockphoto.com/Hamza Türkkol

PART 4
Communication through Reports and Business Presentations 148

9 Understanding the Report Process and Research Methods 148

10 Managing Data and Using Graphics 168

11 Organizing and Preparing Reports and Proposals 182

© iStockphoto.com/Rouzes

12 Designing and Delivering Business Presentations 206

Establishing a Framework for Business Communication

OBJECTIVES

1-1 Define communication and describe the value of communication in business.

1-2 Explain the communication process model and the ultimate objective of the communication process.

1-3 Discuss how information flows in an organization.

1-4 Explain how legal and ethical constraints, diversity challenges, changing technology, and team environment act as contextual forces that influence the process of business communication.

1-1 Value of Communication

We communicate to satisfy needs in both our work and private lives. Each of us wants to be heard, appreciated, and wanted. We also want to accomplish tasks and achieve goals. Generally people communicate for three basic purposes: to inform, to persuade, and to entertain. However, in the professional workplace some of these purposes have greater importance. Informing and persuading are common purposes of communication in the workplace; entertainment is less so. In addition, establishing and maintaining our credibility and positive relationships with others are also important purposes in an organizational setting.

What is communication? Communication is the process of exchanging and interpreting information and meaning between or among individuals through a system of symbols, signs, and behavior. In ideal situations, the goal is to reach mutual understanding. Studies indicate that managers typically spend 60% to 80% of their time involved in communication. In your career activities, you will communicate in a wide variety of ways, including

- attending meetings and listening and contributing to decision making and problem solving;
- writing various types of messages to inform and persuade others about your ideas and the services and products your organization provides;
- presenting information and persuasive messages to large and small groups in face-to-face and virtual environments;
- explaining and clarifying management procedures and work assignments;
- coordinating the work of various employees, departments, and other work groups;
- evaluating and counseling employees;
- promoting the company's products/services and image using a variety of channels in various contexts.

1-2 The Communication Process

Effective business communication is essential to success in today's work environments. Recent surveys of executives document that abilities in writing and speaking are major determinants of career success in many fields.[1] Although essential to personal and professional success, effective business communication does not occur automatically. Your own experiences likely have taught you that a message is not interpreted correctly just because you transmitted it. An effective communicator anticipates possible breakdowns in the communication process—the unlimited ways the message can be misunderstood. This mind-set provides the concentration to plan and design the initial message effectively and to be prepared to intervene at the appropriate time to ensure that the message received is on target.

Consider the transactional process model of communication presented in Figure 1-1. These seemingly simple steps actually represent a very complex process.

A number of communication process models exist. The transactional model is useful, though, because it illustrates the complexity of the communication process and reveals some of the challenges to effective communication that might emerge in a communication encounter.

Log onto www.cengagebrain.com for additional resources, including flashcards, games, self-quizzing for chapter review, grammar exercises, and more.

BCOM

Figure 1-1 The Transactional Process Model of Communication

Sender ⟷ **Message** ⟷ **Receiver**

Feedback

interferences
also called *barriers*; numerous factors that hinder the communication process

organizational communication
the movement of information within the company structure

According to the transactional process model, two parties involved in a communication encounter are potentially both communicating at the same time, particularly if the encounter is face to face. That's because in face-to-face communication situations, parties to the encounter are continuously interpreting each other's nonverbal signals. Some scholars say more than 90% of the information in a face-to-face encounter may be sent nonverbally. But even in a cell-phone conversation, silences and tone of voice may be interpreted in various ways. Even a written message may provide information about the writer that he or she did not intend to convey.

In an ideal communication situation, one party would be able to **encode** his or her message in such a way that the receiving party would understand it exactly as intended. However, this goal can be challenging for a variety of reasons, or what are called **interferences** or *barriers* to effective communication. For example,

- differences in educational level, experience, culture, and other characteristics of the sender and the receiver increase the complexity of encoding and decoding a message;
- physical interferences in the channel, including a noisy environment, interruptions, and uncomfortable surroundings, can occur;
- mental distractions, such as being preoccupied with other matters and developing a response, rather than listening, create barriers to understanding.

Because of these barriers and because both parties to a communication encounter may be sending information both orally and nonverbally simultaneously, it can be very challenging to ensure that the information is received as intended. For this reason, it is particularly important to check for understanding rather than assume that it has taken place, particularly when communicating important messages or to audiences that are less familiar to us.

You can surely compile a list of other barriers that affect your ability to communicate with friends, instructors, coworkers, supervisors, and others. By being aware of them, you can concentrate on removing these interferences.

1-3 Communicating within Organizations

To be successful, organizations must create an environment that energizes and encourages employees to accomplish tasks by promoting genuine openness and effective communication. **Organizational communication** is concerned with the movement of information within the company structure. Regardless of your career or level within an organization, your ability to communicate will affect not only the success of the organization but also your personal success and advancement within that organization.

1-3a Communication Flow in Organizations

Communication occurs in a variety of ways within an organization. Some communication flows are planned and structured; others are not. Some communication flows can be formally depicted, whereas some defy description.

What nonverbal signals are being shown in this photo?

© Peter Bernik/Shutterstock.com

Formal and Informal Communication Networks

Communication within an organization involves both formal and informal networks.

- **Formal communication network.** This channel is typified by the formal organization chart, which is created by management to define individual and group relationships and to specify lines of responsibility. Essentially, the formal system is dictated by the managerial, technical, cultural, and structural environment of the organization. Within this system, people are required to behave and to communicate in certain ways simply to get work done.

- **Informal communication network.** This network, which is commonly called "the grapevine," continuously develops as people interact within the formal system to accommodate their social and psychological needs. Because the informal network undergoes continual changes and does not parallel the organizational chart, it cannot be depicted accurately by any graphic means.

When employees rely almost entirely on the formal communication system as a guide to behavior, the system might be identified as a *bureaucracy*. Procedures manuals, job descriptions, organization charts, and other written materials dictate the required behavior. Communication channels are followed strictly, and red tape is abundant. Procedures are generally followed exactly; terms such as *rules* and *policies* serve as sufficient reasons for actions. Even the most formal organizations, however, cannot function long before an informal communication system emerges. As people operate within the organized system, they interact on a person-to-person basis and create an environment conducive to meeting their personal emotions, prejudices, likes, and dislikes.

In a workplace, employees are generally expected to satisfy a formal system of arriving at work on time, fulfilling their job duties, working well with others, and addressing their supervisor's requests. However, some employees may not openly accept these expectations and may arrive at work late and spend an undue amount of time "around the water cooler." If these informal practices become more widely spread, the purposes of the group may move from a focus on completing tasks to that of socializing with others. Obviously, the informal system benefits people because it meets their needs, but it also may affect the overall communication of the group in important ways.

The Informal Communication Network

As people talk casually during breaks, text one another, or chat online, the focus usually shifts from topic to topic. One of the usual topics is work—job, company, supervisor, fellow employees. Even though the formal system includes definite communication channels, the grapevine tends to develop and operate within all organizations. Consider these points related to the accuracy and value of grapevine communication:

- As a communication network, the grapevine has a reputation for being speedy but inaccurate. In the absence of alarms, the grapevine might be the most effective way to let occupants know that the building is on fire. It certainly beats sending an email.

- Although the grapevine often is thought of as a channel for inaccurate communication, in reality it is no more or less accurate than other channels. Even formal communication can become inaccurate and filtered as it passes from level to level in the organizational hierarchy.

- The inaccuracy of the grapevine has more to do with the message input than with the output. For example, the grapevine is noted as a carrier of rumors, primarily because it carries informal messages. If the input is a rumor, and nothing more, the output obviously will be inaccurate. But the output might be an accurate description of the original rumor.

- In a business office, news about promotions, personnel changes, company policy changes, and annual salary adjustments often is communicated through the grapevine long before being conveyed through formal channels. The process works similarly in colleges, where information about choice instructors typically is not officially published but is known by students through the grapevine. How best to prepare for examinations, instructor attitudes on attendance and homework, and even faculty personnel changes are messages that travel over the grapevine.

- A misconception about the grapevine is that the message passes from person to person until it finally reaches a person who can't pass it on—the end of the line. Actually, the grapevine works as a network channel. Typically, one person tells two or three others, who each tell two or three others, who each

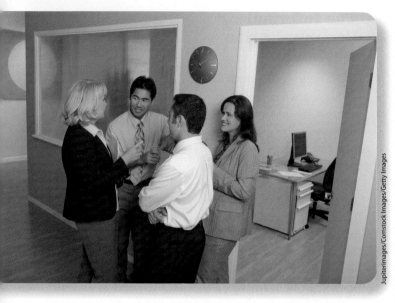

An informal communication network will emerge from even the most carefully designed formal system. Managers who ignore this fact are attempting to manage blindfolded. Instead of denying or condemning the grapevine, the effective manager will learn to *use* the informal communication network. The grapevine, for instance, can be useful in counteracting rumors and false information.

Directions of Communication Flow

The direction in which communication flows in an organization can be downward, upward, or horizontal, as shown in Figure 1-2. Because these three terms are used frequently in communication discussions, they deserve clarification. Although the concept of flow seems simple, direction has meaning for those participating in the organizational communication process.

Downward Communication

Downward communication flows from supervisor to employee, from policy makers to operating personnel, or from top to bottom on the organization chart. A simple policy statement from the top of the organization might grow into a formal plan for operation at lower levels. Teaching people how to perform their specific tasks is an element of downward communication. Another element is orientation to a company's rules, practices, procedures, history, and goals. Employees learn about the quality of their job performance through downward communication. Downward communication normally involves both written and spoken methods and makes use of the following assumptions:

Downward Communication

- People at high levels in the organization usually have greater knowledge of the organization's mission and goals than do people at lower levels.

- Both spoken and written messages tend to become larger as they move downward through organizational levels. This expansion results from attempts to prevent distortion and is more noticeable in written messages.

- Spoken messages are subject to greater changes in meaning than are written messages.

tell two or three others, and so on. Thus, the message might spread to a huge number of people in a short time, especially now that the grapevine has gone hi-tech and social networking sites have become "gossip central."

- The grapevine has no single, consistent source. Messages might originate anywhere and follow various routes.

Due at least in part to widespread downsizing and corporate scandals during the last few years, employees in many organizations are demanding that they be better informed. Some companies have implemented new formal ways, such as newsletters and intranets, as well as informal ways, including blogs and Twitter, for sharing information with their internal constituents. Company openness with employees about management decisions and financial issues means conveying more information through the formal system rather than risking its miscommunication through informal channels. The Internet juggernaut Google has taken the number one spot on *Fortune's* list of the 100 best companies to work for for the past four years and not just for the subsidized massages it doles out to employees. It also offers three wellness centers and a 7-acre sports complex. "We have pretty lofty goals—to create the happiest and healthiest work environment in the world, and to ensure a really innovative work environment where people can do their best work," says Michelle DeBeyer, Human Resources business partner at Google Canada.[2]

downward communication
a type of communication that flows from supervisor to employee, from policy makers to operating personnel, or from top to bottom on the organization chart

Figure 1-2 Flow of Information within an Organization

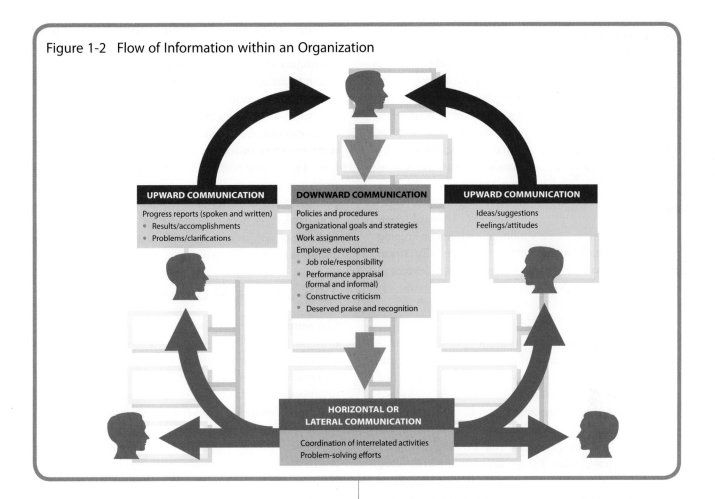

UPWARD COMMUNICATION	DOWNWARD COMMUNICATION	UPWARD COMMUNICATION
Progress reports (spoken and written) • Results/accomplishments • Problems/clarifications	Policies and procedures Organizational goals and strategies Work assignments Employee development • Job role/responsibility • Performance appraisal (formal and informal) • Constructive criticism • Deserved praise and recognition	Ideas/suggestions Feelings/attitudes

HORIZONTAL OR LATERAL COMMUNICATION

Coordination of interrelated activities
Problem-solving efforts

When a supervisor sends a message to a subordinate employee who then asks a question or nods in agreement, the employee has given signs of feedback. Feedback can flow both downward and upward in organizational communication through traditional as well as informal channels.

Upward Communication

Upward communication flows from the front lines of an organization to the top. When management requests information from lower organizational levels, the resulting information becomes feedback to that request. Employees talk to supervisors about themselves, their fellow employees, their work and methods of doing it, customer needs and perceptions, and their own perceptions of the organization. These comments are commonly feedback to the downward flow transmitted in both spoken and written forms by group meetings, procedures or operations manuals, company news releases, the company intranet, and the grapevine.

Although necessary and valuable, upward communication involves risks. The following factors are

important to consider when upward communication flow is involved:

Upward Communication

- Upward communication is primarily feedback to requests and actions of supervisors.
- Upward communication can be misleading because lower-level employees often tell their superiors what they think their superiors want to hear. Therefore, their messages might contradict their true observations and perceptions.
- Upward communication frequently involves risk to an employee and is dependent on trust in the supervisor.
- Employees will reject superficial attempts by management to obtain feedback.

© iStockphoto.com/Pali Rao

upward communication
a type of communication that is generally a response to requests from supervisors

When effectively used, upward communication keeps management informed about the feelings of lower-level employees, taps the expertise of employees, helps management identify both difficult and potentially promotable employees, and paves the way for even more effective downward communication. Upward communication is key to keeping employees engaged and informed and is especially critical in tapping the power of younger employees who expect to collaborate rather than to be supervised.[3]

Horizontal Communication

Horizontal, or lateral, communication describes interactions between organizational units on the same hierarchical level. These interactions reveal one of the major shortcomings of organizational charts: They do not recognize the role of horizontal communication when they depict authority relationships by placing one box higher than another and define role functions by placing titles in those boxes. Yet management should realize that horizontal communication is the primary means of achieving coordination in a functional organizational structure. Units coordinate their activities to accomplish task goals just as adjacent workers in a production line coordinate their activities. So for horizontal communication to be maximally effective, the people in any system or organization should be available to one another.

Many companies realize that the traditional hierarchy organized around functional units is inadequate for competing in increasingly competitive global markets. They value work teams that integrate work-flow processes rather than specialists in a single function or product. Such work teams can break down communication barriers between isolated functional departments, and communication patterns take on varying forms to accommodate team activities.

1-3b Levels of Communication

Communication can involve sending messages to both large and small audiences. **Internal messages** are intended for recipients within the organization. **External messages** are directed to recipients outside the organization. When considering the intended audience, communication can be described as taking place on five levels: intrapersonal, interpersonal, group, organizational, and public. Figure 1-3 depicts the five audience levels. An effective communicator has a clearly defined purpose for each message and selected strategies for targeting his or her intended audience.

Figure 1-3   Levels of Communication

COMMUNICATION LEVELS	EXAMPLES
INTRAPERSONAL	
• Communication within oneself	*Individual considers how others respond to his or her verbal and/or nonverbal communication.*
• Not considered by some to be true communication as it does not involve a separate sender and receiver	
INTERPERSONAL	
• Communication between two people	*Supervisor and subordinate, two coworkers*
• Task goal to accomplish work confronting them	
• Maintenance goal to feel better about themselves and each other because of their interaction	
GROUP	
• Communication among more than two people	*Work group, project team, department meeting*
• Goal of achieving greater output than individual efforts could produce	
ORGANIZATIONAL	
• Groups combined in such a way that large tasks may be accomplished	*Company, organization*
• Goal of providing adequate structure for groups to achieve their purposes	
PUBLIC	
• The organization reaching out to its public to achieve its goals	*Media advertisement, website communication, annual report*
• Goal of reaching many with the same message	

1-4 Contextual Forces Influencing Business Communication

All communication occurs within a **context**, which is the situation or setting. Context can influence the content, the quality, and the effectiveness of a communication event. The effective communicator will recognize the importance of context, identify the contextual elements that will influence communication, and adjust messages in response. Four important contextual forces influence the communication process today and help determine and define the nature of the communication that should occur, as shown in Figure 1-4. These forces are legal and ethical constraints, diversity challenges, changing technology, and team environment.

1-4a Legal and Ethical Constraints

Legal and ethical constraints act as contextual or environmental forces on communication because they set boundaries in which communication rightfully occurs. International, federal, state, and local laws affect the way that various business activities are conducted. For instance, laws specify that certain information must be stated in messages that reply to credit applications and those dealing with the collection of outstanding debts. Furthermore, one's own ethical standards will often influence what he or she is willing to say in a message. For example, a system of ethics built on honesty might require that the message provides full disclosure rather than a shrouding of the truth. Legal responsibilities, then, are the starting point for appropriate business communication. One's ethical belief system, or personal sense of right and wrong behavior, provides further boundaries for professional activity.

The press is full of examples of unethical conduct in business and political communities, but unethical behavior is not relegated to the papers—it has far-reaching consequences. Those affected by decisions, the **stakeholders**, can include people inside and outside the organization. Employees and stockholders are obvious losers when a company fails. Competitors in the same industry also suffer, because their strategies are based on what they perceive about their competition. Beyond that, financial markets as a whole suffer due to erosion of public confidence.

Business leaders, government officials, and citizens frequently express concern about the apparent erosion of ethical values in society. Even for those who want to do the right thing, matters of ethics are seldom clear-cut decisions of right versus wrong, and they often contain ambiguous elements. In addition, the pressure appears to be felt most strongly by lower-level managers, often recent business school graduates who are the least experienced at doing their jobs.

The Foundation for Legal and Ethical Behavior

Although ethics is a common point of discussion, many find defining ethics challenging. Most people immediately associate ethics with standards and rules of conduct, morals, right and wrong, values, and honesty. Dr. Albert Schweitzer defined *ethics* as "the name we

> **stakeholders**
> people inside and outside the organization who are affected by decisions

---

Figure 1-4 Factors Influencing Business Communication

LEGAL AND ETHICAL CONSTRAINTS	**CHANGING TECHNOLOGY**	**DIVERSITY CHALLENGES**	**TEAM ENVIRONMENT**
• International Laws	• Accuracy and Security Issues	• Cultural Differences	• Trust
• Domestic Laws	• Telecommunications	• Language Barriers	• Team Roles
• Codes of Ethics	• Software Applications	• Gender Issues	• Shared Goals and Expectations
• Stakeholder Interests	• "High-Touch" Issues	• Education Levels	• Synergy
• Ethical Frameworks	• Telecommuting	• Age Factors	• Group Reward
• Personal Values	• Databases	• Nonverbal Differences	• Distributed Leadership

ethics
the principles of right and wrong that guide one in making decisions that consider the impact of one's actions on others as well as on the decision maker

give to our concern for good behavior. We feel an obligation to consider not only our own personal well-being, but also that of others and of human society as a whole."[4] In other words, **ethics** refers to the principles of right and wrong that guide you in making decisions that consider the impact of your actions on others as well as yourself.

Although the recorded accounts of legal and ethical misconduct would seem to indicate that businesses are dishonest and unscrupulous, keep in mind that millions of business transactions are made daily on the basis of honesty and concern for others. Why should a business make ethical decisions? What difference will it make? James E. Perrella, executive vice president of Ingersoll-Rand Company, gave a powerful reply to these questions:[5]

> Many people, including many business leaders, would argue that such an application of ethics to business would adversely affect bottom-line performance. I say nay.... Good ethics, simply, is good business. Good ethics will attract investors. Good ethics will attract good employees. You can do what's right. Not because of conduct codes. Not because of rules or laws. But because you know what's right.

Causes of Illegal and Unethical Behavior

Understanding the major causes of illegal and unethical behavior in the workplace will help you become sensitive to signals of escalating pressure to compromise your values. Unethical corporate behavior can have a number of causes:

- **Excessive emphasis on profits.** Business managers are often judged and paid on their ability to increase business profits. This emphasis on profits might send a message that the end justifies the means.

- **Misplaced corporate loyalty.** A misplaced sense of corporate loyalty might cause an employee to do what seems to be in the best interest of the company, even if the act is illegal or unethical.

- **Obsession with personal advancement.** Employees who wish to outperform their peers or are working for the next promotion might feel that they cannot afford to fail. They might do whatever it takes to achieve the objectives assigned to them.

- **Expectation of not getting caught.** Thinking that the end justifies the means, employees often believe illegal or unethical activity will never be discovered. Unfortunately, a great deal of improper behavior escapes detection in the business world. Believing no one will ever find out, employees are tempted to lie, steal, and perform other illegal acts.

- **Unethical tone set by top management.** If top managers are not perceived as highly ethical, lower-level managers might be less ethical as a result. Employees have little incentive to act legally and

Ethical Dilemmas ...

Identifying ethical issues in typical workplace situations can be difficult, and coworkers and superiors might apply pressure for seemingly logical reasons. To illustrate, examine each of the following workplace situations for a possible ethical dilemma:

© StockLite/Shutterstock.com

- In order to achieve profit expectations, a stockbroker hides the financial risk of an investment product from potential clients.
- To prevent an adverse effect on stock prices, corporate officers deliberately withhold information concerning a possible corporate takeover.
- To protect the organization, management decides not to publicize a design flaw in an automobile that could lead to possible injury and even death to consumers because the announcement might result in legal action.
- A supervisor takes advantage of his position and threatens an employee with dismissal if she does not acquiesce to his inappropriate requests and language use.
- Angry because of an unfavorable performance appraisal of a colleague, an employee leaks confidential information to the colleague that creates distrust among others in the department and results in a lawsuit.

Your fundamental morals and values provide the foundation for making ethical decisions. However, as the previous examples imply, even seemingly minor concessions in day-to-day decisions can gradually weaken an individual's ethical foundation.

ethically if their superiors do not set an example and encourage and reward such behavior. The saying "the speed of the leader is the speed of the pack" illustrates the importance of leading by example.

- **Uncertainty about whether an action is wrong.** Many times, company personnel are placed in situations in which the line between right and wrong is not clearly defined. When caught in this gray area, the perplexed employee asks, "How far is too far?"

- **Unwillingness to take a stand for what is right.** Often employees know what is right or wrong but are not willing to take the risk of challenging a wrong action. They might lack the confidence or skill needed to confront others with sensitive legal or ethical issues. They might remain silent and then justify their unwillingness to act.

Framework for Analyzing Ethical Dilemmas

Determining whether an action is ethical can be difficult. Learning to analyze a dilemma from both legal and ethical perspectives will help you find a solution that conforms to your own personal values. Figure 1-5 shows the four conclusions you might reach when considering the advisability of a particular behavior.

Dimension 1: Behavior that is illegal and unethical

When considering some actions, you will reach the conclusion that they are both illegal and unethical. The law specifically outlines the "black" area—those alternatives that are clearly wrong—and your employer will expect you to become an expert in the laws that affect your particular area. When you encounter an unfamiliar area, you must investigate any possible legal implications. Obviously, obeying the law is in the best interest of all concerned: you as an individual, your company, and society. Contractual agreements between two parties also offer guidance for legal decision making. Frequently, your own individual sense of right and wrong will also confirm that the illegal action is wrong for you personally. In such situations, decisions about appropriate behavior are obvious.

Dimension 2: Behavior that is illegal yet ethical

Occasionally, a businessperson will decide that even though a specific action is illegal, there is a justifiable reason to break the law. A case in point is a law passed in Vermont that makes it illegal for a pharmaceutical company to give any gift valued at more than $25 to doctors or their personnel.[6] Those supporting the law charge that the giving of freebies drives up medical costs by encouraging doctors to prescribe new, more expensive brand-name drugs. The law's opponents contend that the gifts do not influence doctors and are merely educational tools for new products. Although a pharmaceutical firm and its employees might see nothing wrong with providing gifts worth in excess of $25, they would be well advised to consider the penalty of $10,000 per violation before acting on their personal ethics. A better course of action would be to act within the law, possibly while lobbying for a change in the law.

Dimension 3: Behavior that is legal yet unethical

If you determine that a behavior is legal and complies with relevant contractual agreements and company policy, your next step is to consult your company's or profession's *code of ethics*. This written document summarizes the company's or profession's *standards of ethical conduct*. Some companies refer to this document as a *credo*. If the behavior does not

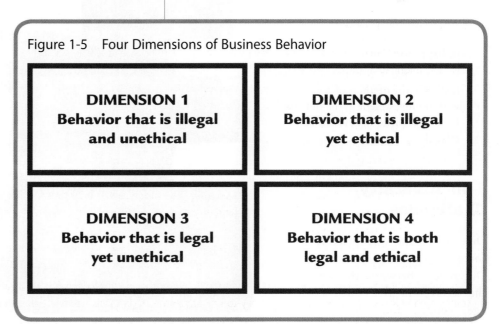

Figure 1-5   Four Dimensions of Business Behavior

DIMENSION 1
Behavior that is illegal and unethical

DIMENSION 2
Behavior that is illegal yet ethical

DIMENSION 3
Behavior that is legal yet unethical

DIMENSION 4
Behavior that is both legal and ethical

violate the code of ethics, then put it to the test of your own personal integrity. You may at times reject a legal action because it does not "feel right." Most Americans were appalled to learn that the marketing of sub-prime loans packaged as reputable securities has been blamed for causing the "Great Recession." Although they might have acted legally, their profiting at the expense of company employees, stockholders, and the public hardly seemed ethical. You might be faced with situations in which you reject a behavior that is legal because you would not be proud to have your family and community know that you engaged in it.

Dimension 4: Behavior that is both legal and ethical

Decisions in this dimension are easy to make. Such actions comply with the law, company policies, and your professional and personal codes of ethics.

The Pagano Model offers a straightforward method for determining whether a proposed action is advisable.[7] For this system to work, you must answer the following six questions honestly:

1. Is the proposed action legal? (This is the core starting point.)
2. What are the benefits and costs to the people involved?
3. Would you want this action to be a universal standard, appropriate for everyone?
4. Does the action pass the light-of-day test? That is, if your action appeared on television or others learned about it, would you be proud?
5. Does the action pass the Golden Rule test? That is, would you want the same to happen to you?
6. Does the action pass the ventilation test? Ask the opinion of a wise friend with no investment in the outcome. Does this friend believe the action is ethical?

1-4b Diversity Challenges

Diversity in the workplace is another force influencing communication. Differences between the sender and the receiver in areas such as culture, age, gender, and education require

sensitivity on the part of both parties so that the intended message is the one that is received.

Understanding how to communicate effectively with people from other cultures has become more integral to the work environment as many U.S. companies are increasingly conducting business with international companies or becoming multinational. Candy manufacturer Jelly Belly learned a great deal about cultural differences when the company opened business operations in Thailand. In Thailand, many more employee amenities are required than U.S. employers are accustomed to providing. For example, a Thai employer is expected to provide transportation to and from work as well as free meals and a workout facility for its employees.[8] When addressing cultural differences, successful communication must often span barriers of language and differing worldviews resulting from societal and religious beliefs and practices. When a person fails to consider these factors, communication suffers, and the result is often embarrassing and potentially costly. To be successful on an international scale, managers had to be aware of cultural differences and be willing to work to ensure that effective communication occurred despite these barriers.

Occasionally, however, a whopper of an intercultural communication faux pas occurs. In 2011, Puma, a German sports gear and apparel company, decided that it was going to launch a shoe in the United Arab Emirates with the colors of the national flag to celebrate the country's 40th anniversary. The problem was that feet are considered to be unclean in Islam. In fact, there is a passage in the Koran that mandates Muslims to wash their feet before offering As-Salat, or prayers. Therefore, placing the colors of the national flag on the feet was seen as "walking on their flag" and associating the colors of the flag with the lowest of insults. The launching of the shoe in the Emirates stores immediately provoked a wave of indignation, which forced Puma to withdraw it from the market and publish a statement to apologize.[9]

This example shows how much "homework" is involved in maintaining good relations with customers or clients from other cultures. The potential barrier of language is obvious; however, successful managers know that much more is involved in communicating with everyone—across cultures, genders, ages, abilities, and other differences.

Communication Opportunities and Challenges in Diversity

As world markets continue to expand, U.S. employees at home and abroad will be doing business with more people from other countries. You might find yourself working abroad for a large American company, an international company with a plant in the United States, or a company with an ethnically diverse workforce. Regardless of the workplace, your **diversity skills**—that is, your ability to communicate effectively with both men and women of all ages, cultures, and minority groups—will affect your success in today's culturally diverse global economy.

Workplace diversity can lead to misunderstandings and miscommunications, but it also poses opportunities to improve both workers and organizations. Managers must be prepared to communicate effectively with workers of different nationalities, genders, races, ages, abilities, and other characteristics.

Managing a diverse workforce effectively will require you to communicate with *everyone* and to help all employees reach their fullest potential and contribute to the company's goals. To lessen miscommunication, which inevitably occurs, increasing numbers of companies have undertaken *diversity initiatives* and are providing diversity training seminars to help workers understand and appreciate gender and age differences and the cultures of coworkers.

Culture and Communication

Managers with the *desire* and the *skill* to conduct business in new international markets and to manage a diverse workforce effectively will confront problems created by cultural differences. The way messages are decoded and encoded is not just a function of the experiences, beliefs, and assumptions of the person sending or receiving those messages but also is shaped by the society in which he or she lives.

People learn patterns of behavior from their culture. The *culture* of a people is the product of their living experiences within their own society. Culture could be described as "the way of life" of a people and includes a vast array of behaviors and beliefs. These patterns affect how people perceive the world, what they value, and how they act. Differing patterns can also create barriers to communication.

Barriers to Intercultural Communication

Because cultures give different definitions of such basics of interaction as values and norms, people raised in two different cultures can clash in various ways.

- **Ethnocentrism.** Problems occur between people of different cultures primarily because people tend to assume that their own cultural norms are the right way to do things. They wrongly believe that the specific patterns of behavior desired in their own cultures are universally valued. This belief, known as **ethnocentrism**, is certainly natural; but learning about other cultures and developing sensitivity will help minimize ethnocentric reactions when dealing with other cultures.

- **Stereotypes.** We often form a mental picture of the main characteristics of another group, creating preformed ideas of what people in this group are like. These pictures, called **stereotypes**, influence the way we interact with members of the other group. When we observe a behavior that conforms to the stereotype, the validity of the preconceived notion is reinforced. We often view the other person as a representative of a class of people rather than as an individual. People of all cultures have stereotypes about other cultural groups they have encountered. These stereotypes can interfere

diversity skills
the ability to communicate effectively with both men and women of all ages, cultures, and minority groups

ethnocentrism
the assumption that one's own cultural norms are the right way to do things

stereotypes
mental pictures that one group forms of the main characteristics of another group, creating preformed ideas of what people in this group are like

Valeriy Lebedev/Dreamstime.com

with communication when people interact on the basis of the imagined representative and not the real individual.

• **Interpretation of time.** The study of how a culture perceives time and its use is called **chronemics**. In the United States, we have a saying that "time is money." Canadians, like some northern Europeans who are also concerned about punctuality, make appointments, keep them, and complete them, and waste no time in the process. In some other cultures, time is the cheapest commodity and an inexhaustible

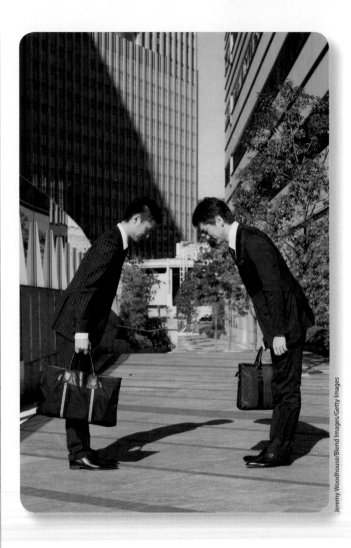

Jeremy Woodhouse/Blend Images/Getty Images

> YOUR ABILITY TO COMMUNICATE EFFECTIVELY WITH BOTH MEN AND WOMEN OF ALL AGES, CULTURES, AND MINORITY GROUPS WILL AFFECT YOUR SUCCESS IN TODAY'S CULTURALLY DIVERSE GLOBAL ECONOMY.

resource; time represents a person's span on Earth, which is only part of eternity. To these cultures, engaging in long, casual conversations prior to serious discussions or negotiations is time well spent in establishing and nurturing relationships. On the other hand, the time-efficient American businessperson is likely to fret about wasting precious time.

• **Personal space requirements.** Space operates as a language just as time does. The study of cultural space requirements is known as **proxemics**. In all cultures, the distance between people functions in communication as "personal space" or "personal territory." In the United States, for example, for intimate conversations with close friends and relatives, individuals are willing to stay within about a foot and a half of each other; for casual conversations, up to two or three feet; for job interviews and

personal business, four to twelve feet; and for public occasions, more than twelve feet. However, in many cultures outside the United States, closer personal contact is accepted, or greater distance might be the norm.

• **Body language.** The study of body language is known as **kinesics**. Body language is not universal, but instead is learned from one's culture. Even the most basic gestures have varying cultural meanings—the familiar North American symbol for "okay" means zero in France, money in Japan, and an expression of vulgarity in Brazil. Similarly, eye contact, posture, and facial expressions carry different meanings throughout the world.

• **Translation limitations.** Words in one language do not always have an equivalent meaning in other languages, and the concepts the words describe are often different as well. Translators can be helpful, but keep in mind that a translator is working with a second language and must listen to one language, mentally cast the words into another language, and then speak them. This process is difficult and opens the possibility that the translator will fall victim to one or more cultural barriers.

Even if you cannot speak or write another language fluently, people from other cultures will appreciate simple efforts to learn a few common phrases.

1-4c Changing Technology

Electronic tools have not eliminated the need for basic communication skills; they can, in fact, create new obstacles or barriers to communication that must be overcome. These tools, however, also create opportunities that range from new kinds of communications to improved quality of the messages themselves. Electronic tools, such as the Internet, intranets, document production software, multimedia presentations, Web publishing tools, and email, can help people in various ways, such as by (1) collecting and analyzing data, (2) shaping messages to be clearer and more effective, and (3) communicating quickly and efficiently with others in geographically dispersed locations.

Using various communication technologies, individuals can often work in their homes or other remote locations and send and receive work from the company office electronically. **Telecommuting** (also referred to as *teleworking*) offers various advantages, including reduced travel time and increased work flexibility. Laptops and smartphones provide computing power and connectivity for professionals wherever they are. While the public Internet is accessible to everyone and offers a wide array of information, private databases provide specialized and advanced information on specific topics. Databases enable decision makers to obtain information quickly and accurately and offer these advantages:

> **telecommuting**
> also called *teleworking*; working at home or other remote locations and sending and receiving work from the company office electronically

- **Data organization**—the ability to organize large amounts of data.
- **Data integrity**—assurance that the data will be accurate and complete.
- **Data security**—assurance that the data are secure because access to a database is controlled through several built-in data security features.

Internal databases contain proprietary information that is pertinent to the particular business or organization and its employees. External databases (networks) allow users to access information from remote locations literally around the world and in an instant transfer that information to their own computers for further manipulation or storage. Information is available on general news, stocks, financial markets, sports, travel, weather, and a variety of publications.

Knowing how to "tunnel" through the vast amounts of irrelevant information available on the Internet to find what you want can be overwhelming. The experience can also be expensive in terms of human time

Legal and Ethical Implications of Technology

In addition to its many benefits, technology poses some challenges for the business communicator. For instance, technology raises issues of ownership, as in the case of difficulties that arise in protecting the copyright of documents transmitted over the Internet. Technology poses dilemmas over access, that is, who has the right to certain stored information pertaining to an individual or a company.

Technology threatens our individual privacy, our right to be left alone, free from surveillance or interference from other individuals or organizations. Common invasions of privacy caused by technology include

Miluxian/Dreamstime.com

- monitoring your Internet use, infiltrating your information, and sending advertising based on your browsing history;
- monitoring the exact time employees spend on a specific task and between tasks and the exact number and length of breaks, and supervisors' or coworkers' reading of another employee's email and computer files;
- and spreading of spyware and various computer "bugs" through the Internet.[10]

Is it possible to pin down how technology will affect the future?

spent and charges incurred for online time. Locating information from electronic sources requires that you know the search procedures and methods for constructing an effective search strategy.

Effective use of various communication technologies helps ensure timely, targeted messages and responses and helps build interpersonal relationships. This responsiveness leads to positive interactions with colleagues and strong customer commitment.

1-4d Team Environment

As firms around the world face problems of decreasing productivity, faltering product quality, and worker dissatisfaction, work teams are seen as a way to help firms remain globally competitive. Decentralized decision making enables teams of people to communicate in a peer-to-peer fashion, rather than following traditional lines of authority, and new technologies give employees the ability to communicate easily and openly with one another and with those outside the firm.

Although worker involvement in the management process has long been the hallmark of Japanese business, many businesses in the United States and elsewhere are empowering self-directed work teams to accomplish various assignments.[11] The list of companies using self-directed work teams is diverse, including Hunt-Wesson, the Internal Revenue Service, the San Diego Zoo, Hewlett-Packard, Southwest Airlines, Toyota, Motorola, General Electric, and Corning.

Work Team Defined

The terms *team*, *work team*, *group*, *work group*, *cross-functional team*, and *self-directed team* are often used interchangeably.[12] Whatever the title, a **team** is a small number of people with complementary skills who work together for a common purpose. Team members set their own goals, in cooperation with management, and plan how to achieve those goals and how their work is to be accomplished. The central organizing element of a team is that it has a common purpose and measurable goals for which the team can be held accountable, independent of its individual members. Employees in a self-directed work team handle a wide array of functions and work with a minimum of direct supervision.[13]

Some major strengths of teams are as follows:[14]

- Teams make workers happier by causing them to feel that they are shaping their own jobs.
- Teams increase efficiency by eliminating layers of managers whose job was once to pass orders downward.
- Teams enable a company to draw on the skills and imagination of a whole workforce.

A key element in team success is the concept of **synergy**, defined as a situation in which the whole is greater than the sum of the parts. Teams provide a depth of expertise that is unavailable at the individual level. Teams open lines of communication that then lead to increased interaction among employees and between employees and management. The result is that teams help companies reach their goals of delivering higher-quality products and services faster and with more cost-effectiveness.

Communication Differences in Work Teams

In the past, most businesses were operated in a hierarchical fashion, with most decisions made at the top and communication following a top-down/bottom-up

team
a small number of people with complementary skills who work together for a common purpose

synergy
a situation in which the whole is greater than the sum of the parts

pattern. Communication patterns are different in successful team environments as compared with traditional organizational structures:

- Trust building is the primary factor that changes the organization's communication patterns.
- Open meetings are an important method for enhancing communication, as they educate employees about the business while building bridges of understanding and trust.
- Shared leadership, which involves more direct and effective communication between management and its internal customers, is common.
- Listening, problem solving, conflict resolution, negotiation, and consensus become important factors in group communication.
- Information flows vertically up to management and down to workers, as well as horizontally among team members, other teams, and supervisors.

Communication is perhaps the single most important aspect of successful teamwork. Open lines of communication increase interaction between employees and management. All affected parties should be kept informed as projects progress.

Maximization of Work Team Effectiveness

Grouping employees into a team structure does not mean that they will automatically function as a team. A group must go through a developmental process to begin to function as a team. Members need training in such areas as problem solving, goal setting, and conflict resolution. Teams must be encouraged to establish the "three Rs"—roles, rules, and relationships.[15]

The self-directed work team can become the basic organizational building block to best ensure success in dynamic global competition. Skills for successful participation in team environments are somewhat different from those necessary for success in old-style organizations:

- Ability to give and take constructive criticism, listen actively, clearly impart one's views to others, and provide meaningful feedback.
- Skills in breaking down emotional barriers, such as insecurity or condescension.
- Ability to promote team functioning by removing process barriers, such as rigid policies and procedures.

To improve group communication, time needs to be set aside to assess the quality of interaction. Questions to pose about the group process might include the following:

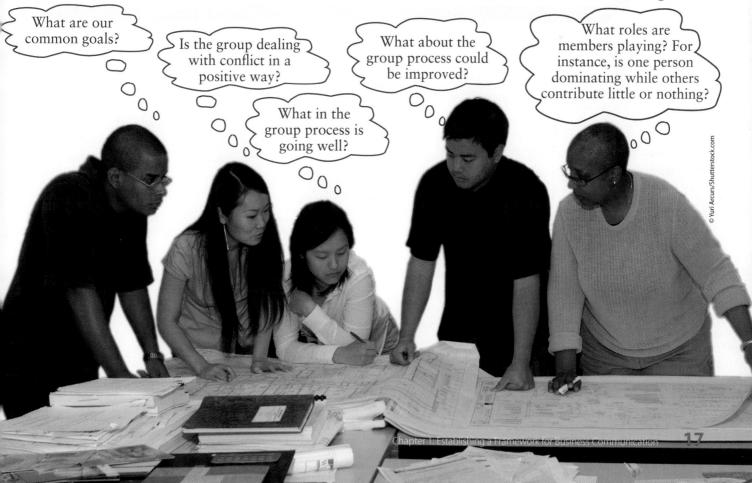

What are our common goals?

Is the group dealing with conflict in a positive way?

What in the group process is going well?

What about the group process could be improved?

What roles are members playing? For instance, is one person dominating while others contribute little or nothing?

- Understanding the feelings and needs of coworkers so members feel comfortable stating their opinions and discussing the strengths and weaknesses of the team.

- Skills in overcoming cultural barriers, such as stereotyped roles and responsibilities, that can separate workers from management.[16]

- Application of leadership skills that apply to a dynamic group setting and lead to team success. In dynamic team leadership, referred to as *distributed leadership*, the role of leader can alternate among members, and more than one leadership style can be active at any given time.[17]

Gender, cultural, and age differences among members of a team can present barriers to team communication. Knowing what behaviors can limit the group process is imperative to maximizing results. Team members might need awareness training to assist in recognizing behaviors that may hinder team performance and in overcoming barriers that can limit the effectiveness of their communication.

STUDY TOOLS
CHAPTER 1

Located at back of the textbook

❑ **Rip out Chapter Review Card**

Located at www.cengagebrain.com

❑ **Review Key Terms Flashcards (Print or Online)**

❑ **Download Audio Summaries for on-the-go review**

❑ **Complete Practice Quizzes to prepare for tests**

❑ **Play "Beat the Clock" to master concepts**

❑ **Complete the Crossword Puzzle to review key terms**

❑ **Watch the video about McDonaldson, a fictitious but all-too-realistic ad agency whose employees struggle with contemporary business communication issues**

4LTR Press solutions are designed for today's learners through the continuous feedback of students like you. Tell us what you think about BCOM6 and help us improve the learning experience for future students.

YOUR FEEDBACK MATTERS.

Focusing on Interpersonal and Group Communication

OBJECTIVES

2-1 Explain how behavioral theories about human needs, trust and disclosure, and motivation relate to business communication.

2-2 Describe the role of nonverbal messages in communication.

2-3 Identify aspects of effective listening.

2-4 Identify factors affecting group and team communication.

2-5 Discuss aspects of effective meeting management.

2-1 Behavioral Theories That Impact Communication

Interpersonal intelligence pertains to the ability to read, empathize with, and understand others.[1] People with interpersonal intelligence are good with people and thrive in social interaction. Rather than being a quality that some are born with and others are not, interpersonal intelligence can be improved by broadening your understanding of human behavior and motivation and practicing certain behaviors when in interpersonal situations. Knowledge from the fields of sociology and psychology is helpful to understanding human needs and providing you with valuable insights about how to achieve effective communication in the workplace.

2-1a Recognizing Human Needs

Psychologist Abraham Maslow developed the concept of a hierarchy of needs through which people progress. In our society, most people have reasonably satisfied their two lower-level needs: (1) physiological needs (food and basic provision) and (2) security and safety needs (shelter and protection from the elements and physical danger). Beyond these two basic need levels, people progress to satisfy the three upper-level needs: (3) social needs for love, acceptance, and belonging; (4) ego or esteem needs to be heard, appreciated, and wanted; and (5) self-actualizing needs, including the need to achieve one's fullest potential through professional, philanthropic, political, educational, and artistic channels.

As people satisfy needs at one level, they move on to the next. The levels that have been satisfied still are present, but their importance diminishes. Effective communicators are able to identify and appeal to need levels in various individuals or groups. Advertising is designed to appeal to need levels. Luxury car and dream vacation ads appeal to ego needs, teeth whitening and anti-aging product messages appeal to social needs, and identity theft, health and fitness, and environmentally friendly commercials appeal to security and safety needs. Efforts to help employees satisfy their needs are essential, since a satisfied worker is generally more productive than a dissatisfied one. In communication activities, a sender's message is more likely to appeal to the receiver if the receiver's need is accurately identified.

2-1b Stroking

People engage in communication with others in the hope that the outcome might lead to mutual trust, mutual pleasure, and psychological well-being. The communication exchange is a means of sharing information about things, ideas, tasks, and selves.

Each communication interaction, whether casual or formal, provides an emotional **stroke** that can have either a positive or a negative effect on your feelings about yourself and others. Getting a pat on the back from the supervisor, receiving a congratulatory phone call or text message, and being listened to by another person are examples of everyday positive strokes. Negative strokes might include receiving a hurtful comment, being avoided or left out of conversation, and receiving a reprimand

interpersonal intelligence
the ability to read, empathize, and understand others

stroke
emotional response one gets in a communication interaction that has either a positive or negative effect on feelings about oneself and others

BCOM

from a superior. By paying attention to the importance of strokes, managers can greatly improve communication and people's feelings about their work.

2-1c Exploring the Johari Window

As relationships develop, the people involved continue to learn about each other and themselves, as shown by the Johari Window in Figure 2-1. Area I, the free or open area, represents what we know about ourselves and what others know about us. Area II, the blind area, designates those things others know about us but that we don't know about ourselves; for example, you are the only person who can't see your physical self as it really is. Things we know about ourselves but that others don't know about us occupy the hidden or secret area III. Area IV includes the unknown: things we don't know about ourselves and others don't know about us, such as our ability to handle emergency situations if we've never been faced with them.

Each of the window areas can vary in size according to the degree to which we learn about ourselves and are willing to disclose things about ourselves to others. Reciprocal sharing occurs when people develop *trust* in each other. When a confidant demonstrates that he or she can be trusted, trust is reinforced and leads to an expansion of the open area of the Johari Window. Usually we are willing to tell people about various things that aren't truly personal. But we share personal thoughts, ambitions, and inner feelings only with selected others—those whom we have learned to trust. The relationships existing between supervisor and employee, doctor and patient, and lawyer and client are those of trust, but only in specific areas. In more intimate relationships with significant others, siblings, and parents, deeper, personal feelings are entrusted to each other.

The idea that trust and openness lead to better communication between two people also applies to groups. Managers engaged in *organizational development* (OD) are concerned with developing successful organizations by building effective small groups. They believe small-group effectiveness evolves mostly from a high level of mutual trust among group members. The aim of OD is to open emotional as well as task-oriented communication. To accomplish this aim, groups often become involved in encounter sessions designed to enlarge the open areas of the Johari Window.[2]

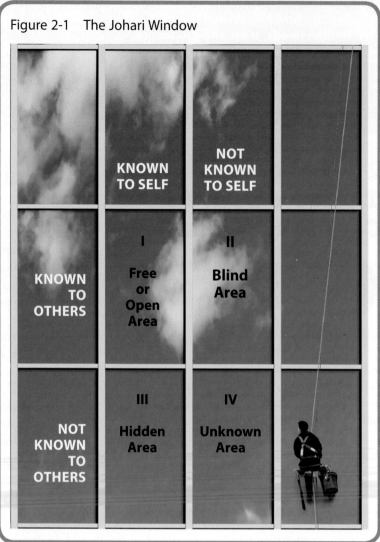

Figure 2-1   The Johari Window

2-1d Contrasting Management Styles

Douglas McGregor, a management theorist, attempted to distinguish between the older, traditional view that workers are concerned only about satisfying lower-level needs and the more contemporary view that productivity can be enhanced by assisting workers in satisfying higher-level needs. Under the older view, management exercised strong control, emphasized the job to the exclusion of concern for the individual, and sought to motivate solely through external incentives—a job and a paycheck. McGregor labeled this management style Theory X. Under the contemporary style, Theory Y, management strives to balance control and individual freedom. By treating the individual as a mature person, management lessens the need for external motivation; treated as adults, people will act as adults.

The situational leadership model developed by Paul Hersey and Kenneth Blanchard does not prescribe a single leadership style, but advocates that what is appropriate in each case depends on the follower (subordinate) and the task to be performed. **Directive behavior** is characterized by the leader's giving detailed rules and instructions and monitoring closely that they are followed. The leader decides what is to be done and how. In contrast, **supportive behavior** is characterized by the leader's listening, communicating, recognizing, and encouraging. Different degrees of directive and supportive behavior can be desirable, given the situation.[3] Combining the ideas of Maslow and McGregor with those of Hersey and Blanchard leads to the conclusion that "the right job for the person" is a better philosophy than "the right person for the job."

The **Total Quality Management** movement focuses on creating a more responsible role for the worker in an organization. In a Total Quality Management environment, decision-making power is distributed to the people closest to the problem, who usually have the best information sources and solutions. Each employee, from the president to the custodian, is expected to solve problems, participate in team-building efforts, and expand the scope of his or her role in the organization. The goal of employee empowerment is to build a work environment in which all employees take pride in their work accomplishments and begin motivating themselves from within rather than through traditional extrinsic incentives.[4] Managers of many companies understand that empowering employees to initiate continuous improvements is critical for survival. Only companies producing quality products and services will survive in today's world market.

Leadership studies have taken a new turn in recent years with the emergence of the social constructionist view of leadership. A social constructionist view sees leadership differently than the psychological approach of the management discipline. A social constructionist view sees leadership as a co-constructed reality that emerges from the interaction of social actors. What this means is that certain leadership behaviors are acceptable to group members while others are not. Because of this, a person may position him or herself as a leader, but others may not perceive these communication behaviors as corresponding with their perception of a leader.

From this perspective, the leader of a group may not be the formally appointed manager or in certain situations, as discussed in Chapter 1, leadership may be distributed among team members. The value of this approach to leadership is its focus on the importance of communication practices in creating leadership.

2-2 Nonverbal Communication

Managers use verbal and nonverbal messages to communicate ideas to employees. *Verbal* means "through the use of words," either written or spoken. *Nonverbal* means "without the use of words." Although major attention in communication study is given to verbal messages, studies show that nonverbal elements can account for more than 90 percent of the total meaning of a message.[5] Nonverbal communication includes *metacommunication* and *kinesic messages*.

2-2a Metacommunication

A **metacommunication** is a message that, although *not* expressed in words, accompanies a message that *is* expressed in words. For example, "Don't be late for work" communicates caution; yet the sentence might imply (but not express in words) such additional ideas as "You are frequently late, and I'm warning you," or "I doubt your dependability." "Your solution is perfect" might also convey a metacommunication such as "You are efficient," or "I certainly like your work." Whether you are speaking or writing, you can be confident that those who receive your messages will be sensitive to the messages expressed in words and to the accompanying messages that are present but not expressed in words.

directive behavior
characterized by leaders who give detailed rules and instructions and monitor closely that they are followed

supportive behavior
characterized by leaders who listen, communicate, recognize, and encourage their followers

Total Quality Management
focuses on creating a more responsible role for the worker in an organization by distributing decision-making power to the people closest to the problem, empowering employees to initiate continuous improvements

metacommunication
a nonverbal message that, although not expressed in words, accompanies a message that is expressed in words

2-2b Kinesic Messages

People constantly send meaning through kinesic communication, an idea expressed through nonverbal behavior. In other words, receivers gain additional meaning from what they see and hear—the visual and the vocal:

- **Visual kinesic communication**—gestures, winks, smiles, frowns, sighs, attire, grooming, and all kinds of body movements.
- **Vocal kinesic communication**—intonation, projection, and resonance of the voice.

Following are some examples of kinesic messages and the meanings they can convey.

Action	Possible Kinesic Message
A wink or light chuckle follows a statement.	"Don't believe what I just said."
A manager is habitually late for staff meetings and with email replies.	"My time is more important than yours. You can wait for me." Alternately, the action might be ordinary for a manager not born in the United States.
A group leader sits at a position other than at the head of the table.	"I want to demonstrate my equality with other members."
An employee wears clothing that reveals tattoos, which violates the company's dress code.	"Rules are for other people; I can do what I want." Alternately, "I do not understand the expectations."
A job applicant submits a résumé containing errors.	"My language skills are deficient." Alternately, "I didn't care to do my best."

2-2c Understanding Nonverbal Messages

Metacommunications and kinesic messages have characteristics that all communicators should take into account.

- **Nonverbal messages cannot be avoided.** Both written and spoken words convey ideas in addition to the ideas contained in the words used. All actions—and even the lack of action—have meaning to those who observe them.

- **Nonverbal messages can have different meanings for different people.** If a team member smiles after making a statement, one member might conclude that the speaker was trying to be funny; another might conclude that the speaker was pleased about having made such a great contribution; another might see the smile as indicating friendliness.

- **Nonverbal messages vary between and within cultures.** Not only do nonverbal messages have different meanings from culture to culture, but men and women from the same culture typically exhibit different body language. As a rule, U.S. men make less body contact with other men than do women with women. Acceptable male body language might include a handshake or a pat on the back, while women are afforded more flexibility in making body contact with each other.

- **Nonverbal messages can be intentional or unintentional.** "You are right about that" can be intended to mean "I agree with you" or "You are right on *this* issue, but you have been wrong on all others discussed."

- **Nonverbal messages can contradict the accompanying verbal message and affect whether your message is understood or believed.** The adage "actions speak louder than words" reveals much about how people perceive messages. Picture a person who says, "I'm happy to be here," but looks at the floor, talks in a weak and halting voice, and clasps his hands timidly in front of his body. Because his verbal and nonverbal messages are contradictory, his audience might not trust his words. Similarly, consider the negative effect of a sloppy personal appearance by a job candidate.

- **Nonverbal messages can receive more attention than verbal messages.** If a supervisor repeatedly glances at his cell phone for text messages or rhythmically taps a pen while making a statement, the words might not register in the employee's mind. An error in basic grammar might receive more attention than the idea that is being transmitted.

- **Nonverbal messages provide clues about the sender's background and motives.** For example, excessive use of big words might suggest that a person reads widely or has an above-average education; it might also suggest a need

visual kinesic communication
gestures, winks, smiles, frowns, sighs, attire, grooming, and all kinds of body movements

vocal kinesic communication
intonation, projection, and resonance of the voice

© cozyta/Shutterstock.com

for social recognition or insecurity about his or her social background.

- **Nonverbal messages are influenced by the circumstances surrounding the communication.** Assume that two men, Ganesh and Jacob, are friends at work. When they are together on the job, Ganesh sometimes puts his hand on Jacob's shoulder. To Jacob, the act could mean nothing more than "We are close friends." But suppose Ganesh is a member of a committee that subsequently denies a promotion for Jacob. Afterward, the same act could mean "We are still friends," but it could also cause resentment. Because of the circumstances, the same act could now mean something such as "Watch the hand that pats; it can also stab."

- **Nonverbal messages can be beneficial or harmful.** Words or actions can be accompanied by nonverbal messages that help or hurt the sender's purpose. Metacommunications and kinesic communications can convey something such as "I am efficient in my business and considerate of others," or they can convey the opposite. They cannot be eliminated, but you can make them work for you instead of against you.

2-3 Listening as a Communication Skill

Despite the fact that many professionals believe incorrectly that business communication is about presentation and not interaction, most managers spend a major part of their day listening and speaking with others. Listening to supervisors, employees, customers, and colleagues commonly consumes more of business employees' time than reading, writing, and speaking combined. Listening is an interpersonal skill as critical as the skill of speaking. According to Peter Nulty, a former board member of *Fortune* magazine and a blogger for Wells Fargo *Daily Advantage*, "Of all the skills of leadership, listening is the most valuable—and one of the least understood. Most captains of industry only listen sometimes, and they remain ordinary leaders. But a few, the great ones, never stop listening. That's how they get word before anyone else of unseen problems and opportunities."[6]

Listening depends on your abilities to receive and decode both verbal and nonverbal messages. The best-devised

EFFECTIVE LISTENING HABITS PAY OFF IN SEVERAL WAYS:

- ☑ Good listeners are liked by others because they satisfy the basic human needs of being heard and being wanted.

- ☑ People who listen well are able to separate fact from fiction, cope effectively with false persuasion, and avoid having others use them for personal gain.

- ☑ Effective listening leads to sensitivity and tolerance toward key individuals who are critical to the organization's success, such as employees, customers, and suppliers.

- ☑ Effective listeners are engaged and constantly learning—gaining knowledge and skills that lead to increased creativity, job performance, advancement, and satisfaction.

- ☑ Job satisfaction increases when people know what is going on, when they are heard, and when they participate in the mutual trust that develops from good communication.

messages and sophisticated communication systems will not work unless people on the receiving end of spoken messages actually listen. Senders of spoken messages must assume their receivers can and will listen, just as senders of written messages must assume their receivers can and will read.

© Rido/Shutterstock.com

2-3a Listening for a Specific Purpose

Individuals satisfy a variety of purposes through listening: (1) interacting socially, (2) receiving information, (3) solving problems, and (4) sharing feelings with others. Each activity may call for a different style of listening or for a combination of styles.

- **Casual listening.** Listening for pleasure, recreation, amusement, and relaxation is casual listening. Some people listen to music all day long for relaxation and to mask unwanted sounds during daily routines, work periods, and daily commutes. Aspects of casual listening are as follows:

    - It provides relaxing breaks from more serious tasks and supports our emotional health.

    - It illustrates that people are selective listeners. You listen to what you want to hear. In a crowded room in which everyone seems to be talking, you can block out all the noise and engage in the conversation you are having with someone.

    - It doesn't require much emotional or physical effort.

- **Listening for information.** Listening for information involves the search for data or material. In a lecture class, for example, the instructor usually has a strategy for guiding the class to desired goals. The instructor will probably stress several major points and use supporting evidence to prove or to reinforce them. When engaged in this type of listening, you could become so focused on recording every detail that you take copious notes with no organization. When listening for information:

    - Use an outlining process to help you capture main ideas and supporting subpoints in a logical way.

    - Watch the speaker as you listen to him or her, since most speakers exhibit a set of mannerisms composed of gestures and vocal inflections to indicate the degree of importance or seriousness that they attach to portions of their presentations.

- **Intensive listening.** When you listen to obtain information, solve problems, or persuade or dissuade (as in arguments), you are engaged in intensive listening. Intensive listening involves greater use of your analytical ability to proceed through problem-solving steps. When listening intensively:

    - Become a good summarizer.

    - Trace the development of the discussion and then move from there to your own analysis.

- **Empathetic listening.** *Empathy* occurs when a person attempts to share another's feelings or emotions. Counselors attempt to use empathetic listening in dealing with their clients, and good friends listen empathetically to each other. Empathy is a valuable trait developed by people skilled in interpersonal relations. When you take the time to listen to another, the courtesy is usually returned. When listening empathetically:

    - Avoid preoccupation with your own problems. Talking too much and giving strong nonverbal signals of disinterest destroy others' desire to talk.

    - Remember that total empathy can never be achieved simply because no two people are exactly alike. The more similar our experiences, however, the better the opportunity to put ourselves in the other person's shoes. Listening with empathy involves some genuine tact along with other good listening habits.

You might have to combine listening intensively and listening empathetically in some situations. Performance appraisal interviews, disciplinary conferences, and other sensitive discussions between supervisors and employees require listening intensively for accurate understanding of the message and listening for feelings, preconceived points of view, and background.

2-3b Bad Listening Habits

Most of us have developed bad listening habits in one or more of the following areas:

- **Faking attention.** Have you ever been introduced to someone only to realize 30 seconds later that you missed the name? We can look directly at a person, nod, smile, and *pretend* to be listening.

- **Allowing disruptions.** We welcome disruptions of almost any sort when we are engaged in somewhat difficult listening. The next time someone enters your classroom or meeting room, notice how almost everyone in the room turns away from the speaker and the topic to observe the latecomer.

- **Overlistening.** When we attempt to record many details in writing or in memory, we can *overlisten* and miss the speaker's major points.

- **Stereotyping.** We make spontaneous judgments about others based on such issues as appearances, mannerisms, dress, and speech delivery. If a speaker doesn't meet our standards in these areas, we simply turn off our listening and assume the speaker can't have much to say.

casual listening
listening for pleasure, recreation, amusement, and relaxation

listening for information
listening that involves the search for data or material

intensive listening
listening to obtain information, solve problems, or persuade or dissuade

empathetic listening
listening to others in an attempt to share their feelings or emotions

- **Dismissing subjects as uninteresting.** People tend to use disinterest as a rationale for not listening. Unfortunately, the decision is usually made before the topic is ever introduced. A good way to lose an instructor's respect when you have to miss class is to ask, "Are we going to do anything important in class today?"
- **Failing to observe nonverbal aids.** To listen effectively, you must observe the speaker. Facial expressions and body motions always accompany speech and contribute much to messages.

Many bad listening habits develop simply because the speed of spoken messages is far slower than our ability to receive and process them. Normal speaking speeds are between 100 and 150 words a minute. The human ear can actually distinguish words in speech in excess of 500 words a minute, and many people read at speeds well beyond 500 words a minute. Finally, our minds process thoughts at thousands of words a minute.

Because individuals can't speak fast enough to challenge our ability to listen, listeners have a responsibility to make spoken communication effective. Good listening typically requires considerable mental and emotional effort.

2-4 Group Communication

Although much of your spoken communication in business will occur in one-to-one relationships, another frequent spoken communication activity will likely occur when you participate in groups, committees, and teams.

2-4a Increasing Focus on Groups

In recent years, developments among U.S. businesses have shifted attention away from the employment of traditional organizational subunits as the only mechanisms for achieving organizational goals and toward the increased use of groups.

- **Flat organizational structures.** Many businesses today are downsizing and eliminating layers of management. Companies implementing Total Quality Management programs are reorganizing to distribute the decision-making power throughout the organization. The trend is to eliminate functional or departmental boundaries. Instead, work is reorganized in cross-disciplinary teams that perform broad

Although much research has been conducted in the area of group size, no optimal number of members has been identified. Groups of five to seven members are thought to be best for decision-making and problem-solving tasks. An odd number of members is often preferred because decisions are possible without tie votes.

core processes (e.g., product development and sales generation) and not narrow tasks (e.g., forecasting market demand for a particular product).

In a flat organizational structure, communicating across the organization chart (among the cross-disciplinary teams) becomes more important than communicating up and down in a top-heavy hierarchy. An individual can take on an expanded **role** as important tasks are assumed. This role can involve power and authority that surpass the individual's **status**, or formal position in the organizational chart. Much of the communication involves face-to-face meetings with team members rather than numerous, time-consuming "handoffs" as the product moves methodically from one department to another. Companies such as IKEA, the Swedish furniture manufacturer and retailer, are using flat organizational structures within stores to build an employee attitude of job involvement and ownership.

- **Heightened focus on cooperation.** Competition has been a characteristic way of life in U.S. companies. Organizations and individuals compete for a greater share of scarce resources, for a limited number of positions at the top of organizations, and for esteem in their professions. Such competition is a healthy sign of the human desire to succeed, and, in terms of

role
tasks employees assume that can involve power and authority that surpass their formal position on the organization chart

status
one's formal position in the organization chart

SUGGESTIONS FOR EFFECTIVE LISTENING

You can enhance the effectiveness of your face-to-face listening by following these suggestions:

- Minimize environmental and mental distractions. Take time to listen. Move to a quiet area where you are not distracted by noise or other conversation. Avoid becoming so preoccupied with what you will say next that you fail to listen.

- Get in touch with the speaker. Maintain an open mind while attempting to understand the speaker's background, prejudices, and points of view. Listen for emotionally charged words and watch for body language, gestures, facial expressions, and eye movements as clues to the speaker's underlying feelings.

- Use your knowledge of speakers to your advantage. Some people seem to run on and on with details before making the point. With this kind of speaker, you must anticipate the major point but not pay much attention to details. Other speakers give conclusions first and perhaps omit support for them. In this case, you must ask questions to obtain further information.

- Let the speaker know you are actively involved. Show genuine interest by remaining physically and mentally involved; for example, avoid daydreaming, yawning, frequently breaking eye contact, looking at your cell phone or papers on your desk, or whispering.

- Do not interrupt the speaker. Try to understand the speaker's full meaning, and wait patiently for an indication of when you should enter the conversation.

- Ask reflective questions that assess understanding. Simply restate in your own words what you think the other person has said. This paraphrasing will reinforce what you have heard and allow the speaker to correct any misunderstanding or add clarification.

- Use probing prompts to direct the speaker. Use probing statements or questions to help the speaker define the issue more concretely and specifically.

- Use lag time wisely. Listening carefully should be your primary focus; however, you can think ahead at times as well. Making written or mental notes allows you to provide useful feedback when the opportunity arises. If you cannot take notes during the conversation, record important points as soon as possible so you can summarize the speaker's key points.

economic behavior, competition is fundamental to the private enterprise system. At the same time, when excessive competition replaces the cooperation necessary for success, communication can be diminished, if not eliminated.

Just as you want to look good in the eyes of your coworkers and supervisors, units within organizations want to look good to one another. This attitude can cause behavior to take the competitive form, a "win/lose" philosophy. When excessive competition has a neg-

ative influence on the performance of the organization, everyone loses.

Although competition is appropriate and desirable in many situations, many companies have taken steps through open communication and information and reward systems to reduce competition and to increase cooperation. Cooperation is more likely when the competitors (individuals or groups within an organization) have an understanding of and appreciation for others' importance and functions. This cooperative spirit is

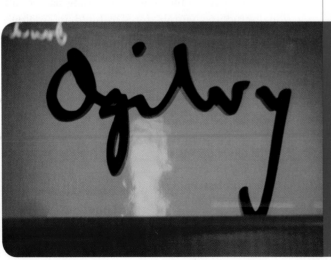

VIRTUAL TEAMS AT OGILVY & MATHER

More than a decade ago, David Ogilvy, the late founder of the advertising company Ogilvy & Mather, invested in an internal IT-based community he called Truffles. As a gourmet, Mr. Ogilvy believed that people should search for knowledge with as much energy and enthusiasm as a pig searches for truffles in the oak forests of France. Truffles includes sites dedicated to individual projects in which virtual teams are able to share their plans, modify a shared piece of work, and informally exchange ideas. This ensures that at any time, people can rapidly understand where their own work is and how it fits with that of others.[7]

characterized as a "win/win" philosophy. One person's success is not achieved at the expense or exclusion of another. Groups identify a solution that everyone finds satisfactory and is committed to achieving. Reaching this mutual understanding requires a high degree of trust and effective interpersonal skills, particularly empathetic and intensive listening skills, and the willingness to communicate long enough to agree on an action plan acceptable to everyone.

2-4b Characteristics of Effective Groups

Groups form for synergistic effects. Through pooling their efforts, members can achieve more collectively than they could individually. At the same time, the social nature of groups contributes to the individual as well. While communication in small groups leads to decisions that are generally superior to individual decisions, the group process can motivate members, improve thinking, and assist attitude change.

As you consider the following factors of group communication, try to visualize their relationship to the groups to which you have belonged, such as in school, religious organizations, athletics, and social activities.

- **Common goals.** In effective groups, participants share a common goal, interest, or benefit. This focus on goals allows members to overcome individual differences of opinion and to negotiate acceptable solutions.
- **Role perception.** People who are invited to join groups have perceptions of how the group should operate and what it should achieve. In addition, each member has a self-concept that dictates how he or she will behave. Those known to be aggressive will attempt to be confrontational and forceful; those who like to be known as moderates will behave in moderate ways by settling arguments rather than initiating them. In successful groups, members play a variety of necessary roles and seek to eliminate nonproductive ones.
- **Longevity.** Groups formed for short-term tasks, such as arranging a dinner and program, will spend more time on the task than on maintenance. However, groups formed for long-term assignments, such as an accounting team auditing a major corporation, may devote much effort to maintenance goals. Maintenance includes division of duties, scheduling, record keeping, reporting, and assessing progress.
- **Size.** The smaller the group, the more its members have the opportunity to communicate with each other. Large groups often inhibit communication

because the opportunity to speak and interact is limited. However, when broad input is desired, large groups can be good if steps are taken to ensure that there is effective communication. Interestingly, large groups generally divide into smaller groups for maintenance purposes, even when the large group is task oriented.

- **Status.** Some group members will appear to have higher ranking than others. Consider a group in which the chief executive of the organization is a member. When the chief executive speaks, members agree. When members speak, they tend to direct their remarks to the one with high status—the chief executive. People are inclined to communicate with peers as their equals, but they tend to speak upward to their supervisor and downward to lower-level employees. In general, groups require balance in status and expertise.
- **Group norms.** A **norm** is a standard or average behavior. All groups possess norms. An instructor's behavior helps establish classroom norms. If some students are allowed to arrive late for class, others will begin to arrive late. If some are allowed to talk during lectures, the norm will be for students to talk. People conform to norms because conformity is easy and nonconformity is difficult and uncomfortable. Conformity leads to acceptance by other group members and creates communication opportunities.
- **Leadership.** The performance of groups depends on several factors, but none is more important than leadership. Some hold the mistaken view that leaders are not necessary when an organization moves to a group concept. The role of leaders changes substantially, but they still have an important part to play. The ability of a group leader to work toward task goals while contributing to the development of group and individual goals is often critical to group success. Leadership activities may be shared among several participants, and leadership may also be rotated, formally or informally. As part of the group, the leader can affect the establishment of norms by determining who can speak and when, encouraging contribution, and providing motivation for effective group activity.[8]

2-4c Group Roles

Groups are made up of members who play a variety of roles, both positive and negative. Negative roles detract from the group's purposes and include those listed below.

Negative Group Roles

- **Isolator**—one who is physically present but fails to participate
- **Dominator**—one who speaks too often and too long
- **Free rider**—one who does not do his or her fair share of the work
- **Detractor**—one who constantly criticizes and complains
- **Digresser**—one who deviates from the group's purpose
- **Airhead**—one who is never prepared
- **Socializer**—one who pursues only the social aspect of the group

A list of positive group roles can be found below.

Positive Group Roles

- **Facilitator** (also known as *gatekeeper*)—one who makes sure everyone gets to talk and be heard
- **Harmonizer**—one who keeps tensions low
- **Record keeper**—one who maintains records of events and activities and informs members
- **Reporter**—one who assumes responsibility for preparing materials for submission
- **Leader**—one who assumes a directive role

In healthy groups, members may fulfill multiple roles, which rotate as the need arises. Negative roles are extinguished as the group communicates openly about its goals, strategies, and expectations. The opinions and viewpoints of all members are encouraged and expected.

2-4d From Groups to Teams

Some use the terms *group* and *team* interchangeably; others distinguish between them. The major distinction between a group and a team is in members' attitudes and level of commitment. A team is typified by a clear identity and a high level of commitment on the part of members. A variety of strategies has been used for organizing workers into teams:

- A **task force** is generally given a single goal and a limited time to achieve it.
- A **quality assurance team**, or *quality circle*, focuses on product or service quality, and projects can be either short or long term.
- A **cross-functional team** brings together employees from various departments to solve a variety of problems such as productivity issues, contract estimations and planning, and multidepartment difficulties.
- A **product development team** concentrates on innovation and the development cycle of new products, and is usually cross-functional in nature. Consider the impact of team structures, as illustrated in the organizational chart in Figure 2-2 on the next page.

While chain of command is still at work in formal organizational relationships and responsibilities, team structures unite people from varying portions of the organization. Work teams are typically given the authority to act on their conclusions, although the level of authority varies, depending on the organization and the purpose of the team. Typically, the group supervisor retains some responsibilities, some decisions are made completely by the team, and the rest are made jointly.

Merely placing workers into a group does not make them a functional team. A group must go through a developmental process to begin to function as a team. The four stages of team development include:

1. **Forming**—becoming acquainted with each other and the assigned task
2. **Storming**—dealing with conflicting personalities, goals, and ideas
3. **Norming**—developing strategies and activities that promote goal achievement
4. **Performing**—reaching the optimal performance level

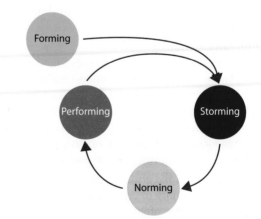

task force
a team of workers that is generally given a single goal and a limited time to achieve it

quality assurance team
a team that focuses on product or service quality; projects can be either short or long term

cross-functional team
a team that brings together employees from various departments to solve a variety of problems

Figure 2-2   Organizational Chart with Hierarchical and Team Structures

Board of Directors

Chief Executive Officer

VP of Information Technology

VP of Operations

VP of Finance

Networks

Communications

Systems Design

Human Resources

Marketing

Public Relations

Accounting

Finance

Stockholder Relations

Product Development Team

Employee Relations Team

Anniversary Celebration Task Force

- **Cooperation.** They have a shared sense of purpose, mutual gain, and teamwork.
- **Communication.** They know that information must flow smoothly between top management and workers. Team members are willing to face confrontation and unpleasantness when necessary.
- **Contribution.** All members share their different backgrounds, skills, and abilities with the team.

Teams have existed for hundreds of years throughout many countries and cultures. Teams are more flexible than larger organizational groupings because they can be assembled, deployed, refocused, and disbanded more quickly, usually in ways that enhance rather than

For a variety of reasons, teams are often unable to advance through all four stages of development. Even long-term teams might never reach the optimal performing stage, settling instead for the acceptable performance of the norming stage.

Research into what makes workplace teams effective indicates that training is beneficial for participants in such areas as problem solving, goal setting, conflict resolution, risk taking, active listening, and recognizing the interests and achievements of others. Participants need to be able to satisfy one another's basic needs for belonging, personal recognition, and support. Team members at the performing stage of team development exhibit the following behaviors:[9]

- **Commitment.** They are focused on the mission, values, goals, and expectations of the team and the organization.

disrupt more permanent structures and processes. Organizational changes are often necessary, however, since support must be in place for performance evaluation, recognition, communication, and training systems. Strategies for bringing about needed change might include arranging site visits to similar organizations that already have teams, bringing in a successful team to speak to the organization, and bringing in consultants to discuss the team development process.

product development team
usually cross-functional in nature; a group of employees who concentrate on innovation and the development cycle of new products

forming
stage one of team development in which team members become acquainted with each other and the assigned task

storming
stage two of team development in which team members deal with conflicting personalities, goals, and ideas

norming
stage three of team development in which team members develop strategies and activities that promote goal achievement

performing
stage four of team development in which team members reach the optimal performance level

2-5 Meeting Management

Meetings are essential for communication in organizations. They present opportunities to acquire and disseminate valuable information, develop skills, and make favorable impressions on colleagues, supervisors, and subordinates. U.S. businesses spend more money on conducting meetings than do businesses in any other country in the world, and they also spend more time in meetings than do people of other countries.[10] International meetings are imperative for solid business reasons but are facing greater planning scrutiny because of tightening travel budgets and a recovering global economy.

Workers frequently have negative attitudes toward meetings because they are perceived as a waste of time. Studies support this opinion, revealing that as much as one-third of the time spent in meetings is unproductive. Negative attitudes toward meetings can be changed when meetings are conducted properly, giving attention to correct procedures and behavior. Successful meetings don't just happen; rather, they occur by design. Careful planning and attention to specific guidelines can help ensure the success of your meetings, whether they are conducted in a face-to-face format or electronically.

2-5a Face-to-Face Meetings

Face-to-face meetings continue to be the most-used meeting format in most organizations. They offer distinct advantages and are appropriate in the following situations:[11]

☑ When you need the richest nonverbal cues, including body, voice, proximity, and touch.

☑ When the issues are especially sensitive.

☑ When the participants don't know one another.

☑ When establishing group rapport and relationships is crucial.

☑ When the participants can be in the same place at the same time.

Face-to-face meetings can be enhanced with the use of various media tools such as flip charts, handouts, and electronic slide decks. While face-to-face meetings provide a rich nonverbal context and direct human contact, they also have certain limitations. In addition to the obvious logistical issues of schedules and distance, face-to-face meetings may be dominated by overly vocal, quick-to-speak, and high-status members.

2-5b Electronic Meetings

Electronic meetings allow companies to reduce travel budgets, save professional time, and minimize the environmental impact caused by travel. A variety of technologies is available to facilitate electronic meetings. Participants may communicate with one another through telephones, computers, or video broadcast equipment using groupware or meeting management software applications. Electronic meetings offer certain advantages. They facilitate geographically dispersed groups because they provide the choice of meeting at different places/same time, different places/different times, same place/same time, or same place/different times. Electronic meetings also speed up meeting follow-up activities because decisions and action items can be recorded electronically.

Electronic meetings also have certain limitations:[12]

- They cannot replace face-to-face contact, especially when group efforts are just beginning and when groups are trying to build group values, trust, and emotional ties.

- They can make it harder to reach consensus, because more ideas are generated and because it might be harder to interpret the strength of other members' commitment to their proposals.

- The success of same-time meetings is dependent on all participants having excellent keyboarding skills to engage in rapid-fire, in-depth discussion. This limitation might be overcome as the use of voice input systems becomes more prevalent.

Figure 2-3 **SAMPLE :-)** Formal Generic Agenda for Meetings

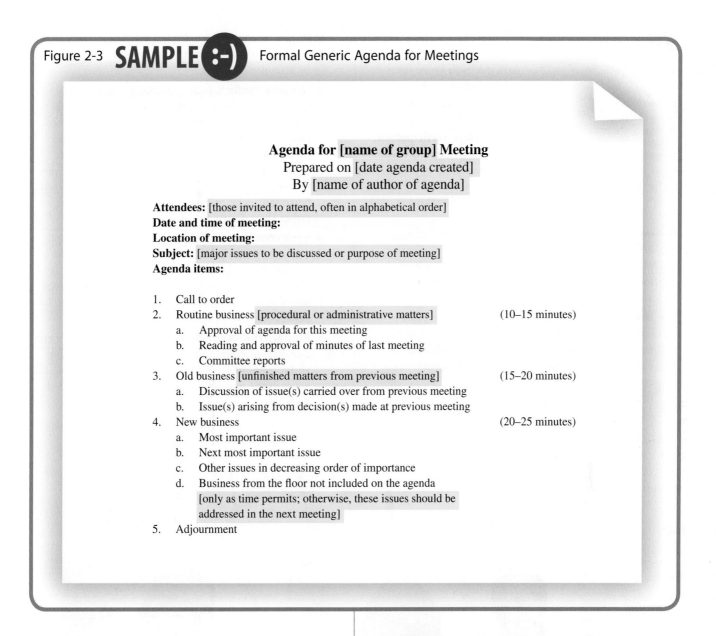

Agenda for [name of group] Meeting
Prepared on [date agenda created]
By [name of author of agenda]

Attendees: [those invited to attend, often in alphabetical order]
Date and time of meeting:
Location of meeting:
Subject: [major issues to be discussed or purpose of meeting]
Agenda items:

1. Call to order
2. Routine business [procedural or administrative matters]   (10–15 minutes)
   a. Approval of agenda for this meeting
   b. Reading and approval of minutes of last meeting
   c. Committee reports
3. Old business [unfinished matters from previous meeting]   (15–20 minutes)
   a. Discussion of issue(s) carried over from previous meeting
   b. Issue(s) arising from decision(s) made at previous meeting
4. New business   (20–25 minutes)
   a. Most important issue
   b. Next most important issue
   c. Other issues in decreasing order of importance
   d. Business from the floor not included on the agenda
      [only as time permits; otherwise, these issues should be
      addressed in the next meeting]
5. Adjournment

Meetings of one 16-person department cost one company $1.6 million a year in lost productivity.[13]

2-5c Suggestions for Effective Meetings

Whether you engage in face-to-face or electronic meetings, observing the following guidelines can help ensure that your meetings are productive:

- **Limit meeting length and frequency.** Any meeting held for longer than an hour or more frequently than once a month should be scrutinized. Ask yourself whether the meeting is necessary. Perhaps the purpose can be achieved in another way, such as email, instant messaging, or telephone.

- **Make satisfactory arrangements.** Select a date and time convenient for the majority of expected participants. For face-to-face meetings, plan the meeting site with consideration for appropriate seating for attendees, media equipment, temperature and lighting, and necessary supplies. For electronic meetings, check hardware and software and connectivity components.

- **Distribute the agenda well in advance.** The **agenda** is a meeting outline that includes important information: date, beginning and ending times, place, topics to be discussed, and responsibilities of those

agenda
a meeting outline that includes important information (e.g., date, beginning and ending times, place, topics to be discussed, and responsibilities of those involved)

involved. Having the agenda prior to the meeting allows participants to know what is expected of them. A sample agenda template is provided in Figure 2-3.

- **Encourage participation.** While it is certainly easier for one person to make decisions, the quality of the decision making is often improved by involving the team. Rational decision making may begin with **brainstorming**, the generation of many ideas from among team members. Brainstormed ideas can then be discussed and ranked, followed by some form of voting.

- **Maintain order.** An organized democratic process ensures that the will of the majority prevails, the minority is heard, and group goals are achieved as expeditiously as possible. Proper parliamentary procedure may be followed in formal meetings, as outlined in sources such as *Robert's Rules of Order* and *Jones' Parliamentary Procedure at a Glance*. For less

formal meetings, the use of parliamentary procedure may not be necessary to ensure effective contribution by attendees.

- **Manage conflict.** In an autocratic organization, conflict might be avoided because employees are conditioned to be submissive. Such an environment, however, leads to smoldering resentment. On the other hand, conflict is a normal part of any team effort and can lead to creative discussion and superior outcomes. Maintaining focus on issues and not personalities helps ensure that conflict is productive rather than destructive.

- **Seek consensus.** While unanimous agreement on decisions is an optimal outcome, total agreement cannot always be achieved. **Consensus** represents the collective opinion of the group, or the informal rule that all team members can live with at least 70 percent of what is agreed upon.

- **Prepare thorough minutes.** Minutes provide a concise record of meeting actions, ensure the tracking and follow-up of issues from previous meetings, and assist in the implementation of previously reached decisions.

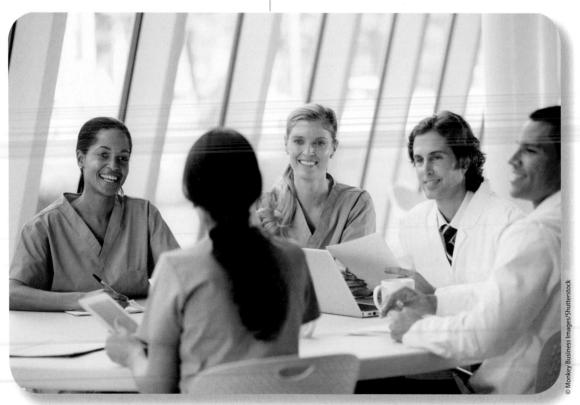

Face-to-face meetings continue to be a frequently used format in most organizations.

© Monkey Business Images/Shutterstock

Meetings are an important management tool and are useful for idea exchange. They also provide opportunities for you, as a meeting participant, to communicate impressions of power and status. Knowing how to present yourself and your ideas and exhibiting knowledge about correct meeting management will assist you in your career advancement.

STUDY TOOLS
CHAPTER 2

Located at back of the textbook

❑ **Rip out Chapter Review Card**

Located at www.cengagebrain.com

❑ **Review Key Terms Flashcards (Print or Online)**

❑ **Download Audio Summaries for on-the-go review**

❑ **Complete Practice Quizzes to prepare for tests**

❑ **Play "Beat the Clock" to master concepts**

❑ **Complete the Crossword Puzzle to review key terms**

❑ **Watch the video about McDonaldson, a fictitious but all-too-realistic ad agency whose employees struggle with contemporary business communication issues**

Planning Spoken and Written Messages

OBJECTIVES

3-1 Consider contextual forces that may affect whether, how, to whom, and when a message is sent.

3-2 Identify the purpose of the message and the appropriate channel and medium.

3-3 Develop clear perceptions of the audience to enhance the impact and persuasiveness of the message, improve goodwill, and establish and maintain the credibility of the communicator.

3-4 Apply tactics for adapting messages to the audience, including those for communicating ethically and responsibly.

3-5 Recognize the importance of organization when planning the first draft.

In a report titled "Writing: A Ticket to Work... or a Ticket Out," the National Commission on Writing reported that two-thirds of salaried employees in large companies have some writing responsibilities, and getting hired and promoted in many industries requires strong writing abilities. While writing is important in most managerial-level jobs, the Commission also concluded that one-third of employees in corporate America write poorly. Knowing that effective communication is tied to the corporate bottom line and many employees can't write well, businesses are investing $3.1 billion annually to train employees to write.[1] Remedies are needed to prevent confusion, waste, errors, lost productivity, and a damaged corporate image—all caused by employees, customers, and clients muddling their way through unreadable messages.

As a capable communicator, you can immediately add value to your organization and set yourself apart from your peers who are struggling to articulate ideas in writing and in presentations. Communication that commands attention and can be understood easily is essential for survival during the information explosion we are experiencing today. On the job, you will be expected to process volumes of available information and shape useful messages that respond to the needs of customers or clients, coworkers and supervisors, and other key business partners. Additionally, increased use of electronic communication (email, texts, instant messages, blogs, videoconferences, etc.) will require you to be technologically savvy and capable of adapting the rules of good communication to the demands of emerging technology.

How can you learn to plan and prepare powerful business messages? The systematic analysis process as outlined in Figure 3-1 will help you develop messages that save you and your organization valuable time and resources and portray you as a capable, energetic professional. A thorough analysis of the audience and your specific communication assignment will empower you to create a first draft efficiently and to revise and proofread your message for accuracy, conciseness, and appropriate tone.

3-1 Step 1: Consider the Applicable Contextual Forces

Chapter 1 discussed four contextual forces that may affect whether, how, to whom, and when a message is sent. These were legal and ethical constraints, diversity challenges, changing technology, and team environment. In addition to these four forces, communication patterns within an organization are a contextual force that should also be considered when planning a message. The organizational culture as well as the four dimensions of context may influence how, whether, and when a message is sent. These two issues are discussed in the sections that follow.

3-1a Organizational Culture

Organizational culture is "a pattern of shared basic assumptions that the group learned as it solved its problems of external adaptation and internal integration and which has worked well enough to be taught to new members as the correct way to perceive, think, and feel in relation to these problems" (Schein, 1992, p. 12).[2]

BCOM

Figure 3-1   Process for Planning and Preparing Spoken and Written Messages

STEP 1	STEP 2	STEP 3	STEP 4	STEP 5	STEP* 6
Consider the applicable contextual forces	Determine the purpose and select an appropriate channel and medium	Envision the audience	Adapt the message to the audience's needs and concerns	Organize the message	Prepare the first draft

*You will focus on the planning process (Steps 1–5) in this chapter; you will learn to prepare the message in Chapter 4 (Step 6).

> "COMMUNICATION THAT COMMANDS ATTENTION AND CAN BE UNDERSTOOD EASILY IS ESSENTIAL FOR SURVIVAL DURING THE INFORMATION EXPLOSION WE ARE EXPERIENCING TODAY."

Boreham and Morgan (2004)[3] note that "Schein makes the crucial claim that an organization's culture determines what it can and cannot do, and that the extent of individual members' socialization into that culture determines what they can and cannot do" (p. 309). This is true of actions and behaviors as well as communicative practices and behaviors.

In other words, organizational culture affects the type, amount, and quality of communication within an organization. The culture of a business provides part of the *context* for interpreting the meaning of everyday organizational life, as well as determining what are considered appropriate messages and the proper or expected ways to convey them.

For example, SAS Institute, the world's largest privately held software company, touts an "employee-friendly" corporate culture. "If you treat employees as if they make a difference to the company, they will make a difference to the company," according to cofounder and CEO Jim Goodnight. SAS Institute's founders set out to create the kind of workplace where employees would enjoy spending time.[4] Compare these values with the type of culture that you might find in an investment banking firm in which competition, individualism, and the drive for profits and bonuses would likely be key elements, and it should be easy to see how culture might affect how communication occurs and what is expected and accepted within an organization in terms of behaviors.

Research suggests that there are seven primary characteristics that, when taken as a whole, capture the essence of an organization's culture. These are

1. **Innovation and risk taking**, or the degree to which employees are encouraged to innovate and take risks

2. **Attention to detail**, or the degree to which employees are expected to exhibit precision, analytical skills, and attention to detail

3. **Outcome orientation**, or the degree to which management focuses on results or outcomes rather than on the techniques and processes used to achieve these outcomes

4. **People orientation**, or the degree to which management decisions consider the effect of outcomes on people within the organization

5. **Team orientation**, or the degree to which work activities are organized around teams rather than individuals

6. **Aggressiveness**, or the degree to which people are aggressive and competitive rather than easygoing

7. **Stability**, or the degree to which organizational activities emphasize maintaining the status quo rather than focusing on change

organizational culture
a pattern of shared basic assumptions that the group learned as it solved its problems of external adaptation and internal integration and which has worked well enough to be taught to new members as the correct way to perceive, think, and feel in relation to these problems

Appraising the organization on each of these characteristics can provide a picture of the organization's culture.

More generally speaking, the culture of business can be characterized as typically having a bias toward action, a demand for confidence, and a results orientation. The culture of business can be seen in everyday office interactions. Being knowledgeable about an organization's culture can help you gauge the type and quality of communication that takes place as well as whether you are a good match with an organization. For example, does the organization have an "open door" policy or are you expected to obey the hierarchical order of management when communicating concerns? Does the office have an open floor plan or do employees have private offices? Do people wear T-shirts and shorts or suits to work every day? The first situation in each of these cases probably signals that the culture is less formal in terms of its expectations and communication patterns, while the second situation may indicate a culture that is more formal in terms of its expectations regarding punctuality and communication choices and behaviors.

3-1b Dimensions of Context

In addition to the other elements of context discussed in previous chapters and sections, there are several dimensions to context, including the physical, social, chronological, and cultural. The *physical* context or setting can influence the content and quality of interaction. For example, if you were to ask your boss for a raise, the effect of the setting might dramatically affect your chances for success. How might the following settings affect the success of such an interaction, how it might take place, or whether it should take place: In the boss's office? At a company picnic? Over lunch at a restaurant? In your work area with others observing?

The *social context* refers to the nature of the relationship between the communicators as well as who is present. In the same situation mentioned above, imagine how the relationship between your manager and yourself might affect your request for a raise if

- You and the manager have been friends for several years, as opposed to a situation in which you and your manager have no personal relationship.
- You are the same age as your manager, *or* she or he is 15 years older (or younger) than you.

Zappos is a company that is well-known for its unique corporate culture, and this is clearly reflected in its fun-filled and hectic activities. Here Kate Gosselin with Cirque du Soleil cast members pose at the Zappos.com Rock 'n' Roll Las Vegas Marathon.

- You and the manager have gotten along well in the past, compared to a situation in which you and the manager have been involved in an ongoing personal conflict.

The *chronological context* refers to the ways time influences interactions. For example, how might the time of day affect the quality of an interaction? How might the communicator's personal preferences regarding time affect communication and its success? Is it a busy time of year for employees and managers? Has there just been a major layoff, downsizing, or profit loss? In this last case, you might want to put off your request for a raise until conditions improve.

The *cultural context* includes both the organizational culture as well as the cultural backgrounds of the people with whom you may be communicating. A person's cultural influences also can affect the kind and quality of communication that takes place, and they can help determine approaches that will be more effective. For example, young people have different expectations than seniors, Hispanics have different expectations than Asians, Californians have different expectations than people from the Midwest or East Coast, and men may communicate differently than women.

Environmental factors may also affect what should be communicated and how. For example, if the economy is doing poorly, then some messages may be inappropriate or may have little chance for success. If you work in a highly litigious environment or one that is strongly regulated, then constraints may exist for what you can communicate and how. Larger social, political, or historical events may affect whether certain messages are appropriate or have a chance of success. As mentioned earlier, in an economic downturn, it may be difficult depending on the industry to be successful at negotiating a pay raise, since the employer may feel that employees should feel lucky to simply have a job during difficult times.

As this discussion shows, context is a complex, multidimensional force that should be considered when planning a message to consider whether it should be sent, when it should be sent, to whom, and how.

3-2 Step 2: Determine the Purpose, and Select an Appropriate Channel and Medium

To speak or write effectively, you must think through what you are trying to say and understand it thoroughly before you begin. Ask yourself why you are preparing the message and what you hope to accomplish. Is the purpose to get information, to answer a question, to accept an offer, to deny a request, to seek support for a product or idea? Condense the answers into a brief sentence that outlines the purpose for writing or the central idea of your message. You will use the central idea to organize your message to achieve the results you desire.

The major purpose of many business messages is to have the receiver understand logical information. Informative messages are used to convey the vast amounts of information needed to complete the day-to-day operations of the business—explain instructions to employees, announce meetings and procedures, acknowledge orders, accept contracts for services, and so forth. Some messages are intended to persuade—to influence or change the attitudes or actions of the receiver. These messages include promoting a product or service and seeking support for ideas and worthy causes presented to supervisors, employees, stockholders, customers or clients, and others. Additional purposes include establishing a good relationship with your audience, which is discussed later in this chapter, and establishing and maintaining your own credibility as a professional, both of which can help increase persuasiveness. You will learn to prepare messages that are for and that consider each of these purposes later in this text. In addition to identifying the purposes of the message, it is also important to decide which channel and medium would be most effective and appropriate.

3-2a Selecting the Channel and Medium

Broadly speaking, four channels of communication exist: visual, written, oral, and nonverbal. However, these broad categories can be broken down further. For example, written communication can be disseminated using a variety of media or forms, including memos, letters, emails, instant or text messaging, faxes, press releases, company Web sites, blogs, blog applications, and reports. Oral communication can also use various media or forms such as face-to-face or interpersonal, telephone, voice messages, teleconferences and videoconferences, speeches, meetings, and podcasts. Typically, nonverbal communication supplements oral forms, but it shouldn't be underestimated because most communication in face-to-face situations is often

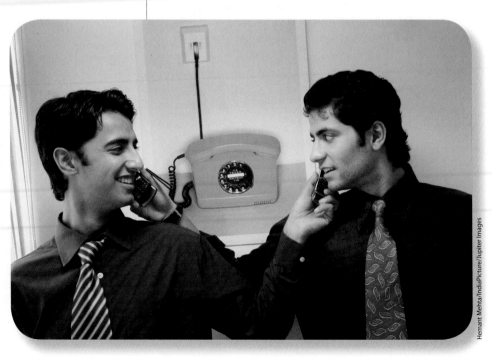

Hemant Mehta/IndiaPicture/Jupiter Images

nonverbal. Similarly, visual communication supplements both written and oral forms of communication in the form of diagrams, photographs, charts, tables, video, and artwork.

Channel choice might be influenced or informed by earlier steps in the planning process. For instance, the contextual forces may affect how a message is sent. For example, if the organization typically conveys most routine messages using email, this may be the most obvious choice. The purpose of communication might affect channel choice as well; in a situation in which the purpose is primarily to establish relationship or convey goodwill, a face-to-face meeting might be the best choice to achieve this goal. Audience analysis might yield information that indicates it prefers a particular medium of communication such as email or phone discussions. Common channel choice considerations are

- **Richness versus leanness.** Some channels of communication provide more information than others. Generally, the richest channels of communication provide nonverbal information in addition to that provided in written or oral form. For this reason, the richest channel of communication is face-to-face, or interpersonal. Face-to-face communication provides participants a rich source of information, including vocal cues, facial expressions, bodily movement, bodily appearance, the use of space, the use of time, touching, and clothing and other artifacts. In addition, face-to-face communication provides opportunities to facilitate feedback and establish a personal focus. These aspects also contribute to the richness of interpersonal communication as a channel of communication.

- **Need for interpretation.** Some channels of communication are more ambiguous or leave more room for interpretation of the message being sent than others. Nonverbal communication may be the most ambiguous channel of communication because it requires the audience to interpret almost the entirety of the message. Nonverbal communication is difficult to interpret for a variety of reasons, mainly because it is not generally considered a coded language. Because of this, one nonverbal code may communicate a variety of meanings. Similarly, nonverbal communication can be difficult to interpret because a variety of codes may communicate the same meaning. A third issue that may affect a person's ability to interpret nonverbal codes accurately is intentionality. Some nonverbal codes are sent intentionally, and others unintentionally.

- **Speed of establishing contact.** Another important consideration, particularly in the business world, is the time it will take for a message to be delivered.

For this reason, electronic forms of communication have become popular. Using the telephone, writing an email or text message, using blogs and blog applications (such as Twitter) or other social media such as Facebook or LinkedIn, posting to wikis, Skyping, using virtual team applications, or sending a fax are nearly instantaneous channels of communication. In contrast, sending a written message or package by mail may take days.

- **Time required for feedback.** Just as we may need to contact someone immediately, we may also need a response from that person just as rapidly. The most rapid forms of communication, as explained above, are generally electronic. However, depending on the person with whom you are communicating, his or her personality, and your relationship, communicating with a person via an electronic channel does not guarantee prompt feedback. In other words, corporate cultures and individual people may have preferences for specific communication channels or mediums and differing communication practices.

- **Cost.** Many channels of communication are relatively inexpensive for business users. Mail, email, text messages, telephones, faxes, wikis, blogs and blog applications, social media, videoconferencing and teleconferencing tools, and Skype are generally considered inexpensive forms of communication. These tools have made it much less expensive for stakeholders both inside and outside organizations to communicate with each other, regardless of their location. Still, there are times when it may be appropriate to choose the greater expense of arranging a face-to-face meeting, such as when introducing members of a virtual team who will be working on an important project for some time or interviewing job applicants for key positions.

- **Amount of information conveyed.** The best channel for conveying large amounts of information is generally a written one. One reason is that most of us are generally poor listeners. Studies indicate that we retain only 10% or so of what we hear. Therefore, if you want people to have the opportunity to process and remember the information you have to deliver, particularly if the message is long or complex, then it is generally best delivered using a written channel rather than an oral one.

- **Need for a permanent record.** Businesspeople are often involved in situations where they must keep records of what occurred during various work activities throughout the day or week. These situations include the need to record what occurred at a department meeting, an employee's work history, the findings of an audit of a client's financial records, and an employee's travel expenses. Most legal documents,

Figure 3-2   Use of Communication Media

MEDIUM	BEST USES
Memo	• Simple, routine messages • Confirming policies • Distributing to a large, internal audience • Providing information when a response isn't required
Letter	• Communicating with an external audience • Conveying formality • Providing a written record • Writing a complaint • Communicating condolences or thanks
Email	• Sending brief, impersonal, or routine messages • Providing a hard copy
Fax	• Sending a visual display of information • Communicating general information about a company and its products or services
Web page	• Sharing information with large audiences in an economical fashion • Inspiring and motivating others • Demonstrating products or training

MEDIUM	BEST USES
Oral presentation	• Introducing a persuasive message or following up on one when goodwill and credibility are especially important • Delivering bad news to a large audience when goodwill and credibility are especially important
Face-to-face	• Communicating confidential information • Negotiating • Promoting or firing an employee • Communicating personal warmth or care • Reading nonverbal communication cues
Telephone	• Providing quick feedback or response • Sending confidential information • Discussing bad news • Confirming
Voice mail	• Informing when feedback isn't needed • Confirming • Sending a simple message
Videoconferencing	• Making a personal connection with a large audience • Economical and efficient • Training

including contracts, use the written channel of communication for this reason: the need to maintain a record. Email messages and other electronic forums such as Web sites, social networking sites, and blogs, if stored and backed up properly, can also serve as a record.

• **Control over the message.** Written channels of communication also are often the best choice when you wish to maintain greater control of the message that you send. The reason? If information is presented orally and interpersonally, you have a greater chance of persons who disagree with you speaking out and potentially derailing or confusing the message. That is why many negative messages, such as informing a job applicant that he or she was not selected, are sent using a written channel of communication.

Figure 3-2 provides a summary of the proper use of differing media within an organizational context.

3-3 Step 3: Envision the Audience

Perception is the part of the communication process that involves how we look at others and the world around us. It's a natural tendency to perceive situations from our own limited viewpoint. We use the context of the situation and our five senses to absorb and interpret the information bombarding us in unique ways.

Individual differences in perception account for the varied and sometimes conflicting reports given by eyewitnesses to the same accident. Our senses can be tricked when there is a difference in what we expect and what really is happening. For example, consider how your *perception* affects your ability to accurately or completely interpret an optical illusion.

Perception of reality is also limited by previous experiences and our attitudes toward the sender of the message. We support ideas that are in line with our own and decide whether to focus on the positive or the negative of a situation. We may simply refuse to hear a message that doesn't fit into our view of the world.

Much of the confusion in communication is caused by differences in the sender's and receiver's perceptions. For example, a manager's brief email requesting a status report on a task may come across as curt to the employees. Perceptions vary between individuals with similar backgrounds, and even more so when people from different cultures, generations, and genders communicate.

Overcoming perceptual barriers is difficult but essential if you are to craft messages that meet the needs and concerns of your audience. To help you envision the audience, first focus on relevant information you know about the receiver. The more familiar you are with the receiver, the easier this task will be. When communicating with an individual, you immediately recall a clear picture of the receiver—his or her physical appearance, background (education, occupation, religion, culture), values, opinions, preferences, and so on. Most importantly, your knowledge of the receiver's reaction in similar, previous experiences will aid you in anticipating how this receiver is likely to react in the current situation. Consider the following audience characteristics:

- **Age.** A message answering an elementary-school student's request for information from your company would not be worded the same as a message answering a similar request from an adult.

- **Economic level.** A solicitation for a business donation for a charity project written to a small business owner would likely differ from one written to a representative of a major corporation.

- **Educational/occupational background.** The technical jargon and acronyms used in a financial proposal sent to bank loan officers may be inappropriate in a proposal sent to a group of private investors.

- **Needs and concerns of the audience.** Just as successful sales personnel begin by identifying the needs of the prospective buyer, an effective manager attempts to understand the receiver's frame of reference as a basis for organizing the message and developing the content.

- **Culture.** The vast cultural differences between people (e.g., language, expressions, customs, values, and religion) increase the complexity of the communication process. An email containing typical American expressions (e.g., "The estimate is in the ballpark," and "Our new sales director really knows all the ropes.") would likely confuse a manager from a different culture. Differences in values influence communication styles and message patterns. For example, Japanese readers value the beauty and flow of words and prefer an indirect writing approach, unlike Americans who prefer clarity and conciseness.[5]

- **Rapport.** A sensitive message prepared for a long-time client may differ significantly from a message prepared for a newly acquired client. Emails discussing expectations for completing an assignment may be briefer and more direct when sent to an employee with whom you share a strong business relationship built on mutual trust. The rapport created by previous dealings with the recipient aids understanding in a current situation.

- **Expectations.** Because accountants, lawyers, and other professionals are expected to meet high standards, a message from one of them containing errors in grammar or spelling would likely cause a receiver to question the credibility of the source.

You may find that envisioning an audience you know well is often such a conscious action that you may not even recognize that you are doing it. On the other hand, envisioning those you do not know well requires additional effort. In these cases, simply assume an

© R. Gino Santa Maria/Shutterstock.com

It can be difficult to see the world as others do.

empathetic attitude toward the receiver to assist you in identifying his or her frame of reference (knowledge, feelings, and emotions). In other words, project mentally how you believe you would feel or react in a similar situation and use that information to communicate understanding back to the person.

Consider the use (or lack) of empathy in the following workplace examples:

SAMPLE MESSAGE

Example 1: A U.S. manager's instructions to a new employee from an Asian culture:

We are **neck and neck** with our competitors, so we really need to work hard to maintain our market share. That means that we really cannot **take our eye off the ball** with this deal, as it will be a real winner for us. The **ball is in our court** now. Do you understand?

Example 2: An excerpt from a message sent to M. Bobby Christiansen, who happens to be female:

Mr. Christensen

The video-on-demand system that you expressed interest in is now available as an option in our minivans. Our sales manager would be happy to provide a demonstration at your convenience. Please stop by on your next maintenance visit.

PROBLEM ANALYSIS

- *The use of expressions peculiar to U.S. environment confuse and intimidate.*
- *Open-ended question at the end disregards importance of saving face to a person of Asian culture. Cultural influences may prevent employee from asking questions that might indicate lack of understanding.*

- *Misspelling receiver's name, misinterpreting gender, and showing disrespect for receiver.*
- *Omission of contact information reduces writer's credibility and shows lack of genuine concern for sender's needs.*
- *Overlooking mechanical errors implies incompetence or carelessness.*

Taking the time and effort to obtain a strong mental picture of your audience through firsthand knowledge or your empathetic attitude *before* you write will enhance your message in the following ways:

1. **Establishes rapport and credibility needed to build long-lasting personal and business relationships.** Your receivers will appreciate your attempt to connect and understand their feelings. A likely outcome is mutual trust, which can greatly improve communication and people's feelings about you, your ideas, and themselves (as shown in the discussion of the Johari Window in Chapter 2).

2. **Permits you to address the audience's needs and concerns.** Such knowledge allows you to select relevant content and to communicate in a suitable style.

3. **Simplifies the task of organizing your message.** From your knowledge of yourself and from your experiences with others, you can reasonably predict receivers' reactions to various types of messages. To illustrate, ask yourself these questions:

   - Would I react favorably to a message saying my request is being granted or that a new client is genuinely pleased with a job I'd just completed?

   - Would I experience a feeling of disappointment when I learn that my request has been refused or that my promised pay raise is being postponed?

   - Would I need compelling arguments to convince me to purchase a new product or support a new company policy?

Now, reread the questions as though you were the message recipient. Because you know *your* answers, you can predict *others'* answers with some degree of accuracy. Such predictions are possible because of commonality in human behavior.

Your commitment to identifying the needs and concerns of your audience before you communicate is invaluable in today's workplace. Organizations must focus on providing quality customer service and developing work environments supportive of talented, diverse workers. Alienating valuable customers and talented employees as a result of poor audience analysis is not an option in today's competitive environment.

3-4 Step 4: Adapt the Message to the Audience's Needs and Concerns

After you have envisioned your audience, you are ready to adapt your message to fit the specific needs of your audience. Adaptations include focusing on the audience's point of view; communicating ethically and responsibly; building and protecting goodwill; using simple, contemporary language; writing concisely; and projecting a positive, tactful tone.

3-4a Focus on the Audience's Point of View

Ideas are more interesting and appealing if they are expressed from the audience's viewpoint. Developing a "you attitude" rather than a "me attitude" involves thinking in terms of the other person's interests and trying to see a problem from the other's point of view. A letter, memo, email, or phone call reflecting a "you attitude" sends a direct signal of sincere concern for the receiver's needs and interest.

The use of the word *you* (appropriately used) conveys to receivers a feeling that messages are specifically for them. However, if the first-person pronoun *I* is used frequently, especially as the subject, the sender may impress others as being self-centered—always talking about self. Compare the following examples of sender-centered and receiver-centered statements:

"I"- or Sender-Centered	"You"- or Receiver-Centered
I wanted to congratulate you on your recent promotion.	Congratulations on your promotion to sales manager!
We are changing our operating hours and dates.	You will find the new hours and days of operation below.

Compliments (words of deserved praise) are another effective way of increasing an audience's receptiveness to ideas that follow. Give sincere compliments judiciously as they can do more harm than good if paid at the wrong time, in the wrong setting, in the presence of the wrong people, or for the wrong reasons. Likewise, avoid flattery (words of undeserved praise). Although the recipient may accept your flattery as a sincere compliment, it is more likely that the recipient will interpret your undeserved praise as an attempt to seek to gain favor or special attention. Suspicion of your motive makes effective communication less likely.

3-4b Communicate Ethically and Responsibly

The familiar directive "with power comes responsibility" applies to your use of communication skills. Because business communication affects the lives of many, you must accept responsibility for using it to uphold your own personal values and your company's standards of ethical conduct. Before speaking or writing, use the following guidelines to help you communicate ethically and responsibly.

HOW TO CULTIVATE A "YOU ATTITUDE"

To cultivate a "you attitude," concentrate on the following questions:

- Does the message address the receiver's major needs and concerns?
- Would the receiver feel this message is receiver-centered? Is the receiver kept clearly in the picture?
- Will the receiver perceive the ideas to be fair, logical, and ethical?
- Are ideas expressed clearly and concisely (to avoid lost time, money, and possible embarrassment caused when messages are misunderstood)?
- Does the message promote positive business relationships—even when the message is negative? For example, are *please, thank you*, and other courtesies used when appropriate? Are ideas stated tactfully and positively and in a manner that preserves the receiver's self-worth and cultivates future business?
- Is the message sent promptly and through the preferred channel to indicate courtesy?
- Does the message reflect the high standards of a business professional: accurate and appealing document design, quality printing, and absence of misspellings and grammatical errors?

- **Is the information stated as truthfully, honestly, and fairly as possible?** Good communicators recognize that ensuring a free flow of essential information is in the interest of the public and the organization. Merck, the manufacturer of the prescription pain reliever Vioxx, was sued by thousands of patients and patients' families for withholding information about known heart risks associated with taking the drug.[6] LifeLock, which advertises itself as "#1 in Identity Theft Protection," was charged by the Federal Trade Commission with engaging in false advertising by promising customers that if they signed up with LifeLock service their personal information would become useless to thieves. According to the FTC, the promises were deceptive because thieves could still rack up unauthorized charges on existing accounts—the most common type of identity theft.[7] Your honor, honesty, and credibility will build strong, long-lasting relationships and lead to the long-term success of your company. Sending complete, accurate, and timely information regardless of whether it supports your interests will help you build credibility.

- **Does the message embellish or exaggerate the facts?** Legal guidelines related to advertising provide clear guidance for avoiding *fraud*, the misrepresentation of products or services; however, overzealous sales representatives or imaginative writers can use language skillfully to create less-than-accurate perceptions in the minds of receivers. Businesses have learned the hard way that overstating the capabilities of a product or service (promising more than can be delivered) is not good for business in the long run. Researchers are at times tempted to overstate their findings to ensure continued funding or greater publicity. Dutch psychologist Diederik Stapel resigned in 2011 after an investigation revealed that he made up the results in many of his eye-catching social psychology studies. So far, 25 of his papers have been retracted; a commission is still investigating others. Stapel also received €2.2 million in grants from the Netherlands Organisation for Scientific Research, and investigators are trying to establish whether he defrauded the government by collecting grant money for research he did not carry out.[8]

While surveys indicate many job seekers believe companies expect résumé padding, companies repeatedly report that this perception is not true. Marilee Jones, dean of admissions at Massachusetts Institute of Technology, and David Edmonson, the former CEO of Radio Shack, resigned high-profile jobs for misstating their academic records. George O'Leary stepped down five days after been named head football coach at Notre Dame, admitting he lied about receiving a master's degree and playing college football.[9]

Skill in communicating persuasively will be important throughout your profession. The techniques you will read about in this text, such as those related to writing a winning résumé and application message, will be helpful as you begin your career; however, these techniques should *not* be used if your motive is to exploit the receiver.

- **Are the ideas expressed clearly and understandably?** If a message is to be seen as honest, you must be reasonably confident that the receiver can understand it. Ethical communicators select words that convey the exact meaning intended and that are within the reader's vocabulary.

- **Is your viewpoint supported with objective facts?** Are facts accurately documented to allow the reader to judge the credibility of the source and to give credit where credit is due? Can opinions be clearly distinguished from facts? Have you evaluated honestly any real or perceived conflict of interest that could prevent you from preparing an unbiased message?

- **Are ideas stated with tact and consideration that preserve the receiver's self-worth?** The metaphor "An arrow, once it is shot, cannot be recalled" describes the irrevocable damage caused by cruel or unkind words.[10] Ego-destroying criticism, excessive anger, sarcasm, hurtful nicknames, betrayed secrets, rumors, and malicious gossip pose serious ethical problems in the workplace because they can ruin reputations, humiliate, and damage a person's self-worth. Serious legal issues arise when negative statements are false, constituting defamation. Written defamatory remarks are referred to as **libel**, and similar spoken remarks are referred to as **slander**. If you choose to make negative statements about a person, be sure the facts in question are supported. Additionally, you'll hone your abilities to convey negative information and to handle sensitive situations in a constructive, timely manner rather than ignoring them until they are out of control. For considerate, fair, and civilized use of words, follow this simple rule: Communicate with and about others with the same kindness and fairness that you wish others to use when communicating with and about you.

- **Are graphics carefully designed to avoid distorting facts and relationships?** Communicating ethically involves reporting data as clearly and accurately as possible. Misleading graphics result either from the developers' deliberate attempt to confuse the audience or from their lack of expertise in constructing ethical graphics.

Communication's Golden Rule: Communicate with and about others with the same kindness and fairness that you wish others to use when communicating with and about you.

libel
written defamatory remarks

slander
spoken defamatory remarks

3-5 Step 5: Organize the Message

After you have identified the specific ways you must adapt the message to your particular audience, you are ready to organize your message. In a discussion of communication, the word *organize* means "the act of dividing a topic into parts and arranging them in an appropriate sequence." Before undertaking this process, you must be convinced that the message is the right message—that it is complete, accurate, fair, reasonable, ethical, and logical. If it doesn't meet these standards, it should not be sent. Good organization and good writing or speaking cannot be expected to compensate for a bad decision.

If you organize and write simultaneously, the task seems hopelessly complicated. Writing is much easier if questions about the organization of the message are answered first: What is the purpose of the message, what is the receiver's likely reaction, and should the message begin with the main point? Once these decisions have been made, you can concentrate on expressing ideas effectively.

3-5a Outline to Benefit the Sender and the Audience

When a topic is divided into parts, some parts will be recognized as central ideas and the others as minor ideas (details). The process of identifying these ideas and arranging them in the right sequence is known as **outlining**. Outlining *before* communicating provides numerous benefits. It:

- **Encourages accuracy and brevity.** Outlining reduces the chance of leaving out an essential idea or including an unessential idea.

- **Permits concentration on one phase at a time.** Having focused separately on (a) the ideas that need to be included, (b) the distinction between major and minor ideas, and (c) the sequence of ideas, total concentration can now be focused on the next challenge—expressing.

- **Saves time in structuring ideas.** With questions about which ideas to include and their proper sequence already answered, little time is lost in moving from one point to the next.

- **Provides a psychological lift.** The feeling of success gained in preparing the outline increases confidence that the next step—writing or speaking—will be successful, too.

- **Facilitates emphasis and de-emphasis.** Although each sentence makes its contribution to the message, some sentences need to stand out more vividly in the receiver's mind than others. An effective outline ensures that important points will appear in emphatic positions.

The preceding benefits derived from outlining are sender oriented. Because a message has been well outlined, receivers benefit, too:

- The message is more concise and accurate.

- Relationships between ideas are easier to distinguish and remember.

- Reactions to the message and its sender are more likely to be positive.

A receiver's reaction to a message is strongly influenced by the sequence in which ideas are presented. A beginning sentence or an ending sentence is in an emphatic position.

3-5b Sequence Ideas to Achieve Desired Goals

When planning your communication, you should strive for an outline that will serve you in much the same way a blueprint serves a builder or an itinerary serves a traveler. Organizing your message first will ensure that your ideas are presented clearly and logically and all vital components are included. To facilitate your determining an appropriate sequence for a business document or presentation, follow the three-step process illustrated in Figure 3-3. This process involves answering the following questions in this order:

1. **What is the central idea of the message?** Think about the *reason* you are writing or speaking—the first step in the communication process. What

outlining
the process of identifying central ideas and details and arranging them in the right sequence; should be completed prior to writing

Figure 3-3   Process of Selecting an Outline for a Spoken or Written Message

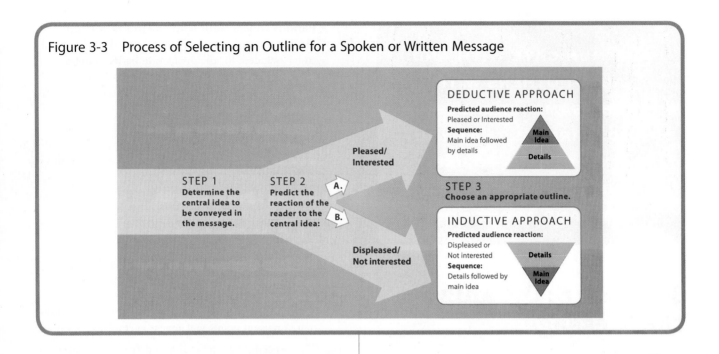

is your purpose—to extend a job offer, decline an invitation, or seek support for an innovative project? The purpose is the central idea of your message. You might think of it as a message condensed in one brief statement.

2. **What is the most likely audience reaction to the message?** Ask, "If I were the one receiving the message I am preparing to send, what would *my* reaction be?" Because you would react with pleasure to good news and displeasure to bad news, you can reasonably assume a receiver's reaction would be similar. By considering anticipated audience reaction, you build goodwill with the receiver. Almost every message will fit into one of four categories of anticipated audience reaction, as shown in Figure 3-3: pleasure, displeasure, interest but neither pleasure nor displeasure, or no interest.

3. **In view of the predicted audience reaction, should the central idea be listed first in the outline or should it be listed as one of the last items?** When a message begins with the major idea, the sequence of ideas is called **deductive.** When a message withholds the major idea until accompanying details and explanations have been presented, the sequence is called **inductive.**

Consider the audience to determine whether to use the inductive or deductive sequence. If an audience might be antagonized by the main idea in a deductive message, lead up to the

deductive
a message in which the major idea precedes the details

inductive
a message in which the major idea follows the details

main idea by making the message inductive. If a sender wants to encourage audience involvement (to generate a little concern about where the details are leading), use the inductive approach. Inductive organization can be especially effective if the main idea confirms the conclusion the audience has drawn from the preceding details—a cause is worthy of support, a job applicant should be interviewed, a product/service should be selected, and so on. As you learn in later chapters about writing letters, memos, and email messages and about planning spoken communications, you will comprehend the benefits of using the appropriate outline for each receiver reaction:

Deductive Order (main idea first)	Inductive Order (details first)
When the message will *please* the audience	When the message will *displease* the audience
When the message is *routine* (will not please nor displease)	When the audience *might not be interested* (will need to be persuaded)

For determining the sequence of minor ideas that accompany the major idea, the following bases for idea sequence are common:

- **Time.** When writing a report or email message about a series of events or a process, paragraphs proceed from the first step through the last step.
- **Space.** If a report is about geographic areas, ideas can proceed from one area to the next until all areas have been discussed.

MEETING DIVERSE AUDIENCES' NEEDS

Kentucky Fried Chicken has achieved market dominance in China over McDonald's and local competitors. This success can be traced to the fast-food giant's use of local ingredients—both for its management team and on its menus. In the 24 years it has been operating in China, KFC's parent company, Louisville, Kentucky–based Yum! Brands, Inc. has hired Chinese managers to build partnerships with local companies in its drive to expand and used their expertise to offer a selection of regional dishes that cater to domestic tastes. Today, KFC's Chinese customers can purchase a bowl of congee , a rice porridge that can feature pork, pickles, mushrooms, and preserved egg, as well as order a bucket of its famous fried chicken. "They got in early, they adapted the product, they expanded aggressively and they gave their Chinese managers real decision-making power, " James McGregor, a former chairman of the American Chamber of Commerce in China and author of *One Billion Customers: Lessons from the Front Lines of Doing Business in China.*[11]

- **Familiarity.** If a topic is complicated, the presentation can begin with a known or easy-to-understand point and proceed to progressively more difficult points.

- **Importance.** In analytical reports in which major decision-making factors are presented, the factors can be presented in order of most important to least important, or vice versa.

- **Value.** If a presentation involves major factors with monetary values, paragraphs can proceed from those with greatest values to those with least values, or vice versa.

The same organizational patterns are recommended for written and spoken communication. These patterns are applicable in email messages, blogs, letters, memos, and reports.

STUDY TOOLS

CHAPTER 3

Located at back of the textbook

❑ Rip out Chapter Review Card

Located at www.cengagebrain.com

❑ Review Key Terms Flashcards (Print or Online)

❑ Download Audio Summaries for on-the-go review

❑ Complete Practice Quizzes to prepare for tests

❑ Play "Beat the Clock" to master concepts

❑ Complete the Crossword Puzzle to review key terms

❑ Watch the video about McDonaldson, a fictitious but all-too-realistic ad agency whose employees struggle with contemporary business communication issues

Preparing Written Messages

OBJECTIVES

4-1 Apply techniques for developing effective sentences and unified and coherent paragraphs.

4-2 Prepare visually appealing documents that grab the audience's attention and increase comprehension.

4-3 Identify factors affecting readability and revise messages to improve readability.

4-4 Revise and proofread a message for content, organization, style, and tone; mechanics; and format and layout.

In Chapter 3, you learned about the importance of following a systematic process to develop business messages. The applications in Chapter 3 guided you in developing a clear, logical plan for your message that focuses on the needs of the receiver (Steps 1–5). Effectively capturing your ideas for various business communication situations involves skillful use of language and careful attention to accuracy and readability issues—the remaining two steps in this important process are shown in Figure 4-1 on the next page.

4-1 Step 6: Prepare the First Draft

Once you have determined whether the message should be presented deductively (main idea first) or inductively (explanation and details first) and have planned the logical sequence of minor points, you are ready to begin composing the message.

Normally, writing rapidly (with intent to rewrite certain portions, if necessary) is better than slow, deliberate writing (with intent to avoid any need for rewriting portions). The latter approach can be frustrating and can reduce the quality of the finished work. Time is wasted in thinking of one way to express an idea, discarding it either before or after it is written, waiting for new inspiration, and rereading preceding sentences.

Concentrating on getting your ideas down as quickly as you can is an efficient approach to writing. During this process, remember that you are preparing a draft and not the final copy. If you are composing at the computer, you can quickly and easily revise your draft throughout the composition process. This seamless approach to writing allows you to continue to improve your working draft until the moment you are ready to submit the final copy. Numerous electronic writing tools are available, and technology will continue to unfold to enhance the writing process.

4-1a Craft Powerful Sentences

Well-developed sentences help the receiver understand the message clearly and react favorably to the writer or speaker. In this section, you will learn about predominant use of active voice and emphasis of important points, which affect the clarity and human relations of your message.

Rely on Active Voice

Business communicators normally use active voice more heavily than passive voice because active voice conveys ideas more vividly. In sentences in which the subject is the *doer* of action, the verbs are called *active*. In sentences in which the subject is the *receiver* of action, the verbs are called *passive*. Review the differences in the impact of **passive voice** and **active voice**:

Passive Voice	Active Voice
Free refills of soft drinks are expected by our customer base and shouldn't be the focus of cutbacks.	Our customers expect free refills of soft drinks, so we shouldn't consider eliminating that offering.

The active sentence invites the receiver to see the consumer as actively engaged in setting expectations, while the passive sentence draws attention to the soft drink refills. Using active voice makes the subject the actor, which

passive voice
when the subject of a sentence is the receiver of an action

active voice
when the subject of a sentence is the doer of an action

Log onto www.cengagebrain.com for additional resources including flashcards, games, self-quizzing for chapter review, grammar exercises, and more.

BCOM

Figure 4-1 Process for Planning and Preparing Spoken and Written Messages

STEP 1	STEP 2	STEP 3	STEP 4	STEP 5	STEP* 6	STEP* 7
Consider the applicable contextual forces	Determine the purpose and select an appropriate channel and medium	Envision the audience	Adapt the message to the audience's needs and concerns	Organize the message	Prepare the first draft	Revise and proofread for accuracy and desired impact

*You focused on the planning process (Steps 1–5) in Chapter 3; you will learn to prepare the message (Steps 6–7) in this chapter.

places greater emphasis on his or her concerns. In the passive sentence, the receiver becomes aware that soft drink refills are an issue, but it does not reveal who is concerned.

Even when a passive sentence contains additional words to reveal the doer, the imagery is less distinct than it would be if the sentence were active: *Free refills of soft drinks are expected by our customer base and shouldn't be the focus of cutbacks.* "Free refills" gets the most attention because it is the subject. The sentence seems to let a receiver know the *result* of the action before revealing the doer; therefore, the sentence is less emphatic.

Although active voice conveys ideas more vividly, passive voice is useful for the following purposes:

- Concealing the doer. ("Shortages in inventory have been found," rather than "Shortages in inventory have been found by auditors.")

- Placing more emphasis on *what* was done and who or what it was *done to* than on who *did* it. ("The reports have been compiled by our sales representatives.")

- Subordinating an unpleasant thought or avoiding finger-pointing. ("The printer on the second floor is not working properly," rather than "Lucy apparently fouled up the printer on the second floor.")

Emphasize Important Ideas

A landscape artist wants some features in a picture to stand out boldly and others to get little attention. A musician sounds some notes loudly and others softly. Likewise, a writer or speaker wants some ideas to be *emphasized* and others to be *de-emphasized*. Normally, pleasant and important ideas should be emphasized; unpleasant and insignificant ideas should be de-emphasized. Emphasis techniques include

© Dusit/Shutterstock.com

sentence structure, repetition, words that label, position, and space and format.

Sentence Structure For emphasis, place an idea in a simple sentence. The simple sentence in the following example has one independent clause. Because no other idea competes with it for attention, this idea is emphasized.

Simple Sentence Is More Emphatic	Compound Sentence Is Less Emphatic
Jeanette is an excellent auditor.	Jeanette is an excellent auditor, but sometimes she finds the work tedious and boring.

For emphasis, place an idea in an independent clause; for de-emphasis, place an idea in a dependent clause. In the following compound sentence, the idea of auditing work is in an independent clause. Because an independent clause makes sense if the rest of the sentence is omitted, an independent clause is more emphatic than a dependent clause. In the complex sentence, the idea of auditing work is in a dependent clause. Compared with the independent clause that follows ("Jeanette is an excellent . . ."), the idea in the dependent clause is de-emphasized.

Compound Sentence Is More Emphatic	Complex Sentence Is Less Emphatic
Jeanette is an excellent auditor, but sometimes she finds the work tedious and boring.	Although she finds the work tedious and boring at times, Jeanette is an excellent auditor.

Repetition

To emphasize a word, let it appear more than once in a sentence. For example, a clever advertisement by OfficeMax used the word *stuff* repeatedly to describe generically several types of office-supply needs ranging from paper clips to color copies, and then ended succinctly with "OfficeMax ... for your office stuff." Likewise, in the following example, "reception" receives more emphasis when the word is repeated.

Less Emphatic	More Emphatic
Her promotion was well received because of ...	Her promotion was well received; this reception is attributed to ...

Words that Label

For emphasis or de-emphasis, use words that label ideas as significant or insignificant. Note the labeling words used in the following examples to emphasize or de-emphasize an idea:

> But most important of all ...
> A less significant aspect was ...

Position

To emphasize a word or an idea, position it first or last in a sentence, clause, paragraph, or presentation. Note that the additional emphasis placed on the words "sales goals" or "sales quotas" and "loss" (or its equivalent) in the examples in the right column because these phrases appear early or late in their clauses.

Less Emphatic	More Emphatic
His daily monitoring of <u>sales quotas</u> helped the company reach monthly <u>goals</u> that otherwise may not have been attained.	Monthly <u>sales goals</u> were reached due to careful monitoring; <u>losses</u> may have resulted without it.
<u>Sales quotas</u> were reached because of his daily monitoring: without that, <u>losses</u> may have been the result.	Monthly <u>sales goals</u> were reached; without his daily monitoring, there may have been a <u>loss</u>.

In paragraphs, the first and last words are in particularly emphatic positions. An idea that deserves emphasis can be placed in either position, but an idea that does not deserve emphasis can be placed in the middle of a long paragraph. The word *I*, which is frequently overused in messages, is especially noticeable if it appears as the first word. *I* is more noticeable if it appears as the first word in *every* paragraph. Avoid using the word *However* as the first word in a paragraph if the preceding paragraph is neutral or positive. These words imply that the next idea will be negative. Unless the purpose is to place emphasis on negatives, such words as *denied*, *rejected*, and *disappointed* should not appear as the last words in a paragraph.

Likewise, the central idea of a written or spoken report appears in the introduction (the beginning) and the conclusion (the end). Good transition sentences synthesize ideas at the end of each major division.

Space and Format

The various divisions of a report or spoken presentation are not expected to be of equal length, but an extraordinary amount of space devoted to a topic attaches special significance to that topic. Similarly, a topic that receives an especially small amount of space is de-emphasized. The manner in which information is physically arranged affects the emphasis it receives and consequently the overall impact of the message.

4-1b Develop Coherent Paragraphs

Well-constructed sentences are combined into paragraphs that discuss a portion of the topic being covered. To write effective paragraphs, you must learn to (a) develop deductive or inductive paragraphs consistently, (b) link ideas to achieve coherence, (c) keep paragraphs unified, and (d) vary sentence and paragraph length.

Position the Topic Sentence Appropriately

Typically, paragraphs contain one sentence that identifies the portion of the topic being discussed and presents the central idea. That sentence is commonly called a **topic sentence**. For example, consider operating instructions prepared for company-owned GPS navigation systems. The overall topic is how to get satisfactory performance from the device. One portion of that topic is setup, another portion (paragraph) discusses operation, and so forth. Within each paragraph, one sentence serves a special function. Sentences that list the steps can appear as one paragraph, perhaps with steps numbered as follows:

To set up the system, take the following steps:

1. Connect …

2. Go to menu settings to …

In this illustration, the paragraphs are **deductive**; that is, the topic sentence *precedes* details. When topic sentences *follow* details, the paragraphs are **inductive**. As discussed previously, the receiver's likely reaction to the main idea (pleased, displeased, interested, not interested) aids in selecting the appropriate sequence.

When the subject matter is complicated and the details are numerous, paragraphs sometimes begin with a main idea, follow with details, and end with a summarizing sentence. But the main idea might not be in the first sentence; the idea could need a preliminary statement. Receivers appreciate consistency in the placement of topic sentences. Once they catch on to the writer's or speaker's pattern, they know where to look for main ideas.

These suggestions seldom apply to the first and last sentences of letters, memos, and email messages. Such sentences frequently appear as single-sentence paragraphs. But for reports and long paragraphs of letters, strive for paragraphs that are consistently deductive or inductive. Regardless of which is selected, topic sentences are clearly linked with details that precede or follow.

topic sentence
a sentence that identifies the portion of the topic being discussed and presents the central idea of the paragraph

deductive paragraph
a paragraph in which the topic sentence precedes the details

inductive paragraph
a paragraph in which the topic sentence follows the details

coherence
cohesion, so that each sentence in some way is linked to the preceding sentences

Link Ideas to Achieve Coherence

Careful writers use coherence techniques to keep receivers from experiencing abrupt changes in thought. Although the word **coherence** is used sometimes to mean "clarity" or "understandability," it is used throughout this text to mean "cohesion." If writing or speaking is coherent, the sentences stick together; each sentence is in some way linked to the preceding sentences. Avoid abrupt changes in thought, and link each sentence to a preceding sentence.

The following techniques for linking sentences are common:

1. **Repeat a word that was used in the preceding sentence.** The second sentence in the following example is an obvious continuation of the idea presented in the preceding sentence.

   … to take responsibility for the decision. This responsibility can be shared …

2. **Use a pronoun that represents a noun used in the preceding sentence.** Because "it" means "responsibility," the second sentence below is linked directly with the first.

   … to take this responsibility. It can be shared …

3. **Use connecting words.** Examples include *however, therefore, yet, nevertheless, consequently, also,* and *in addition.* "However" implies "We're continuing with the same topic, just moving into a different phase." Remember, though, that good techniques can be overused. Unnecessary connectors are space consuming and distracting. Usually they can be spotted (and crossed out) in proofreading.

   … to take this responsibility. However, few are willing to …

Just as sentences within a paragraph must link, paragraphs within a document must also link. Unless a writer or speaker is careful, the move from one major topic to the next will seem abrupt. A good transition sentence can bridge the gap between the two topics by summing up the preceding topic and leading a receiver to expect the next topic:

Once the new accounting system is put into place, training employees in its operation is vital.

This sentence could serve as a transition between the "Installation" and "Training" division headings. Because a transition sentence comes at the end of one segment and before the next, it emphasizes the central idea of the preceding segment and confirms the relationship of the two segments. While transition sentences are helpful if properly used, they can be overused. For most reports, transition sentences before major headings are sufficient. Normally, transition sentences before subheadings are unnecessary.

© valdis torms/Shutterstock.com

Keep Paragraphs Unified

Receivers expect the first paragraph of a message to introduce a topic, additional paragraphs to discuss it, and a final paragraph to tie all of the paragraphs together. The middle paragraphs should be arranged in a systematic sequence, and the end must be linked easily to some word or idea presented in the beginning. The effect of a message that is *not* unified is like that of an incomplete circle or a picture with one element obviously missing.

- A unified email message, letter, memo, or report covers its topic adequately but does not include extraneous material. The document should have a beginning sentence appropriate for the expected receiver reaction, paragraphs that present the bulk of the message, and an ending sentence that is an appropriate closing for the message presented.

- A unified report or presentation begins with an introduction that identifies the topic, reveals the thesis, and previews upcoming points. The introduction often includes some background, sources of information, and the method of treating data. Between the beginning and the ending, a unified report should have paragraphs arranged in a systematic sequence. A summary or conclusion brings all major points together.

Vary Sentence and Paragraph Length

Sentences of short or average length are easy to read and preferred for communicating clearly. However, keeping *all* sentences short is undesirable, because the message might sound monotonous, unrealistic, or elementary. A 2-word sentence is acceptable; so is a 60-word sentence—if it is clear. Just as sentences should vary in length, they should also vary in structure. Some complex or compound sentences should be included with simple sentences.

Variety is just as desirable in paragraph length as it is in sentence length. A paragraph can be from one line in length to a dozen lines or more. However, just as with sentence length, average paragraph length also should be kept short, as appropriate to the document type:

- Paragraphs in letters, memos, and email messages are typically shorter than paragraphs in business reports.
  - First and last paragraphs are normally short (one to four lines), and other paragraphs are normally no longer than *six lines*. A short first paragraph is more inviting to read than a long first paragraph, and a short last paragraph enables a writer to emphasize parting thoughts.

- The space between paragraphs is a welcome resting spot. Long paragraphs are difficult to read and make a message appear uninviting. Paragraph length will vary depending on the complexity of the subject matter. However, as a general rule paragraphs should be no longer than *eight to ten lines*. This length usually allows enough space to include a topic sentence and three or four supporting statements. If the topic cannot be discussed in this space, divide the topic into additional paragraphs.

To observe the effect large sections of unbroken text have on the overall appeal of a document, examine the memos in Figure 4-2 on the next page. Without question, the memo with the short, easy-to-read paragraphs is more inviting than the memo with one bulky paragraph.

Although variety is a desirable quality, it should not be achieved at the expense of consistency. Using *I* in one part of a message and then without explanation switching to *we* is inadvisable. Using the past tense in one sentence and the present tense in another sentence creates variety at the expense of consistency—unless the shift is required to indicate actual changes in time. Unnecessary changes from active to passive voice and from third to first person are also discouraged.

Figure 4-2 Contrast the Readability and Appeal of Bulky (left) versus Broken (right) Text

---

New Message

To: All employees
From: Kim Andrews, Marketing Manager
Subject: Harassment Training Available Online

Hi, all,

You can now access the required Harassment and Discrimination seminar online. Not only will this change make the training more convenient for you by enabling you to take it at your leisure, but it should also save you time. To access the online training module, go to the Training link on the company intranet. You should see the course listing, "Harassment and Discrimination," which you can click on to begin the course. The course should take you one hour to complete. Your completion will automatically be recorded, and Human Resources will be notified. Hopefully, you will find this new option for fulfilling this training requirement better suits your schedule. Please complete the survey at the end of the training to enable us in Human Resources to serve you, our valued employees, better.

New Message

To: All employees
From: Kim Andrews, Marketing Manager
Subject: Harassment Training Available Online

Hi, all,

You can now access the required Harassment and Discrimination seminar online. Not only will this change make the training more convenient for you by enabling you to take it at your leisure, but it should also save you time.

To access the online training module, go to the Training link on the company intranet. You should see the course listing, "Harassment and Discrimination," which you can click on to begin the course. The course should take you one hour to complete. Your completion will automatically be recorded, and Human Resources will be notified.

Hopefully, you will find this new option for fulfilling this training requirement better suits your schedule. Please complete the survey at the end of the training to enable us in Human Resources to serve you, our valued employees, better.

4-2 Revise and Proofread

Professional writers often recognize that the real work of writing occurs during the revision process. It is this step, however, that is often overlooked or given short shrift by those who do not write for a living. Revising and proofreading effectively therefore requires a change in mind-set.

4-2a Cultivate a Frame of Mind for Effective Revising and Proofreading

The following suggestions will guide your efforts to develop business documents that achieve the purpose for which they are intended.

- **Attempt to see things from your audience's perspective rather than from your own.** Being empathetic with your audience isn't as simple as it seems, particularly when dealing with today's diverse workforce. Erase the mind-set, "I know what *I* need to say and how *I* want to say it." Instead, ask, "How would

my audience react to this message? Is this message worded so that my audience can easily understand it? Does it convey a tone that will build goodwill?"

- **Revise your documents until you cannot see any additional ways to improve them.** Resist the temptation to think of your first draft as your last draft. Instead, look for ways to improve and be willing to incorporate valid suggestions once you have completed a draft. Experienced writers believe that there is no such thing as good writing, but there is such a thing as good rewriting. Author Dorothy Parker, who wrote for *Vanity Fair* and *Esquire*, once said, "I can't write five words but that I change seven."[1] Skilled speech writers might rewrite a script 15 or 20 times. Writers in public relations firms revise brochures and advertising copy until perhaps only a comma in the final draft is recognizable from the first draft. Even simple email messages require revision for clarity and mechanical errors, with extra passes needed depending on the number of recipients and the context of the message. Regardless of the message type, your careful revising will aid you in creating accurate, readable documents that produce results.

- **Be willing to allow others to make suggestions for improving your writing.** Because most of us consider our writing personal, we often feel reluctant to share it with others and can be easily offended if they suggest changes. This syndrome, called *writer's pride of ownership*, can prevent us from seeking needed assistance from experienced writers—a proven method of improving communication skills. On the job, especially in today's electronic workplace, your writing will be showcased to your supervisor, clients/customers, members of a collaborative writing team, and more. You have nothing to lose but much to gain by allowing others to critique your writing. This commitment is especially important considering the mistake hardest to detect is your own. However, you have the ultimate responsibility for your document; don't simply trust that someone else will catch and correct your errors.

The ability you've gained in following a systematic process for developing effective business messages will prove valuable as you direct your energies to developing effective messages as a member of a team. Refer to the "Check Your Communication" checklist on the Chapter 4 Review Card to review the guidelines for preparing and proofreading a rough draft.

The speed and convenience of today's electronic communication have caused many communicators to confuse informality with sloppiness. Sloppy messages contain misspellings, grammatical errors, unappealing and incorrect formats, and confusing content—all of which create a negative impression of the writer and the company and affect the receiver's ability to understand the message. Some experts believe the increased use of email is leading to bosses becoming ruder. To combat against the harsh tone that often sets in when managers must respond to 300 to 500 emails weekly, Unilever is providing writing training and urging staff to think before they press the send button.[2]

As the sender, you are responsible for evaluating the effectiveness of each message you prepare. You must not use informality as an excuse to be sloppy. Instead, take one consultant's advice: "You can still be informal and not be sloppy. You can be informal and correct."[3] Take a good hard look at the messages you prepare. Commit to adjusting your message to the audience, designing appealing documents that are easily read, and following a systematic proofreading process to ensure error-free messages. This effort could save you from being embarrassed or jeopardizing your credibility.

4-2b Apply Visual Enhancements to Improve Readability

The vast amount of information created in today's competitive global market poses a challenge to you as a business writer. You must learn to create visually appealing documents that entice the audience to read rather than discard your message. Additionally, an effective design will enable you to highlight important information for maximum attention and to transition a receiver smoothly through sections of a long, complex document. These design techniques can be applied easily using word processing software. However, add visual enhancements only when they aid in comprehension. Overuse will cause your document to appear cluttered and will defeat your purpose of creating an appealing, easy-to-read document.

Enumerations

To emphasize units in a series, place a number, letter, or bullet before each element. Words preceded by numbers, bullets, or letters attract the receiver's special attention and are easier to locate when the page is reviewed.

Original	Highlighted
To download your copy, please click on the link below, check the "agreement" box, and click on "Next."	To download your copy, please 1. Click on the link below 2. Check the "agreement" box 3. Click on "Next."

Enumerated or Bulleted Lists

Writers often want to save space; however, cluttered text is unappealing and difficult to read. *Chunking*—a desktop publishing term—is an answer to the problem. Chunking involves breaking down information into easily digestible pieces. It's the communication equivalent of Butterfinger BBs rather than the whole candy bar. The added white space divides the information into blocks, makes the page look more organized, and increases retention by 50 percent.[4]

Enumerated or bulleted lists can be used to chunk and add even greater visual impact to items in a series. Items appear on separate lines with numerals, letters, or various types of bullets (•, ◊, □, ✓, and so on) at the beginning. Multiple-line items often are separated by a blank line. This design creates more white space, which isolates the items from other text and demands attention. Bullets are typically preferred over numerals unless the sequence of the items in the series is critical (e.g., steps in a procedure that must be completed in the correct order). In the following excerpt from a long analytical report, the four supporting reasons for a conclusion are highlighted in a bulleted list:

Original	Highlighted
Although moving to a robotic manufacturing system will be costly up front in terms of initial equipment outlays and installation fees, there are many advantages, including increased efficiency of processes, greater reliability, enhanced safety, and dramatically lower costs for employee benefits.	Although moving to a robotic manufacturing system will be costly up front in terms of initial equipment outlays and installation fees, there are many advantages, including • increased efficiency of processes • greater reliability • enhanced safety • dramatically lower costs for employee benefits

Headings

Headings are signposts that direct the receiver from one section of the document to another. Studies have shown that readers find documents with headings easier to grasp and that they are more motivated to pay attention to the text, even in a short document such as a half-page warranty.[5] You'll find that organizing the content of various types of documents with logical, well-written headings will make the documents more readable and appealing. Follow these general guidelines for writing effective headings:

- Compose brief headings that make a connection with the receiver, giving clear cues as to the usefulness of the information (e.g., "How Do I Apply?"). Consider using questions rather than noun phrases to let readers know they are reading the information they need (i.e., choose "Who Is Eligible to Apply?" rather than "Eligible Loan Participants").[6] Consider talking headings that reveal the conclusions reached in the following discussion rather than general topic headings. For example, "Costs Are Prohibitive" is more emphatic than "Cost Factors."
- Strive for parallel structure of readings within a section. For example, mixing descriptive phrases with questions requires additional mental effort and distracts readers who expect parallel writing.
- Follow a hierarchy, with major headings receiving more attention than minor headings or paragraph headings. To draw more attention to a major heading, center it and use a heavier, larger typestyle or brighter text color.

Tables and Graphs

Tables and graphs are used to simplify and clarify information and to add variety to long sections of dense text. The clearly labeled rows and columns in a table organize large amounts of specific numeric data and facilitate analysis. Graphics such as pie, line, and bar charts visually depict relationships within the data; they provide quick estimates rather than specific information.

Lines and Borders

Horizontal and vertical lines can be added to partition text or to focus attention on a specific line or lines. For example, a thin line followed by a thick line effectively separates the identification and qualifications sections of a résumé. Placing a border around a paragraph or section of text sets that information apart; adding shading inside the box adds greater impact. For example, a pull-quote format might spotlight a testimonial from a satisfied customer in a sales letter, important dates to remember in a memorandum, or a section of a document that must be completed and returned.

Relevant Images

A variety of interesting shapes can be used to highlight information and add appeal. Examples include creating a rectangular callout box highlighting a key idea with an arrow pointing to a specific number in a table, surrounding a title with a shaded oval for added impact, and using built-in designs to illustrate a process, cycle, hierarchy, or other relationship. Clip art or photos can also be added to reinforce an idea and add visual appeal. The following example from the Plain Language Web site shows how visual communication can convey important safety information more effectively than words can.

Battling to manage an avalanche of information, the recipients of your messages will appreciate your extra effort to create an easy-to-read, appealing document. These fundamental techniques will be invaluable as you enhance printed documents such as letters, memos, reports, agendas, handouts, and minutes for meetings.

4-2c Improve Readability

Although sentences are arranged in a logical sequence and are written coherently, the receiver might find reading the sentences difficult. Several programs have been developed to measure the reading difficulty of your writing. Electronic tools aid you in making computations and identifying changes that will improve readability.

The grammar and style checker feature of leading word-processing software calculates readability measures to aid you in writing for quick and easy reading and listening. The Fog index, a popular readability index developed by Robert Gunning, and the Flesch–Kincaid Grade Level calculator available in Microsoft Word consider the length of sentences and the difficulty of words to produce the approximate grade level at which a person must read in order to understand the material. For example, a grade level of 10 indicates a person needs to be able to read at the tenth-grade level to understand the material. Fortunately, you don't have to calculate

Before

This is a multipurpose passenger vehicle which will handle and maneuver differently from an ordinary passenger car, in driving conditions which may occur on streets and highways and off road. As with other vehicles of this type, if you make sharp turns or abrupt maneuvers, the vehicle may roll over or may go out of control and crash. You should read driving guidelines and instructions in the Owner's Manual, and WEAR YOUR SEAT BELTS AT ALL TIMES.

After

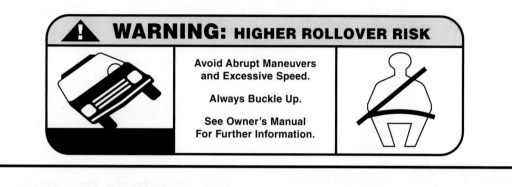

Courtesy of National Highway Traffic Safety Administration

readability manually, but understanding the manual calculation of the Fog index will illustrate clearly how sentence length and difficulty of words affect readability calculations and guide you in adapting messages.

Trying to write at the exact grade level of the receiver is not advised. You may not know the exact grade level, and even those who have earned advanced degrees appreciate writing they can read and understand quickly and easily. Also, writing a passage with a readability index appropriate for the audience does not guarantee the message will be understood. Despite simple language and short sentences, the message can be distorted by imprecise words, biased language, jargon, and translations that ignore cultural interpretations, to name just a few. The value of calculating a readability measure lies in the feedback you gain about average length of sentences and the difficulty of the words. Revise and recalculate

the readability index and continue revising until you feel the reading level is appropriate for the intended audience.

The grammar and style feature in word processing programs also locates grammatical errors, including misspellings and common usage errors, such as the use of fragments, run-on sentences, subject-verb disagreement, passive voice, double words, and split infinitives. Because it can only guess at the structure of a sentence and then apply a rigid set of rules, a grammar and style checker, such as a spell-checker, must be used cautiously. It is not a reliable substitute for a human editor who has an effective writing style and is familiar with the rules the software displays. Allow the software to flag misspellings and writing errors as you write, accept or reject the suggested changes based on your knowledge of effective writing, and use the readability measures to adjust your writing levels appropriately as shown in Figure 4-3 below.

Figure 4-3   Improving Readability Through Cautious Use of a Grammar and Style Checker

Spelling and Grammar: English (U.S.)

Subject-Verb Agreement:

Only one or two more questions is necessary to finalize the survey.

[Ignore Once]
[Ignore Rule]
[Next Sentence]

Suggestions:

are

[Change]
[Explain...]

☑ Check grammar

[Options...] [Undo]   [Cancel]

Readability Statistics

Counts
Words	309
Characters	1572
Paragraphs	4
Sentences	12

Averages
Sentences per Paragraph	3.0
Words per Sentence	25.7
Characters per Word	4.9

Readability
Passive Sentences	8%
Flesch Reading Ease	43.2
Flesch-Kincaid Grade Level	13.6

[OK]

4-3 Step 7: Revise for Style and Tone

4-3a Eliminate Outdated Expressions

Using outdated expressions will give your message a dull, stuffy, unnatural tone. Instead, substitute fresh, original expressions that reflect today's language patterns.

Outdated Expressions	Improvement
As per your request, the report has been submitted to the client.	As you requested, the report has been submitted to the client.
Enclosed please find a copy of my transcript.	The enclosed transcript should answer your questions.
Very truly yours (used as the complimentary close in a letter)	Sincerely

4-3b Curb Clichés

Clichés, or overused expressions, are common in our everyday conversations and in business messages. These handy verbal shortcuts are convenient, quick, easy to use, and often include simple metaphors and analogies that effectively communicate the most basic idea or emotion or the most complex business concept. However, writers and speakers who routinely use stale clichés may be perceived as unoriginal, unimaginative, lazy, and perhaps even disrespectful. Less frequently used words capture the receiver's attention because they are original, fresh, and interesting.

Clichés present another serious problem. Consider the scenario of shoppers standing in line at a discount store with the cashier saying to each, "Thanks for shopping with us today; please come again." Because the last shopper has heard the words several times already, he or she may not consider the statement genuine. The cashier has used an expression that can be stated without thinking and possibly without meaning. A worn expression can convey messages such as "You are not special," or "For you, I won't

> **clichés**
> overused expressions that can cause their users to be perceived as unoriginal, unimaginative, lazy, and perhaps even disrespectful

bother to think; the phrases I use in talking with others are surely good enough for you." Original expressions convey sincerity and build strong human relations.

Cliché	Improvement
Pushed (or stretched) the envelope	Took a risk or considered a new option
Skin in the game	Committed to the project
Cover all the bases	Get agreement/ input from everyone
That sucks!	That's unacceptable/needs improvement

4-3c Eliminate Profanity

Increasing tolerance of profanity is an issue of concern to society as a whole and also for employers and employees as they communicate at work. You must consider the potential business liabilities and legal implications resulting from the use of profanity that may offend others or create a hostile work environment. Recognize that minimizing or eliminating profanity is another important way you must adapt your language for communicating effectively and fostering human relations in a professional setting.

4-3d Use Simple, Informal Words

Business writers prefer simple, informal words that are readily understood and less distracting than more difficult, formal words. If a receiver questions the sender's motive for using formal words, the impact of the message may be diminished. Likewise, the impact would be diminished if the receiver questioned a sender's use of simple, informal words. That distraction is unlikely, however, if the message contains good ideas that are well organized and well supported. Under these conditions, simple words enable a receiver to understand the message clearly and quickly.

To illustrate, consider the unnecessary complexity of a notice that appeared on a corporate bulletin board: "Employees impacted by the strike are encouraged to utilize the hotline number to arrange for alternative transportation to work. Should you encounter difficulties in arranging for alternative transportation to work, please contact your immediate supervisor." A simple, easy-to-read revision would be, "If you can't get to work, call the hotline or your supervisor." For further illustration, note the added clarity of the following words:

Formal Words	Informal Words
terminate	end
procure	get
remunerate	pay
corroborate	support

Using words that have more than two or three syllables when they are appropriate is acceptable. However, you should avoid regular use of a long, infrequently used word when a simpler, more common word conveys the same idea. Professionals in some fields often use specialized terminology, referred to as **jargon**, when communicating with colleagues in the same field. In this case, the audience is likely to understand the words, and using the jargon saves time. However, when communicating with people outside the field, professionals should select simple, common words to convey messages. Using clear, jargon-free language that can be readily understood by non-native recipients and easily translated is especially important in international communication.

You should build your vocabulary so that you can use just the right word for expressing an idea and can understand what others have said. Just remember the purpose of business messages is not to advertise a knowledge of infrequently used words but to transmit a clear and tactful message. For the informal communication practiced in business, use simple words instead of more complicated words that have the same meaning.

4-3e Communicate Concisely

Concise communication includes all relevant details in the fewest possible words. Abraham Lincoln's two-minute *Gettysburg Address* is a premier example of concise communication. Mark Twain alluded to the skill needed to write concisely when he said, "I would have written a shorter book if I had had time."

Some executives have reported that they read memos that are two paragraphs long but may only skim or discard longer ones. Yet it's clear that this survival technique can lead to a vital message being discarded or misread. Concise writing is essential for workers struggling to handle an avalanche of information that often is read on the run on a Blackberry or iPhone. Concise messages save time and money for both the sender and the receiver, as the receiver's attention is directed toward the important details and is not distracted by excessive words and details.

The following techniques will produce concise messages:

- **Eliminate redundancies.** A **redundancy** is a phrase in which one word unnecessarily repeats an idea contained in an accompanying word. "Absolutely necessary" and "negative misfortune" are redundant because both words have the same meaning; only "necessary" and "misfortune" are needed. A few of the many redundancies in business writing are shown in the following list. Be conscious of redundancies in your speech and writing patterns.

Redundancies to Avoid

Needless repetition:	advance forward, it goes without saying, best ever, cash money, important essentials, each and every, dollar amount, pick and choose, past experience
Unneeded modifiers:	new innovations, personal friend, actual experience, brief summary, complete stop, collaborate together, disappear from sight, honest truth, trickle down, month of May, personal opinion, red in color, severe crisis, currently available
Repeated acronyms:	ATM machine, PIN number, SAT tests, SIC code

Redundancy is not to be confused with repetition used for emphasis. In a sentence or paragraph, you may need to use a certain word again. When repetition serves a

jargon
specialized terminology that professionals in some fields use when communicating with colleagues in the same field

redundancy
a phrase in which one word unnecessarily repeats an idea contained in an accompanying word (e.g., "exactly identical")

specific purpose, it is not an error. Redundancy serves no purpose and *is* an error.

- **Use active voice to reduce the number of words.** Passive voice typically adds unnecessary words, such as prepositional phrases. Compare the sentence length in each of these examples:

Passive Voice	Active Voice
Work schedules will be updated by department supervisors.	Department supervisors will update work schedules.
The project planning department will be transferred to the third floor next month by a moving company.	Next month, movers will transfer the project planning department to the third floor.

- **Review the main purpose of your writing, and identify relevant details needed for the receiver to understand and take necessary action.** More information is not necessarily better information. You may be so involved and perhaps so enthusiastic about your message that you believe the receiver needs to know everything that you know. Or perhaps you just need to devote more time to audience analysis and empathy.

- **Eliminate clichés that are often wordy and not necessary to understand the message.** For example, "Thank you for your letter," "I am writing to," "May I take this opportunity," "It has come to my attention," and "We wish to inform you" only delay the major purpose of the message.

- **Do not restate ideas that are sufficiently implied.** Notice how the following sentences are improved when ideas are implied. The revised sentences are concise, yet the meaning is not affected.

Wordy	Concise
John prepared PowerPoint slides and practiced his presentation.	John prepared for his presentation.
The manager reviewed team reports and revised the project schedule.	The manager revised the project schedule.

tone
the way a statement sounds; it conveys the writer's or speaker's attitude toward the message and the receiver

- **Shorten sentences by using suffixes or prefixes, making changes in word form, or substituting precise words for phrases.** In the following examples, the expressions in the right column provide useful techniques for saving space and being concise. However, the examples in the left column are not grammatically incorrect. Sometimes their use provides just the right emphasis.

Wordy	Concise
She completed her work in a competent manner.	She was a competent worker.
His style of writing was quite florid.	He had a florid writing style.
He believes the new policy guidelines to be of little value.	He believes the new policy guidelines are valueless.
Sales staff with high energy levels ...	Energetic sales staff ...
... arranged in chronological order.	... arranged chronologically ...

- **Use a compound adjective.** By using the compound adjective, you can reduce the number of words required to express your ideas and thus save the reader a little time.

Wordy	Concise
The corporation values employees who use their time efficiently.	The corporation values efficient employees.
Karen Lewis, who is well liked by her colleagues, will take ...	Well-liked Karen Lewis will take ...
The intranet will be down for two days for routine upgrades on July 23 and 24.	The two-day intranet upgrade will occur on July 23 and 24.

4-3f Project a Positive, Tactful Tone

Being adept at communicating negative information will give you the confidence you need to handle sensitive situations in a constructive manner, resulting in a positive **tone**. The following suggestions reduce the sting of an unpleasant thought:

- **State ideas using positive language.** Rely mainly on positive words—words that speak of what can be done instead of what cannot be done, of the pleasant instead of the unpleasant. In each of the following pairs, both sentences are sufficiently clear, but the positive words in the improved sentences make the message more diplomatic and promote positive human relations.

Negative Tone	Positive Tone
<u>You forgot</u> to fill in the last column of the annual budget report.	**Please fill in the last column of the annual budget report.**
We <u>cannot</u> complete your order without your email address.	**Please supply your email address so that we can complete your order.**
You <u>failed</u> to submit your expense report by the monthly deadline.	**Please submit your expense report by the next monthly deadline.**

- **Avoid using second person when stating negative ideas.** Use second person for presenting pleasant ideas; use third person for presenting unpleasant ideas. Note the following examples:

Pleasant Idea (Second Person Preferred)

You delivered a compelling presentation.	*The person will appreciate the emphasis placed on his or her excellent performance.*

Unpleasant Idea (Third Person Preferred)

The supply order was incorrectly filled out.	*"You filled out the supply order incorrectly" directs undiplomatic attention to the person who made the error.*

- **Use passive voice to convey negative ideas.** Presenting an unpleasant thought emphatically (as active verbs do) makes human relations difficult. Compare the tone of the following negative thoughts written in active and passive voices:

Active Voice	Passive Voice (Preferred for Negative Ideas)
Juanita did not complete the order form correctly.	**The order needed revision.**
Shelly missed the deadline for proposal submission by a week.	**The proposal was submitted a week after deadline.**

- Positive words are normally preferred, but sometimes the addition of negative words can sharpen a contrast (and thus increase clarity):
Please complete the online order form; phone and email requests will take longer to process. Original copies are to be submitted to the certification board; photocopies will not be accepted.

    Because the subject of each active sentence is the doer, the sentences are emphatic. Since the idea is negative, Shelly probably would appreciate being taken out of the picture. The passive voice sentences place more emphasis on the job than on who failed

to complete it; they retain the essential ideas, but the ideas seem less irritating. For negative ideas, use passive voice.

- **Use active voice to promote positive ideas.**

    Just as emphasis on negatives hinders human relations, emphasis on positives promotes human relations. Which sentence makes the positive idea more vivid?

Passive Voice	Active Voice (Preferred for Positive Ideas)
The proposal was submitted before the deadline.	**Shelly submitted the proposal before the deadline.**

Because "Shelly" is the subject of the active voice sentence, the receiver can easily envision the action. Shelly is recognized for meeting the deadline in this sentence. In the passive message, the fact that the deadline was met receives emphasis.

- **Use the subjunctive mood.** Sometimes the tone of a message can be improved by switching to the subjunctive mood. **Subjunctive sentences** speak of a wish, necessity, doubt, or condition contrary to fact and use such conditional expressions as *I wish*, *as if*, *could*, *would*, and *might*. In the following examples, the sentence in the right column conveys a negative

> **subjunctive sentences** sentences that speak of a wish, necessity, doubt, or condition contrary to fact and employ such conditional expressions as *I wish, as if, could, would,* and *might*

© iStockphoto.com/iqoncept

idea in positive language, which is more diplomatic than negative language.

Negative Tone	Subjunctive Mood Conveys Positive Tone
I can't complete the report.	When the information is made available, I can complete the report.
I cannot attend the planning meeting.	I could attend the planning meeting if the date were changed to next week.
I don't believe his statements about the product's efficiency.	I wish I could believe his statements about the product's efficiency.

Sentences in subjunctive mood often include a reason that makes the negative idea seem less objectionable and thus improves the tone. Tone is important, but clarity is even more important. The revised sentence in each of the preceding pairs sufficiently *implies* the unpleasant idea without stating it directly. If for any reason a writer or speaker suspects the implication is not sufficiently strong, a direct statement in negative terms is preferable.

- **Include a pleasant statement in the same sentence.** A pleasant idea is included in the following examples to improve the tone:

Negative Tone	Positive Tone
Your ability to meet deadlines is satisfactory.	While your ability to meet deadlines was satisfactory, your work to motivate your team was excellent.
Increased health-care costs have decreased funds available for salary adjustments.	Increased health-care costs have decreased funds available for salary adjustments, but we hope a shorter workweek will offset employee expectations.

4-3g Use Euphemisms Cautiously

A **euphemism** is a kind word substituted for one that may offend or suggest something unpleasant.

euphemism
a kind word substituted for one that may offend or suggest something unpleasant

doublespeak
also called doubletalk or corporate speak; euphemisms that deliberately mislead, hide, or evade the truth

For example, the idea of picking up neighborhood garbage does not sound especially inviting. Someone who does such work is often referred to as a *sanitation worker*. This term has a more pleasant connotation than *garbage collector*.

Choose the euphemistic terms rather than the negative terms shown in the following examples:

Negative Tone	Euphemistic Tone
aged or elderly	senior citizen
dying	fading away/near the end
used or secondhand	pre-owned
prison	correctional facility
disabled or handicapped	physically challenged/ differently abled
patient management	care coordination/ supportive services

Generally, you can recognize such expressions for what they are—unpleasant ideas presented with a little sugarcoating. Knowing the sender was simply trying to be polite and positive, receivers are more likely to react favorably. You should avoid, however, euphemisms that excessively sugarcoat and those that suggest subtle sarcasm. For example, to refer to a janitor as a *maintenance engineer* is to risk conveying a negative metacommunication, such as "This person does not hold a very respectable position, but I did the best I could to make it sound good." To the receiver (and to the janitor), just plain *janitor* would sound better.

You will also want to avoid **doublespeak**, also known as *doubletalk* or *corporate speak*. Such terms refer to euphemisms that deliberately mislead, hide, or evade the truth. This distortion of the truth is often found in military, political, and corporate language. A loss of credibility may result when a police officer refers to "nontraditional organized crime" rather than gang activity. Another example would be a politician who talks of an "enhanced interrogation technique" rather than "torture," or "collateral damage" or "friendly fire" rather than civilians killed accidentally by the military's own weapons. Companies use doublespeak when they make "workforce reductions" or offer workers a "career opportunity adjustment" or "voluntary termination." One company called the permanent shutdown of a steel plant an "indefinite idling" in an attempt to avoid paying severance or pension benefits to the displaced workers.

Despite your training in writing, you may fall into the trap of mirroring the writing of people above you on the career ladder who prefer writing in doublespeak. They often choose doublespeak over clear, concise writing because of the misguided belief that doublespeak makes them sound informed and professional. Such vagueness protects them when they're unsure how their messages will be received and makes writing easy once they learn the code. Instead of falling into doublespeak, learn to develop clear, concise messages that clarify ideas and provide direction to recipients regardless of their culture while enhancing your credibility as an honest communicator. A CEO of a writing training company has another interesting angle on clear writing. He contends that "articulation of thought is an element of intelligence, and you can increase your intelligence through writing." Working to articulate ideas clearly and logically through writing makes people smarter! That is a motivating reason for perfecting writing (and speaking) skills in our professional and personal lives.

4-3h Avoid Condescending or Demeaning Expressions

Condescending words seem to imply that the communicator is temporarily coming down from a level of superiority to join the receiver on a level of inferiority; such words damage efforts to build and protect **goodwill**. Note how the reminders of inequality in the following examples hamper communication:

Ineffective Examples

- My team always outshines others in the company, due, in part, to my experience as a leader.
- You did not receive the promotion because Lisa was a much better choice.

A demeaning expression (sometimes called a *dysphemism*) makes an idea seem negative or disrespectful. Avoid demeaning expressions because they divert attention from the real message to emotional issues that have little to do with the message. Many examples can be taken as contempt for an occupation or a specific job or position ("bean counters" for accountants, "ambulance chasers" for lawyers, "spin doctors" for politicians or public relations directors, and "shrinks" for psychiatrists). Like words that attack races or nationalities, words that ridicule occupations work against a communicator's purpose.

Many demeaning expressions are common across regions, ages, and perhaps even cultures. Some demeaning expressions belong to a particular company; for example, "turtles" was coined in one firm to mock first-year employees for their slow work pace. President Obama quickly recognized and apologized for his late-night talk show quip that equated his bowling skills to those of athletes with disabilities. Seeing the president's gaffe as a "teachable moment" for the country, Special Olympics Chairman Tim Shriver emphasized that "words hurt and words do matter and these words that in some respect can be seen as humiliating … do cause pain."[7] Effective communicators choose respectful expressions that build and protect goodwill.

4-3i Use Connotative Tone Cautiously

Human relations can suffer when connotative words are inadvertently or intentionally used instead of denotative words. The **denotative meaning** of a word is the literal meaning that most people assign to it. The **connotative meaning** is the literal meaning plus an extra message that reveals the speaker's or writer's qualitative judgment, as shown in this example:

Connotative Meaning with Negative Implication	Denotative Meaning (Preferred)
Please don't hassle the customer service representatives with too frequent questions.	Please don't question the customer service representatives too frequently.

The connotative meaning of "hassle" carries an additional message that the writer has a bias against asking questions. The connotation may needlessly introduce thoughts about whether asking questions is beneficial and distract the receiver from paying sufficient attention to the statements that follow. Connotations, like meta-communications discussed in Chapter 2, involve messages that are implied. In the preceding example, the connotation seems to be more harmful than helpful.

goodwill
arises when a business is worth more than its tangible assets

denotative meaning
the literal meaning of a word that most people assign to it

connotative meaning
the literal meaning of a word plus an extra message that reveals the speaker's or writer's qualitative judgment

At times, however, connotations can be helpful, as seen in the following examples:

Connotative Meaning with Positive Meaning (Preferred)	Denotative Meaning
Our <u>corporate think tank</u> has developed an outstanding production process.	<u>Research and Development</u> has developed an outstanding production process.
Rita is a <u>real spark plug</u> when it comes to sales.	Rita's <u>drive and enthusiasm</u> make her successful at sales.

In crafting business messages, rely mainly on denotative or connotative words that will be interpreted in a positive manner. To be sure that your connotative words are understood and will generate goodwill, consider your audience, the context, and the timing of the message.

- **Connotative words may be more easily misinterpreted than denotative words.** Because of differences in peoples' perceptions based on their life experiences, words that are perceived positively by one person may be perceived negatively by another. In some cases, receivers may simply not understand the connotative words. Damaged human relations occur when managers repeatedly convey connotative messages without considering whether employees can interpret the meanings as they are intended.

- **The appropriateness of connotations varies with the audience to which they are addressed and the context in which they appear.** For example, referring to a car as a "foreign job" or "sweet" might be received differently by teenagers than by senior citizens. Such expressions are less appropriate in a research report than in a blog or popular magazine.

4-3j Use Specific Language Appropriately

To help the receiver understand your message easily, select words that paint intense, colorful word pictures. Creating clear mental images adds energy and imagination to your message, thus increasing its overall impact.

General	Specific (Preferred)
The <u>public outcry</u> was huge.	<u>More than 3 million emails were received from the public.</u>
Please get back to me <u>soon</u> about your proposal changes.	Please supply me with the changes to the proposal by <u>this Friday at noon.</u>

Sam is a great manager.	Sara shines as a manager because of her <u>ability to stay on task and yet make people feel supported</u>.

Sometimes, using general statements can be useful in building and protecting goodwill. General words keep negative ideas from receiving more emphasis than they deserve. In addition, senders who don't have specific information or for some reason don't want to divulge it use general words.

General (Preferred)	Specific
Three customers complained about their <u>service</u>.	Three customers complained because their <u>food order was incomplete and the food was delivered cold</u>.
I look forward to <u>working with you again</u>.	I look forward to <u>working with you again because of your easygoing manner and attention to details</u>.

4-3k Use Bias-Free Language

Being responsive to individual differences requires you to make a conscious effort to use bias-free (nondiscriminatory) language. Using language that does not exclude, stereotype, or offend others permits them to focus on your message rather than to question your sensitivity. Goodwill can be damaged when biased statements are made related to gender, race or ethnicity, religion, age, or disability. The following guidelines will help you avoid bias:

1. **Avoid referring to men and women in stereotyped roles and occupations.** The use of *he* to refer to anyone in a group was once standard and accepted; however, this usage is considered insensitive and, to some, offensive. Therefore, do not use the pronoun *he* when referring to a person in a group that may include women or the pronoun *she* to refer to a group that may include men; otherwise you may unintentionally communicate an insensitive message that only women or only men can perform certain tasks or serve in certain professions. Follow these four approaches to avoid gender bias:

© iStockphoto.com/photomak

Guideline	Gender-Biased	Improved
Avoid using a pronoun	Each employee must complete <u>his</u> vacation request form.	Employees must complete a vacation request form.
Repeat the noun	Expect promptness from your guide. Ask <u>him</u> to . . .	Expect promptness from your <u>guide</u>. Ask the <u>guide</u> to . . .
Use a plural noun	Each employee should update and confirm <u>his</u> contact information.	Employees should update and confirm <u>their</u> contact information.
Use pronouns from both genders (when necessary, but not repeatedly)	Please page a doctor. <u>He</u> should respond . . .	Please page a doctor. <u>He or she</u> should respond . . .

2. **Use occupational titles that reflect genuine sensitivity to gender.** Note the gender-free titles that can be easily substituted to avoid bias:

Gender-Biased	Gender-Free
salesman	salesperson
chairman	chair

3. **Avoid designating an occupation by gender.** For example, omit "woman" in "A woman doctor has initiated this research." The doctor's profession, not the gender, is the point of the message. Similarly, avoid using the -ess ending to differentiate genders in an occupation:

Gender-Biased	Gender-Free
waiter or waitress	server
hostess	host

4. **Avoid using expressions that may be perceived to be gender-biased.** Avoid commonly used expressions in which "man" represents all humanity, such as "To go where no man has gone before," and stereotypical characteristics, such as "man hours," "man-made goods," and "work of four strong men." Note the improvements made in the following examples by eliminating the potentially offensive words.

Gender-Biased	Improved
Our energy products will benefit <u>all of mankind</u>.	Our energy products will benefit <u>humanity</u>.
Laurence is the best <u>man for</u> the job.	Laurence is the best <u>person</u> for the job.

5. **Avoid racial or ethnic bias.** Include racial or ethnic identification only when relevant, and avoid referring to these groups in stereotypical ways.

Racially or Ethnically Biased	Improved
The salespeople ran around like a bunch of wild <u>Indians</u>.	The salespeople were extremely busy on the floor today.
Please give your form to Sheila, the Asian woman.	Please give the form to Sheila, the woman at that desk.
The articulate <u>African American</u> engineer overseeing the product redesign plans suggested . . .	The engineer overseeing the product redesign plans suggested . . .

6. **Avoid age bias.** Include age only when relevant, and avoid demeaning expressions related to age.

Age-Biased	Improved
George is <u>the older gentleman</u> who works downstairs.	George works downstairs in the office on the right.

7. **Avoid disability bias.** When communicating about people with disabilities, use people-first language. That is, refer to the person first and the disability second so that focus is appropriately placed on the person's ability rather than on the disability. Also avoid words with negative or judgmental connotations, such as *handicap*, *unfortunate*, *afflicted*, and *victim*. When describing people without disabilities, use the word *typical* rather than *normal*; otherwise you may inadvertently imply that people with disabilities are abnormal. Consider these more sensitive revisions:

Insensitive	Sensitive (People-First)
<u>Blind</u> employees receive . . .	Employees <u>with vision impairments</u> receive . . .
The elevator is for the exclusive use of <u>handicapped</u> employees and should not be used by <u>normal</u> employees.	The elevator is for the exclusive use of employees <u>with disabilities</u>.

4-4 Proofreading for Mechanical Correctness

Errors in writing and mechanics may seem isolated, but the truth is, proofreading *is* important. You don't have to look far to see silly typos or obvious instances of writers relying only on the computer spell-checker. The classifieds in a small-town newspaper advertised "fully fascinated and spade damnation puppies." The advertisement was for fully vaccinated and spayed Dalmatian puppies. These errors clearly illustrate how spell-check can fail, but goofs such as this one are not limited to small-town newspapers.

It was not a spelling error but a simple transposition in a telephone number that created an unbelievably embarrassing situation for a telecommunications giant. AT&T customers calling to redeem points earned in a True Rewards program were connected to pay-by-the-minute erotic phone entertainment.[8] Mistakes ranging from printing ordinary typos to running entirely erroneous ads forced newspapers to refund $10.6 million to dissatisfied advertisers and to print $10.5 million in free, make-good ads.[9] The University of California at San Diego inadvertently sent an acceptance email message to all 28,000 students it had rejected, raising their hopes only to dash them when the mistake was discovered and corrected.[10] Each of these actual mistakes illustrates that inattention to proofreading can be potentially embarrassing and incredibly expensive.

Following systematic revision procedures will help you produce error-free documents that reflect positively on the company and you. Using the procedures that follow, you will see that effective proofreading must be done several times, each time for a specific purpose.

Follow these simple procedures to produce a finished product that is free of errors in content, organization, and style; mechanics; and format and layout:

1. **Use the spell-checker to locate simple keying errors and repeated words.** When the software cannot guess the correct spelling based on your incorrect attempt,

you will need to consult a dictionary, other printed source, or online reference such as the Merriam-Webster online language center at http://m-w.com.

2. **Proofread the document onscreen, concentrating first on errors in content, organization, and style.** To locate errors, ask the following questions:

   - **Content.** Is the information complete? Have I included all the details the receiver needs to understand the message and to take necessary action? Is the information accurate? Have I checked the accuracy of any calculations, dates, names, addresses, and numbers? Have words been omitted?

   - **Organization.** Is the main idea presented appropriately, based on the receiver's likely reaction (deductive or inductive organization)? Are supporting ideas presented in a logical order?

   - **Style.** Is the message clear? Will the receiver interpret the information correctly? Is the message concise and written at an appropriate level for the receiver? Does the message reflect a considerate, caring attitude and focus primarily on the receiver's needs? Does the message treat the receiver honestly and ethically?

3. **Proofread a second time concentrating on mechanical errors.** You are searching for potentially damaging errors that the spell-checker cannot detect. These problem areas include:

   - **Grammar, capitalization, punctuation, number usage, and abbreviations.** Review the grammatical principles presented in the appendix if necessary.

   - **Word substitutions.** Check the proper use of words such as *your* and *you* and words that sound alike (*there*, *they're*, or *their*; *affect* or *effect*).

   - **Parts of the document other than the body. Proofread the entire document.** Errors often appear in the opening and closing sections of documents because writers typically begin proofreading at the first paragraph.

4. **Display the document in print preview mode, and edit for format and layout.** Follow these steps to be certain the document adheres to appropriate business formats and is visually appealing:

   - Format according to a conventional format. Compare your document to the conventional business formats shown on your Style and Formatting cards, and make any revisions. Are all standard parts of the document included and presented in an acceptable format? Are all necessary special parts (e.g., attention line, enclosure) included? Does the message begin on the correct line? Should the right margin be justified or jagged?

   - Be sure numbered items are in the correct order. Inserting and deleting text might have changed the order of these items.

- Evaluate the visual impact of the document. Could you increase the readability of long, uninterrupted blocks of text by using enumerated or indented lists, headings, or graphic borders or lines? Would adding images or varying print styles add visual appeal? View Web documents on several different browsers to ensure readability and appeal.

- Be certain the document is signed or initialed (depending on the document). Ensure that email messages are addressed to the appropriate person or persons.

5. **Print a draft copy and proofread a third time if the document is nonroutine and complex.** Read from *right to left* to reduce your reading speed, allowing you to concentrate deliberately on each word. If a document is extremely important, you might consider reading the document aloud, spelling names and noting capitalization and punctuation, while another person verifies the copy.

6. **Print written documents on high-quality paper.** The message in Figure 4-4 has been revised for

Figure 4-4 Rough Draft of a Letter (excerpt)

May 28, 2014
Fax Transmission

Jerry Lainger, President
Spa Resorts
2054 Beach Boulevard
Miami, Florida 09982

Dear Mr. Linger:
Congratulations on the recent opening of the latest Spa Resort Hotel in Palm Springs, CA! Because of your national branding and reach, we are contacting you to let you know about the benefits of becoming a Speedster hotel partner.

Speedster is the world's leading online travel company with more than 100 localized points of sale in more than 70 countries. Speedster connects you with the largest travel marketplace and demand covering North America, Latin America, Europe, Middle East, Africa, and Asia Pacific.

As a Speedster hotel partner, you'll benefit from ~~new, incremental business; unmatched exposure; above-the-line marketing exposure; and access to different types of consumers.~~

- New, incremental business: More than 90 million gross room nights are booked annually on Speedster's Web sites.
- Unmatched exposure: More people shop for travel on Speedster websites worldwide than on any other online travel company. On average, more than 72 million global travelers come to Speedster branded points of sale every month. Hotels that join the Speedster marketplace also benefit from distribution through Speedster's 15,000 global affiliate sites.
- Above-the-line marketing exposure: Speedster invests in local advertising, such as television commercials, billboard campaigns, and search engine optimization strategies to increase our brand awareness and ultimately drive shoppers to our websites.
- Access to different types of consumers: Speedster has a portfolio of consumer brands, which includes Speedster, besthotels.com, Travelese, Hotwire, and accommodationone.com, and reaches consumers with different purchasing patterns and travel profiles—everything from luxury-minded early bookers and business travelers to last-minute deal seekers.

To start your hotel partnership, please click Contact Us on the Join Speedster page (www.speedster.com/join) to connect with a representative who can work with you to get all of your property information, room types, and rate plans into our system so travelers can start booking your rooms on Speedster's Web sites. We look forward to working together with you!

Annotations:
- Adds mailing notation.
- Uses two-letter state abbreviation.
- Corrects spelling of name.
- Adds smooth transition to next paragraph.
- Bullet list for emphasis and conciseness.
- Eliminates unnecessary comma.
- Adds additional explanation to bullet-list items for clarity and persuasiveness.
- Correct proofreading error.
- Check correctness of word substitutions: "to" for "too" and "your" for "you."

(1) content, organization, and style; (2) mechanics; and (3) format and layout. Study the revisions made using the track-changes feature in word processing software. The commentary makes it easy to see how revising this draft improved the document's quality.

STUDY TOOLS

CHAPTER 4

Located at back of the textbook

❑ **Rip out Chapter Review Card**

Located at www.cengagebrain.com

❑ **Review Key Terms Flashcards (Print or Online)**

❑ **Download Audio Summaries for on-the-go review**

❑ **Complete Practice Quizzes to prepare for tests**

❑ **Play "Beat the Clock" to master concepts**

❑ **Complete the Crossword Puzzle to review key terms**

❑ **Watch the video about McDonaldson, a fictitious but all-too-realistic ad agency whose employees struggle with contemporary business communication issues.**

THE CROWD IN-

Share your 4LTR Press story on Facebook at www.facebook.com/4ltrpress for a chance to win.

To learn more about the In-Crowd opportunity 'like' us on Facebook.

Communicating Electronically

OBJECTIVES

5-1 Discuss the effective use of email, instant messaging, and text messaging in business communication.

5-2 Explain principles for writing effectively for the Web.

5-3 Discuss the effective use of voice and wireless technologies in business communication.

5-4 Consider legal and ethical implications associated with the use of communication technology.

5-1 Electronic Mail Communication

As you read in Chapter 1, the continuous evolution of technology has expanded communication options. Email, instant messaging, Web communications, and voice and wireless technologies are important tools for accomplishing company goals. In fact, email has overtaken the telephone in terms of the most common workplace communication tool.[1] The ability to use email communications effectively is essential to success in virtually every career.

5-1a Advantages of Email

Electronic mail, or email, offers numerous advantages. Its ready availability, convenience, and ease of use have resulted in its skyrocketing popularity. The advantages of email are numerous:

- **It facilitates the fast, convenient flow of information among users at various locations and time zones.** Mail service is often too slow for communicating timely information, and the telephone system is inconvenient and costly when communicating with people located in several locations and time zones. For these reasons, email is especially effective when sending a single message to several recipients and when needing to communicate 24 hours a day, 365 days a year.

- **It increases efficiency.** Email reduces "telephone tag" and unnecessary telephone interruptions caused when delivering messages that are unlikely to require a verbal response.

- **It reduces costs.** Sending email messages represents a substantial savings to companies in long-distance telephone costs and postal mail-outs.

- **It reduces paper waste.** Often an electronic message can be read and immediately discarded without the need for a printed copy.

5-1b Guidelines for Preparing Email Messages

Following these guidelines will enable you to use email efficiently and effectively when communicating with both valued coworkers and outside parties:

- **Send to single or multiple addressees.** The same message can be sent to one or many recipients simultaneously. Sending an email message to multiple recipients routinely involves keying the email address of each recipient into a distribution list and selecting the distribution list as the recipient.

- **Provide a useful subject line.** A descriptive subject line assists the receiver's understanding of the message and is helpful for future reference to it. Additionally, a well-written subject line in an email message will help the receiver sort through an overloaded mailbox and read messages in priority order. When writing a subject line, think of the five Ws—Who, What, When, Where, and Why—to give you some clues for wording. For instance, "Budget Committee Meeting on Thursday" is a more meaningful subject line than "Meeting."

- **Restate the subject in the body of the message.** The body of the message should be a complete thought and should not rely on the subject line for elaboration. A good opening sentence might be a repetition of most of the subject line. Even if the reader skipped the subject line, the message would still be clear, logical, and complete.

- **Focus on a single topic directed toward the receiver's needs.** An email message is generally limited to one

BCOM

netiquette
the buzzword for proper
behavior on the Internet

idea rather than addressing several issues. If you address more than one topic in a single email message, chances are the recipient will forget to respond to all points discussed. Discussing one topic allows you to write a descriptive subject line, and the receiver can file the single subject message in a separate mailbox if desired. If you must send a lengthy email, preview the topics to be covered in the introduction and then divide the message into logical sections for easy comprehension.

- **Sequence your ideas based on anticipated reader reaction.** As you learned previously, ideas should be organized deductively when a message contains good news or neutral information; inductive organization is recommended when the message contains bad news or is intended to persuade. Email messages should be organized according to the sequence of ideas—for example, time order, order of importance, or geography. As a general rule, present the information in the order it is likely to be needed. For example, describe the nature and purpose of an upcoming meeting before giving the specifics (date, place, time).

- **Make careful use of jargon, technical words, and shortened terms.** The use of jargon and technical terms is more common in email messages than in business letters. Such shortcuts save time with audiences who will understand the intent. In practicing empathy, however, consider whether the receiver will likely understand the terms used.

- **Use graphic highlighting to add emphasis.** Enumerated or bulleted lists, tables, graphs, pictures, or other images can be either integrated into the content of the email or attached as supporting material.

- **Revise your email before sending.** Even the average email requires at least one pass to ensure that the intended message is clear, concise, and error-free. The number of passes increases depending on the number of people receiving the email and the complexity of

the message. Revising for brevity and conciseness is a primary goal for messages that are often read on the run and on mobile devices. Keep to one screen, eliminate redundancies, and tighten wording. Avoid off-topic material that detracts from the email's single subject, as well as clever or amusing statements that are funny only to the writer.[2] Direct, concise messages sometimes sound impersonal and curt if not revised for goodwill. Question whether a phone call would be more appropriate for the message; a businesslike, yet conversational tone might sound less aggressive or demanding. Revise emails to achieve a similar tone.[3] Use the email spell-checker and then proofread onscreen for content and grammatical errors.

5-1c **Effective Use of Email**

The email message in Figure 5-1 illustrates guidelines for using professional email. The sender begins the email message reminding the receiver of an employment interview. The paragraphs that follow include timely information about the interview and instructions for an alternate meeting, if needed.

While email offers various advantages in speed and convenience, problems arise when it is managed inappropriately. Learning fundamental **netiquette**, the buzzword for proper behavior on the Internet, will ensure your online success. The following guidelines will assist you in using email effectively:

- **Check mail promptly.** Generally, a response to email is expected within 24 hours. Ignoring messages from coworkers can erode efforts to create an open, honest, and cooperative work environment. On the other hand, responding every second could indicate that you are paying more attention to your email than your job.

- **Do not contribute to email overload.** To avoid clogging the system with unnecessary messages, follow these simple guidelines:

  - Be certain individuals need a copy of the email, and forward an email from another person only with the original writer's permission.

  - Never address an email requesting general action to more than one person if you want to receive an individual response. Sharing responsibility will lead to no one taking responsibility.

  - Avoid sending formatted documents. Messages with varying fonts, special print features (e.g., bold, italics, etc.), and images take longer to download, require more storage space, and could be unreadable on some computers. In addition, enhancing routine email messages does not support the goals of competitive organizations, and

---

TO RECAP—EMAIL ADVANTAGES

- ☑ Allows communication 24 hours a day, 365 days a year.
- ☑ Reduces telephone interruptions by delivering messages that are unlikely to require a verbal response.
- ☑ Saves companies the costs of long-distance telephone bills and postal mail-outs.
- ☑ Reduces the need to print messages.

Figure 5-1

GOOD :-) Good Example of an Email Message

New Message

To: James Frederick
From: Li Wong
Subject: Finalist Interviews on Tuesday ─────────────── ● *Provides subject line that is meaningful to reader and writer.*

Interview schedule.docx

Hi Jim,

You will find attached to this message the schedule for Tuesday's interviews with finalists for the marketing analyst position. Please confirm your times of 2 and 2:30 p.m. ─────── ● *Includes salutation and closing to personalize message.*

The interviews will be held in the Human Resources conference room on the third floor. Interviews are limited to 30 minutes. Please be aware of these time limits so that we can stay on schedule throughout the day. ● *Conveys short, concise message limited to one idea and one screen.*

If your scheduled time is not convenient, please let me know ASAP. Although the time blocks are currently filled, you can interview in tandem with another person.

Regards,

Li Wong, Human Resources

---

employees and clients or customers might resent such frivolous use of time.

- Edit the original message when you reply to email if the entire body of the original message is not needed for context. Instead, you can cut and paste pertinent sections within a reply that you believe will help the recipient understand your reply. You can also key brief comments in all caps below the original section.

- Follow company policy for personal use of email. Obtain a private email account if you are job hunting or sending many private messages to friends and relatives.

- **Use email selectively.** Send short, direct messages for routine matters that need not be handled immediately (scheduling meetings, giving your supervisor quick updates, or addressing other uncomplicated issues).

- **Do not send messages when you are angry.** Email containing sensitive, highly emotional messages could be easily misinterpreted because of the absence

of nonverbal communication (facial expressions, voice tone, and body language). Sending a *flame*, the online term used to describe a heated, sarcastic, sometimes abusive message or posting, might prompt a receiver to send a retaliatory response. Email messages written in anger and filled with emotion and sarcasm could result in embarrassment or even end up as evidence in litigation. Because of the potential damage to relationships and legal liability, read email messages carefully before sending them. Unless a response is urgent, store a heated message for an hour until you have cooled off and thought about the issue clearly and rationally. When you *must* respond immediately, you might acknowledge that your response is emotional and has not been thoroughly considered. Give this warning by using words such as "I need to vent my frustration for a few paragraphs" or "flame on—I'm writing in anger."[4]

- **Exercise caution against email viruses and hoaxes.** An ounce of prevention can avert the problems caused by deadly *viruses* that destroy data files or annoying messages that simply waste your time while they

social networking sites
Web sites that provide virtual communities in which people with shared interests can communicate

instant messaging
a real-time email technology that blends email with conversation; sender and receiver who are online at the same time can type messages that both see immediately

are executing. Install an *antivirus software program* that will scan your hard drive each time you start the computer or access external devices, and keep backups of important files. Be suspicious of email messages that contain attachments if they are from people you don't know. Email text is usually safe to open, but the attachment could contain an executable file that can affect your computer's operations. **Social networking sites** such as Facebook and MySpace are also common sources of viruses and spyware.

Additionally, be wary of *computer hoaxes*—email messages that incite panic, typically related to risks of computer viruses or deadly threats, and urge you to forward them to as many people as possible. Forwarding a hoax can be embarrassing and causes inefficiency by overloading email boxes and flooding computer security personnel with inquiries from alarmed recipients of your message. Investigate the possible hoax by visiting Web sites such as the following that post virus alerts and hoax information and provide tips for identifying a potential hoax:

- Urban legends: www.urbanlegends.com
- Snopes: www.snopes.com
- Truth or Fiction: www.truthorfiction.com

If a bogus message is forwarded to you, reply to the person politely that the message is a hoax. This

TO RECAP—EFFECTIVE USE OF EMAIL

- ☑ Check email promptly.
- ☑ Do not contribute to email overload.
- ☑ Use email selectively.
- ☑ Do not send messages when you are angry.
- ☑ Exercise caution against email viruses and hoaxes.
- ☑ Develop an effective system for handling email.

action allows you to help stop the spread of the malicious message and will educate one more person about the evils of hoaxes.

- **Develop an effective system for handling email.** Some simple organization will allow you to make better use of your email capability:
  - Set up separate accounts for receiving messages that require your direct attention.
  - Keep your email inbox clean by reading an email and taking action immediately. Delete messages you are not using and those not likely to be considered relevant for legal purposes.
  - Move saved messages into a limited number of email folders for quick retrieval. The email search feature is also useful for identifying saved messages quickly. If you receive many messages, consider setting up your account to sort and prioritize messages, send form letters as replies to messages received with a particular subject line, automatically forward specified email, and sound an alarm when you receive a message from a particular person.

5-1d Instant and Text Messaging

Business use of **instant messaging (IM)** has experienced phenomenal growth. Analysts estimate that in 90 percent of companies, some employees use IM, whether to close a sale, collaborate with a colleague, or just trade pleasantries with a colleague.[5] This real-time email technology allows the sender to know when someone is available to respond immediately.

The best known IM programs are free and require no special hardware and little training. With some programs, users can exchange graphics and audio and video

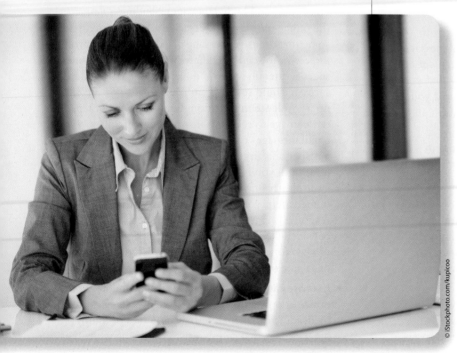

© iStockphoto.com/kupicoo

Figure 5-2 **GOOD** :-) Good Example of an Instant Message

Output Interaction Box	Users Logged On
Rodney: Is this a good time to talk about report revisions?	Rodney
Tina: Sure. What's up?	Tina
Rodney: I have new info from marketing that needs to be added.	
Tina: Do you have time to do it today?	
Rodney: No. I was hoping you could.	
Tina: Maybe this afternoon. How much?	
Rodney: A paragraph or two. I'll email you the info.	
Tina: OK. Get it to me by 1, pls.	
Rodney: Will do.	
Tina: Thx.	

☐ Entry Chime

Enter your message below

Send URL
Quit

- *Opens message by "knocking" to ask if he is interrupting.*
- *Keeps conversation brief by limiting it to a few short sentences.*
- *Uses a few easily recognized abbreviations and acronyms but avoids informal slang that could be confusing and unprofessional.*
- *Uses instant messaging to arrange for sudden report revisions.*

clips. To use instant messaging, you maintain a list of people with whom you want to interact. You can send messages to any or all of the people on your list as long as the people are online. Sending a message opens up a window in which you and your contact can key messages that you both can see immediately. Figure 5-2 illustrates a sample IM conversation that occurred to arrange for last-minute report changes.

Many of the guidelines that apply to the use of email for business purposes also apply to instant messaging. With IM, however, spelling and grammar matter less when trading messages at high speed. IM users often use shorthand for common words and phrases. IM and telephone communication also share common challenges: being sure that the sender is who he or she claims to be and that the conversation is free from eavesdropping.

Some managers worry that employees will spend too much work time using IM to chat with buddies inside and outside the company. They also emphasize that IM is not the right tool for every business purpose; employees should still rely on email when they need a record and use the telephone for a personal touch.

5-1e Text Messaging

Text messaging has grown in popularity as cell phones and other handheld devices with text capability have proliferated. Messages can be sent from one cell phone to another, a cell phone to a computer, or computer to computer. **Text messaging** on a cell phone or personal digital assistant is a refinement of computer instant messaging. The typical cell phone screen can accommodate no more than 160 characters, and because the keypad is far less versatile, text messaging puts an even greater premium on conciseness. An entire code book of acronyms and abbreviations has emerged, ranging from CWOT (complete waste of time) to DLTBBB (don't let the bed bugs bite). The use of emoticons has also advanced far beyond the traditional smiley face and includes drooling (:-) . . .) and secrecy (:X). Inventive and young users frequently insert their own style, substituting "z" for "s," or "d" for "th." Shortened lingo or

text messaging
messages that can be sent from one cell phone to another, a cell phone to a computer, or computer to computer; a refinement of computer instant messaging

text gets right to the point. For instance, a sender might send the following message that can be easily deciphered by most: "Pk u up @730." Cell phone programs are also available to assist in efficiency when texting. T9 (text on nine keys) and similar programs use predictive text to finish words after the first few characters are keyed. T9 can be "trained" to recognize new vocabulary.[6]

Texting is a viable alternative to phone calls for those with hearing impairments. Economic and cultural factors have also driven the advancement of text messaging in some parts of the world where voice conversations are more expensive than texting and short conversations are considered impolite. Some of the most avid text messagers are clustered in Southeast Asia. The Chinese language is particularly well suited to text messaging, because in Mandarin the names of the numbers are also close to the sounds of certain words.[7] Japanese commuters use their cell phones to text silently, as talking on the phones on the train would be impolite. In the United States, teenagers have popularized texting and carry the habit into places of work. Both abroad and at home, text messaging can be used as an avoidance mechanism that preserves the feeling of communication without the burden for actual intimacy or substance. Most text messages are superficial greetings and are often sent when the two parties are within speaking distance of each other. Like a wave or nod, they are meant to merely establish connection without getting specific.

While text messaging is generally considered a social communication tool, it is finding more use for business. Text messages can be sent or retrieved in situations when a ringing phone would be inappropriate, such as during meetings. With research showing that many more text messages are opened than are email messages, advertisers are using text messages to send their marketing messages.[8] Refer to Figure 5-3, which compares the completeness and relative formality of an email message to the informal nature of the instant message and

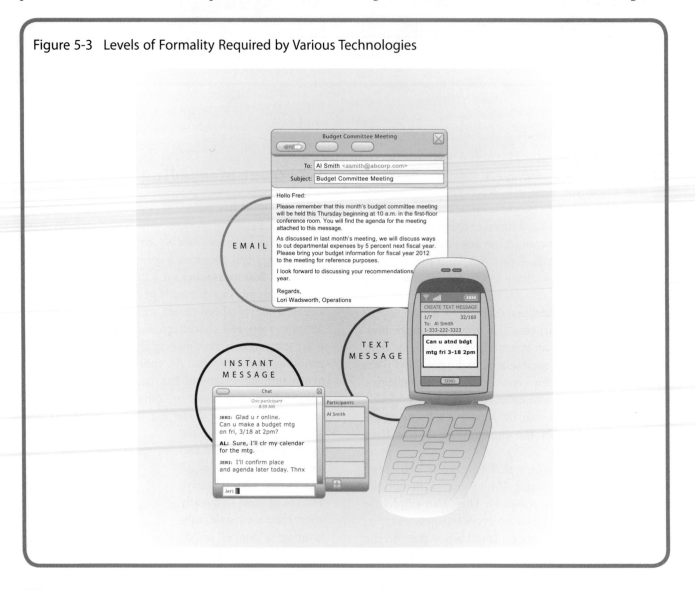

Figure 5-3 Levels of Formality Required by Various Technologies

EMAIL

Budget Committee Meeting

send

To: Al Smith <asmith@abcorp.com>

Subject: Budget Committee Meeting

Hello Fred:

Please remember that this month's budget committee meeting will be held this Thursday beginning at 10 a.m. in the first-floor conference room. You will find the agenda for the meeting attached to this message.

As discussed in last month's meeting, we will discuss ways to cut departmental expenses by 5 percent next fiscal year. Please bring your budget information for fiscal year 2012 to the meeting for reference purposes.

I look forward to discussing your recommendations year.

Regards,

Lori Wadsworth, Operations

TEXT MESSAGE

CREATE TEXT MESSAGE

1/7   32/160
To: Al Smith
1-333-222-3323

Can u atnd bdgt mtg fri 3-18 2pm

SEND

INSTANT MESSAGE

Chat

One participant
8:39 AM

Participants:
Al Smith

JERI: Glad u r online. Can u make a budget mtg on fri, 3/18 at 2pm?

AL: Sure, I'll clr my calendar for the mtg.

JERI: I'll confirm place and agenda later today. Thnx

Jeri:

the abbreviated style of the text message. Each medium requires its own appropriate writing style to maximize effectiveness and social expectations.

5-1f Electronic Messages and the Law

U.S. courts have established the right of companies to monitor the electronic mail of an employee because they own the facilities and intend them to be used for job-related communication only. On the other hand, employees typically expect that their email messages will be kept private. To protect themselves against liability imposed by the Electronic Communications Privacy Act (ECPA), employers simply provide a legitimate business reason for the monitoring (e.g., preventing computer crime, retrieving lost messages, and regulating employee morale) and obtain written consent to intercept email or at least notify employees. Employees who use the system after the notification may have given implied consent to the monitoring.[9]

The legal status of text messaging has been murkier. A 2008 court ruling made a distinction between electronic communications employers store on their servers and communication that is contracted out to third parties. Employers must have either a warrant or the employee's permission to view messages stored by someone other than the employer. Employers who intend to monitor electronic communications must be specific in their written employee policy statements that they intend to access text messages sent with company-issued devices.[10]

Remember that you are responsible for the content of any electronic message you send. Because electronic messages move so quickly between people and often become very informal and conversational, individuals might not realize (or might forget) their responsibility. If a person denies commitments made via an electronic message, someone involved can produce a copy of the message as verification.

Electronic communicators must abide by copyright laws. Be certain to give credit for quoted material and seek permission to use copyrighted text or graphics from printed or electronic sources. Unless you inform the reader that editing has occurred, do not alter a message you are forwarding or reposting, and be sure to ask permission before forwarding it.

Federal and state bills related to employee privacy are frequently introduced for legislative consideration. Although litigation related to present privacy issues is underway, the development of law is lagging far behind technology; nevertheless, employers can expect changes in the laws as technology continues to develop. Electronic messages have often become the prosecutor's star witness, the corporate equivalent of DNA evidence, as it and other forms of electronic communication are subject to subpoena in litigation. Referring to this issue, former New York Attorney General Eliot Spitzer had this to say: "Never write when you can talk. Never talk when you can nod. And never put anything in an email [that you don't want on the front page of the newspaper]."[11] Several perils of "evidence" mail that companies must address are illustrated in these cases:

• Including inappropriate content in an email can humiliate and lead to indictment. Detroit Mayor Kwame Kilpatrick and his chief of staff were charged in a 12-count indictment

> NEVER WRITE WHEN YOU CAN TALK. NEVER TALK WHEN YOU CAN NOD. AND NEVER PUT ANYTHING IN AN EMAIL [THAT YOU DON'T WANT ON THE FRONT PAGE OF THE NEWSPAPER].

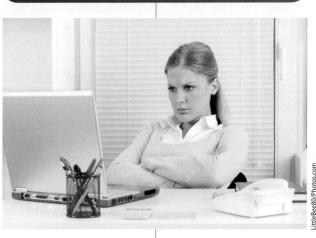

including perjury and obstruction of justice when text messages exchanged between the two were revealed. The pair's secret love affair played out in the messages was also disclosed to a shocked public.[12] The press dubbed the resulting disastrous professional result as "death by Blackberry."

• Failing to preserve or destroying email messages in violation of securities rules is a sure path to destruction. Deleting Enron scandal-related messages led to Arthur Andersen's criminal conviction and eventually to Enron's implosion.

• Inability to locate emails and other relevant documents demanded by the courts is unacceptable and considered negligence by the courts. Penalties have included monetary fines, assessment of court costs or attorney's fees, and dismissal of the case in favor of the opposing side.[13]

On the other hand, evidence mail can protect a company from lawsuits. A company being sued by a female employee because a male executive had allegedly sexually abused her retrieved a trail of emails with lurid attachments sent by the female employee to the male executive named in the case.[14]

To avoid the legal perils of electronic communications, employees must be taught not to write loose, potentially rude, and overly casual messages; to avoid carelessly deleting messages; and to take the time to identify and organize relevant messages for quick retrieval.

5-2 Web Page Communication and Social Media

Although effective Web page development is a highly specialized activity, understanding the process will be useful to any business communicator. Organizations can use the Web not only to communicate with customers and clients but also to interact with business associates.

The World Wide Web is truly a universal communication medium, reaching a broad audience in diverse locations. The familiar Web platform can also be used for offering a company **intranet** to distribute various types of information to employees at numerous locations.

Business associates such as vendors, suppliers, and customers can utilize the Web to access a company's **extranet**. Both intranets and extranets restrict access to only authorized viewers; those viewers are provided passwords to access the sites. An organization can also establish a public Web site to extend its reach significantly and provide potential customers or clients with an always available resource for contact and product information.

Designing Web pages that are accessible by the millions of people with permanent or temporary disabilities, including visual impairments, is good for business.[15] Research by the 2004 Disability Rights Commission has found that the Web sites that were most accessible for users with disabilities were also easier for people without disabilities to operate, with some online tasks performed 35 percent faster on the more accessible sites.[16] U.S. businesses have legal requirements for online content to be available to everyone under equal opportunity and anti-discrimination laws. The National Federation of the Blind filed a class action suit against Target Corporation because the online store offered values that could not be accessed by screen reader software.[17] The Web Content Accessibility Guidelines provided by The World Wide Web Consortiums (W3C) at **www.w3.org** are helpful resources for ensuring Web accessibility. The same group has also developed Mobile Web Accessibility Guidelines for making Web sites usable from mobile devices.

5-2a Writing for a Web Site

Many of the same standard rules for writing apply, whether writing for the Web or print. However, some important differences exist between readers of paper material and Web users:[18]

• Web users do not want to read. They skim, browse, and hop from one highlighted area to another trying to zero in on the word or phrase that relates to their search.

• English-speaking readers typically start scanning at the top left side of the main content area. Their attention moves from top to bottom and left to right. Given this pattern, placing frequently accessed items close to the top of the content area is important. Information should follow the pyramid style of writing common in newspaper writing: The main idea or conclusion is presented first, and subsequent sections and pages expand upon it.

• Users can more quickly scan items in columns rather than rows, especially if they are categorized, grouped, and have headings. You can have more lists on the Web than in a typical print document.

• Users refer infrequently to directions. It is unlikely they will read little notes, sidebars, and help files, so directions must appear in simple, numbered steps.

- In recognition of these Web user characteristics, writers should tailor their styles accordingly.

Effective Web writing involves moving beyond the paper mode into the Web mode of thinking. Understanding the distinctive expectations of Web readers will allow you to structure your ideas effectively and efficiently.

5-2b Social Media

Web 2.0, which encourages online interaction, made it possible for people to participate on the Web. Unlike Web pages, which are not generally interactive, social media enables people to connect online and have a conversation. Web 2.0 technologies include blogs, wikis, video, and social networking sites that enable users to generate their own content.

More and more organizations are using social media tools to communicate with customers. Seventy-nine percent of the Fortune Global 100 companies use at least one of four social platforms—Facebook, videos, Twitter, and blogs—for this purpose.[19]

Writing for Weblogs

A **weblog, or blog,** is a type of online journal typically authored by an individual and does not allow visitors to change the original posted material, but to only add comments. Some of the millions of blogs now

© 1000 Words/Shutterstock.com

populating the Web are online scrapbooks for pasting links, information, and quotes. Some resemble personal diaries, often illustrated with digital snapshots; others serve as digital soapboxes, providing a platform for airing opinions and commentary about the world at large or on a special topic of interest. Users (known as bloggers) add entries (referred to as posts) using a simple online form in their browsers, while the weblog publishing software takes care of formatting the page layout and creating archive pages.[21]

Blogs differ from Web sites in that blogs are dynamic, with rapidly changing content that does not require authorization to post. The creator of the message does not have to be familiar with special coding and uploads a message simply by clicking the "Publish" button.[22] Blogging allows average citizens to become publishers. Bloggers, however, should write each post with the realization that it is publicly available.

Blog formats have been adapted for business uses, including commercial publishing, marketing, and as a knowledge management tool. Blogs can store knowledge in searchable archives for future use. This function can be helpful, for example, for service teams as they search

weblog (or blog)
a type of online journal typically authored by an individual that does not allow visitors to change the original material posted, but to only add comments

An effective corporate blog begins with a clear goal, such as winning business or building customer loyalty.

past communications to troubleshoot current problems. Many companies, such as Microsoft, Sun Microsystems, and General Motors, encourage blogging among employees.[23] An effective corporate blog begins with a clear goal, such as winning business or building customer loyalty, and then provides relevant, frequently updated information for the target audience to return to regularly. Like other effective Web communications, blogs must be promoted creatively to attract avid readers.[24]

Internal blogs can be established that are not published to anyone outside the company. They present similar legal issues to those surrounding email and instant messaging. One of the most important considerations is whether posts are truly anonymous. The potential for anonymous speech creates an atmosphere that can encourage irresponsible behavior, such as harassment, defamation, and gossip. To reduce this problem, IT professionals can configure internal blogs so that all users can be identified, at least by the company.[25]

Writing Wikis

While a traditional Web site's content is usually controlled by the sponsoring individual or agency, a wiki is a collaborative Web site that hosts the collective work of many authors. Similar to a blog in structure and logic, a wiki allows anyone to edit, delete, or modify content, even the work of previous authors. While allowing everyday users to create and edit a Web site encourages cooperative use of electronic information, the content posted at such sites should not be considered authoritative. When wiki writing, avoid the first-person blogging style and conform to the tone and flow of the existing article. Wikis are not typically the place for personal opinion and analysis. Instead, present factual information in clear, concise, and neutral language.[26]

Many businesses make use of wikis to encourage free flow of ideas within the organization. Content in a wiki can be updated in real time, without any real administrative effort, and without the need for deliberate distribution. Contributors simply visit and update a common Web site. Wikis facilitate the exchange of information within and between teams. They allow maintenance of a series of unique documents with evolving content. Placing a document in a wiki does not necessarily make it editable by everyone with access to the wiki. For example, the marketing department can make a PowerPoint slide deck available to the sales team or the company at large without letting them change or overwrite it. Most companies implement their wikis behind a firewall to limit participation to their internal user base.[27]

Social Networking

Social networking sites are for communities of people who share common interests or activities. Common social networking sites include Facebook, LinkedIn, Twitter, and YouTube. Early on, social networking sites were used largely for making personal connections, but more and more, companies are using them to interact with customers. Companies such as Dell and Southwest Airlines employ "communities and conversation teams" or a "social media team" who track comments posted on sites such Twitter, YouTube, Flickr, and Facebook, verify facts, and respond quickly to any customer complaint appearing in cyberspace. In addition to being an early warning system, these online conversations are sources of feedback on customer needs and pain points that lead to innovation in products and services.[28]

5-3 Voice and Wireless Communication

Not so long ago, voice communication referred strictly to communication over phone lines, and using the telephone effectively is still an important skill in any profession. Although the traditional telephone still plays an important role in business activity, voice communication extends to voice mail systems and cell phone usage. Both voice and data can be transmitted now using wireless communication systems.

5-3a Voice Mail Communication

Voice mail technology allows flexibility in staying in touch without the aid of a computer and reduces telephone tag. Just as email communication can be enhanced by adhering to some basic principles, voice mail communication can be more effective by following recommended guidelines:[29]

- Update your greeting often to reflect your schedule and leave special announcements.
- Leave your email address, fax number, or mailing address on your greeting if this information might be helpful to your callers.
- Encourage callers to leave detailed messages. If you need certain standard information from callers, use your greeting to prompt them for it. Such information often eliminates the need to call back.
- Instruct callers on how to review their message or be transferred to an operator.
- Check your voice mail regularly, and return all voice messages within 24 hours.

When leaving a message, you can improve your communication by following these tips:[30]

- Speak slowly and clearly, and repeat your name and phone number at the beginning and end of the message.
- Spell your name for the recipient, who might need the correct spelling.
- Leave a detailed message, not just your name and number, to avoid prolonged phone tag.
- Keep your message brief, typically 60 seconds or less.
- Ensure that your message will be understandable. Don't call from places with distracting background noise or an inadequate signal connection.

The sound of your voice makes a lasting impression on the many people who listen to your greeting or the messages you leave. To ensure that the impression you leave is a professional one, review your voice greeting before you save it. Rerecord to eliminate verbal viruses ("um," "uh," stumbles), flat or monotone voice, and garbled or rushed messages that are difficult to understand. Consider scripting the message to avoid long, rambling messages. As you are recording, stand, smile, and visualize the person receiving the message; you'll hear the added energy, enthusiasm, and warmth in your voice.[31]

Remember that the voice mail message you leave should be seen as permanent. In some systems the digital files are backed up and stored for possible retrieval by managers or other company personnel. A voice mail message can also be used as evidence in a lawsuit or other legal proceeding.[32]

5-3b Cell Phone Communication

Mobile telephones, once a rarity, are now a standard accessory for many people throughout the world. In the United States, cell phones are as commonplace as landline phones, and the number continues to rise.

The increasing functionality and ease of use of cell phones have outstripped the development of rules for proper cell phone etiquette. According to a recent poll, almost 7 out of 10 Americans say they observe poor cell phone etiquette at least once every day.[33] Cell phone abuse in the workplace causes much annoyance and intrusion that leads to ineffectiveness and can endanger employee safety. Your attention to a few commonsense guidelines will help ensure that you are not seen as a rude phone user.[34]

- **Observe wireless-free quiet zones.** This obviously includes theaters, performances, and religious services, but can also include meetings, restaurants, hospitals, and other public places. Exercise judgment about silencing your ringer, switching to vibrate mode, or turning off your phone. To increase the effectiveness of meetings, cell phone policies in some businesses ask that employees leave their cell phones at their desks; vibrating mode is acceptable for an anticipated emergency. To encourage proper cell phone etiquette, one business requires managers to deposit a designated amount of money in a jar should their cell phones ring during a meeting; monies collected are donated to a charity.

- **Respect others in crowded places.** Speak in low conversational tones, and consider the content of your conversation.

- **Think safety.** Some states and municipalities have banned the use of cell phones while driving. Others allow the use of hands-free devices only. Even if not illegal, cell phone usage increases the risk of accident by distracting the driver. Some companies

are implementing cell phone policies that prohibit operators of company-owned vehicles from using cell phones or other communication devices while driving in order to minimize risks to their employees and liability resulting from accidents.

Cell phone users should remember that the technology is not secure. Perhaps you have overheard another party's phone conversation when using your cell phone. The radio frequencies that transmit the voice signals can be picked up by other equipment. For this reason, information that is confidential or sensitive should be shared using an alternate communication channel.

5-3c Wireless Communication and the Future

With the many communication innovations that have occurred in the last 20 years, one can only wonder what the next 20 years will hold. Whatever the breakthroughs, wireless technology will figure strongly in the changes. Wireless communication has freed us from the necessity of being literally plugged in while enabling us to communicate voice and high-speed data transmission virtually anytime, anywhere.

Wireless technology drives many of the significant changes that are affecting today's businesses. Smartphones offer advanced capabilities beyond a typical mobile phone, with PC-like functionality. Applications include email access, data processing, and entertainment. Other functionality might include an additional interface such as a miniature QWERTY keyboard, touch screen or D-pad, built-in camera, contact management, navigation hardware and software, media software for playing music, browsing and viewing capability for photos and video clips, and Internet browsers. Phone data can be synchronized with a computer and other communication devices for easy information access and manipulation. The future promises increased use of smartphones, especially touch-screens, by both consumers and professionals as well as the development of many innovative phone apps (shorthand for phone applications) that customize smartphone capabilities to fit users' needs. Security will continue to be a challenging consideration as workers use their phones to hold and transmit confidential information.[35]

Ronnie Kaufman/Flirt/Corbis

The impact of wireless communication will be even more significant as voice-to-text and text-to-voice technology continues to develop. Voice input and output technology offers the ability to communicate through a computer system without a keyboard. Although such technology has been around for more than two decades, newer systems have more powerful processors, are smaller in size, and better tolerate variances in speakers' accents and inflections without sacrificing speed and accuracy.

Wireless capability will increase the timeliness of key business decisions, resulting in greater revenues and profitability. However, being able to make decisions quickly does not ensure that they will be the right decisions. As in the past, workers will need to have correct and timely information for making decisions. An additional challenge for the wireless era will be balancing electronic communication capabilities with the need for human interaction.

© iStockphoto.com/DRB Images, LLC

5-4 Appropriate Use of Technology

Technology offers numerous advantages, but a technological channel is not always the communication method of choice. Before sending a message, be certain the selected channel of communication is appropriate by considering the message's purpose, confidentiality issues, and human relations factors.

5-4a Determine the Purpose of the Message

If a message is straightforward and informative, chances are a technological option might be appropriate. Although the use of instantaneous and efficient communication methods is quite compelling, keep in mind that written communication, printed or online, cannot replace the personal interaction so essential in today's team-based work environments. Employees floors apart or in different offices or time zones benefit from email and Web communications, but two people sitting side by side or on the same floor shouldn't have to communicate solely by electronic means.

A second question when selecting among communication options is whether a permanent record of the message is needed or if a more temporary form such as a phone call or instant message would suffice.

5-4b Determine Whether the Information Is Personal or Confidential

As a general guideline, keep personal correspondence off-line if you don't want it to come back and haunt you. The content of an email message could have embarrassing consequences since such documents often become a part of public records and wireless communications might be unexpectedly intercepted. Your company technically "owns" your electronic communications and thus can monitor them to determine legitimate business use or potential abuse. Undeliverable email messages are delivered to a mail administrator, and many networks routinely store backups of all email messages that pass through them.

Even deleted messages can be "resurrected" with little effort, as several public figures discovered when investigators retrieved archived email as evidence in court cases. For sensitive situations, a face-to-face encounter is often preferred.

5-4c Decide Whether Positive Human Relations Are Sacrificed

Be wary of using an electronic communication tool as an avoidance mechanism. Remember, too, that some people do not regularly check their email or voice mail, and some have unreliable systems that are slow or

SOCIAL APPS FOR WORK

Tomfoolery, a mobile-first enterprise app lab, has introduced a piece of software called Anchor that it describes as a "social app for work." According to a description posted to the Tomfoolery Web site, Anchor is a combination of Twitter, Facebook, and Google+ that users can employ to share photos, create groups, post updates, and chat with co-workers. The app also provides a directory function to access company-wide contact information. The idea behind Anchor, says Tomfoolery CEO and cofounder Kakul Srivastava, is to create a stronger connection among colleagues.[36]

prone to losing messages. Some news will be received better in person than through an electronic format that might be interpreted as cold and impersonal.

Additionally, some people, especially those of certain cultures, prefer a personal meeting even if you perceive that an electronic exchange of information would be a more efficient use of everyone's time. Choose the communication channel carefully to fit both your purpose and the preference of the receiver.

STUDY TOOLS
CHAPTER 5

Located at back of the textbook

❑ Rip out Chapter Review Card

Located at www.cengagebrain.com

❑ Review Key Terms Flashcards (Print or Online)

❑ Download Audio Summaries for on-the-go review

❑ Complete Practice Quizzes to prepare for tests

❑ Play "Beat the Clock" to master concepts

❑ Complete the Crossword Puzzle to review key terms

❑ Watch the video about McDonaldson, a fictitious but all-too-realistic ad agency whose employees struggle with contemporary business communication issues

Delivering Good- and Neutral-News Messages

OBJECTIVES

6-1 Describe the deductive outline for good and neutral news and its adaptations for specific situations and for international audiences.

6-2 Prepare messages that convey good news, including thank-you and appreciation messages.

6-3 Write messages presenting routine claims and requests and favorable responses to them.

6-4 Write messages acknowledging customer orders, providing credit information, and extending credit.

6-5 Prepare procedural messages that ensure clear and consistent application.

6-1 Deductive Organizational Pattern

You read in Chapter 4 that you can organize business messages either *deductively* or *inductively* depending on your prediction of the receiver's reaction to your main idea. Learning to organize business messages according to the appropriate outline will improve your chances of preparing a document that elicits the response or action you desire.

In this chapter, you will learn to compose messages that convey ideas that a receiver likely will find either *pleasing* or *neutral*. Messages that convey pleasant information are referred to as **good-news messages**. Messages that are of interest to the receiver but are not likely to generate an emotional reaction are referred to as **neutral-news messages**. The strategies discussed for structuring good-news and neutral-news messages generally can be applied to North American audiences. Because message expectations and social conventions differ from culture to culture, the effective writer will adapt as necessary when writing for various audiences. People in organizations use a number of channels to communicate with internal and external audiences. When sending a message that is positive or neutral, you have numerous choices, as shown in Figure 6-1. Depending on the message, recipient, and constraints of time and location, the best channel might be spoken or electronic. In addition to the electronic and verbal tools presented in Chapter 5 (email, instant messaging, Web communications, and phone), companies also use written documents such as memorandums and letters to communicate information.

The principles for preparing memorandums (commonly referred to as *memos*) are similar to those you've already applied when composing email messages, as both are channels for sharing information of a somewhat informal nature. Memos provide a tangible means of sharing information with people inside an organization. Letters are more formal, because they are used to convey information to external audiences such as customers, clients, business partners, or suppliers. Regardless of whether the audience is an internal or external one, communication should be carefully structured to achieve the desired purpose.

Good-news or neutral-news messages follow a **deductive** or **direct sequence**—the message begins with the main idea. To present good news and neutral information deductively, begin with the major idea, followed by supporting details as depicted in Figure 6-1. In both outlines, the third point (closing thought) might be omitted without seriously impairing effectiveness; however, including it unifies the message and avoids abruptness.

The deductive pattern has several advantages:

- The first sentence is easy to write. After it is written, the details follow easily.

- The first sentence gets the attention it deserves in this emphatic position.

- Encountering good news in the first sentence puts receivers in a pleasant frame of mind, and they are receptive to the details that follow.

- The arrangement might save receivers some time. Once they understand the important idea, they can move rapidly through the supporting details.

good-news messages
messages that convey pleasant information

neutral-news messages
messages that are of interest to the reader but are not likely to generate an emotional reaction

deductive (or direct) sequence
when the message begins with the main idea followed by supporting details

Log onto www.cengagebrain.com for additional resources, including flashcards, games, self-quizzing for chapter review, grammar exercises, and more.

BCOM

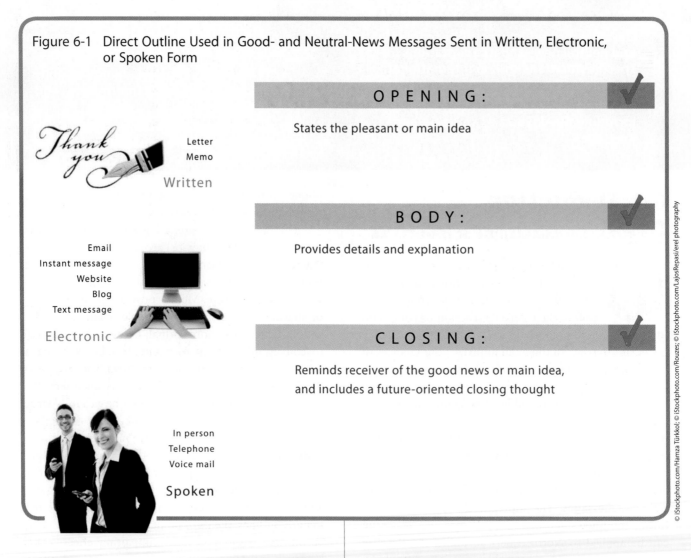

Figure 6-1 Direct Outline Used in Good- and Neutral-News Messages Sent in Written, Electronic, or Spoken Form

Letter
Memo
Written

Email
Instant message
Website
Blog
Text message
Electronic

In person
Telephone
Voice mail
Spoken

OPENING:
States the pleasant or main idea

BODY:
Provides details and explanation

CLOSING:
Reminds receiver of the good news or main idea, and includes a future-oriented closing thought

© iStockphoto.com/Hamza Türkkol; © iStockphoto.com/Rouzes; © iStockphoto.com/LajosRepasi/erel photography

As you study sample deductive messages in this chapter, note the *poor example* notations that clearly mark the examples of ineffective writing. Detailed comments highlight important writing strategies that have been applied or violated. While gaining experience in developing effective messages, you will also learn to recognize standard business formats. Fully formatted messages are shown as printed documents (letters on company letterhead or paper memos) or as electronic formats (email messages or online input screens).

6-2 Good-News Messages

Messages delivering good news are organized using a direct approach as illustrated in Figure 6-1. For illustration, you'll study examples of messages that convey positive news as well as thank-you and appreciation messages that generate goodwill.

6-2a Positive News

The memo sent to all employees in Figure 6-2 begins directly with the main idea: the approval of a flex-time work schedule policy. The discussion that follows includes a brief review of the policy and ends positively by encouraging employees to seek additional information from the company Web site or contact the writer.

6-2b Thank-You and Appreciation Messages

Empathetic managers take advantage of occasions to write goodwill messages that build strong, lasting relationships with employees, clients, customers, and various other groups. People are usually not reluctant to

Figure 6-2 GOOD :-) Good Example of a Good-News Message

INTEROFFICE MEMORANDUM

TO: All Employees
FROM: Dina Lombard, CEO
DATE: February 2, 2014
SUBJECT: Merger with PubPRO moves forward

As you know, Chastain Publishing has been in talks with the online publishing company PubPRO regarding a possible merger. It is my pleasure to announce that Chastain and PubPRO have reached an agreement, and the two companies will formally merge July 1, 2014.

This agreement will enable Chastain to move to more efficiently take advantage of digital delivery of its current product offerings and to offer a variety of new product lines. We expect that these opportunities will lead to greater profitability for Chastain and a more secure working environment for our employees.

- The merger will not affect our current operations here at headquarters. Beginning in April, employees will begin receiving training to learn more about PubPRO's capabilities and product line. Product development teams will begin working with counterparts at PubPRO soon after the merger to identify potential synergies in current product offerings that may be leveraged for product enhancements. Later in the year, we plan to create product development teams comprised of employees from both PubPRO and Chastain to begin identifying and developing new product opportunities.

- You will be updated as more information about the merger becomes available. In the meantime, please visit the HR Web site for the most recent information about the merger and to learn more about PubPRO.

- I hope you will join me in welcoming PubPRO employees to the Chastain team!

Format Pointers

Uses template with standard memo headings for efficient production.

Includes writer's initials after printed name and title.

Starts with main idea—announcement of new policy.

Provides clear explanation to ensure policy is understood. Formats as bullet list for quick, easy reference to specific. details.

Encourages readers to ask questions or view additional information on company intranet.

To Express Thanks for a Gift

Thank you for the gift certificate to Coco's Coffee. You know how much I love their double chocolate mocha! I was happy to fill in for you during the hiring meeting, since our choices are so important to our team. I hope Lisa is feeling better.

say, "Thank you," "What a great performance," "You have certainly helped me," and so on. Despite good intentions, however, often people don't get around to sending thank-you and appreciation messages. Because of their rarity, written appreciation messages are especially meaningful— even treasured.

© ever/Shutterstock.com

Thank-You Messages

After receiving a gift, being a guest, attending an interview, or benefiting in various other ways, a thoughtful person will take the time to send a written thank-you message. A simple handwritten or electronically sent note is sufficient for some social situations. However, when written from a professional office to respond to a business situation, the message might be printed on company letterhead. Your message should be written deductively and reflect your sincere feelings of gratitude. The thank-you messages shown on this page (1) identify the circumstances for which the writer

To Extend Thanks for Hospitality

Thank you for opening your home for our department barbecue. Your beautiful garden and inviting pool made the event one of our best summer parties yet. I enjoyed meeting your lovely family and especially wanted to thank your husband for grilling all those delicious burgers and brats. Thanks again for your generosity in sharing your home and family with your colleagues.

is grateful and (2) provide specific reasons the action is appreciated.

Appreciation Messages

You will write appreciation messages to recognize, reward, and encourage the receiver; however, you will also gain happiness from commending a deserving person. Such positive thinking can be a favorable influence on your own attitude and performance. In appropriate situations, you might wish to address an appreciation message to an individual's supervisor and send a copy of the document to the individual to share the positive comments. In any case, an appreciation message should be sent to commend deserving people and not for possible self-gain.

For full potential value, follow these guidelines for appreciation messages:

- **Send in a timely manner.** Sending an appreciation message within a few days of the circumstance will emphasize your genuineness. The receiver might question the sincerity of appreciation messages that are sent long overdue.

- **Avoid exaggerated language that is hardly believable.** You might believe the exaggerated statements to be true, but the recipient might find them unbelievable and insincere. Strong language with unsupported statements raises questions about your motive for the message.

- **Make specific comments about outstanding qualities or performance.** Compared to Figure 6-3, the following message might lack the impact of one that contains more detail and is written with more care. Although the sender cared enough to say thank you, the message could have been given to any speaker, even if the sender had slept through the entire seminar. Similarly, a note merely closed with "sincerely" does not necessarily make the ideas seem sincere. Including specific remarks about understanding and applying the speaker's main points makes the message meaningful and sincere.

Original: Your workshop on using the new database software program was very much appreciated. I'm sure it will help staff tremendously. Thanks.

Improved: Your workshop on the use of our new database software program has enabled staff to apply its broad array of features much more quickly.

One of the most important takeaways from the class was the emphasis you placed on creating and communicating clear procedures for work processes. Based upon your suggestions, our team created a draft of these guidelines during our first meeting. Thank you for the suggestions that have put my colleagues and me on the path to becoming a more effective virtual team.

Figure 6-3 **GOOD** :-) Good Example of an Appreciation Message

---

New Message

To: Rose Neilsen <rneilsen@ecosolutions.com>
From: Ned Sherman <nsherman@tslcorp.com>
Subject: Appreciation for Outstanding Work

Hello Ms. Neilsen,

Staff members have been elated by the new heating and air conditioning system your company recently installed in our building. I am particularly pleased, since I am no longer swamped with complaints about too-hot or too-cool offices.

Management has expressed its appreciation regarding the swiftness with which the retrofit was accomplished, resulting in minimal interruption of operations. Management and I also look forward to the reduced costs we expect from installation of your energy-efficient system.

One final benefit is that our public relations department expects to gain positive exposure by increasing our profile as a "green" company in part because of the installation of our new energy-efficient heating and cooling system. Thank you for helping us to see this potential.

Best wishes,

Ned Sherman
Operations Manager
TSL Corporation
901-555-1616, Fax 901-555-1302
nsherman@tslcorp.com

• *Extends appreciation for company's provision of quality service and installation.*

• *Provides specific example without exaggerating or using overly strong language or insincere statements.*

• *Assures reader of tangible benefits gained.*

Format Pointers
Uses short lines, mixed case; omits special formatting such as emoticons and email abbreviations for improved readability.

The appreciation message in Figure 6-3 sent from a manager to the owner of a heating and cooling company conveys warmer, more sincere compliments than a generic, exaggerated message. The net effects of this message are positive: The sender feels good for having passed on a deserved compliment, and the receiver is encouraged by the client's satisfaction with its new heating and cooling system.

An apology is written much like an appreciation message. A sincere written apology is needed to preserve relationships when regrettable situations occur. However difficult to prepare, a well-written apology will usually be received favorably.

Minerva Studio/Fotolia LLC

6-3 Routine Claims

A **claim** is a request for an adjustment. When business communicators ask for something to which they think they are entitled (such as a refund, replacement, exchange, or payment for damages), the message is called a *claim message*.

6-3a Claim Message

Requests for adjustments can be divided into two groups: **routine claims** and **persuasive claims**. Persuasive claims, which are discussed in Chapter 8, assume that a request will be granted only after explanations and persuasive arguments have been presented. Routine claims (possibly because of guarantees, warranties, or other contractual conditions) assume that a request will be granted quickly and willingly, without persuasion. Because you expect routine claims to be granted willingly, a forceful, accusatory tone is inappropriate.

claim
a request for an adjustment

routine claims
messages that assume that a claim will be granted quickly and willingly, without persuasion

persuasive claims
messages that assume a claim will be granted only after explanations and persuasive arguments have been presented

adjustment messages
messages that are fair responses by businesses to legitimate requests in claim messages by customers

When the claim is routine, the direct approach shown in Figure 6-1 is appropriate. Let's consider the situation referred to in Figures 6-4 and 6-5. Surely, the office furniture company intended its office chairs to be fully functioning. Because the damage—a broken pneumatic lift and fabric tear—are obvious, the office furniture company can be expected to correct the problem without persuasion. Thus the manager can ask for an adjustment before providing an explanation, as shown in Figure 6-5. Beginning with the request for an adjustment gives it the emphasis it deserves. Note, however, that the message in Figure 6-4 is written inappropriately using an indirect approach—the details are presented before the main idea, and ends abruptly.

6-3b Favorable Response to a Claim Message

Businesses *want* their customers to communicate when merchandise or service is not satisfactory. They want to learn of ways in which goods and services can be improved, and they want their customers to receive value for the money they spend. With considerable confidence, they can assume that writers of claim messages think their claims are valid. By responding fairly to legitimate requests in **adjustment messages**, businesses can gain a reputation for standing behind their goods and services. A loyal customer is likely to become even more loyal after a business has demonstrated its integrity.

Figure 6-4 **BAD :-(** Poor Example of a Routine Claim

Dear Ms. Jonas,

We recently purchased five office chairs from your company. Four of the chairs work perfectly, but the fifth is not functioning properly.

The pneumatic height adjustment on the chair appears to be stuck or broken. There is also a small tear in the fabric upholstery on the edge of the seat that may have occurred during shipping.

This message is to request that you replace or repair the chair as soon as possible. How would you like to proceed?

- *Introduction does not state the purpose of the message. Instead, it provides unneeded background.*

- *Paragraph provides more unnecessary background information.*

- *The routine request comes at the end of the message rather than at the beginning.*

Figure 6-5

GOOD :-) Good Example of a Routine Claim

New Message

To: Theodora Jonas <tjonas@OfficePlus.com>
From: Wang Chong <wchong@globaltravel.com>
Subject: Chair Repair or Replacement Needed

Ms. Jonas,

Please repair or send us a replacement for a chair we purchased from your company and that was delivered on May 12. The pneumatic height adjustment on the chair appears to be broken. There is also a small tear in the fabric upholstery on the edge of the seat that may have occurred during shipping.

The chair was part of an order for five Big and Tall Office Chairs, model number H-3643, placed on April 28, 2014.

We have hired five new customer-service employees, who will be starting on May 20 and will need seating for their workspaces. Therefore, I look forward to a prompt solution to this problem.

Thanks,
Wang Chong
Manager

- Limits message to a single idea expressed in meaningful subject line.
- Emphasizes main idea (request for adjustment) by placing it in first sentence.
- Provides explanation.
- Ends on positive note, reminding reader of immediate need.

Format Pointers
Composes short, concise message that fits on one screen.

Includes salutation and closing to personalize message.

Ordinarily, a response to a written message is also a written message. Sometimes people communicate to confirm ideas they have already discussed on the phone. When the response to a claim is favorable, present ideas in the direct sequence. Although the word *grant* is acceptable when talking about claims, its use in adjustment messages is discouraged. An expression such as "Your claim is being granted" unnecessarily implies that you are in a position of power.

Because the subject of an adjustment is related to the goods or services provided, the message can include a brief sales idea. With only a little extra space, the message can include resale or sales promotional material. **Resale** refers to a discussion of goods or services already bought. It reminds customers and clients that they made a good choice in selecting a company with which to do business, or it reminds them of the good qualities of their purchase. **Sales promotional material** refers to statements made about related merchandise or service. For example,

a message about a company's recently purchased office furniture might also mention available office equipment. Mentioning the office equipment is using sales promotional material. Subtle sales messages that are included in adjustments have a good chance of being read, whereas direct sales messages might not be read at all.

Consider the ineffective response in Figure 6-6 to Wang Chong's claim letter and the message it sends about the company's commitment. Now notice the deductive outline and the explanation in the revision in Figure 6-7. Because the writer knows that Wang Chong will be pleased the office chair has been repaired and shipped, the good news appears in the first sentence. The details and closing sentence follow naturally and show a desire to correct the problem.

resale
a discussion of goods or services already bought

sales promotional material
statements made about related merchandise or service

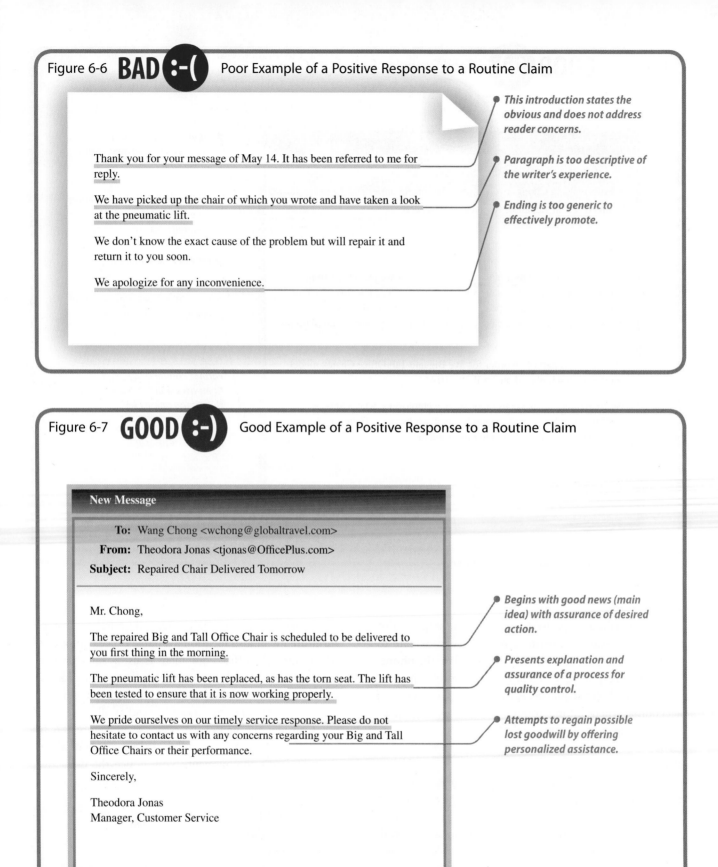

Figure 6-6 BAD :-(Poor Example of a Positive Response to a Routine Claim

Thank you for your message of May 14. It has been referred to me for reply.

- This introduction states the obvious and does not address reader concerns.

We have picked up the chair of which you wrote and have taken a look at the pneumatic lift.

- Paragraph is too descriptive of the writer's experience.

We don't know the exact cause of the problem but will repair it and return it to you soon.

- Ending is too generic to effectively promote.

We apologize for any inconvenience.

Figure 6-7 GOOD :-) Good Example of a Positive Response to a Routine Claim

New Message

To: Wang Chong <wchong@globaltravel.com>
From: Theodora Jonas <tjonas@OfficePlus.com>
Subject: Repaired Chair Delivered Tomorrow

Mr. Chong,

The repaired Big and Tall Office Chair is scheduled to be delivered to you first thing in the morning.

- Begins with good news (main idea) with assurance of desired action.

The pneumatic lift has been replaced, as has the torn seat. The lift has been tested to ensure that it is now working properly.

- Presents explanation and assurance of a process for quality control.

We pride ourselves on our timely service response. Please do not hesitate to contact us with any concerns regarding your Big and Tall Office Chairs or their performance.

- Attempts to regain possible lost goodwill by offering personalized assistance.

Sincerely,

Theodora Jonas
Manager, Customer Service

6-4 Routine Requests

Like claims, requests are divided into two groups: **routine requests** and **persuasive requests**. Persuasive requests, which are discussed in Chapter 8, assume that action will be taken after persuasive arguments are presented. Routine requests and favorable responses to them follow the deductive sequence.

6-4a Requests for Information

Requests for information about people, prices, products, and services are common. Because these requests

from customers and clients are door openers for future business, businesses accept them optimistically. At the same time, they arrive at an opinion about the sender based on the quality of the message. Follow the points in the deductive outline for preparing effective requests you are confident will be fulfilled.

The message in Figure 6-8 does not follow the deductive outline that is appropriate for a routine request. The request is too vague and the sales manager receiving the message is not provided with enough useful information.

Note that the revision in Figure 6-9 starts with a direct request for specific information. Then as much detail as necessary is presented to enable the receiver to answer specifically. The revision ends confidently with appreciation for the action requested. The email message is short, but because it conveys enough information and has a tone of politeness, it is effective.

routine requests
messages that assume that a request will be granted quickly and willingly, without persuasion

persuasive requests
messages that assume that a requested action will be taken after persuasive arguments are presented

---

Figure 6-8 **BAD :-(** Poor Example of a Routine Request

Subject: Need information

I have been searching for a relaxing location for my organization's national conference to be held in late May of next year. From looking at your Web site, it appears that Virginia Beach meets almost all our criteria. However, I am uncertain as to whether your hotel can accommodate our needs.

We expect that we may have as many as 700 attendees and perhaps half may need hotel accommodations. In addition, we expect as many as 200 travel and travel-related companies to purchase booths to showcase their products and services. Does your hotel have facilities to meet these needs?

I look forward to receiving your reply as quickly as possible.

- *The subject line could be more informational.*

- *The introduction could more clearly state the purpose of the message.*

- *The writer's needs could be stated more clearly and systematically.*

- *The generic close fails to build goodwill or a sense of urgency.*

Figure 6-9 **GOOD :-)** Good Example of a Routine Request

New Message

To: Deann Summers <dsummers@vbresort.com>

From: Larry Taylor <ltaylor@ncpa.org>

Subject: Information Needed for Planning Large Convention in Virginia Beach

Ms. Summers,

The helpful information on your Web site describing the panoramic views of the ocean and unique shopping and restaurant possibilities offered on Palisades Avenue suggests that Virginia Beach could be an ideal location for our three-day annual consumer products convention. To assist us in selecting the site for this event scheduled for late May 2013, please provide the following information:

- Does your hotel contain a conference center with space for 200 sales booths and three smaller rooms for concurrent sales presentations and press announcements?

- Can the conference hotel provide a block of 350 rooms, preferably at conference rate? If not, are there other suitable hotels nearby?

- Does the hotel have the capacity to feed 700 attendees during the three-day event at its in-house cafes and restaurants? If not, could you please provide a list of other nearby establishments that might meet the needs of attendees for breakfast, lunch, and dinner?

- Could your concierge staff provide a list of attractions and other venues that attendees might visit during the conference dates?

The information you provide could likely confirm our expectation that the Virginia Beach Resort can meet our conference needs. At that point you will be contacted to assist us in making necessary reservations. Should you wish to talk to me directly, please call (307) 213-6770.

Thanks,

Larry Taylor, Executive Director
National Consumer Products Association
307-213-6770, Fax: 307-213-6775
token@nta.org

- States request clearly.

- Asks specific questions with necessary explanation; uses list for emphasis.

- Expresses appreciation and alludes to benefits for quick action.

- Opens door for personal dialogue by providing telephone number.

Format Pointers
Provides salutation appropriate for company.

Includes a complete signature block below writer's name for complete reference.

6-4b Favorable Response to a Routine Request

The message in Figure 6-10 on page 99 responds favorably but with little enthusiasm to an online request for detailed information related to conference accommodations at a Pacific Coast hotel. With a little planning and consideration for the executive planning a major event, the message in Figure 6-11 on page 100 could have been written just as quickly. Note the specific answers

RE: Information Needed

Mr. Taylor,

I read your request and hopefully my hurried response will provide you the information you need.

Virginia Beach Resort can serve your needs with a 10,000-square foot conference center and accommodations for more than 700 guests. We also have three restaurants in the hotel as well as a coffee kiosk in the lobby. We are near shopping and restaurants on Palisade Avenue and North Beach Drive as well as local area attractions, such as the Virginia Beach Art Museum and Virginia Beach Aquarium.

We are happy you're considering Virginia Beach and the Virginia Beach Resort for your annual convention. Please contact either me or my staff to make the necessary reservations.

- *The subject line could be more informational.*
- *The introduction could be more positive and speak more narrowly to the reader's concerns.*
- *This discussion could be more specific and presented in an easier-to-read format.*
- *The close could be more effective at building goodwill and demonstrating a sincere interest in meeting the organization's needs.*

to the manager's questions prepared in the convenient Q&A format and the helpful, sincere tone.

6-4c Positive Response to a Favor Request

Occasionally, as a business professional, you will be asked for special favors. You might receive invitations to speak at various civic or education events, spearhead fund-raising and other service projects, or offer your expertise in other ways. If you say "Yes," you might as well say it enthusiastically. Sending an unplanned, stereotyped acceptance suggests that the contribution will be similar.

If you find yourself responding to invitations frequently, you can draft a form message that you'll revise for each invitation you receive. Go to www.cengage-brain.com to view a TV production manager's gracious acceptance of an invitation to emcee an awards program for a civic group. This well-written acceptance illustrates how form messages can be effectively individualized to enable businesses to communicate quickly and efficiently.

6-4d Form Messages for Routine Responses

Form messages are a fast and efficient way of transmitting frequently recurring messages to which receiver reaction is likely favorable or neutral. Inputting the customer's name, address, and other variables (information that differs for each receiver) personalizes each message to meet the needs of its receiver. Companies might use form paragraphs that have been saved as template documents. When composing a document, select the appropriate paragraph according to your receiver's request. After assembling the selected files on the computer screen, input the particular information for the situation (e.g., name and address) and print a copy of the personalized message on letterhead to send to the receiver.

Form letters have earned a negative connotation because of their tendency to be impersonal. Many people simply refuse to read such letters for that reason. Personalizing a form letter can circumvent this problem.

Figure 6-11 GOOD :-) Good Example of a Positive Response to a Routine Request

---

New Message

To: Larry Taylor <ltaylor@ncpa.org>

From: Deann Summers <dsummers@vbresort.com>

Subject: Assistance for Planning Exciting Convention in Virginia Beach

---

Mr. Taylor,

Virginia Beach and the Virginia Beach Resort are the ideal location for the National Consumer Products Association's annual convention. My staff and I can assist you with all your lodging, conference, and entertainment reservations.

Q: Does your hotel contain a conference center with space for 200 sales booths and three smaller rooms for sales presentations/press announcements?

A: Virginia Beach Resorts' Conference Center can easily meet your needs. We have a 10,000-square-foot conference space as well as 10 smaller meeting rooms.

Q: Can the hotel provide a block of 350 rooms at conference rate?

A: Yes, the Virginia Beach Resorts has 700 boutique-style rooms that are available for conferences of 200 people or more at a 15 percent rate reduction.

Q: Does the hotel have the capacity to feed 700 attendees during the three-day event at its in-house cafes and restaurants?

A: Virginia Beach Resort provides a unique dining experience in its three restaurants: The Car-Hop Diner, the Keys Grill, and the Blue Crab Bistro. A coffee bar is conveniently located in our lobby. Just outside our door on Palisade Avenue, more than a dozen restaurants are within easy walking distance.

Q: Could your concierge staff provide a list of attractions and other venues that attendees might visit during the conference?

A: Virginia Beach Resort is within walking distance of the Virginia Beach Museum of Art that houses the world's largest collection of folk art. Nearby is Virginia Beach Aquarium with more than 3,000 species of marine animals. A short bus or taxi ride takes visitors to world-class shopping and restaurants on North Beach Drive. Of course, other attractions include the beach and various water sports, such as surfing, kayaking, and paddle-boarding.

Please call my direct line (509) 569-6768 for more advice on organizing an exciting event on the shores of the beautiful Atlantic Ocean.

Thanks,

Deann Summers, Sales Manager
Virginia Beach Resort

• Revises subject line after clicking "reply" to communicate enthusiasm for providing exceptional personalized service.

• Shows sincere interest in request and person.

• Highlights specific answers to recipient's questions using an articulate, concise writing style.

• Encourages direct call and provides more useful information that communicates genuine interest in person and event.

Format Pointer
Uses Q&A format to enhance readability of response to series of detailed questions.

6-5 Routine Messages about Orders and Credit

Routine messages, such as customer order acknowledgments, are written deductively. Normally, credit information is requested and transmitted electronically from the national credit reporting agencies to companies requesting credit references. However, when companies choose to request information directly from other businesses, individual credit requests and responses must be written.

6-5a Acknowledging Customer Orders

When customers place orders for merchandise, they expect to get exactly what they ordered as quickly as possible. Most orders can be acknowledged by shipping the order; no message is necessary. For an initial order and for an order that cannot be filled quickly and precisely, companies typically send an **acknowledgment message**, a document that indicates the order has been received and is being processed. Typically, acknowledgment messages are preprinted letters or copies of the sales order. An immediate email message acknowledges an order placed online and confirms the expected date of shipment as shown in Figure 6-12 on page 102. Individualized letters are not cost effective and will not reach the customer in a timely manner. Although the form message is impersonal, customers appreciate the order acknowledgment and information as to when the order will arrive.

Nonroutine orders, such as initial orders, custom orders, and delayed orders, require individualized acknowledgment messages. When well-written, these messages not only acknowledge the order but also create customer goodwill and encourage the customer to place additional orders.

6-5b Providing Credit Information

Replies to requests for credit information are usually simple—just fill in the blanks and return the document. If the request does not include a form, follow a deductive plan in writing the reply: the major idea first, followed by supporting details.

When providing credit information, you have an ethical and legal obligation to yourself, the credit applicant, and the business from which credit is requested. You must be able to document any statement you make to defend yourself against a defamation charge. Thus, good advice is to stick with facts; omit any opinions. "I'm sure he will pay promptly" is an opinion that should be omitted, but include the documentable fact that "His payments are always prompt." Can you safely say a customer is a good credit risk when all you know is that the customer had a good credit record when purchasing from you?

acknowledgment message
a document that indicates an order has been received and is being processed

Figure 6-12 **GOOD** :-)   Good Example of an Online Order Confirmation

New Message

To: Jessica Burns <jburns@pmail.com>
From: Manuel Ortega <mortega@happykidz.com>
Subject: Happy Kidz welcomes Jessica as valued customer

Provides warm, personal subject line.

Hi, Jessica,

Welcome to Happy Kidz and our line of unique clothing for children!
We have received your order for the purchase of the items listed below:

Welcomes new customer and acknowledges receipt of online order.

1.   1 Windblown Heart top with necklace, size 7, color White
2.   1 Flip Sequin Appliqué top, size 7, color Purple
3.   1 Color-Blocked Sequin top, size 7, color Black and White
4.   1 Essential Knit legging, size 7, color Black

The items are expected to be delivered within 7 or 10 days of receipt of the order. The statement of order and return documents will be delivered along with the items. Please report any defects in the items or any problems with the order by contacting customer service at happykidz .com/customerservice at your earliest convenience.

New products are listed weekly, so please check out our "New Arrivals" on our Web site, happykidz.com. We are pleased to provide you unique, quality kids' clothing designs, all made in America.

Thank you again for your order.

Best regards,

Manuel Ortega
Customer Service Manager
Happy Kidz, Inc.

P.S. Be sure to watch your mailbox for notices of special sales offered only to our online customers. Our online customers receive an additional 10 percent off of sales items.

6-5c Extending Credit

A timely response is preferable for any business document, but it is especially important when communicating about credit. The Equal Credit Opportunity Act (ECOA) requires that a credit applicant be notified of the credit decision within 30 days of receipt of the request or application. The party granting the credit must also disclose the terms of the credit agreement, such as the address for sending or making payments, due dates for payments, and the interest rate charged.

When extending credit, follow these guidelines as you write deductively:

1. **Open by extending credit and acknowledging shipment of an order.** Because of its importance, the credit aspect is emphasized more than the acknowledgment of the order. In other cases (in which the order is for cash or the credit terms are already clearly understood), the primary purpose of writing might be to acknowledge an order.

2. **Indicate the basis for the decision to extend credit and explain the credit terms.** Indicating that you are extending credit on the basis of an applicant's prompt paying habits with present creditors might encourage this new customer to continue these habits with you.

3. **Present credit policies.** Explain policies (e.g., credit terms, authorized discounts, payment dates). Include any legally required disclosure documents.

4. **Communicate a genuine desire to build a strong business relationship.** Include resale, sales promotional material, and comments that remind the customer of the benefits of doing business with you and encourage additional orders.

The letter in Figure 6-13 was written to a retailer; however, the same principles apply when writing to a

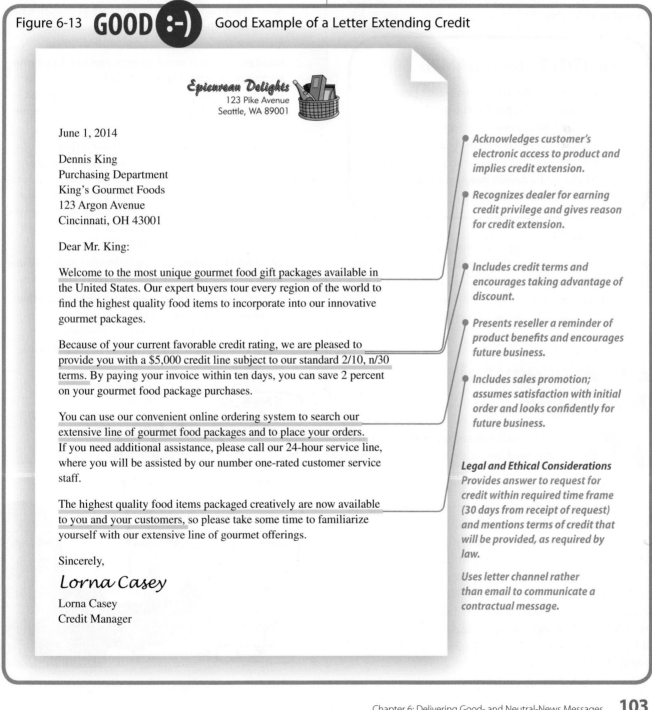

Figure 6-13 **GOOD :-)** Good Example of a Letter Extending Credit

Epicurean Delights
123 Pike Avenue
Seattle, WA 89001

June 1, 2014

Dennis King
Purchasing Department
King's Gourmet Foods
123 Argon Avenue
Cincinnati, OH 43001

Dear Mr. King:

Welcome to the most unique gourmet food gift packages available in the United States. Our expert buyers tour every region of the world to find the highest quality food items to incorporate into our innovative gourmet packages.

Because of your current favorable credit rating, we are pleased to provide you with a $5,000 credit line subject to our standard 2/10, n/30 terms. By paying your invoice within ten days, you can save 2 percent on your gourmet food package purchases.

You can use our convenient online ordering system to search our extensive line of gourmet food packages and to place your orders. If you need additional assistance, please call our 24-hour service line, where you will be assisted by our number one-rated customer service staff.

The highest quality food items packaged creatively are now available to you and your customers, so please take some time to familiarize yourself with our extensive line of gourmet offerings.

Sincerely,

Lorna Casey

Lorna Casey
Credit Manager

Acknowledges customer's electronic access to product and implies credit extension.

Recognizes dealer for earning credit privilege and gives reason for credit extension.

Includes credit terms and encourages taking advantage of discount.

Presents reseller a reminder of product benefits and encourages future business.

Includes sales promotion; assumes satisfaction with initial order and looks confidently for future business.

Legal and Ethical Considerations
Provides answer to request for credit within required time frame (30 days from receipt of request) and mentions terms of credit that will be provided, as required by law.

Uses letter channel rather than email to communicate a contractual message.

consumer. Each message should be addressed in terms of individual interests. Dealers are concerned about markup, marketability, and display; consumers are concerned about price, appearance, and durability. Individual consumers might require a more detailed explanation of credit terms.

Companies receive so many requests for credit that the costs of individualized letters are prohibitive; therefore, most favorable replies to credit requests are form letters. To personalize the letter, however, the writer should merge the customer's name, address, amount of loan, and terms into the computer file containing the form letter information. Typically, form messages read something like this:

> ## Dear [TITLE] [LAST NAME]:
>
> Tuttle Electronics is pleased to extend credit privileges to you. Initially, you may purchase up to [CREDIT LIMIT] worth of merchandise. Our credit terms are [TERMS]. We welcome you as a credit customer at Tuttle Electronics and look forward to serving your needs for the latest electronics devices designed and manufactured by the world's top companies.

Although such form messages are effective for informing the customer that credit is being extended, they do little to build goodwill and promote future sales. Managers can personalize form messages that recipients do not perceive as canned responses.

6-6 Procedural Messages

Memos or email messages are the most frequently used methods of communicating standard operating procedures and other instructions, changes related to personnel or the organization, and other internal matters for which a written record is needed.

Instructions to employees must be conveyed clearly and accurately to facilitate the day-to-day operations of business and to prevent negative feelings that occur when mistakes are made and work must be redone. Managers must take special care in writing standard operating procedures to ensure that all employees complete the procedures accurately and consistently.

Before writing instructions, walk through each step to understand it and to locate potential trouble spots. Then attempt to determine how much employees already know about the process and to anticipate any questions or problems. Then as you write instructions that require more than a few simple steps, follow these guidelines:

1. **Begin each step with an action statement to create a vivid picture of the employee completing the task.** Using an action verb and the understood subject *you* is more vivid than a sentence written in the passive voice. For example, a loan officer attempting to learn new procedures for evaluating new venture loans can more easily understand "*identify* assets available to collateralize the loan" than "assets available to collateralize the loan should be identified."

2. **Itemize each step on a separate line to add emphasis and to simplify reading.** Number each step to indicate that the procedures should be completed in a particular order. If the order of steps is not important, use bullets rather than numbers.

3. **Consider preparing a flow chart depicting the procedures.** The cost and effort involved in creating a sophisticated flow chart might be merited for extremely important and complex procedures. For example, take a look at the flow chart in Figure 10-8, which simplifies the steps involved in processing a telephone order in an effort to minimize errors.

4. **Complete the procedure by following your instructions step-by-step.** Correct any errors you locate.

5. **Ask a colleague or employee to walk through the procedures.** This walk-through will allow you to identify ambiguous statements, omissions of relevant information, and other sources of potential problems.

© Tom Wang/Shutterstock.com

Figure 6-14

GOOD :-)   Good Example of a Procedural Email with an Attachment

---

New Message

To: All Employees
From: Milton Bergman <mbergman@procorp.com>
Subject: New Procedure for Requesting Vacation Leave

Attachment: Vacation_Leave_Request_Procedures.docx 📎

Includes attached file of document requiring involved formatting.

Hi all,

With the recent and dramatic growth in the company, the challenge of processing employee requests for vacation leave has become a concern. To solve this issue, we have instituted an online process for requesting vacation leave, beginning March 31.

Introduces main idea.

To request vacation leave, please follow the procedure outlined in the attached file. (This file can also be found on the company intranet under "Human Resources.") You can complete these procedures at any computer, including your home machine.

Explains new procedures outlined in attached file.

Thanks,
Milton Bergman
Human Resource Manager

Procedures for Requesting Vacation Leave

1. Access http://www.procorp.com/hr and click the Forms link.
2. Scroll down the list that appears and click on Vacation Leave Request.
3. Provide the information requested in the form. Be certain to complete the required items denoted with asterisks.
4. Check your email for the response to your request, which typically will arrive within 48 hours.
5. Make sure that you notify your manager of your approved leave time so that he or she may plan accordingly.

If you have questions, please contact a human resource coordinator by emailing hrinfo@procorp.com. A coordinator will contact you within 24 hours.

Dated 02/22/2014

Provides descriptive title that clearly identifies procedures

Enumerates to direct attention to each step and emphasize need for sequence.

Begins each item with action verb to help employees visualize completing procedures.

Includes date of last revision to ensure currency.

Consider the seemingly simple task of requesting vacation leave. The human resource manager might respond to such a request, "No need for written instructions; just request vacation leave any way you wish." Ambiguous verbal instructions (reported in haste) could lead to confusion about vacation schedules and bad feelings about the efficiency of the process. The clear, consistent procedure in Figure 6-14 was prepared after the manager anticipated employee issues in requesting vacation leave. The policy is sent as an email attachment and posted to the company intranet for easy reference.

STUDY TOOLS
CHAPTER 6

Located at back of the textbook
❑ **Rip out Chapter Review Card**

Located at www.cengagebrain.com
❑ **Review Key Terms Flashcards (Print or Online)**
❑ **Download Audio Summaries for on-the-go review**
❑ **Complete Practice Quizzes to prepare for tests**
❑ **Play "Beat the Clock" to master concepts**
❑ **Complete the Crossword Puzzle to review key terms**
❑ **Watch the video about McDonaldson, a fictitious but all-too-realistic ad agency whose employees struggle with contemporary business communication issues**

WHY CHOOSE?

Every 4LTR Press solution comes complete with a visually engaging textbook in addition to an interactive eBook. Go to CourseMate for BCOM6 to begin using the eBook.
Access at **www.cengagebrain.com**

Delivering Bad-News Messages

OBJECTIVES

7-1 Explain the steps in the inductive outline, and understand its use for specific situations.

7-2 Discuss strategies for developing the five components of a bad-news message.

7-3 Prepare messages refusing requests and claims.

7-4 Prepare messages handling problems with customers' orders and denying credit.

7-5 Prepare messages providing constructive criticism, communicating negative organizational news, and responding to crises.

7-1 Choosing an Appropriate Channel and Organizational Pattern

An organization's ability to handle difficult situations with tact and empathy powerfully influences the perceptions of employees, local citizens, and the public at large. As a skilled communicator, you will attempt to deliver bad news in such a way that the recipient supports the decision and is willing to continue a positive relationship. To accomplish these goals, allow empathy for the receiver to direct your choice of an appropriate channel and an outline for presenting a logical discussion of the facts and the unpleasant idea. Use tactful and effective language to aid you in developing a clear, yet sensitive, message.

7-1a Channel Choice and Commitment to Tact

Personal delivery has been the preferred medium for delivering bad news because it signals the importance of the news and shows empathy for the recipient. Face-to-face delivery also provides the benefit of nonverbal communication and immediate feedback, which minimizes the misinterpretation of these highly sensitive messages. Personal delivery, however, carries a level of discomfort and the potential for escalation of emotion.

A voice on the telephone triggers the same discomfort as a face-to-face meeting, and the increased difficulty of interpreting the intensity of nonverbal cues over the telephone only adds to the natural discomfort associated with delivering negative information.

You must be cautious when you deliver bad news electronically, whether by email or electronic postings. While you might feel more comfortable avoiding the discomfort of facing the recipient, the impersonal nature of the computer might lead to careless writing that is tactless and lacking in empathy, and perhaps even defamatory. Stay focused and follow the same communication strategies you would apply if you were speaking face to face or writing a more formal message. Regardless of the medium, your objective is to help the receiver understand and accept your message, and this requires empathy and tact.

"You're fired" became a familiar phrase immortalized by Donald Trump on the hit show *The Apprentice*. Though such bluntness might work on television, it is rarely recommended in actual work situations. Tactlessness can have serious effects when your personal response fails to soothe negative feelings and ensure a harmonious relationship with a customer, client, or employee. You might find it difficult to show tact when you doubt the legitimacy of a request or simply don't have the time to prepare an effective bad-news message. When this conflict exists, you must remember that your message delivered on behalf of the company is a direct reflection on the company's image.

7-1b Use of the Inductive Approach to Build Goodwill

Just as good news is accompanied by details, bad news is accompanied by supporting reasons and explanations. If the bad news is presented in the first sentence, the reaction is likely to be negative: "They never gave me a fair chance," "That's unfair," "This just can't be." Having made a value judgment on reading the first sentence, receivers are naturally reluctant to change their minds before the last sentence—even though the

BCOM

intervening sentences present a valid basis for doing so. Once disappointed by the idea contained in the first sentence, receivers are tempted to concentrate on *refuting* (instead of *understanding*) supporting details.

From the communicator's point of view, details that support a refusal are very important. If the supporting details are understood and believed, the message might be readily accepted and good business relationships preserved. Because the reasons behind the bad news are so important, the communicator needs to organize the message in such a way as to emphasize the reasons.

The chances of getting the receiver to understand the reasons are much better *before* the bad news is presented than *after* the bad news is presented. If the bad news precedes the reasons, the message might be discarded before this important portion is even read, or the disappointment experienced when reading the bad news might interfere with the receiver's ability to comprehend or accept the supporting explanation.

The five-step outline shown in Figure 7-1 simplifies the process of organizing bad-news messages. These five steps are applied in messages illustrated in this chapter.

Although the outline has five points, a bad-news message may or may not have five paragraphs. More than one paragraph might be necessary for conveying supporting reasons. In the illustrations in this chapter, note that the first and final paragraphs are seldom longer than two sentences. In fact, one-sentence paragraphs at the message's beginning look inviting to read.

You might speculate that receivers might become impatient when a message is inductive. Concise, well-written explanations are not likely to make a receiver impatient. They relate to the receiver's problem, present information not already known, and help the receiver understand. However, if a receiver becomes impatient while reading a well-written explanation, that impatience is less damaging to understanding than would be the anger or disgust that often results from encountering bad news in the first sentence.

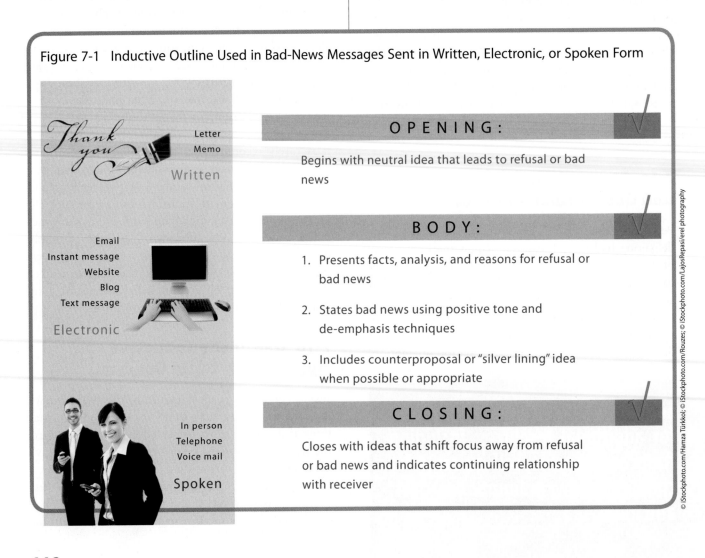

Figure 7-1   Inductive Outline Used in Bad-News Messages Sent in Written, Electronic, or Spoken Form

OPENING:

Begins with neutral idea that leads to refusal or bad news

BODY:

1. Presents facts, analysis, and reasons for refusal or bad news

2. States bad news using positive tone and de-emphasis techniques

3. Includes counterproposal or "silver lining" idea when possible or appropriate

CLOSING:

Closes with ideas that shift focus away from refusal or bad news and indicates continuing relationship with receiver

The Inductive Sequence of Ideas Has the Following Advantages:

- Sufficient identification of the subject of the message without first turning off the receiver.
- Presentation of the reasons *before* the refusal, where they are more likely to be understood and will receive appropriate attention.
- Avoidance of a negative reaction. By the time the reasons are read, they seem sensible, and the refusal is foreseen. Because it is expected, the statement of refusal does not come as a shock.
- De-emphasis of the refusal by closing on a neutral or pleasant note. By showing a willingness to cooperate in some way, the sender conveys a desire to be helpful.

7-1c Exceptions to the Inductive Approach

Normally, the writer's purpose is to convey a clear message and retain the recipient's goodwill; thus, the inductive outline is appropriate. In the rare circumstances in which a choice must be made between clarity and goodwill, clarity is the better choice. When the deductive approach will serve a communicator's purpose better, it should be used. For example, if you submit a clear and tactful refusal and the receiver submits a second request, a deductive presentation might be justified in

Placing a Refusal in the First Sentence Can Be Justified when One or More of the Following Circumstances Exist:

- The message is the second response to a repeated request.
- A very small, insignificant matter is involved.
- The request is obviously ridiculous, immoral, unethical, illegal, or dangerous.
- The sender's intent is to "shake" the receiver.
- The sender–recipient relationship is so close and longstanding that satisfactory human relations can be taken for granted.
- The sender *wants* to demonstrate authority.

the second refusal. Apparently, the refusal needs the emphasis provided by a deductive outline.

In most situations, the preceding circumstances do not exist. When they do, a sender's goals might be accomplished by stating bad news in the first sentence.

7-2 Developing a Bad-News Message

Developing a bad-news message following the inductive outline is challenging. The following suggestions will aid you in writing the (1) introductory paragraph, (2) explanation, (3) bad-news statement, (4) counterproposal or "silver lining" idea, and (5) closing paragraph.

7-2a Writing the Introductory Paragraph

The introductory paragraph in the bad-news message should accomplish the following objectives: (1) provide a buffer to cushion the bad news that will follow, (2) let the receiver know what the message is about without stating the obvious, and (3) serve as a transition into the discussion of reasons without revealing the bad news or leading the receiver to expect good news. If these objectives can be accomplished in one sentence, that sentence can be the first paragraph.

© lenetstan/Shutterstock.com

Avoid the Following Weaknesses When Writing the Introductory Paragraph:

- **Empty acknowledgments of the obvious.** *"I am writing in response to your letter requesting …"* or *"Your message of the 14th has been given to me for reply"* wastes space to present points of no value. Beginning with *I* signals the message might be writer-centered.
- **Tipping off the bad news too early.** *"Although the refund requested in your letter of May 1 cannot be approved …"* might cause an immediate emotional reaction resulting in the message being discarded or interfering with understanding the explanations that follow.

   The neutral statement *"Your request for an adjustment has been considered. However, …"* does not reveal whether the answer is "Yes" or "No," but the use of "however" signals that the answer is "No" before the reasons are presented. Such a beginning has about the same effect as an outright "No."
- **Starting too positively so as to build false hopes.** Empathetic statements such as *"I can understand how you felt when you were asked to pay an extra $54"* might lead the receiver to expect good news. When a preceding statement has implied that an affirmative decision will follow, a negative decision is all the more disappointing.

Study the Following Examples That Use Transition Statements to Achieve a Coherent Opening:

Your employment application package has been reviewed by Human Resources.	Reveals the topic as a reply to a recipient's employment application.
Human Resources personnel …	Uses "Human Resources personnel" to transition from first to second paragraph.
Following your request for permission to submit a proposal to continue subsidizing employees' access to exercise facilities, we reviewed recent records of attendance.	Reveals subject of message as reply to employee's request.
In the past two years, attendance …	Uses "recent" and "attendance" to tie second paragraph to first.

Here are several ideas that can be incorporated into effective beginning paragraphs:

- **Compliment.** A message denying a customer's request could begin by recognizing the customer's promptness in making payments.
- **Point of agreement.** A sentence that reveals agreement with a statement made in the message could get the message off to a positive discussion of other points.
- **Good news.** When a message contains a request that must be refused and another that is being answered favorably, beginning with the favorable answer can be effective.
- **Resale.** A claim refusal could begin with some favorable statement about the product.
- **Review.** Refusal of a current request could be introduced by referring to the initial transaction or by reviewing certain circumstances that preceded the transaction.
- **Gratitude.** In spite of the unjustified request, the receiver might have done or said something for which you are grateful. An expression of gratitude could be used as a positive beginning.

7-2b Presenting the Facts, Analysis, and Reasons

The reasons section of the bad-news message is extremely important because people who are refused want to know why. When people say "No," they usually do so because they think "No" is the better answer for all concerned. They can see how recipients will ultimately benefit from the refusal. If a message is based on a sound decision, and if it has been well written, recipients will understand and accept the reasons and the forthcoming refusal statement as valid.

To accomplish this goal, begin with a well-written first paragraph that transitions the receiver smoothly into the reasons section. Then develop the reasons section following these guidelines:

- **Provide a smooth transition from the opening paragraph to the explanation.** The buffer should help set the stage for a logical movement into the discussion of the reasons.

- **Include a concise discussion of one or more reasons that are logical to the receiver.** Read the section aloud to identify flaws in logic or the need for additional explanation.

- **Show receiver benefit and/or consideration.** Emphasize how the receiver will benefit from the decision. Avoid insincere, empty statements such as "To improve our service to you, …"

- **Avoid using "company policy" as the reason.** Disclose the reason behind the policy, which likely will include benefits to the receiver. For example, a customer is more likely to understand and accept a 15% restocking fee if the policy is not presented as the "reason" for the refusal.

The principles for developing the reasons section are illustrated in Figure 7-2, a letter written by travel agent refusing visa procurement service.

7-2c Writing the Bad-News Statement

A paragraph that presents the reasoning behind a refusal at least partially conveys the refusal before it is stated directly or indirectly. Yet one sentence needs to convey (directly or by implication) the conclusion to which the preceding details have been leading. A refusal (bad news) needs to be clear; however, you can subordinate the refusal so that the reasons get the deserved emphasis. The following techniques will help you achieve this goal.

- **Position the bad-news statement strategically.** Using the inductive outline positions the bad-news statement in a less important position—sandwiched between an opening buffer statement and a positive closing. Additionally, the refusal statement should be included in the same paragraph as the reasons, since placing it in a paragraph by itself would give too much emphasis to the bad news. When the preceding explanation is tactful and relevant, resentment over the bad news is minimized. Positioning the bad-news statement in the dependent clause of a complex sentence will also cushion the bad news. This technique places the bad news in a less visible,

Figure 7-2   Developing the Components of a Bad-News Message

You want your upcoming trip to India to be a memorable celebration of you and your husband's 25th anniversary. For this reason, it is imperative that you work with a travel planner who is able to guarantee delivery of the needed travel documents to make this trip a success.

Unfortunately, the process for securing a visa for travel to India has recently become more uncertain. We have been assured that the Indian government will be switching to a new process soon. When that operation is in place, we can proceed with the process of securing your travel documents.

Due to unrest in a number of foreign countries, we suggest that you begin your trip planning at least a year in advance. We hope you will contact us for your future travel needs.

- Begins with statement with which both can agree. Sets stage for reasons by presenting importance of timely vacation planning.

- Reveals subject of message and transitions into reasons.

- Supports refusal with logical reasoning.

- States refusal positively and clearly using complex sentence and positive language.

- Includes counterproposal as alternative.

- Closes with focus on continuing business relationship.

less emphatic position. In the sentence, *"Although the company's current financial condition prevents us from providing raises this year, we hope to make up for the freeze when conditions improve,"* the emphasis is directed toward a promise of raises at another time.

- **Use passive voice, general terms, and abstract nouns.** Review the *emphasis techniques* that you studied in Chapter 3 as you consider methods for presenting bad news with human relations in mind.

- **Use positive language to accentuate the positive.** Simply focus on the good instead of the bad, the pleasant instead of the unpleasant, or what can be done instead of what cannot be done. Compared with a negative idea presented in negative terms, a negative idea presented in positive terms is more likely to be accepted. When you are tempted to use the following terms, search instead for words or ideas that sound more positive:

Words that Evoke Negative Feelings

complaint incompetent misled regrettable
error inexcusable mistake unfortunate
failure lied neglect wrong

Words that Evoke Positive Feelings

accurate concise enthusiasm productive
approval durable generous recommendation
assist energetic gratitude respect

- **Imply the refusal when the receiver can understand the message without a definite statement of the bad news.** By *implying* the "No" answer, the response has the following positive characteristics: (1) it uses positive language, (2) it conveys reasons or at least a positive attitude, and (3) it seems more respectful. For example, during the noon hour one employee says to another, "Will you go with me to see this afternoon's baseball game?" "No, I won't," communicates a negative response, but it seems unnecessarily direct and harsh. The same message (invitation is rejected) can be clearly stated in an *indirect* way (by implication) by saying "I must get my work done," or even, "I'm a football fan." Note the positive tone of the following implied refusals:

counterproposal
in a bad-news message, an alternative to the action requested that follows the negative news and can assist in preserving future relationships with the receiver

Implied Refusal	Underlying Message
I wish I could.	• Other responsibilities prohibit, but recipient would like to accept.
Had you selected our newest calling plan, you could have reduced your monthly rates by 10% or more.	• States a condition under which answer would have been "Yes" instead of "No." Note use of subjunctive words "had" and "could."
By accepting the new terms, Southern Wood Products would have doubled its energy costs.	• States the obviously unacceptable results of complying with request.

7-2d Offering a Counterproposal or "Silver Lining" Idea

Following negative news with an alternative action, referred to as a **counterproposal**, will assist in preserving a relationship with the receiver. Because it states what you *can* do, including a counterproposal might eliminate the need to state the refusal directly. The counterproposal can follow a refusal stated in a tactful, sensitive manner. When global Internet services and media company AOL was faced with laying off 2,000 workers, the silver lining offered was a generous severance package and aid in transitioning to other job opportunities.[1]

While the counterproposal might represent a tangible benefit, at times it is more intangible in nature. For instance, in a letter that informs a job applicant that he or she was not selected to fill the position, the counterproposal might be an offer to reconsider the applicant's résumé when other appropriate positions become available. Any counterproposal must, of course, be reasonable. For instance, when informing a customer of an inability to meet a promised delivery deadline, an unreasonable counterproposal would be to offer the merchandise at no charge. A reasonable counterproposal might be to include some additional items at no charge or to offer a discount certificate good on the customer's next order.

When no reasonable counterproposal is apparent, the sender might be able to offer a silver lining thought that turns the discussion back into the positive direction. For instance, a statement to tenants announcing an increase in rent might be followed by a description of improved lighting that will be installed in the

Offering a counterproposal or "silver lining" idea can assist in preserving a relationship with the receiver of bad news.

parking lot of the apartment complex. When offering a counterproposal or silver lining statement, care must be taken to ensure that the idea does not seem superficial or minimize the recipient's situation.

7-2e Closing Positively

After presenting valid reasons and a tactful refusal followed with a counterproposal or silver lining statement, a closing paragraph should demonstrate empathy without further reference to the bad news. A pleasant closing paragraph should close with an empathetic tone and achieve the following goals:

- **De-emphasize the unpleasant part of the message.** End on a positive note that takes the emphasis away from the bad news previously presented. A statement of refusal (or bad news) in the last sentence or paragraph would place too much emphasis on it. Preferably, *reasons* (instead of bad news) should remain uppermost in the receiver's mind. Placing bad news last would make the ending seem cold and abrupt.

When no reasonable counterproposal is apparent, the sender might be able to offer a silver lining thought that turns the discussion back into the positive direction.

- **Add a unifying quality to the message.** Make your final sentence an *appropriate* closing that brings a unifying quality to the whole message. Repetition of a word or reference to some positive idea that appears early in the message serves this purpose well.

Avoid restatement of the refusal or direct reference to it. This paragraph is usually shorter than the preceding explanatory paragraphs, often one or two sentences.

- **Include a positive, forward-looking idea.** This idea might include a reference to some pleasant aspect of the preceding discussion or a future aspect of the business relationship, resale or sales promotion, or an offer to help in some way. Consider the following closures that apply these suggestions:

Reference to some pleasant aspect of the preceding discussion:
"*Your decision to refinance your mortgage last year was a wise choice.*" Home mortgage and other provisions had been mentioned in the early part of a letter to a client who was refused a double-indemnity settlement.

Use of resale or sales promotional material:
"*Selecting our new hybrid Breeze with its 50-miles-per-gallon fuel usage was a wise decision with today's gas prices.*" A reminder that the hybrid has superior gas mileage will assist in regaining goodwill after a customer's request for free repair has been refused.

An expression of willingness to assist in some other way:
Specifically, you might offer an alternative solution to the receiver's problem or useful information that could not be presented logically with the bad news. "*Our representative will show you some samples during next week's sales call.*" The samples are being proposed as a possible solution to the receiver's problem.

Note the closing paragraph in Figure 7-2 is a positive, forward-looking statement that includes promotion of vacation planning the travel agency can offer.

7-3 Refusing a Request

I t's a good idea to use the inductive approach (reasons before refusal) for refusing requests for a favor, an action, or even a donation. Present clear, understandable reasons in a way that minimizes the receiver's disappointment.

You can examine a company's refusal to provide an executive to speak to a group in Figure 7-3 on page 117. This *response* to prior correspondence uses the same principles of sequence and style that are recommended for messages that *initiate* communication about unpleasant topics. The same principles apply whether the communication is a spoken message, letter, memo, or email message.

Companies have learned that building employee relationships is just as important as developing customer goodwill. Refusing employees' requests requires sensitivity and complete, honest explanations, qualities not included in the bad email in Figure 7-4 on page 118. The manager's hasty and vague response to a valued employee's request to create an employee wellness center uses a direct, blunt approach. In the revision illustrated in

Figure 7-5 (on page 119), the manager takes the time to prepare a response that reflects detailed explanation supporting the refusal and genuine respect for the employee.

7-4 Denying a Claim

ompanies face a challenging task of refusing claims from customers while maintaining goodwill and building customer loyalty. Claim refusals are necessary when a

Figure 7-3 **GOOD :-)** Good Example of a Refusal for a Favor

Blades Real Estate, Inc. 2700 Ridgeway • Kansas City, MO 69909 • Phone 425 555-8700 •

March 18, 2014

Linda Weiser, President
Kansas City Women Business Owners
4375 Devon Street, Suite 5
Kansas City, MO 69912

Dear Ms. Weiser:

Emphasizing the value of sales and marketing skills is critical for the success of today's small business. Your organization's commitment to helping women successfully start up small businesses by exposing them to sales and marketing experts is to be commended.

The success of this endeavor depends on a sales professional who has the needed time to prepare a persuasive and engaging message for your group. Unfortunately, I will be leaving the country for a month for a long-planned tour of Europe, so I will not be available during your requested time.

One of my sales associates, Leena Trip, has agreed to speak to your group in my place. Leena has worked for Blades Real Estate for ten years and has been earned a "Million-Dollar Club" designation in annual sales for the past five years.

If you are interested in Leena's help, please call her at 555-8700, extension 65.

Sincerely,

Glenda

Glenda Blades
Blades Real Estate, Inc.
President

● *Introduces subject without revealing whether answer will be "Yes" or "No."*

● *Gives reasons that will seem logical to reader.*

● *Subordinates refusal by placing it in dependent clause of complex sentence. Alludes to help in another form.*

● *Closes positively with counterproposal. Conveys genuineness by summarizing executive's responsibilities and providing telephone number.*

Format Pointer
Signs first name only because writer knows receiver well.

warranty does not apply or has expired or a customer has misused the product. Companies must also write refusals when customers ask for something that a company simply can't do. For example, many retailers charge customers a $25–$40 fee on returned checks. A retailer who receives a customer's request to waive the charge must refuse because the claim is inconsistent with the retailer's policies and objectives.

The inductive approach is helpful in communicating this disappointing news to customers. Presenting

Figure 7-4   **BAD** 8-(Poor Example of a Refusal to an Employee's Request

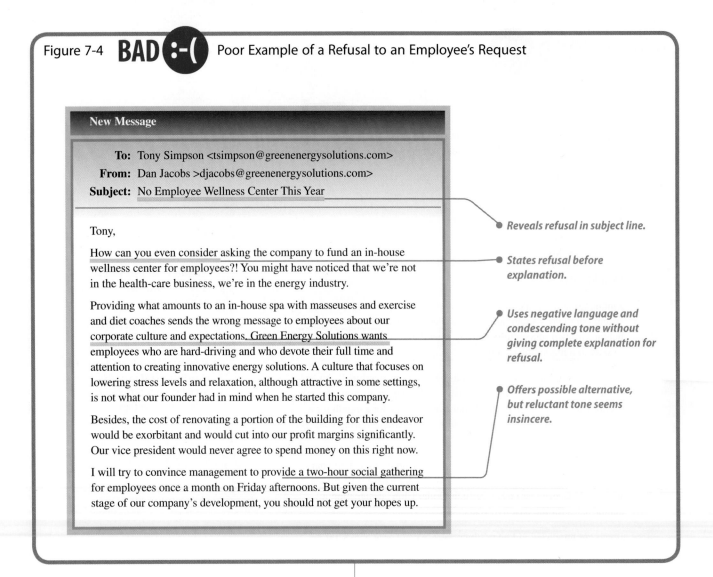

New Message

To: Tony Simpson <tsimpson@greenenergysolutions.com>
From: Dan Jacobs >djacobs@greenenergysolutions.com>
Subject: No Employee Wellness Center This Year

Tony,

How can you even consider asking the company to fund an in-house wellness center for employees?! You might have noticed that we're not in the health-care business, we're in the energy industry.

Providing what amounts to an in-house spa with masseuses and exercise and diet coaches sends the wrong message to employees about our corporate culture and expectations. Green Energy Solutions wants employees who are hard-driving and who devote their full time and attention to creating innovative energy solutions. A culture that focuses on lowering stress levels and relaxation, although attractive in some settings, is not what our founder had in mind when he started this company.

Besides, the cost of renovating a portion of the building for this endeavor would be exorbitant and would cut into our profit margins significantly. Our vice president would never agree to spend money on this right now.

I will try to convince management to provide a two-hour social gathering for employees once a month on Friday afternoons. But given the current stage of our company's development, you should not get your hopes up.

- Reveals refusal in subject line.
- States refusal before explanation.
- Uses negative language and condescending tone without giving complete explanation for refusal.
- Offers possible alternative, but reluctant tone seems insincere.

the explanation for the refusal first leads customers through the reasoning behind the decision and helps them *understand* the claim is unjustified by the time the refusal is presented. Tone is especially important when denying claims. Present the reasons objectively and positively without casting blame or judgment on the customer for the problem. Avoid lecturing a customer on the actions he or she should have taken to have avoided the problem. Finally, close the message with resale or sales promotional material that indicates you expect future business. Although disappointed with your decision, customers continue doing business with companies who make fair, objective decisions and communicate the reasons for those decisions in a positive, respectful manner.

Assume a manufacturer of LED screens receives the following email from a customer.

New Message

To: Craig Turner [cturner@electronicsplus.com]
From: Jon Frakes [jfrakes@tvoptions.com]
Subject: Refund Error

Please issue a credit to my account for $535.24. Although you accepted $3,405 of LED screens I returned, you only credited my account for $2,869.76. Because I could find no explanation for the discrepancy, I assume an error has been made.

Figure 7-5 **GOOD :-)** Good Example of a Refusal to an Employee's Request

New Message

To: Tony Simpson <tsimpson@greenenergysolutions.com>
From: Dan Jacobs >djacobs@greenenergysolutions.com>
Subject: No Employee Wellness Center This Year

Hi, Tony,

Because we want employees to work at the highest level possible, your suggestion to create an onsite wellness center has been carefully considered. Taking a break from work to relax and de-stress is an excellent way to create a healthy, positive work environment.

Constructing a wellness center on site would be a time-consuming and expensive project because of architectural, labor, and building material and equipment costs. It would mean that we would need to take much-needed work space out of use and convert it for this purpose. Doing so may require renting or constructing additional office space, which might cost in excess of $200,000.

In response to your idea, I have proposed to Human Resources that we hold a weekly social gathering on Friday afternoons. This event would enable employees to relax and get to know each other better on a personal level. The cost of refreshments would be minimal, and the potential for a more relaxed working environment and the resulting enhanced morale and productivity should offset the reduction in work hours.

Tony, I will get back to you as soon as I hear back from Human Resources regarding my proposal for a weekly employee social.

Regards,
Dan Jacobs
Operations Manager
Green Energy Solutions, Inc.
Las Vegas, NV 80349
509-823-4211, Fax 509-823-4200
djacobs@greenenergysolutions.com

- *Cushions bad news with sincere compliment for suggestion.*
- *Transitions to reasons and provides complete explanation for refusal.*
- *Restates reason to justify refusal.*
- *Includes logical alternative and closes with positive look toward future expansion.*

Format Pointers
Sends message by email—medium preferred by recipient.

Includes .sig file to identify writer and provide contact information.

The company's return policy allows customers to return unsold merchandise at the end of the holiday season, subject to a 15% restocking charge. The return policy is printed clearly on the inside cover of its catalog and in bold print at the bottom of both the printed and Internet order forms. Telephone operators explain the restocking charge to customers placing orders via the company's toll-free number.

Figure 7-6 **BAD** :-(Poor Example of a Claim Denial

Your message questioning your statement has been received. I am sorry, but we cannot adjust your account as you requested. Clearly, the statement is correct.

• *The introduction might be more positive by acknowledging customer's wise decision to buy product.*

Each of the order forms you have completed states that returns are subject to a 15% restocking charge. Surely you saw this information printed in **bold** print on the order forms, and our telephone operators also explain our return policy thoroughly when customers place orders. I am sure you can appreciate the cost and effort we incur to restock merchandise after the holiday season is over.

• *A more tactful explanation of the reason for the refusal might prepare the reader for an implied refusal at the end of the paragraph.*

Thank you for doing business with us. If you have any further questions, please do not hesitate to call or message us.

• *The conclusion does not build goodwill because it is too generic.*

The customer's inquiry shows a lack of understanding of the return policy. Although a frustrated company representative might question why the customer can't read the return policy, the response must be more tactful than that illustrated in Figure 7-6. The example in Figure 7-7 reveals the subject of the message in the first sentence and leads into a discussion of the reasons. Reasons for the restocking fee, including benefits to the customer, precede the refusal. The tone is positive and respectful. The refusal statement uses several de-emphasis techniques to cushion its impact, and the final sentence turns the discussion away from the refusal with reference to future business with the customer.

7-5 **Denying Credit**

O nce you have evaluated a request for credit and have decided "No" is the better answer, your primary writing challenge is to refuse credit so tactfully that you keep the business relationship on a cash basis. When requests for credit are accompanied with an order, your credit refusals might serve as order acknowledgments. Of course, every business message is directly or indirectly a sales message. Prospective customers will be disappointed when they cannot buy on a credit basis. However, if you keep them sold on your goods and services, they might prefer to buy from you on a cash basis instead of seeking credit privileges elsewhere.

When the credit investigation shows that applicants are poor credit risks, too many credit writers no longer regard them as possible customers. They write to them in a cold, matter-of-fact manner. They do not consider that such applicants might still be interested in doing business on a cash basis and might qualify for credit later.

In credit denials, as in other types of refusals, the major portion of the message should be an explanation for the denial. You cannot expect your receiver to agree that your "No" answer is the right answer unless you give the reasons behind it.

Figure 7-7 Good Example of a Claim Denial

HUNTINGTON SURF & SPORTS

1905 BEACH BOULEVARD
HUNTINGTON BEACH, CA 97501-7313

TELEPHONE: 800-555-6000
FAX: 800-555-0583

October 14, 2014

Lonny Checkers
Huntington Surf & Sports
1905 Beach Boulevard
Huntington Beach, CA 97501-7313

Dear Mr. Checkers:

Restocking of Returned Merchandise

The Mantaray wetsuits you stocked this past season are of quality construction and made from the most durable materials available.

Maintaining a wide selection of quality surfwear is an excellent strategy for developing customer loyalty and maximizing your sales. Our refund policies provide you the opportunity to keep a fully stocked inventory at the lowest possible cost. You receive full refunds for merchandise returned within 10 days of receipt. For unsold merchandise returned after the primary selling season, a modest 15% restocking fee is charged to cover our costs for holding this merchandise until next season. The credit applied to your account for $3,069.75 covers merchandise you returned at the end of February.

While relaxing from another great surf season, take a look at our new Mantaray surfwear and accessories and other items available in the enclosed catalog for the 2015 season. You can save 10% by ordering products before November 1.

Sincerely,

Gina Treos

Gina Treos
Credit Manager
Enclosure: Catalog

Legal and ethical consideration avoids corrective language that might insult, belittle, or offend.

Uses subject line that identifies subject without revealing refusal.

Uses resale to cushion bad news and lead into explanation.

Presents clear explanation of reasons behind policy with emphasis on ways reader benefits.

Implies refusal by stating amount credited to account.

Shifts emphasis away from refusal by presenting silver lining sales promotion for next season's merchandise.

Specifies enclosure to emphasize importance of exact items.

Why Explain Credit Denial?

☑ Writers can show fairness of the decision.

☑ Receivers are entitled to the truth.

☑ Receivers can learn to adjust bad habits.

Both writers and readers benefit from the explanation of the reasons behind the denial. For writers, the explanation helps to establish fair-mindedness; it shows that the decision was not arbitrary. For receivers, the explanation not only presents the truth to which they are entitled, it also has guidance value. From it they learn to adjust habits and, as a result, qualify for credit purchases later.

© iStockphoto.com/DNY59

credit reporting agency whose name, address, and telephone number are provided.

7-6 Delivering Constructive Criticism

A person who has had a bad experience as a result of another person's conduct might be reluctant to write or speak about that experience. However, because one person took the time to communicate, many could benefit. Although not always easy or pleasant, communicating about negatives can be thought of as a social responsibility. For example, a person who returns from a long stay at a major hotel might, upon returning home, write a letter or email message to the management commending certain employees. If the stay had not been pleasant and weaknesses in hotel operation had been detected, a tactful message pointing out the negatives would probably be appreciated. Future guests could benefit from the effort of that one person.

Before communicating about the problem, an individual should recognize the following risks: being stereotyped as a complainer, being associated with negative thoughts and perceived in negative terms, and appearing to challenge management's decisions concerning hotel operations. Yet such risks might be worth taking because of the benefits:

- The communicator gets a feeling of having exercised a responsibility.
- Management learns of changes that need to be made.
- The hotel staff about whom the message is written modifies techniques and is thus more successful.
- Other guests will have more enjoyable stays in the hotel.

In the decision to communicate about negatives, the primary consideration is intent. If the intent is to hurt or to get even, the message should not be sent. Including false information would be *unethical* and *illegal*. To avoid litigation charges and to respond ethically, include only specific facts you can verify and avoid evaluative words that present opinions about the person's character or ability. For example, instead

Because of the legal implications involved in denying credit, legal counsel should review your credit denial messages to ensure that they comply with laws related to fair credit practices. For example, the Equal Credit Opportunity Act (ECOA) requires that the credit applicant be notified of the credit decision within 30 calendar days following application. Applicants who are denied credit must be informed of the reasons for the refusal. If the decision was based on information obtained from a consumer reporting agency (as opposed to financial statements or other information provided by the applicant), the credit denial must include the name, address, and telephone number of the agency. It must also remind applicants that the **Fair Credit Reporting Act** provides them the right to know the nature of the information in their credit file. In addition, credit denials must include a standard statement that the ECOA prohibits creditors from discriminating against credit applicants on the basis of a number of protected characteristics (race, color, religion, national origin, sex, marital status, and age).

To avoid litigation, some companies choose to omit the explanation from the credit denial letter and invite the applicant to call or come in to discuss the reasons. Alternately, they might suggest that the receiver obtain further information from the

Fair Credit Reporting Act
federal law that provides consumers the right to know the nature of the information in their credit file and gives them other protections when they apply for and are denied credit

Figure 7-8 **BAD** :-(Poor Example of a Constructive Criticism

Sarah Frank, a temporary administrative assistant your firm sent to us, is not working out well. She is constantly accepting cell phone calls, even while clients are waiting for help in our lobby. The constant distraction of her phone conversations, sometimes highly personal, has resulted in several complaints from important clients. Sarah has asked clients to wait up to 20 minutes while she finishes personal phone calls.

Although extensive knowledge of administrative duties is important, Sarah's lack of respect for others far outweighs her professional experience. I seriously hope Sarah is able to take steps to correct the situation.

> *A more positive or neutral introduction would help to better maintain goodwill.*

> *This information should be placed in a second paragraph that describes specific behaviors to maintain neutrality.*

> *The close would better maintain goodwill if it were more positive in tone and content.*

of presenting facts, the message in Figure 7-8 judges the staff member sent to perform administrative assistant duties at a client's office. Overall, the message is short, general, and negative. By comparison, the revision in Figure 7-9 on page 124 has positive intent, is factual, uses positive language, and leaves judgment to the recipient.

7-7 Communicating Negative Organizational News

Being able to initiate messages that convey bad news is as important as responding "No" to messages from customers/clients and others outside the company. Employees and the public are seeking, and expecting, *honest* answers from management about situations adversely affecting the company—slumping profits, massive layoffs, bankruptcy, a variety of major changes in the organization, and negative publicity that affects the overall health of the business and retirement plans, to name a few.

Managers who can communicate negative information in a sensitive, honest, and timely way can calm

fears and doubts and build positive employee and public relations. Effective managers recognize that employee morale, as well as public goodwill, is fragile—easily damaged and difficult to repair. If handled well, these bad-news messages related to the organization can be opportunities to treat employees, customers, and the general public with respect, thus building unity and trust.

Strong internal communication is a key to involving employees in corporate strategies and building an important sense of community. Transparency can have a positive effect on an organization's culture. According to a recent workplace survey, open, honest communication between corporate leaders and employees can lead to a more productive and ethical workplace. According to Deloitte Chairman Sharon Allen, motivating communication patterns are "increasingly critical to retaining talent and preserving the health of today's organizations."[2]

Obviously, business and competitive reasons prevent a company from always being completely transparent with its staff, but every attempt should be made to do so when possible. The best companies use a variety of communication tools that promote an open exchange of honest, candid communication and welcome input from employees. Newsletters, email updates, town hall or focus meetings, videoconferencing, phone calls, and

Figure 7-9 **GOOD 😊-)** Good Example of a Constructive Criticism

VSI
Office Systems Incorporated
2500 lincoln Green Road/Austin,
TX 78710-2500 / Phone: 512-555-9000 / Fax: 512-555-6573.

March 24, 2014

Charles Smythe
Smythe and Associates
3504 Elm Street
Chicago, IL 50340

Dear Mr. Smythe:

Your firm has served our temporary personnel needs for nearly 10 years with excellent results. Sarah Frank, a temporary administrative assistant we acquired from your firm, has done an excellent job of scheduling client appointments and following up with phone calls.

While working at the front desk, Sarah's attention is constantly diverted from waiting on clients by her receipt of personal cell phone calls. The constant distraction from these calls—sometimes highly intimate in nature—has caused some of our clients to complain that she is preoccupied with non-business matters.

More specifically, several important clients said that they had waited up to 20 minutes while Sarah completed personal phone calls in their presence. Sarah is obviously quite good at some aspects of her job; her expertise in managing administrative duties explains why she is represented by your firm. Please convey my concerns to Sarah confidentially so that the rest of her time in our office will go smoothly for her and for us.

Sincerely,

Dena Singleton
Human Resources Manager

- Introduces discussion of audit work underway.

- Conveys fair-mindedness and establishes credibility by acknowledging good as well as bad points.

- Presents verifiable statements without labeling them in negative, judgmental terms.

- Ends on pleasant note that seeks to add credibility to preceding negatives.

Legal and Ethical Considerations

- Conveys positive intent to help—not to hurt or get even.

- Avoids potential litigation charges by including specific, verifiable facts and avoiding evaluative, judgmental statements.

- Uses "confidential" as safeguard; information is intended for professional use only, not designed to hurt or to be thought of as gossip.

Format Pointer

- Uses letter channel rather than email to communicate a sensitive message.

discussion boards drive home relevant messages and allow employees to pose questions to management. This quality two-way communication involves employees in corporate strategies; employees who are aware of company goals and potential problems feel connected and accountable. Informed employees are also better prepared for bad news when it must be shared.

7-7a Breaking Bad News

Assuming this long-term commitment to keep employees informed, the following suggestions provide guidance in breaking bad news to employees and the public:[3]

- **Convey the bad news as soon as possible.**
  Timeliness will minimize damage caused by rumors and will give employees the concern and respect they deserve. Nestlé Purina and others in the pet food industry acted early and effectively to recall potentially deadly pet food tainted with wheat gluten from China and to assure pet owners that steps were in place to ensure healthy ingredients would be used in the future.[4]

- **Give a complete, rational explanation of the problem.** Be candid about what is happening, why, and its effect on employees, customers, and the public. Provide enough detail to establish your credibility and provide context so your audience can understand the situation. Stressing positive aspects will provide needed balance and avoid sugarcoating or minimizing the severity of the news to the point that the message is misunderstood. Bridgestone, makers of Firestone tires, was criticized for botching its recovery efforts from claims of accidents being caused by faulty tires when it initially attempted to blame Ford for the problems instead of taking responsibility and seeking corrective actions.[5]

- **Show empathy.** There is really no good way to break bad news, such as the announcement of layoffs or closures, to employees. The economic downturn and job insecurity has resulted in increased stress for many employees, which raises the potential for workplace aggression. However, methods that reflect respect and proper timing reduce the likelihood of an emotional boil over.[6]

- **Respond to the feelings.** Allow people adequate time to react to the bad news. Listen attentively for understanding and then address the concerns, issues, and potential problems presented.

- **Follow up.** Let people know what will happen next—what is expected of employees or customers, and what the company will do and when. Plan to repeat your explanations and assurances that you are available to respond to concerns in several communications that extend over a given time.

Consider the company president who emailed employees about a relocation of the company's manufacturing facility (Figure 7-10). The president should not be surprised to learn that employees are resisting the relocation; some perceive the company to be an enemy uprooting families from their homes simply for financial gain. In his revision (Figure 7-11 on page 126), the president anticipates the employees' natural resistance to this stunning announcement and crafts a sensitive message.

A printed memo is a more effective channel for communicating this sensitive and official information than the efficient, yet informal, email message. The revision indicates that the company's internal communications (newsletters and intranet) have been used to prepare the employees for this negative announcement. Thus the official memo is no surprise; nor is the company's commitment to listen to the employees' concerns and to provide up-to-date information as it develops.

Figure 7-10 **BAD 😟** Poor Example of a Message Announcing Negative Organizational News

New Message

To: <company employees>
From: Marion Lebaron, President
Subject: Company will relocate Nov. 1

Effective November 1, 2014, we will relocate our headquarters to Austin, Texas. Approved by the board of directors at its last meeting, this relocation will enable the company to better retain key employees and reduce tax costs by more than 10 percent.

All employees wishing to relocate should notify their supervisors by the end of the week. We appreciate your support in the move.

- *Bad news should not be announced in subject line. Better to provide reasons for change first.*
- *Introduction should serve as a buffer to naturally lead reader to "bad news."*
- *Additional paragraphs should be added to provide an explanation for the move.*
- *The close should let people know what will happen next and what the company will do.*

INTEROFFICE MEMORANDUM

TO: All Employees

FROM: Marion Lebaron, President

DATE: June 4, 2014

SUBJECT: Proposed Plan for Managing Future Growth

Our location in Detroit has historically provided us the skilled and motivated workforce needed to produce the innovation necessary for success in today's competitive automotive accessories market.

However, this advantage has slowly diminished as skilled workers have moved out of the city, taxes have risen to support bloated city budgets, and safety and housing have become a concern for many. Detroit now has the highest crime rate in the nation. In 2013, it was named the "Most Miserable City in America" by Forbes Magazine. This designation along with the recent city bankruptcy makes it a challenging location for a business such as ours that needs to attract well-educated, innovative engineers to its fold for continue growth.

While relocating could provide a long-term economic benefit to the company in terms of tax savings, moving out of Detroit could enhance the quality of life for all of us. Consequently, we have been working with state and local governments in other parts of the country to identify an area with a well-educated workforce, good housing and schools, and safe neighborhoods. This search has led us to identify Austin, the capital of the state of Texas, as our new headquarters location. With a population of about 900,000 people, Austin has a growing commercial and diversified manufacturing sector. Home to the University of Texas, Austin is a major center for research and development and is nationally recognized as a high-technology center.

Your supervisor will explain the logistics of the relocation at your next team meeting. In the meantime, please visit the Austin link on the company intranet to read more about what Texas can offer us and our families. Check back for updates on the FAQ page designed to provide responses to your concerns. Now let us work together for a smooth transition to Austin.

Annotations (right margin):

- *Uses subject line to introduce topic but does not reveal bad news.*
- *Uses buffer to introduce topic familiar to employees through previous communication and leads into reasons.*
- *Provides rational explanation, including benefits.*
- *Presents bad news while reminding receiver of benefits.*
- *Follows up, assuring continued exchange of timely information through discussions and Web pages.*
- *Ends with positive appeal for unity.*

Legal and Ethical Consideration
Uses memo channel rather than email for conveying sensitive message.

7-7b Responding to Crisis Situations

Crises can occur in any organization, disrupting business activity and posing significant political, legal, financial, or governmental impacts. Crisis situations can result from various events, including accidents, weather-related disasters, equipment failures, procedural errors, and deliberate maliciousness. When crises occur, the communication that is offered can either help ease situations or worsen them. Rather than waiting for a crisis to occur, an organization should examine its state of preparedness and have a carefully considered plan of action that includes the following steps:

- Anticipate potential crises in terms of areas of vulnerability and what could happen.
- Establish emergency procedures, including an alternate command center and chain of command. Ensure that more than one employee is media trained and able to respond appropriately if needed.
- Identify who will need to be contacted and plan for multiple means of disseminating information. Cell phones and text messaging have proven themselves valuable when other contact means might not work,

© Lukiyanova Natalia/frenta/Shutterstock.com

but keep in mind that telecommunication circuits can be overloaded in mass disaster situations, necessitating multiple means for sharing news.

- Ensure current contact information is available for employees, media, and other pertinent parties.
- Maintain an up-to-date fact sheet about the company, its products/services, locations, and operations.

While crises can seldom be predicted, an organization can position itself to respond to them appropriately when they do occur. Having a well-prepared plan of action for dealing with emergencies can make the difference in an organization's survival and collapse.

In responding to a crisis, the message conveyed is extremely important in reassuring employees and business partners and in shaping public opinion. These guidelines can help ensure an effective message:

- Determine what your message is and prepare a checklist of what it should contain before writing.
- Keep the message simple, and arrange it in logical sections.
- Include verbiage that demonstrates your concern, compassion, and control.
- Prepare separate messages for internal and external audiences, including the appropriate level of detail.

STUDY TOOLS
CHAPTER 7

Located at back of the textbook

❏ Rip out Chapter Review Card

Located at www.cengagebrain.com

❏ Review Key Terms Flashcards (Print or Online)
❏ Download Audio Summaries for on-the-go review
❏ Complete Practice Quizzes to prepare for tests
❏ Play "Beat the Clock" to master concepts
❏ Complete the Crossword Puzzle to review key terms
❏ Watch the video about McDonaldson, a fictitious but all-too-realistic ad agency whose employees struggle with contemporary business communication issues.

Delivering Persuasive Messages

OBJECTIVES

8-1 Develop effective outlines and appeals for messages that persuade.

8-2 Write effective sales messages.

8-3 Write effective persuasive requests (making a claim or asking for a favor or information) and persuasion within an organization.

8-1 Persuasion Strategies

Businesspeople regularly seek to persuade others. **Persuasion** is the ability to influence others to accept your point of view. It is not an attempt to trap someone into taking action favorable to the communicator. Instead, it is an honest, organized presentation of information on which a person can choose to act. Professionals in all fields benefit from well-prepared communications that persuade others to accept their ideas or buy their products, services, or ideas.

How do you learn to persuade others through spoken and written communication? Have you ever made a persuasive request, written employment documents or an essay for college entry or a scholarship, or given a campaign speech? If so, you already have experience with this type of communication. While the persuasive concepts discussed in this chapter are directed primarily at written communication, they can also be applied in many spoken communication situations.

For persuasion to be effective, you must understand your product, service, or idea; know your audience; anticipate the arguments that might come from the audience; and have a rational and logical response to those arguments. Remember, persuasion need not be a hard sell; it can simply be a way of getting a client or your supervisor to say yes. Although much of this chapter concentrates on selling products and services, similar principles apply to selling an idea, your organization, and your own abilities.

Log onto www.cengagebrain.com for additional resources, including flashcards, games, self-quizzing for chapter review, grammar exercises, and more.

8-1a Plan Before You Write

Success in writing is directly related to success in preliminary thinking. If the right questions have been asked and answered, the composing will be easier and the message will be more persuasive. Specifically, you need information about (1) your product, service, or idea; (2) your audience; and (3) the desired action.

Know the Product, Service, or Idea

You cannot be satisfied with knowing the product, service, or idea in a general way; you need details. Get your information by (1) reading available literature; (2) using the product and watching others use it; (3) comparing the product, service, or idea with others; (4) conducting tests and experiments; and (5) soliciting reports from users.

Before you write, you need concrete answers to such questions as these:

- What will the product, service, or idea do for the receiver(s)?

  "What is the major difference?"
  "What is the cost to the receiver?"
  "What will it do for the receiver?"
  "What are its superior features?"
  "Who is the competition?"

- What are its superior features (e.g., design and workmanship or receiver benefit)?

- How is the product or service different from its competition? How is the proposed idea superior to other viable alternatives?

- What is the cost to the receiver?

Similar questions must be answered about other viable alternatives or competing products. Of particular importance is the question, "What is the

persuasion
the ability of a sender to influence others to accept his or her point of view

BCOM

major difference?" People are inclined to choose an item (or alternative) that has some distinct advantage. For example, some people might choose a particular car model because of its style and available options; still others might choose the model because of its safety record.

Know the Receiver

Who are the people to whom the persuasive message is directed? What are their wants and needs? Is a persuasive message to be written and addressed to an individual or to a group? If it is addressed to a group, what characteristics do the members have in common? What are their common goals, their occupational levels, and their educational status? To what extent have their needs and wants been satisfied? How might cultural differences affect your message?

Recall the discussion of Maslow's need hierarchy in Chapter 2. Some people might respond favorably to appeals to physiological, security, and safety needs (to save time and money, to be comfortable, to be healthy, or to avoid danger). People with such needs would be impressed with a discussion of the benefits of convenience, durability, efficiency, or serviceability. Others might respond favorably to appeals to their social, ego, and self-actualizing needs (to be loved, entertained, remembered, popular, praised, appreciated, or respected). Consider the varying appeals used in a memo to employees and to supervisors seeking support of teleworking. The memo to employees would appeal to the need for greater flexibility and reduced stress. Appeals directed at supervisors would focus on increased productivity and morale, reduced costs for office space, and compliance with the Clean Air Act, a federal law requiring companies to reduce air pollution and traffic congestion.

Identify the Desired Action

What do you want the receiver to do? Complete an online order and make a payment? Receive a demonstration version for trial? Return a card requesting a representative to call? Email for more information? Approve a request? Accept a significant change in service, style, and procedures? Whatever the desired action, you need to have a clear definition of it before composing your message.

8-1b Use the Inductive Approach

More than 100 years ago, Sherwin Cody summarized the persuasive process into four basic steps called **AIDA**.[1] The steps have been varied somewhat and have had different labels, but the fundamentals remain relatively unchanged. The persuasive approach illustrated in Figure 8-1 is inductive. The main idea, which is the request for action, appears in the *last* paragraph after presenting the details—convincing reasons for the receiver to comply with the request.

Each step is essential, but the steps do not necessarily require equal amounts of space. Good persuasive messages do not require separate sentences and paragraphs for each phase of the outline. The message *could* gain the receiver's attention and interest in the same sentence, and creating desire *could* require many paragraphs.

8-1c Apply Sound Writing Principles

The principles of unity, coherence, and emphasis are just as important in persuasive messages as in other messages. In addition, the following principles seem to be especially helpful in preparing persuasive messages:

- **Keep paragraphs short.** The spaces between paragraphs show the dividing place between ideas, improve appearance, and provide convenient resting places for the eyes. Hold the first and last paragraph to three or fewer lines; a one-line paragraph (even a very short line) is acceptable. You can even use paragraphs less than one sentence long by putting four or five words on the first line and completing the sentence in a new paragraph. Be careful to include key attention-getting words that either introduce the product, service, or idea or lead to its introduction.

- **Use concrete nouns and active verbs.** Concrete nouns and active verbs help receivers see the product, service, or idea and its benefits more vividly than do abstract nouns and passive verbs.

- **Use specific language.** General words won't mean much unless they are well supported with specifics. Specific language is space consuming (saying that something is "great" requires fewer words than telling what makes it so); therefore, persuasive messages are usually longer than other messages. Still, persuasive messages need to be concise; they should say what needs to be said without wasting words.

- **Let receivers have the spotlight.** If receivers are made the subject of some of the sentences, if they can visualize themselves with the product in their hands, or if they

Figure 8-1   Inductive Outline Used in Persuasive Messages Sent in Written, Electronic, or Spoken Form

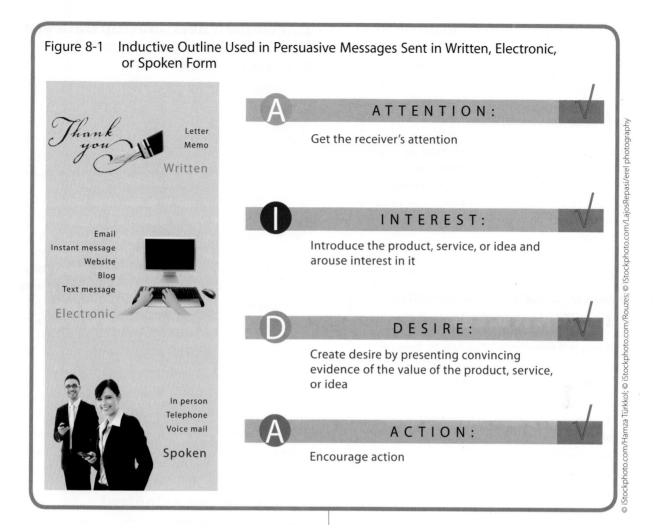

Written
Letter
Memo

Electronic
Email
Instant message
Website
Blog
Text message

Spoken
In person
Telephone
Voice mail

A **ATTENTION:**
Get the receiver's attention

I **INTEREST:**
Introduce the product, service, or idea and arouse interest in it

D **DESIRE:**
Create desire by presenting convincing evidence of the value of the product, service, or idea

A **ACTION:**
Encourage action

can get the feel of using it for enjoyment or to solve problems, the chances of creating a desire are increased.

- **Stress a central selling point or appeal.** A thorough analysis ordinarily will reveal some feature that is unique or some benefit that is not provided by other viable alternatives—the **central selling point.** This point of difference can be developed into a theme that is woven throughout the entire message. Or, instead of using a point of difference as a central selling point, a writer could choose to stress a major satisfaction to be gained from using the item or doing as asked. A central selling point (*theme*) should be introduced early and reinforced throughout the remainder of the message.

8-2 Sales Messages

The four-point persuasive outline is appropriate for an *unsolicited sales message*—a letter, memo, or email message written to someone who has not requested it.

A *solicited sales message* has been requested by a potential buyer or supporter; that is, the message is prepared to answer this interested person's questions.

A person requesting sales information has given some attention to the product, service, or idea already; therefore, an attention-getting sentence is hardly essential. However, such a sentence is needed when the receiver is not known to have expressed an interest previously. The very

central selling point
the primary appeal on which a persuasive message focuses

first sentence, then, is deliberately designed to make a receiver put aside other thoughts and concentrate on the rest of the message.

8-2a Gain Attention

Various techniques have been successful in convincing receivers to consider an unsolicited sales message. Regardless of the technique used, the attention-getter should achieve several important objectives: introduce a relationship, focus on a central selling feature, and use an original approach.

Some Commonly Used Attention-Getting Devices Include:

→ **A personal experience:** When a doctor gives you instructions, how often have you thought, "I wish you had time to explain" or "I wish I knew more about medical matters"?

→ **A solution to a problem (outstanding feature/benefit):** Imagine creating a customized multimedia presentation that. …

→ **A startling announcement:** More teens die as a result of suicide each month than die in auto accidents in the same time period.

→ **A what-if opening:** What if I told you there is a savings plan that will enable you to retire three years earlier?

→ **A question:** Why should you invest in a company that has lost money for six straight years?

→ **A story:** Here's a typical day in the life of a manager who uses an iPad.

→ **A proverb or quote from a famous person:** Vince Lombardi, one of the most successful coaches in the history of football, once said, "If winning isn't everything, why do they keep score?" At Winning Edge, we specialize in making you the winner you were born to be.

→ **A split sentence:** Sandy beaches, turquoise water, and warm breezes … it's all awaiting you on your Mesa cruise.

→ **An analogy:** Like a good neighbor, State Farm is there.

Other attention-getters include a gift, an offer, a bargain, or a comment on an enclosed product sample.

Introduce a Relationship Between the Receiver and the Product, Service, or Idea

Remaining sentences grow naturally from this beginning sentence. If receivers do not see the relationship between the first sentence and the sales appeal, they could react negatively to the whole message—they might think they have been tricked into reading it. For example, consider the following poor attention-getter:

 Would you like to be the chief executive officer of one of America's largest companies? As CEO of Graham Enterprises, you can launch new products, invest in developing countries, or arrange billion dollar buyouts. Graham Enterprises is one of several companies at your command in the new computer software game developed by Creative Diversions Software.

The beginning sentence of the preceding ineffective example is emphatic because it is a short question. However, it suggests the message will be about obtaining a top management position, which it is not. All three sentences combined suggest high pressure. The computer software game has relevant virtues, and one of them could have been emphasized by placing it in the first sentence.

8-2b Focus on a Central Selling Feature

Almost every product, service, or idea will in some respects be superior to its competition. If not, such factors as favorable price, fast delivery, or superior service can be used as the primary appeal. This central selling point must be emphasized, and one of the most effective ways to emphasize a point is by position in the message. An outstanding feature mentioned in the middle of a message might go unnoticed, but it will stand out if mentioned in the first sentence. Note how the following opening sentence introduces the central selling feature and leads naturally into the sentences that follow:

 Like running through a sprinkler on a warm summer day, our latest iced coffee creation combines hot and cold in a way that's totally invigorating. The heat comes from the warm cinnamon notes you taste on first sip, followed by a sweet orange finish. Our classic Orange Spice iced coffee is there to refresh you all the while. Jump in!

8-2c Use an Original Approach

To get the reader's attention and interest, you must offer something new and fresh. Thus, choose an anecdote likely unfamiliar to your receiver or use a unique combination of words to describe how a product, service, or idea can solve the receiver's problem:

The nine-year-old boy rushes to the store's toy department, unaware that his parents are far behind him in housewares. Surrounded by the latest action figures, electronic games, and cartoon DVDs, he hardly knows where to start in his search for the perfect gifts to include on his holiday wish list. For the next hour, his parents indulge his enthusiasm as he tries out every displayed product.

In many ways, Adobe Photoshop Elements is like that toy department. The new Photoshop offers a plethora of powerful, useful features that will hold your attention for hours on end.

8-2d Generate Interest by Introducing the Product, Service, or Idea

A persuasive message is certainly off to a good start if the first sentences cause the receiver to think, "Here's a solution to one of my problems," "Here's something I need," or "Here's something I want." You can lead the receiver to such a thought by introducing the product, service, or idea in the very first sentence. If you do, you can succeed in both getting attention and creating interest in one sentence. An effective introduction of the product, service, or idea is cohesive and action centered, and continues to stress a central selling point.

Be Cohesive

If the attention-getter does not introduce the product, service, or idea, it should lead naturally to the introduction. Note the abrupt change in thought and the unrelatedness of the attention-getter to the second paragraph in the following example:

Employees appreciate a company that provides a safe work environment.

The Adcock Human Resources Association has been conducting a survey for the last six months. Their primary aim is to improve the safety of office work environments.

The last words of the first sentence, "safe work environment," are related to "safety of office work environments"—the last words of the last sentence. No word or phrase in the first sentence connects the words of the second sentence, which creates an abrupt, confusing change in thought. In the following revision, the second sentence is tied to the first by the word *that's*. *Safety* in the second sentence refers to *protection* in the third. The LogicTech low-radiation monitor is introduced as a means of providing a safe work environment. Additionally, notice that the attention-getter leads smoothly to the discussion of the survey results.

Employees appreciate a company that provides a safe work environment.

That's one thing the Tucker Human Resources Association learned from its six-month survey of the safety of the office work environment. For added protection from radiation emissions, more companies are purchasing LogicTech's low-radiation computer monitors ...

Be Action Oriented

To introduce your offering in an interesting way, you must place the product, service, or idea in your receivers' hands and talk about using it or benefiting from accepting your idea. They will get a clearer picture when reading about something happening than when reading a product description. Also, the picture becomes all the more vivid when the receiver is in the spotlight. In a sense, you do not sell products, services, or ideas; instead, you sell the pleasure people derive from their use. Logically, then, you have to focus more on that use than about the offering itself. If you put receivers to work using your product, service, or idea to solve problems, they will be the subject of most of your sentences.

Some product description is necessary and natural. In the following example, the writer focuses on the product and creates an uninteresting, still picture:

The Elise CR is a stripped-back racer that doesn't just deliver on the road. Eibach anti-roll bar and springs plus Bilstein sports dampers mean the Elise CR provides fingertip responsiveness on the racetrack, too.

In the revision, a person is the subject of the message and is enjoying the benefits of the sports car.

Channel your inner Kimi Räikkönen in this stripped-back racer worthy of the best Formula One tracks in the world. The

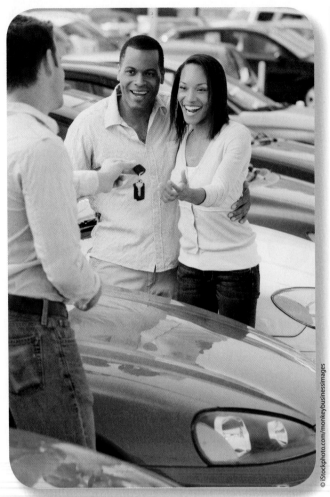

In a sense, you do not sell products, services, or ideas; instead, you sell the pleasure people derive from their use.

Elise CR is an uncompromised sports machine that doesn't just deliver on the road. Eibach anti-roll bar and springs plus Bilstein sports dampers mean the Elise CR provides fingertip responsiveness on the racetrack, too. Handling is assisted further with the latest Lotus Dynamic Performance Management (DPM) system, and selectable Sport setting, giving the driver ultimate power and control.[2]

Stress a Central Selling Point

If the attention-getter does not introduce a distinctive feature, it should lead to it. Note below how the attention-getter introduces the distinctive selling feature (app availability) and how the following sentences keep the receivers' eyes focused on that feature:

 With more than 375,000 apps made just for iPad, there's almost no end to what you can do. These aren't merely scaled-up versions of phone apps that lack features designed for a larger screen. They're powerful apps tailor-made to take full advantage of everything iPad has to offer. And because iPad and iPad mini are so thoughtfully designed, virtually every app works on both devices.

With iPad, all that content is available from one source: Apple. The iTunes Store is the world's largest and most trusted entertainment store. Other mobile platforms have a myriad of fragmented store options, resulting in availability issues, developer frustration, and security risks.[3]

By stressing one main point, you do not limit the message to that point. For example, while app availability is being stressed, other features are also mentioned.

8-2e Create Desire by Providing Convincing Evidence

After you have made an interesting introduction to your product, service, or idea, present enough supporting evidence to satisfy your receivers' needs. Keep one or two main features uppermost in the receivers' minds, and include evidence that supports these features. For example, using fuel economy as an outstanding selling feature of hybrid cars while presenting abundant evidence about performance would be inconsistent.

Present and Interpret Factual Evidence

Few people will believe general statements without having supporting factual evidence. Saying a certain method is efficient is not enough. You must say how it is efficient and present some data to illustrate this. Saying a piece of furniture is durable is not enough. Durability exists in varying degrees. You must present information that shows what makes it durable and also define how durable. Durability can be established, for example, by presenting information about the manufacturing process, the quality of the raw materials, or the skill of the workers:

 If you're looking for plush comfort, then look no further than Ashley's DuraPella® upholstery collection. DuraPella® is a high-tech fabric that is a breakthrough in comfort and durability. DuraPella® consists of 100% MicroDenier Polyester Suede, which gives you the subtle look and elegant feel of suede, yet is durable and stain-resistant ... the best of both worlds! Everyday spills like coffee, wine, and even ballpoint pen are cleaned easily and effectively with a mixture of low pH balance liquid soap and water. You can enjoy luxury in everyday living with DuraPella®.

Presenting research evidence (hard facts and figures) to support your statements is another way to increase your chances of convincing your audience. Presenting results of a research study takes space but makes the message much more convincing than general remarks about superior durability and appearance.

Evidence must not only *be* authentic; it must *sound* authentic, too. Talking about pages treated with special protectants to retard aging and machine-sewn construction suggests the sender is well informed, which increases receiver confidence. Facts and figures are even more impressive if they reflect comparative advantage, as illustrated in the following example:

With thousands of new viruses created every day, relying on traditional security updates isn't enough anymore. Unlike the competition, exclusive McAfee Total Protection™ technology instantly analyzes and blocks new and emerging threats in milliseconds so there's virtually no gap in your protection. McAfee is 99.9% effective in detecting Malware, the best rating among competitors.[4]

Naturally, your receivers will be less familiar with the product, service, or idea and its uses than you will be. Not only do you have an obligation to give information, you should interpret it if necessary and point out how the information will benefit the receiver. Notice how the following example clearly interprets *why* an induction cooktop is superior to electric or gas cooktops. The interpretation makes the evidence understandable and thus convincing.

Cold Statement Without Interpretation	Specific, Interpreted Fact
Cooking with an induction cooktop is the latest in technology for a restaurant environment or for just the average household.	Induction cooking is an entirely new way of cooking. Forget about red-hot electric coils or open gas flames. An induction cooktop converts your cookware into the heating element by using a magnetic field to energize the atoms in the cookware. Your food cooks faster, using less energy, while providing you with instantaneous temperature control.

The previous example uses a valuable interpretative technique—the comparison. You can often make a point more convincing by comparing something unfamiliar with something familiar. Most people are familiar with electric coils and gas flames, so they can now visualize how the cookware becomes the heating element. Comparison can also be used to interpret prices. Advertisers frequently compare the cost of sponsoring a child in a third-world country to the price of a fast-food lunch. An insurance representative might write this sentence: *The monthly premium for $300,000 of term life insurance is $18, the mere cost of two movie tickets.*

Do not go overboard and bore or frustrate your receivers with an abundance of facts or technical data. Never make your receivers feel ignorant by trying to impress them with facts and figures they might not understand.

Be Objective

Use language people will believe. Specific, concrete language makes your message sound authentic. Excessive superlatives, exaggerations, flowery statements, unsupported claims, and incomplete comparisons all make your message sound like high-pressure sales talk. Just one such sentence can destroy confidence in the whole message. Examine the statements in the following paragraphs to see whether they give convincing evidence. Would they make a receiver want to buy? Or do they merely remind the receiver of someone's desire to sell?

This antibiotic is the best on the market today. It represents the very latest in biochemical research. Identifying the best-selling antibiotic requires gathering information about all antibiotics marketed and then choosing the one with superior characteristics. You know the sender is likely to have a bias in favor of the particular drug being sold. However, you do not know whether the sender actually spent time researching other antibiotics or whether he or she would know how to evaluate this information. You certainly do not know whether the sender knows enough about biochemical research to say truthfully what the very best and latest is.

Similarly, avoid preposterous statements (*Gardeners are turning handsprings in their excitement over our new weed killer!*) or subjective claims (*Stretch out on one of our memory foam mattresses. It's like floating on a gentle dream cloud on a warm, sunny afternoon. Ah, what soothing relaxation!*). Even though some people might be persuaded by such writing, many will see it as absurd.

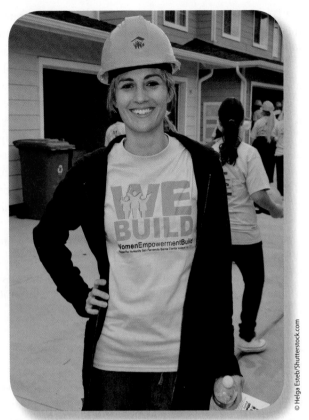

Effective persuasion has enabled Habitat for Humanity to raise in excess of $1 billion annually to support its goal—to provide safe, decent, affordable housing to low-income families.

© Helga Esteb/Shutterstock.com

the usefulness of your offering. Guarantees and free trials convey both negative and positive connotations. By revealing willingness to refund money or exchange an unsatisfactory unit, a writer confesses a negative: the purchase could be regretted or refused. However, the positive connotations are stronger than the negatives: the seller has a definite plan for ensuring that buyers get value for money spent. In addition, the seller conveys willingness for the buyer to check a product, service, or idea personally and compare it with others. The seller also implies confidence that a free trial will result in a purchase and that the product will meet standards set in the guarantee. A long or complex guarantee can be included in an enclosure or attachment.

A message should persuade the receiver to read an enclosure, attachment, or file link that includes more detailed information. Thus, refer to the added material late in the message after the major portion of the evidence has been given. An enclosure or link is best referred to in a sentence that is not a cliché ("Enclosed you will find," or "We have enclosed a brochure") and says something else:

> **The enclosed annual report will help you understand the types of information provided to small- and medium-sized companies by Lincoln Business Data, Inc.**

> **Click here to view the huge assortment of clearance-priced items and other end-of-season specials.**

Subordinate the Price

Logically, price should be introduced late in the message—after most of the advantages have been discussed. Use the following techniques to overcome people's natural resistance to price:

- **Introduce price only after creating a desire for the product, service, or idea and its virtues.** Let receivers see the relationship of features and benefits to the price.

- **Use figures to illustrate that the price is reasonable or that the receiver can save money.** Example: Purigard saves the average pool owner about $50 in chemicals each month; thus, the $200 unit pays for itself in a single swim season.

- **State price in terms of small units.** Thirty dollars a month seems like less than $360 a year.

Note the incomplete comparison in the following example: *SunBlock provides you better protection from the sun's dangerous ultraviolet rays.* Is SunBlock being compared with *all* other sunscreens, *most* other sunscreens, *one* unnamed brand, or others? Unless an additional sentence identifies the other elements in the comparison, you do not know. Too often, the writer of such a sentence hopes the receiver will assume the comparison is with *all* others. Written with that intent, the incomplete comparison is *unethical*. Likewise, statements of certainty are often inaccurate or misleading.

Include Testimonials, Guarantees, and Enclosures

One way to convince prospective customers that they will like your product, service, or idea is to give them concrete evidence that other people like it. Tell what others have said (with permission, of course) about

- **Invite comparison of like products, services, or ideas with similar features.**
- **Consider mentioning price in a complex or compound sentence that relates or summarizes the virtues of the product, service, or idea.**
  Example: For just $79 a year, Amazon Prime brings you access to Instant Videos and Kindle Books as well as free two-day shipping on selected products.

8-2f Motivate Action

For proper clarity and emphasis, the last paragraph should be relatively short. Yet it must accomplish four important tasks: define the specific action wanted, present it as easy to take, encourage quick action, and ask confidently.

Make the Action Clear and Simple to Complete

Define the desired action in specific terms that are easy to complete. For example, you might ask the receiver to complete an order blank and return it with payment, place a phone call, or order online. General instructions such as "Let us hear from you," "Take action on the matter," and "Make a response" are ineffective. Make action simple to encourage receivers to act immediately. Instead of asking receivers to fill in their names and addresses on order forms or return cards and envelopes, do that work for them. Otherwise, they might see the task as difficult or time consuming and decide to procrastinate.

Restate the Reward for Taking Action (Central Selling Point)

The central selling point should be introduced early in the message, interwoven throughout the evidence section, and included in the last paragraph as an emphatic, final reminder of the reason for taking action.

Provide an Incentive for Quick Action

If the receiver waits to take action on your proposal, the persuasive evidence will be harder to remember, and the receiver will be less likely to act. Therefore, you prefer the receiver to act quickly. Reference to the central

selling point (assuming it has been well received) helps stimulate action. Commonly used appeals for getting quick action are to encourage customers to buy while prices are in effect, while supplies last, when a rebate is being offered, when it is a particular holiday, or when they will receive benefits.

Ask Confidently for Action

If you have a good product, service, or idea and have presented evidence effectively, you have a right to feel confident. Demonstrate your confidence when requesting action: "To save time in organizing appointments and tasks, complete and return…." Avoid statements suggesting lack of confidence, such as "If you want to save time in organizing appointments and tasks, complete and return…," "If you agree…," and "I hope you will…."

Observe How the Following Closing Paragraph Accomplishes the Four Important Tasks of an Effective Sales Message:

 refers to the central selling point,

 makes a specific action easy,

 provides an incentive for quick action, and

 asks confidently for action.

Simply dial 1-800-555-8341. Then input the five-digit number printed in the top right corner of the attached card. Your name and address will be entered automatically into our system, a speedy way to get your productivity software to you within five working days along with a bill for payment. When you order by August 12, you will also receive a free subscription to Time Resource Magazine. *TMC's new productivity software is as easy to use as it is to order!*

Figures 8-2 (on the next page) and 8-3 (on page 139) illustrate poor and good *unsolicited sales messages* for a service. Figure 8-4 on page 140 presents an unsolicited sales message promoting a product. The same principles apply in writing a *solicited sales message*, with one exception: because the solicited sales message is a response to a request for information, an attention-getter is not essential. Typically, sales messages are

Figure 8-2

BAD :-(Poor Example of a Sales Message Promoting a Product

Dear Mr. Fielding:

We have all the capabilities of a full-service communication consultant, including strategy assessment, program planning, program implementation, and program evaluation. But we also offer unique services that can truly integrate your corporate communication strategy among all key stakeholders.

We believe that an integrated communication strategy, one that includes both internal and external stakeholders, is a central need of most large organizations today. Most organizations have piecemeal strategies aimed at individual stakeholders. Such an approach fails to communicate the overall vision and brand of the organization in a coherent manner and results in widespread confusion about who or what the organization is, severely inhibiting its ability to compete in today's global economy. Let our team help you create and communicate your message—whether it's driving sales, bringing together people for important causes, or reputation management. There couldn't be a more critical time to plan an integrated communication strategy with the financial insecurity many organizations face today.

Our billing hours are in line with the industry. At just $300 per hour, our team of consultants can help you maximize your communication strategies to attract and retain valuable customers and increase employee morale.

If you contact us before May 15, you will also receive a free assessment of your current marketing program from our proprietary MarkET analysis tool. Please call me at 509-788-1302 to make an appointment with a consultant today.

- *Introduction might better engage the reader by addressing his or her needs in a more personal way.*

- *The language is a bit overblown and vague in terms of concrete actions or results. This approach may damage the writer's credibility in the area of trust.*

- *This paragraph adds little in terms of concrete actions or results.*

- *The cost of the consultant might put off the reader before he or she has a chance to be persuaded by concrete results or actions.*

- *The close might be considered too direct for a "cold-call" message.*

longer than messages that present routine information or convey good news. Specific details (essential in prompting action) require space.

More and more organizations are using email as a means to persuade existing and potential customers to buy their products. While email marketing is a relatively new field, marketers are learning how to use email effectively with various audiences.

To gain desired attention from customers, email messages must be carefully timed to arrive when they will gain the most attention. Over-messaging can be annoying, while under-messaging can cause the company to miss potential sales. The subject line is of utmost importance, as it must catch the attention of the reader and create a desire to learn more.

Figure 8-3 **GOOD :-)** Good Example of a Sales Message Promoting a Service

Strategic Solutions, Inc.
Full-service Communication Consulting
4208 Olympic Boulevard
Springfield, IL 62702
509-788-1302

April 1, 2014

Leonard Fielding, Corporate Communications Manager
First National Bank
2304 Lake Street
Chicago, IL 60322

Dear Mr. Fielding:

Are you looking for help developing your organization's communication strategy?... enhancing employee communication? ... improving communication with your external stakeholder? Then you need the services of the full-service communication consulting firm Strategic Solutions, Inc., to develop an integrated communication plan that ensures your company's continued success.

Uses a series of phrases rather than complete sentences to gain attention. Introduces needs familiar to a corporate communication director.

With Strategic Solutions' full-service capabilities, you will receive support in all of the following areas:

Presents "everything-in-one-place" service as solution to problem and reinforces central selling point.

• **Strategy assessment and identification.** Using our tested data collection techniques, we will assess how well your current communication strategy is working among major stakeholders and identify areas that need development or improvement.

• **Communication planning.** Based on our assessment of your current communication strategy, we will create an integrated plan to help you more effectively communicate your company's mission and brand to both internal and external organizational constituents.

• **Strategy implementation.** Our team of experts will ensure that the integrated communication strategy is implemented properly by holding orientation and training sessions for key players among internal and external constituents.

• **Strategy evaluation.** After the plan has been implemented, our team of experts will evaluate its success and prepare a report that identifies areas where additional work is needed and proposes continuing improvements in those areas that have reached strategic goals.

Uses easy-to-read bulleted list to present evidence that reflects understanding of receiver's desired needs.

Visit www.strategicsolutions.com today and check out the list of consulting services we provide and read real-life stories from past clients about how we enhanced their communication strategy. If you contact us before May 15, you will also receive a free assessment of your current marketing program from our proprietary MarkET analysis tool. Our team is ready to assist you in improving the impact of your communication strategy today. Please call me at 509-788-1302 to make an appointment with a consultant.

States specific action with reward. Makes action easy and provides incentive for quick response.

Sincerely,

Francis Fox

Francis Fox
Engagement Director
Enclosure

Figure 8-4 **GOOD :-)** Good Example of a Sales Message Promoting a Product

---

New Message

To: Bill Jenkins <bjenkins@hotmail.com>
From: Jennifer Reese <jreese@winners.com>
Subject: Meet Your Career Goals through Achievable Change

Bill,

What would you say if I told you that Winners could help you climb that career ladder faster? … feel more fulfilled at work? … improve relationships with friends and partners? People across the country are discovering how to improve their life and careers with the help of Winners patented life coaching program.

You are invited to attend a free dinner at the renowned beach-side restaurant Chez Blu, where you will be introduced to the Winners program and learn how it can help you improve your life. The Winners program will provide you

- Personal coaching wherever you happen to be—anywhere in the world.
- Convenience because there's no travel time or cost involved in meeting with your coach.
- Almost immediate support since telephone coaching sessions can be arranged with minimum prior notice—our coaches are there when you need us.

During your evening with our coaches, you will see how easy it is to take advantage of our program and will meet and talk to people who have experienced success through its use.

Take a moment to visit our website at www.winners.com to view a video presentation of the program and to hear testimonials from satisfied clients. At the same time, please click on the "Winners Evening" link to RSVP your attendance at one of our dinner events. Your invitation acceptance will automatically enter you in a drawing for a free spa service at the Shores Resort, which is adjacent to Chez Blu.

Would you like to join dozens of people who have used the Winners program to accelerate their careers, improve their outlook, and exude more confidence? Register for the Winners Evening today or schedule a personal consultation with one of our life coaches to determine the benefits you might receive from the Winners program. Learn for yourself whether the Winners program could do for you what it has already done for so many.

Best regards,

Jennifer Reese
President

Sends customized email message to customers who may be interested in product.

Gains attention by introducing familiar annoyances; presents life coaching as central selling point.

Introduces program as potential solution to reader's personal growth concerns.

Builds interest by offering an invitation to see the product demonstrated.

Requests specific action and associates it with central selling point.

Legal and Ethical Consideration
Abides by requirements under the Federal Trade Commission Act regarding false and deceptive advertising.

8-3 Persuasive Requests

he preceding discussion of sales messages assumed the product, service, or cause was sufficiently worthy to reward the receiver for taking action. The discussion of persuasive requests assumes requests are reasonable—that compliance is justified when the request is for an adjustment and that compliance will (in some way) be rewarded when the request is for a favor.

Common types of persuasive requests are claim requests and messages that ask for special favors and information. Although their purpose is to get favorable action, the messages invite action only after attempting to create a desire to take action and providing a logical argument to overcome any anticipated resistance.

8-3a Making a Claim

Claim messages are often routine because the basis for the claim is a guarantee or some other assurance that an adjustment will be made without need of persuasion. However, when an immediate remedy is doubtful, persuasion is necessary. In a typical large business, customer service representatives handle claims.

Often, any reasonable claim will be adjusted to the customer's satisfaction. Therefore, venting strong displeasure in the claim message will likely alienate the claims adjuster—the one person whose cooperation is needed. Remember, adjusters might have had little or nothing to do with the manufacture and sale of the product or direct delivery of the service. They did not create the need for the claim.

Companies should welcome claims. Only a small percentage of claims are from unethical individuals; the great bulk is from people who believe they have a legitimate complaint. Research indicates that only 4% of customers complain, so for every complaint received, many more customers have been satisfied. Complaints help companies identify problem areas and correct them. Another advantage that companies derive from the claim process is that when complaints are handled appropriately, complainers can become very loyal customers.[5] Thus, the way a complaint is handled determines, to a large extent, the goodwill toward the company.

Like sales messages, persuasive claims should use an inductive sequence. Unlike routine claim messages, persuasive claims do not begin by asking for an adjustment.

The poor example shown in Figure 8-5 could be improved by (1) writing inductively (to reduce the chance of a negative reaction in the first sentence), and (2) stressing an appeal throughout the message (to emphasize an incentive for taking favorable action). In a persuasive claim, an appeal serves the same purpose that a central selling feature does in a sales message. Both serve as a theme; both remind the receiver of a benefit gained from doing as asked. Note the application of these techniques in the revision in Figure 8-6.

Knowledge of effective claim writing should never be used as a means of taking advantage of someone. Hiding an unjustifiable claim under a cloak of untrue statements is difficult and strictly unethical. Adjusters typically are fair-minded people who will give the benefit of the doubt, but they will not satisfy an unhappy customer simply to avoid a problem.

8-3b Asking a Favor

Occasionally, everyone has to ask someone else for a special favor—action for which there is little reward, time, or inclination. For example, suppose a professional association wants to host its annual fund-raiser dinner at an exclusive country club. The program chair of the association must write the club's general manager requesting permission to use the facility. Will a deductive message be successful?

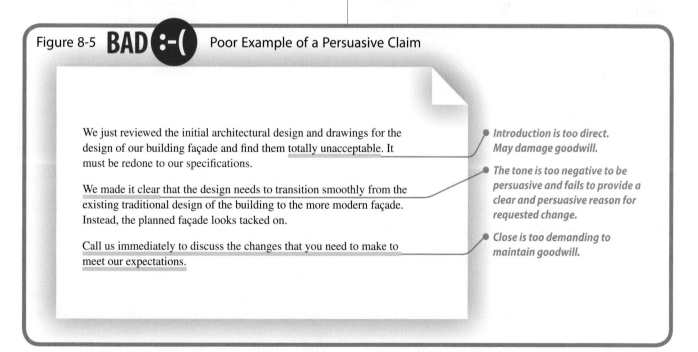

Figure 8-5 **BAD 8-(** Poor Example of a Persuasive Claim

We just reviewed the initial architectural design and drawings for the design of our building façade and find them totally unacceptable. It must be redone to our specifications.

We made it clear that the design needs to transition smoothly from the existing traditional design of the building to the more modern façade. Instead, the planned façade looks tacked on.

Call us immediately to discuss the changes that you need to make to meet our expectations.

- *Introduction is too direct. May damage goodwill.*
- *The tone is too negative to be persuasive and fails to provide a clear and persuasive reason for requested change.*
- *Close is too demanding to maintain goodwill.*

Figure 8-6 **GOOD** :-) Good Example of a Persuasive Claim

Lewis, Lloyd, & Clark
3443 Arbor Street, Boston, MA 22009

Lewis, Lloyd, & Clark

Attorneys at Law
3443 Arbor Street
Boston, MA 22009

March 26, 2014

Doyle Harris
Vice President
Harris and Lowe Architects
234 27th Avenue
New York, NY 03201

Dear Doyle:

When Lewis, Lloyd, and Clark negotiated with your firm to design our new building façade, we were impressed with your previous track record of success. Especially impressive was the building you designed for Tricor Technologies here in Boston with its simplicity of structure and abundant use of glass to bring in natural lighting and provide access to its park-like surroundings.

In our meeting with your architects, we discussed a façade design that incorporated some of these features but relates harmoniously with the existing building. However, after viewing the initial plan and drawings for the façade, we were disappointed with the planned transition from the more traditional design of the existing building with that to the more modern façade.

With Harris and Lowe's reputation for innovative architectural designs, we are confident that the plans can be redrawn to better meet our expectations. We are happy to meet with you again if you would like more specific suggestions regarding changes. Please call me at 330-662-4434 if a meeting would be helpful in this regard.

Sincerely,

Barbara Leland

Barbara Leland
Office Manager

- Seeks attention by giving sincere compliment that reveals subject of message.

- Continues central appeal—commitment to quality design—while providing needed details.

- Presents reasoning that leads to request and subtle reminder of central appeal.

- Connects specific request with firm's commitment to develop a harmonious design.

Legal and Ethical Consideration
- Uses letter rather than less formal email format to add formality to contractual agreement.

When a deductive approach is used in a persuasive situation, chances of getting cooperation are minimal. For example, what might be a probable reaction to the following beginning sentence? *Please send me, without charge, your $450 interactive video training game on workplace safety.*

If the first sentence gets a negative reaction, a decision to refuse might be made instantly. Having thought "No," the receiver might not read the rest of the message or might hold stubbornly to that decision in spite of a well-written persuasive argument that follows the opening sentence. Note that the letter in Figure 8-7 asks the favor before presenting any benefit for doing so. The letter illustrated in Figure 8-8 (on page 144) uses an inductive approach and applies the principles discussed earlier. As this message shows, if the preceding paragraphs adequately emphasize a receiver's reward for complying, the final paragraph need not shout loudly for action.

Figure 8-7 **BAD :-(** Poor Example of a Persuasive Request (Asking a Favor)

Your restaurant does not offer a take-out option. My mother is unable to visit your restaurant due to health problems. Would you consider providing this option so that people such as my mom could enjoy your food?

You've probably already considered this option, but I would be very interested in having it available to meet my mother's current needs.

Does not use an inductive approach to set a more positive tone. Fails to provide clear reasons to comply with the request.

Close does little to build goodwill or encourage compliance.

8-3c Requesting Information

Requests for information are common in business. Information for research reports frequently is obtained by questionnaire, and the reliability of results is strongly influenced by the percentage of return. If a message inviting respondents to complete a questionnaire is written carelessly, the number of responses might be insufficient.

The most serious weakness is asking for action too quickly and providing no incentive for action. Sometimes the reward for taking action is small and indirect, but the message needs to make these benefits evident.

8-3d Persuading within an Organization

The majority of memos are of a routine nature and essential for the day-to-day operation of the business; for example, giving instructions for performing work assignments, scheduling meetings, providing project progress reports, and so on. In many organizations, such matters are handled through the use of email rather than paper memos. These routine messages, as well as messages conveying good news, are written deductively. However, some circumstances require that a supervisor write a persuasive message that motivates employees to accept a change in their jobs that might have a negative effect on the employees or generate resistance (e.g., a job transfer, change in work procedures, software upgrade).

For example, imagine that Pub on the Green restaurant was faced with the challenge of communicating to its employees a significant change in service and style, which included new uniforms. Rather than coercing or demanding that employees accept the change, a letter from the president could emphasize reasons the changes were being made (benefits to guests, the company, and the employees) and the employee's important role in implementing the changes. Using a lighthearted, entertaining approach, the message could include (a) a visual model of the fresh, crisp, and professional look the company expected with the uniform change and (b) helpful information on ways to achieve this look. The following excerpt shows how a "you" orientation and "style flashes" could be interwoven into the letter:

- *Make sure your hair is neatly tied back. Messy hair is a problem for guests—they don't want it getting it into their food. You might even get a better tip.*

© iStockphoto.com/CandyBoxImages

Figure 8-8 **GOOD :-)** Good Example of a Persuasive Request (Asking a Favor)

October 22, 2014

Hernando Ruiz
Owner and Manager
Ruiz Mexican Restaurant
Twin Falls, ID 83330

Dear Mr. Hernandez:

As regular customers of Ruiz Mexican Restaurant, I and my family appreciate your efforts to provide quality food using the freshest ingredients provided by our local farming community. Your efforts to support local farming have extended to your co-sponsorship of the addition of a farmer's market to the annual Taste Twin Falls! event.

My mother particularly enjoys your food and appreciates your support of local farmers, having been one herself. Because of recent health problems, however, she has been unable to visit your restaurant. Adding a takeout option to your menu would not only satisfy my mother's cravings for your delicious food but also may result in increased sales for your restaurant from other residents seeking the convenience of this option.

By broadening your service options, you will continue to build a reputation as a local business that is attentive to its customers' needs and concerns.

Sincerely,

Lucy Thomas

Lucy Thomas

Begins with sincere compliment that sets stage for request that follows.

Explains rationale for request with discussion of benefits to restaurant and its customers.

Connects specific action to rewards for taking action.

- *Don't wear a lot of bling. Guests may think you don't need as large a tip.*

- *Remember to smile. Your smile is the first sign to guests that their Pub on the Green experience will be a memorable one. Your smile tells guests, "I'm glad you came!" But don't just take our word for it. A recent Bay College study found that smiling reflects an awareness of other people and their needs. That's probably why a "winning smile" is so charming!*

The detailed language leaves no doubt in an employee's mind as to what management considers clean, crisp, and professional. However, by continually emphasizing the benefits employees gain from the change, management garners support for the high standards being imposed.

Similarly, employees must often make persuasive requests of their supervisors. For example, they might recommend a change in procedure, acquisition of equipment

Figure 8-9   **GOOD** :-)   Good Example of a Persuasive Memo

To: Karen Moran
From: Donald Regis
Date: January 30, 2014
Subject: Corporate Wellness Program

During our managers' meeting last month, HR Director Wilma Peters expressed concern regarding the rising cost of employee health care. A discussion followed about ways to decrease the cost of health care for the company.

Opens with reference to meeting discussion and company goal.

As you recall, I offered to do some research on how other firms are dealing with this challenge.

Presents a solution to the identified problem.

My research has found that creating a company wellness program can not only reduce health care costs but also provide a number of other benefits:

- Improve employees' overall health
- Reduce the amount of sick days
- Increase productivity
- Raise company morale and camaraderie
- Strengthen employee/employer relations

Developing a company wellness program can take a good deal of time, however, primarily because of a lack of in-house expertise in this area. To help solve this problem, I have identified several companies that provide this service, some for a single one-time fee. If we provide them information on the size of our company, number of employees, and the benefits we seek, they can design a program to suit those needs.

Builds interest by mentioning benefits of the program.

With our goal of reducing employee health-care costs and improving their overall health, would you allow me to create and distribute a survey to employees regarding their interest in taking advantage of an in-house wellness program? I could distribute the survey by the end of the week and likely have the results in time for our meeting next month. The results will allow us to consider whether creating a wellness program would be an attractive offering to employees.

Reduces potential resistance by providing an easy-to-implement, low-cost solution.

Alludes to benefits and closes with specific action to be taken.

or software, or attendance at a professional development program. They might justify a promotion or job reclassification or recommendation for policy changes, and so on. Persuasive memos and email messages are longer than most routine messages because of the extra space needed for developing an appeal and providing convincing evidence.

When preparing to write the memo in Figure 8-9, a manager recognizes that implementation costs could affect the president's reaction to her proposal to implement a wellness program. Anticipating resistance, the manager writes inductively and builds a logical, compelling argument for her proposal.

Deductive sequence (main idea first) works well for routine messages and good-news messages.

Inductive sequence (details first) works well if the reader needs to be persuaded.

STUDY TOOLS
CHAPTER 8

Located at back of the textbook
❑ **Rip out Chapter Review Card**

Located at www.cengagebrain.com
❑ **Review Key Terms Flashcards (Print or Online)**
❑ **Download Audio Summaries for on-the-go review**
❑ **Complete Practice Quizzes to prepare for tests**
❑ **Play "Beat the Clock" to master concepts**
❑ **Complete the Crossword Puzzle to review key terms**
❑ **Watch the video about McDonaldson, a fictitious but all-too-realistic ad agency whose employees struggle with contemporary business communication issues.**

Understanding the Report Process and Research Methods

9-1 Characteristics of Reports

"Hi, Ken. This is Loretta in marketing. Do you know whether the latest sales figures report is ready? My supervisor wants me to review it in preparation for next week's presentation."

"Hi, Loretta. Yes, I just finished a draft of the report yesterday. I will email it to you right now. If there are any changes, I will let you know."

This brief exchange illustrates a simple reporting task. A question has been posed; the answer given (along with supporting information) satisfies the reporting requirement. Although Ken might never have studied report preparation, he did an excellent job; so Loretta can prepare to report the sales figures. Ken's spoken report is a simple illustration of the four main characteristics of reports:

- **Reports typically travel upward in an organization because they usually are requested by a higher authority.** In most cases, people would not generate reports unless requested to do so.
- **Reports are logically organized.** In Ken's case, he answered Loretta's question first and then supported the answer with evidence to justify it. Through your study of message organization, you learned the difference between deductive and inductive organization. Ken's report was deductively organized. If Ken had given the supporting evidence first and followed that

with the answer that he would meet the deadline, the organization of his reply would have been inductive and would still have been logical.

- **Reports are objective.** Because reports contribute to decision making and problem solving, they should be as objective as possible; when nonobjective (subjective) material is included, the report writer should make that known.
- **Reports are generally prepared for a limited audience.** This characteristic is particularly true of reports traveling within an organization and means that reports, like letters, memos, and emails, should be prepared with the receivers' needs in mind.

9-1a Types of Reports

Based on the four characteristics, a workable definition of a *report* is an orderly, objective message used to convey information from one organizational area to another or from one organization to another to assist in decision making or problem solving. Reports have been classified in numerous ways by management and by report-preparation authorities. The form, direction, functional use, and content of the report are used as bases for classification. However, a single report might fit several classifications. The following brief review of classification illustrates the scope of reporting and establishes a basis for studying reports.

- **Formal or informal reports.** The formal/informal classification is particularly helpful because it applies to all reports. A **formal report** is carefully structured; it is logically organized and objective, contains much detail, and is written in a style that tends to eliminate such elements as personal pronouns. An **informal report** is usually a short message written in natural or personal language. An internal memo

> **formal report**
> carefully structured report that is logically organized and objective, contains much detail, and is written in a style that tends to eliminate such elements as personal pronouns
>
> **informal report**
> usually a short message written in natural or personal language

Glossary terms

informational report
a report that carries objective information from one area of an organization to another

analytical report
a report that presents suggested solutions to problems

vertical report
a report that can be upward- or downward-directed

lateral report
a report that travels between units on the same organizational level

internal report
a report that travels within an organization, such as a production or sales report

external report
a report prepared for distribution outside an organization

periodic report
a report that is issued on regularly scheduled dates

---

generally can be described as an informal report. All reports can be placed on a continuum of formality, as shown in Figure 9-1. The distinction among the degrees of formality of various reports is explained more fully in Chapter 11.

- **Short or long reports.** Reports can be classified generally as short or long. A one-page memo is obviously short, and a report of 20 pages is obviously long. What about in-between lengths? One important distinction generally holds true: as it becomes longer, a report takes on more characteristics of formal reports. Thus, the classifications of formal/informal and short/long are closely related.

- **Informational or analytical reports.** An **informational report** carries objective information from one area of an organization to another. An **analytical report** presents suggested solutions to problems. Company annual reports, monthly financial statements, reports of sales volume, and reports of employee or personnel absenteeism and turnover are informational reports. Reports of scientific research, real estate appraisal reports, and feasibility reports by consulting firms are analytical reports.

- **Vertical or lateral reports.** The vertical/lateral classification refers to the directions in which reports travel. Although most reports travel upward in

organizations, many travel downward. Both represent vertical reports and are often referred to as *upward-directed* and *downward-directed* reports. The main function of **vertical reports** is to contribute to management *control*, as shown in Figure 9-2. **Lateral reports**, on the other hand, assist in *coordination* in the organization. A report traveling between units on the same organizational level, as between the production department and the finance department, is lateral.

- **Internal or external reports.** An **internal report**, such as a production or sales report, travels within an organization. An **external report**, such as a company's annual report to stockholders, is prepared for distribution outside an organization.

- **Periodic reports. Periodic reports** are issued on regularly scheduled dates. They are generally directed upward and serve management control purposes. Daily, weekly, monthly, quarterly, semiannual, and annual time periods are typical for periodic reports. Preprinted forms and computer-generated data contribute to uniformity of periodic reports.

Figure 9-1   Report Formality Continuum

Formal ⟵⟶ Informal

| SCIENTIFIC RESEARCH | LONG REPORT/ PROPOSAL | SHORT REPORT/ PROPOSAL | LETTER REPORT/ PROPOSAL | NONROUTINE MEMO REPORT | PERIODIC MEMO REPORT | FORM REPORT |

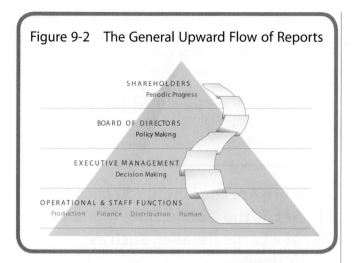

Figure 9-2 The General Upward Flow of Reports

SHAREHOLDERS
Periodic Progress

BOARD OF DIRECTORS
Policy Making

EXECUTIVE MANAGEMENT
Decision Making

OPERATIONAL & STAFF FUNCTIONS
Production   Finance   Distribution   Human

- **Functional reports.** A **functional report** serves a specified purpose within a company. The functional classification includes accounting reports, marketing reports, financial reports, personnel reports, and a variety of other reports that take their functional designation from their ultimate use. For example, a justification of the need for additional personnel or for new equipment is described as a *justification report* in the functional classification.

9-1b Proposals

A **proposal** is a written description of how one organization can meet the needs of another; for example, by providing products or services or solving problems. Businesses issue *calls for bids* that present the specifications for major purchases of goods and certain services. Most governmental and non profit agencies issue *requests for proposals*, or RFPs. Potential suppliers prepare proposal reports telling how they can meet that need. Those preparing the proposal create a convincing document that will lead to obtaining a contract.

In our information-intensive society, proposal preparation is a major activity for many firms. In fact, some companies hire consultants or designate employees to specialize in proposal writing. Chapter 11 presents proposal preparation in considerable detail.

As you review these report classifications, you will very likely decide—correctly—that almost all reports could be included in these categories. A report may be formal or informal, short or long, informational or analytical, vertically or laterally directed, internal or external, periodic or nonperiodic, functionally labeled, a proposal, or some other combination of these classifications. These report categories are in common use and provide necessary terminology for the study and production of reports.

9-2 Basis for Reports: The Problem-Solving Process

T he upward flow of reports provides management with data that someone might use to make a decision. The purpose is to use the data to solve a problem. Some problems are recurring and call for a steady flow of information; other problems might be unique and call for information on a one-time basis. A problem is the basis for a report. The following steps are used for finding a solution:

1. Recognize and define the problem.
2. Select a method of solution.
3. Collect and organize the data and document the sources.
4. Arrive at an answer.

Only after all four steps have been completed is a report written for presentation. Reports represent an attempt to communicate how a problem was solved. These problem-solving steps are completed *before* the report is written in final form.

9-2a Recognizing and Defining the Problem

Problem-solving research cannot begin until the researchers define the problem. Frequently, those requesting a report will attempt to provide a suitable definition. Nevertheless, researchers should attempt to state the problem clearly and precisely to ensure they are on the right track.

Using Problem Statements, Statements of Purpose, and Hypotheses

The **problem statement**, or statement of the problem, is the particular problem that is to be solved by the research. The **statement of purpose** is the goal of the study and includes the aims or objectives the researcher hopes to accomplish.

functional report
a report that serves a specified purpose within a company

proposal
a written description of how one organization can meet the needs of another

problem statement
the particular problem that is to be solved by the research

statement of purpose
the goal of the study; includes the aims or objectives the researcher hopes to accomplish

hypothesis
a statement to be proved or
disproved through research

Research studies often have both a problem statement and a statement of purpose. For example, a real estate appraiser accepts a client's request to appraise a building to determine its market value. The problem is to arrive at a fair market value for the property. The purpose of the appraisal, however, might be to establish a value for a mortgage loan, to determine the feasibility of adding to the structure, or to assess the financial possibility of demolishing the structure and erecting something else. Thus, the purpose might have much to do with determining what elements to consider in arriving at an answer. In other words, unless you know *why* something is wanted, you might have difficulty knowing *what* is wanted. Once you arrive at the answers to the *what* and *why* questions, you will be on your way to solving the problem.

A **hypothesis** is a statement to be proved or disproved through research. For example, a study of a marketing program might determine whether increased use of social media for marketing purposes would increase sales as compared with current marketing methods. For this problem, the hypothesis could be formulated in this way:

> **Hypothesis:** Sales will increase with the use of social media for marketing purposes as compared with our current marketing methods.

Because the hypothesis tends to be stated in a way that favors one possibility or is prejudiced toward a particular answer, many researchers prefer to state hypotheses in the null form. The *null hypothesis* states that no relationship or difference will be found in the factors being studied, which tends to remove the element of prejudice toward a certain answer. The null hypothesis for the previous example could be written as follows:

> **Null hypothesis:** No significant difference will be found in sales between the use of current marketing methods and the introduction of social media for marketing purposes.

Using the problem/purpose approach, the hypothesis approach, or both, is a choice of the researcher. In many ways, the purpose of a study is determined by the intended use of its results.

Limiting the Scope of the Problem

A major shortcoming that often occurs in research planning is the failure to establish or to recognize desirable limits. The *scope* of the report helps to establish boundaries in which the report will be researched and prepared. Assume, for instance, that you want to study salaries of computer technicians. Imagine the enormity of such a task. Millions of people are employed in computer jobs. Perhaps a thousand or so different types of jobs fall into this classification. Use the *what, why, when, where,* and *who* questions to reduce such a problem to reasonable proportions.

> ## Here Are the Limits You Might Set as the Online Sales Manager of a Large Retailer, Such as JCPenney:
>
> **What:** A study of customer attitudes about our online sales Web site.
>
> **Why:** To determine whether the site is easy to navigate and provides desired features and convenience
>
> **When:** Current
>
> **Where:** United States
>
> **Who:** Current online customers
>
> Now you can phrase the problem this way:
>
> **Statement of purpose:** *The purpose of this study is to survey customers to learn their attitudes about the design, features, and convenience of our online sales Web site.*

Note that this process of reducing the problem to a workable size has also established some firm limits to the research. You have limited the problem to Web site functionality, the particular area, and a certain group of users. Note, too, how important the *why* was in helping to establish the limits. Limiting the problem is "zeroing in on the problem."

In some reports, it is desirable to differentiate between the boundaries that were placed on the project outside the control of the researchers and those that were chosen by the researchers. Boundaries imposed outside the control of the researchers are called *limitations;* they might include the assignment of the topic, allotted budget, and time for completion of the report. These boundaries affect what and how the topic can be researched. Boundaries chosen by the researchers to make the project more manageable are called *delimitations;* they might include the sources and methods chosen for research.

Defining Terms Clearly

Words often have more than one meaning, and technical or special-use words might occur in the report that are not widely used or understood. Such terms would require a definition for the reader's understanding of the information presented. In the previously used example concerning the study of computer technicians' salaries, a comparison of one bank's salaries with those paid by others would be meaningful only if the information gathered from other banks relates to identical jobs. A job description defining the duties performed by a computer technician, for example, would help ensure that all banks would be talking about the same job tasks regardless of the job title. In addition, the term *salary* requires definition. Is it hourly, weekly, monthly, or yearly? Are benefits included?

Documenting Procedures

The procedures or steps a writer takes in preparing a report are often recorded as a part of the written report. This **procedures** section, or **methodology**, adds credibility to the research process and also enables subsequent researchers to repeat, or replicate, the study in another setting or at a later time. Reports that study the same factors in different time frames are called **longitudinal studies**.

The procedures section of a report records the major steps taken in the research, and possibly the reasons for their inclusion. It might, for instance, tell the types of printed and electronic sources that were consulted and the groups of people interviewed and how they were selected. Steps in the procedures section are typically listed in chronological order so that the reader has an overall understanding of the timetable that existed for the project.

9-3 Selecting a Method of Gathering Information

After defining the problem, the researcher will plan how to arrive at a solution. The research methods you use to collect necessary information can be secondary, primary, or both.

© iStockphoto.com/Andrey Prokhorov/enot-poloskun

9-3a Secondary Research

Secondary research provides information that has already been created by others. Researchers save time and effort by not duplicating research that has already been undertaken. They can access this information easily through the aid of electronic databases and bibliographic indexes. Suppose that a marketing manager has been asked to investigate the feasibility of implementing a strategic information system. The manager knows other companies are using this technology. By engaging in secondary research, the manager can determine the boundaries of knowledge before proceeding into the unknown.

Certain truths have been established and treated as principles reported in textbooks and other publications. However, because knowledge is constantly expanding, the researcher knows that new information is available. The job, then, is to canvass the literature of the field and attempt to redefine the boundaries of knowledge.

Secondary research can be gathered by means of traditional printed sources or by using electronic tools.

procedures (or methodology)
the steps a writer takes in preparing a report; often recorded as a part of the written report

longitudinal studies
reports that study the same factors in different time frames

secondary research
provides information that has already been reported by others

Printed Sources

Major categories of printed sources are books, periodicals, and government documents. Books are typically cataloged in libraries by call number, with larger libraries using the Library of Congress classification system. Traditional card catalogs in libraries have been replaced by online catalogs, which allow the user to locate desired books by author, title, subject, or keyword. A wide assortment of reference books is typically available for use within libraries; these include dictionaries, encyclopedias, yearbooks, and almanacs. Some of these volumes contain general information on a wide array of topics, while others are designed for a specific field of study.

Periodicals, referred to as *serials* by librarians, include various types of publications that are released on a periodic basis. Newspapers, magazines, and journals are all types of periodicals. Newspapers, which are usually published daily, are a good initial source for investigation, since they give condensed coverage of timely topics. Magazines might be published weekly, monthly, bimonthly, or in some other interval. They are typically written for a general readership, providing expanded coverage in an easy-to-read format. Journals, on the other hand, are written for more specialized audiences, are peer reviewed, and are more research oriented and thus more credible. Journal articles share the results of research studies and provide data that support their findings. They also provide bibliographies or citation lists that can be used to locate related materials. Articles on specific topics can be located using both printed and online indexes. A partial list of these sources is shown in Figure 9-3.

Figure 9-3   Useful Reference Sources

Printed Indexes

Business Periodicals Index
Education Index
The New York Times Index
Readers' Guide to Periodical Literature
Social Science and Humanities Index
The Wall Street Journal Index

Electronic Databases

ABI/INFORM
Academic Search Elite
Business & Company Resource Center
Business Dateline
Business Source Premier
DIALOG Information Services
ERIC
First Search
FSI Online
General BusinessFile
LexisNexis Academic Universe
Periodical Abstracts
ProQuest
Westlaw

Biography

Who's Who in America
Similar directories for specific geographic areas, industries, and professions

General Facts and Statistics

Statistical Abstract of the United States
Bureau of the Census publications
Dictionaries (general and discipline specific)
Encyclopedia (*Americana* or *Britannica*)
Fortune Directories of U.S. Corporations
World Atlas
LexisNexis Statistics
Almanacs

Report Style and Format

American Psychological Association. (2010). *Publication Manual of the American Psychological Association* (6th ed.). Washington, DC: Author. [www.apastyle.org]

Gibaldi, J. (2003). *MLA Handbook for Writers of Research Papers* (6th ed.). New York: Modern Language Association. [www.mla.org/style_faq]

Electronic Sources

The availability of computer-assisted data searches has simplified the time-consuming task of searching through indexes, card catalogs, and other sources. Weekly and monthly updates keep electronic databases current, and they are easy to use. Databases such as LexisNexis Academic Universe have full-text retrieval capability, meaning you can retrieve the entire article for reviewing and printing. Other databases offer only some articles in full text, with citations or abstracts provided for others. Note the list of electronic databases for business users listed in Figure 9-3.

The Internet and its subset, the World Wide Web, have made thousands of reference sources available in a matter of seconds. However, the vastness of this resource can be overwhelming to the novice researcher. The following tips will help make your Internet search more productive:

- **Choose your search engine or database appropriately.** A *search engine* is a cataloged database of Web sites that allows you to search specific topics. Several popular search engines exist, including Yahoo!, Ask, AOL, and MyWebSearch. Megasearch engines such as Google and Bing, which index billions of Web pages, search through a number of other engines to produce "hits."[1] (A *hit* is a located Web site that contains the word or words specified in the search.) You want to obtain a sufficient number of hits, but not thousands. Although the variety of these larger engines is greater, they pose more difficulty in narrowing a search.

Electronic databases provide access to articles from newspapers, magazines, journals, and other types of publications. The database provider might charge a subscription fee or a document delivery fee to access articles. These types of databases are not accessible by a search engine and are often described as the *hidden Internet*. Many libraries provide access to these databases. Some databases are suited for topic searches of general interest; others are geared toward specialized fields. A topic search will produce a listing of references and article abstracts, or even full-text articles in some cases. Databases available through your library might include Business Source Premier (an offering of EBSCO), Academic Search Elite, LexisNexis Academic Universe, ABI Inform First Search, Business and Company Resource Center, General BusinessFile, and others.

- **Structure searches from broad to specific.** Use words for your topic that are descriptive and do not have multiple meanings. Once sites have been located for your general topic, you can use *Boolean logic* to narrow the selection. Boolean operands (*and*, *or*, *not*) serve to limit the identified sites. The following example shows how these delimiters can assist you in locating precisely what you want:

  - Using the key phrase *workplace productivity* will produce all sites that have either of the key words in the title or descriptors.

  - Placing "and" between key words will produce hits that have both words.

  - Keying *workplace productivity not United States* will eliminate hits that refer to the United States.

- **Use quotation marks when literal topics are desired.** Putting quotation marks around your topic words can drastically affect the number of hits. The quotation marks cause the search engine to look for the designated words as a phrase, thus producing only those sites that have the phrase present. Without the quotation marks, the search engine will treat the words individually and produce many more hits, most of which might not be useful. For instance, if you are looking for sites related to "international communication," placing quotation marks around the desired phrase would eliminate the sites that deal with international topics that are not communication oriented.

- **Look for Web pages that have collections of links to other related topics.** Clicking on these hyperlinks will allow you to maximize your time investment in the data-gathering phase of your research.

TELL US MORE ABOUT YOURSELF Social bookmarking Web sites, such as Twitter, Pinterest, and StumbleUpon, provide users with a place to share favorite Web pages and files. The sites track the links users access, and businesses can use this information to target markets and reveal potential markets.

© iStockphoto.com/mattjeacock

- **Be adaptable to the various access format requirements.** Each search engine and database has its own particular format and instructions for use. The method for specifying and narrowing your search will vary.

9-3b Primary Research

After reviewing the secondary data, you might need to collect primary data to solve your problem. **Primary research** relies on firsthand data, such as responses from pertinent individuals or observations of people or phenomena related to your study. Recognized methods to obtain original information are observational studies, experimental research, and normative surveys.

Observational studies are those in which the researcher observes and statistically analyzes certain phenomena to assist in establishing new principles or discoveries. For example, market analysts observe buying habits of certain income groups to determine the most desirable markets. Internal auditors analyze expected patterns in expense reimbursement amounts to identify potential fraud activity. Developing an objective system for quantifying observations is necessary to collect valid data. For example, to gain insight on the effect of a comprehensive ethics program, a researcher might record the number of incidents of ethical misconduct reported or the number of calls made to an ethics help-line designed to provide advice about proper conduct. Observational studies typically involve no contact with the human subjects under study.

Experimental research typically involves the study of two or more samples that have exactly the same components before a variable is added to one of the samples. Any differences observed are viewed as due to the variable. Like scientists, businesses use experimental research to solve various problems. For example, a company conducts new employee training with all new hires. Two training methods are presently used: New hires in one regional office receive their training in a traditional classroom setting with other new employees, while employees at the other regional office take a Web-based training class. Management wants to determine whether one method is superior to the other in terms of learning success. During the period of the study, learning differences in the two study groups are noted. Because the training method is assumed to be the only significant variable, any difference is attributed to its influence. Experimental research involves very careful recordkeeping and can require informed consent from participants who are subjected to experimental methods.

Normative survey research is undertaken to determine the status of something at a specific time. Survey instruments such as questionnaires, opinion surveys, checklists, and interviews are used to obtain information from participants. Election opinion polls represent one type of normative survey research. The term *normative* is used to qualify surveys because surveys reveal "norms" or "standards" existing at the time of the survey. A poll taken two months before an election might have little similarity to one taken the week preceding the election.

Surveys can help verify the accuracy of existing norms. The U.S. Census is conducted every decade to establish an actual population figure, and each person is supposedly counted. In effect, the census tests the accuracy of prediction techniques used to estimate population during the years between censuses. A survey of what employees consider a fair benefits package would be effective only for the date of the survey. People retire, move, and change their minds often; these human traits make survey research of opinions somewhat tentative. Yet surveys remain a valuable tool for gathering information on which to base decisions and policies.

Researchers normally cannot survey everyone, particularly if the population is large and the research budget is limited. **Sampling** is a survey technique that eliminates the need for questioning 100% of the population. Sampling is based on the principle that a sufficiently large number drawn at random from a population will be representative of the total population; that is, the sample will possess the same characteristics in the same proportions as the total population. For example, a company collecting market research data before introducing a new low-fat food product would survey a small number of people. The data are

primary research
data collected for the first time, usually for a specific purpose

observational studies
studies in which the researcher observes and statistically analyzes certain phenomena in order to assist in establishing new principles or discoveries

experimental research
the study of two samples that have exactly the same components before a variable is added to one of the samples

normative survey research
research to determine the status of something at a specific time

sampling
a survey technique that eliminates the need for questioning 100% of the population

number of participants can test the instrument, which can then be revised prior to wide-scale administration.

- **Reliability** refers to the level of consistency or stability over time or over independent samples; that is, reliable data are reasonably accurate or repeatable. Reliability results from asking a large enough sample of people so that the researcher is reasonably confident the results would be the same even if more people were asked to respond or if a different sample were chosen from the same population. For example, if you were to ask 10 people to react to a questionnaire item, the results might vary considerably. If you were to add 90 more people to the sample, the results might tend to reach a point of stability, where more responses would not change the results. Reliability would then be reasonably established.

Responses to surveys conducted by mail often represent only a small percentage of the total mailings. In some cases, a return of 3% to 5% is considered adequate and is planned for by researchers. In other cases, such as employee surveys or questionnaires, a return of considerably more than half the mailings might be a planned result. Selecting an appropriate data collection method and developing a sound survey instrument are crucial elements of an effective research study.

considered *representative* if the sample of people surveyed has the same percentage of ages, genders, purchasing power, and so on as the anticipated target market.

As a researcher, you must be cautious about drawing conclusions from a sample and generalizing them to a population that might not be represented by the sample. For example, early-morning shoppers might differ from afternoon or evening shoppers; young adults might differ from senior citizens; male shoppers might differ from female shoppers. A good researcher defines the population as distinctly as possible and uses a sampling technique to ensure that the sample is representative.

Whether a survey involves personal interviewing or the distribution of items such as checklists or questionnaires, some principles of procedure and planning are common to both methods. These principles assure the researcher that the data gathered will be both valid (i.e., it will measure what the researcher intended to measure) and reliable (i.e., it will measure data accurately).

- **Validity** refers to the degree to which the data measure what you intend to measure. It generally results from careful planning of the questionnaire or interview questions or items. Cautious wording, preliminary testing of items to detect misunderstandings, and some statistical techniques are helpful in determining whether the responses to the items are valid. A *pilot test* of the instrument is often conducted prior to the full-scale survey so that a smaller

9-4 Collecting and Organizing the Data

Collecting the right data and ensuring that they are recorded appropriately is paramount to the success of a business report. Various techniques can assist in this process when collecting both secondary and primary research.

9-4a Collecting Secondary Data

When beginning to collect secondary data, beware of collecting too much information—one of the major deterrents to good report writing. Although you want

validity
the degree to which the data measure what the researcher intends to measure

reliability
the level of consistency or stability over time or over independent samples

to be thorough, you do not want to collect and record such a large amount of information that you will hardly know where to begin your analysis.

The availability of computer-assisted data searches has simplified the time-consuming task of searching through indexes, card catalogs, and other sources. For example, suppose you select an online database such as Business Source Premier or an Internet search engine such as Google to research the role of microblogging in the workplace. By inputting the key term *instant message* in an online database, you receive the screen output in Figure 9-4 below. The screen output contains information that will facilitate your research.

First, you can quickly evaluate the relevance of references by reading each article's title and abstract, if available, to determine appropriateness to your topic. Retrieved full-text articles can be read and analyzed for useful information, saved, and printed for later use. Be sure to record a full bibliographic citation for each reference you obtain to avoid the need to relocate the online source or revisit the library to find it again.

After you have located relevant sources, you can take notes using various methods. When your aim is to *learn*, the following technique for taking notes is effective: (1) read an article rapidly and put it aside, (2) *from memory*, list main and supporting points, and (3) review the article to see whether all significant points have been included.

Rapid reading forces concentration, builds a strong understanding of the topic, and reveals relationships between ideas. Traditionally, researchers read the article and immediately wrote notes on cards. Currently, researchers typically prefer copying and pasting relevant information into a word-processing file or highlighting important points on a photocopy or printout of the article; then from the selected passages, they compose notes at the keyboard.

You can use two kinds of note-taking: direct quotation or paraphrase. The *direct quotation method* involves citing the exact words from a source. This method is useful when the exact words have specific impact or expert appeal. The *paraphrase method* involves summarizing information in your own words without changing the author's intended meaning. Put direct quotes in quotation marks, and indicate the page numbers, if available.

Figure 9-4   A Sample Computer Data Search Using an Online Database

Insert key search term.

Alerts researcher of articles that can be viewed in full text.

Plagiarism is the presentation of someone else's ideas or words as your own. To safeguard your reputation against plagiarism charges, be certain to give credit where credit is due. Specifically, provide a citation for each (1) direct quotation and (2) passage from someone else's work that you stated in your own words rather than using the author's words—the words are your own, but the idea is not. To attribute information to another source, develop complete, accurate citations and a reference page according to some recognized referencing method.

9-4b Collecting Data through Surveys

The method of distribution and the makeup of the questionnaire are critical factors in successful survey research.

Selecting a Data Collection Method

Selecting an appropriate data collection method is crucial to effective research. Researchers must consider various factors when selecting an appropriate method for collecting data, as illustrated in Figure 9-5 on page 160.

Developing an Effective Survey Instrument

No matter which survey technique or combination of techniques is used, the way in which the survey instrument is designed and written has much to do with the validity and reliability of results, response rate, and quality of information received.

The construction of the survey instrument—usually a questionnaire or interview guide—is critical to obtaining reliable and valid data. Before developing items for a questionnaire or opinion survey, a researcher should visualize the ways responses will be compiled and included in a final report. Here are some suggestions for developing an effective questionnaire:

- **Provide brief, easy-to-follow directions.** Explain the purpose of the study in a cover letter or in a brief statement at the top of the questionnaire so that the respondents understand your intent. While a screening question might be needed to determine whether the respondent is qualified to answer a set of questions, minimize confusing "skip-and-jump" instructions such as the following:

  If you answered Yes to item 4, skip directly to item 7; if you answered No, explain your reason in items 5 and 6.

Consider using electronic survey systems that advance respondents to the next question based on answers to screening questions.

- **Arrange the items in a logical sequence.** If possible, the sequence should proceed from easy to difficult items; simple, nonthreatening items involve respondents and encourage them to finish. You might group related items such as demographic questions or those that use the same response options (multiple choice, rating scales, open-ended questions).

- **Create an appealing, easy-to-comprehend design.** Use typefaces, bold, underline, and italics to emphasize important ideas. Use text boxes and graphic lines to partition text so that the reader can identify and move through sections quickly.

- **Use short items that ask for a single answer to one idea.** Include only the questions needed to meet the objectives of your study, since long questionnaires affect the return rate negatively.

- **Design questions that are easy to answer and to tabulate.** Participants might not take the time to answer numerous open-ended questions that require essay-style answers. When open-ended questions are included, provide enough space for respondents to answer adequately.

- **Strive to write clear questions that all respondents will interpret in the same way.** Avoid words with imprecise meanings (e.g., *several*, *usually*) and specialized terms and difficult words that respondents might not understand. Use accurate translations for each concept presented if other cultures are involved. Provide examples for items that might be difficult to understand.

- **Ask for information that can be recalled readily.** Asking for "old" information might not result in sound data.

plagiarism
the presentation of someone else's ideas or words as your own

Figure 9-5   Selecting an Appropriate Data-Collection Method

METHOD	ADVANTAGES	LIMITATIONS
Mailed surveys	• Are relatively inexpensive to administer • Can reach a wide number of people who complete the survey at their convenience • Allow anonymity, which may produce more honest responses • Remove difference-in-status barriers	• Can be expensive if follow-up mailings are required • Yield a low response rate • Are not useful for obtaining detailed information
Telephone surveys	• Provide inexpensive and rapid data collection • Allow personal contact between interviewer and respondent for clarification or follow-up questions	• Must be relatively short to minimize perceived intrusion and to increase typical small return rate • May exclude respondents with unlisted numbers and those without telephones
Personal interviews	• Are useful to obtain in-depth answers and explore sensitive topics • Allow personal contact between interviewer and respondent for clarification and follow-up questions	• Are time-consuming and resource intensive • Require proper interviewer • Vary in value, depending on quality and consistency of interviewer
Email polling	• Is inexpensive • Provides for easy response • Yields quick results that can be updated electronically as responses are received	• Is limited to respondents with computer access

C Squared Studios/Photodisc/Getty Images / Ryan McVay/Photodisc/Getty Images / Duncan Smith/Photodisc/Getty Images / Siede Preis/Photodisc/Getty Images

- **Provide all possible answer choices on multiple-choice items.** Add an "undecided" or "other" category so that respondents are not forced to choose a nonapplicable response.

- **Ask for factual information whenever possible.** Opinions might be needed in certain studies, but

opinions might change daily. As a general rule, the smaller the sample, the less reliable are any conclusions based on opinions.

- **Decide on an optimal number of choices to place on a ranking scale.** Ranking scales, also called Likert scales, allow participants to indicate their opinion on a numbered continuum. When deciding the numbers to place on the scale, consider the tendency of some groups to choose the noncommittal midpoint in a scale with an odd number of response choices (for instance, choosing 3 on a scale from 1 to 5).

- **Avoid questions that might be threatening or awkward to the respondent.** For sensitive issues, such as age and income, allow respondents to select among ranges if possible. Ensure that ranges do not overlap, and provide for all possible selections.

- **Consider the advisability of prompting a forced answer.** A forced-answer question can be used to determine which single factor is most critical to a respondent, as shown in the following examples:

 Of the locations listed, which is the most convenient for your use?

 Do you agree to the terms of use provided in the attached document?

❏ Yes   ❏ No

When using forced-choice items, avoid "leading questions" that cause people to answer in a way that is not their true opinion or situation. The following item is an example of such a question:

 Would you participate in unethical acts, such as insider trading, if this potential were provided?

❏ Yes   ❏ No

- **Include a postage-paid envelope with the mailed questionnaire.** A higher response rate results when this courtesy is provided. Include your return information at the bottom of the questionnaire in the event the envelope is misplaced.

Various types of items can be used in questionnaire design, depending on your purpose and the characteristics of your participants. Figure 9-6 on the next page illustrates the principles of effective questionnaire design.

A final step in questionnaire design is to test the instrument by asking others to complete and critique the questionnaire. For surveys of major importance, researchers typically conduct a pilot study, administering the questionnaire to a small group of the population involved. This process allows them to correct problems in clarity and design, and typically leads to better response and quality of answers. A pilot study might uncover factors affecting your results, which you can

address in the final research design and before conducting the actual survey.

Researchers must select from among the several formats available the one best suited to the situation. Criteria for selecting one alternative over the others might include the following: Which format leaves the least chance for misinterpretation? Which format provides information in the way it can best be used? Can it be tabulated easily? Can it be cross-referenced to other items in the survey instrument?

9-4c Avoiding Data-Gathering Errors

If acceptable data-gathering techniques have been used, data will measure what they are intended to measure (have validity) and will measure it accurately (have reliability). Hopefully, a carefully designed research process will yield useful data for analysis.

Some Common Errors at the Data-Gathering Stage:

- ☒ Using samples that are too small
- ☒ Using samples that are not representative
- ☒ Using poorly constructed data-gathering instruments
- ☒ Using information from biased sources
- ☒ Failing to gather enough information to cover all important aspects of a problem
- ☒ Gathering too much information

9-4d Documenting Sources of Information

A crucial part of ethical, honest research writing is documenting or referencing sources fairly and accurately. Although time consuming and tedious, careful attention to documentation marks you as a respected, highly professional researcher.

An important first step is to pledge that you will not, for any reason, present someone else's ideas as your own. Then develop a systematic checklist for avoiding plagiarism. Carelessly forgetting to enclose someone else's words within quotation marks or failing to paraphrase another's words can cause others to question your ethical conduct. When you feel that the tedious work required to document sources fairly and

Figure 9-6 Example of an Effective Questionnaire

1. **Rank the following job factors in the order of their importance to you. Add other factors important to you in the space provided.**

		1	2	3	4	5	6	7
a.	Wages	○	○	○	○	○	○	○
b.	Health and retirement benefits	○	○	○	○	○	○	○
c.	Job security	○	○	○	○	○	○	○
d.	Ability to maintain balance between work and family life	○	○	○	○	○	○	○
e.	Creativity and challenge of work assignment	○	○	○	○	○	○	○
f.	Perceived prestige of work	○	○	○	○	○	○	○
g.	_____	○	○	○	○	○	○	○
h.	_____	○	○	○	○	○	○	○

   • *Uses variety of items to elicit different types of responses.*

   • *Uses clear, concise language to minimize confusion.*

   • *Provides clear instructions for answering each item.*

2. **Which of the following is the single job satisfaction factor that you feel needs more attention in our company? (Please select only one.)**

   ○ Wages
   ○ Health and retirement benefits
   ○ Job security
   ○ Ability to maintain balance between work and family life
   ○ Creativity and challenge of work assignment
   ○ Perceived prestige of work
   ○ Other (specify) [_____ ▾]

   • *Provides additional lines to allow for individual opinions.*

   • *Provides even number of rating choices to eliminate "fence" responses.*

3. **How would you rate your overall job satisfaction?**

Very unsatisfied 1	Unsatisfied 2	Somewhat unsatisfied 3	Somewhat satisfied 4	Satisfied 5	Very satisfied 6
○	○	○	○	○	○

   • *Asks for easily recalled information.*

4. **How would you rate your overall job satisfaction 12 months ago?**

Very unsatisfied 1	Unsatisfied 2	Somewhat unsatisfied 3	Somewhat satisfied 4	Satisfied 5	Very satisfied 6
○	○	○	○	○	○

5. **Indicate your age group:**

   ○ 20–29
   ○ 30–39
   ○ 40–49
   ○ 50–59
   ○ 60–69
   ○ 70 years and over

   • *Provides nonoverlapping categories of response and open-ended final category.*

6. **Indicate your time with the company:**

   ○ Less than 1 year
   ○ 1–3 years
   ○ 4–6 years
   ○ 7–10 years
   ○ Over 10 years

   Format Pointers
   Provides adequate space for answering open-ended item.

   Keeps length as short as possible while meeting survey objectives.

7. **What could the company do to enhance your satisfaction as a company employee?**

   [_____]

   Includes instructions for submitting completed questionnaire.

   Thanks for your participation. Click to submit your questionnaire.

   [Submit]

accurately is not worth the time invested, remind yourself of the following reasons for documentation:

- **Citations give credit where it is due—to the one who created the material.** People who document demonstrate high standards of ethical conduct and responsibility in scholarship. Those exhibiting this professional behavior will gain the well-deserved trust and respect of peers and superiors.
- **Documentation protects writers against plagiarism charges.** Plagiarism occurs when someone steals material from another and claims it as his or her own writing. Besides suffering embarrassment, the plagiarist might be assessed fines, penalties, or professional sanctions.
- **Documentation supports your statements.** If recognized authorities have said the same thing, your work takes on credibility; you have put yourself in good company.
- **Documentation can aid future researchers pursuing similar material.** Documentation must be complete and accurate so that the researcher can locate the source.

Many style guides are available to advise writers how to organize, document, and produce reports and manuscripts. Figure 9-3 includes two of the most popular authoritative style manuals. The *Publication Manual of the American Psychological Association* has become the most-used guide in the social and "soft" sciences and in many scholarly journals. The *MLA Handbook for Writers of Research Papers* is another authoritative source used in the humanities.

Citations

Two major types of citations are used to document a report: source notes and explanatory notes. Depending on the authoritative style manual used, these notes might be positioned in parentheses within the report, at the bottom of the page, or at the end of the report.

- **Source notes.** These citations acknowledge the contributions of others. They might refer readers to sources of quotations, paraphrased portions of someone else's words or ideas, and quantitative data used in the report. Source notes must include complete and accurate information so that the reader can locate the original source if desired.
- **Explanatory notes.** These citations are used for several purposes: (1) to comment on a source or to provide information that does not fit easily in the text, (2) to support a statistical table, or (3) to refer the reader to another section of the report. The following sample footnote describes the mathematics involved in preparing a table:

*The weighted opinion was derived by assigning responses from high to low as 5, 4, 3, 2, 1; totaling all respondents; and dividing by the number of respondents.

In this case, the asterisk (*) was used rather than a number to identify the explanatory footnote both in the text and in the citation. This method is often used when only one or two footnotes are included in the report. If two footnotes appear on the same page, two asterisks (**) or numbers or letters are used to distinguish the second from the first. An explanatory note that supports a graphic or a source note that provides the reference from which data were taken appears immediately below the graphic.

Referencing Methods

Various reference methods are available for the format and content of source notes: in-text parenthetical citations, footnotes, and endnotes. Note the major differences among the methods in the following discussion.

- **In-text parenthetical citations.** The *APA Publication Manual*, *MLA Handbook*, and some other documentation references eliminate the need for separate footnotes or endnotes. Instead, an in-text citation, which contains abbreviated information within parentheses, directs the reader to a list

---

Follow These General Suggestions for Preparing Accurate Documentation:

- **Decide which authoritative style manual to follow for preparing in-text parenthetical citations or footnotes (endnotes) and the bibliography (references).** Some companies and most journals require writers to prepare reports or manuscripts following a particular style manual. Once you are certain you have selected the appropriate manual, follow it precisely as you prepare the documentation and produce the report.
- **Be consistent.** If you are carefully following a format, you shouldn't have a problem with consistency. For example, one style manual might require an author's initials in place of the first name in a bibliography; another manual requires the full name. The placement of commas and periods and other information varies among manuals. Consult the manual, apply the rules methodically, and proofread carefully to ensure accuracy and consistency.

of sources at the end of a report. This list contains all publication information on every source cited. It is arranged alphabetically by the author's last name or, if no author is provided, by the first word of the article title.

- **Footnote citation method.** Placing citations at the bottom of the page on which they are cited is the footnote citation. The reader can conveniently refer to the source if the documentation is positioned at the bottom of the page. Alternatively, a list of footnotes can be included in an endnotes page at the end of the document in the order they appeared. Footnotes and endnotes are not used in APA and MLA referencing, as these styles permit the use of in-text citations only.

- **References (APA) or Works Cited (MLA).** The APA and MLA styles use different terms to distinguish between these types of lists. This document is an alphabetized list of the sources used in preparing a report. Each entry contains the publication information necessary for locating the source. In addition, the bibliographic entries give evidence of the nature of sources the author consulted. The term *bibliography* (literally "description of books") is sometimes used to refer to this list. A researcher often uses sources that provide information but do not result in citations. To acknowledge that you might have consulted these works and to provide the reader with a comprehensive reading list, you might include them in the list of sources.

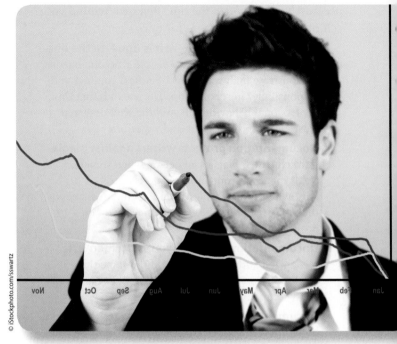
© iStockphoto.com/sswartz

9-5 Arriving at an Answer

Even the most intelligent person cannot be expected to draw sound conclusions from faulty information. Sound conclusions can be drawn only when information has been properly organized, collected, and interpreted.

9-5a Analyzing the Data

Follow a step-by-step approach to the solution of your research problem. Plan your study and follow the plan. Question every step for its contribution to the objective, and keep a record of actions. In a formal research study, the researcher is expected to make a complete report. Another qualified person should be able to make the same study, use the same steps, and arrive at the same conclusion.

Suppose you have conducted a survey and collected several hundred replies to a 30-item questionnaire. Appropriate statistical analysis must be applied to interpret survey results. Statistical analysis is a complex task, involving specialized understanding that is gained through appropriate training, but some of the common terms are identified here. *Tabulation* techniques should be used to reduce quantitative data such as numerous answers to questionnaire items. For instance, you might want to tabulate the number of males and females participating in the study, along with the appropriate percentages for each gender.

For many kinds of studies, *measures of central tendency* might help in describing distributions of quantitative data. The *range* assists the researcher in understanding the distribution of the scores. The *mean*, *median*, and *mode* are descriptions of the average value of the distribution.

Other statistical techniques may be used. For example, *correlation analysis* might be used to determine whether a relationship existed between how respondents answered one item and how they answered another. Were males, for example, more likely to have chosen a certain answer to another item on the survey than were females?

The report process is one of reducing the information collected to a size that can be handled conveniently in a written message, as shown in Figure 9-7. Visualize the report process as taking place in a huge funnel. At the top of the funnel, pour in all the original information. Then through a process of compression within the funnel, take these steps:

1. Evaluate the information for its usefulness.
2. Reduce the useful information through organization of notes and data analysis.

Figure 9-7 The Report Process

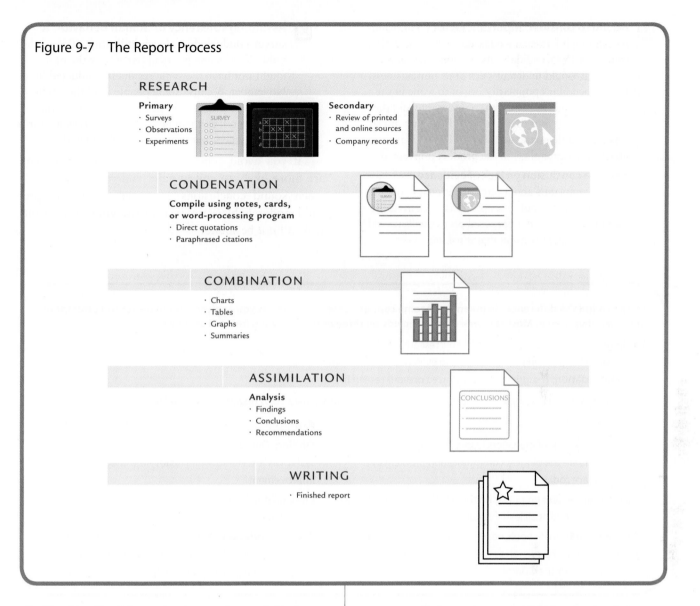

RESEARCH

Primary
· Surveys
· Observations
· Experiments

Secondary
· Review of printed and online sources
· Company records

CONDENSATION

Compile using notes, cards, or word-processing program
· Direct quotations
· Paraphrased citations

COMBINATION
· Charts
· Tables
· Graphs
· Summaries

ASSIMILATION

Analysis
· Findings
· Conclusions
· Recommendations

WRITING
· Finished report

3. Combine like information into understandable forms through the use of tables, charts, graphs, and summaries. (See Chapter 10.)

4. Report in written form the information that remains. (See Chapter 11.)

9-5b Interpreting the Data

Your ethical principles affect the validity of your interpretations. Through all steps in the research process, you must attempt to maintain the integrity of the research. Strive to remain objective, design and conduct an unbiased study, and resist any pressure to slant research to support a particular viewpoint.

Some common errors that seriously hinder the interpretation of data include the following:

☒ **Trying, consciously or unconsciously, to make results conform to a prediction or desire.** Seeing predictions come true might be pleasing, but objectivity is much more important. Facts should determine conclusions.

☒ **Hoping for spectacular results.** An attempt to astonish supervisors by preparing a report with revolutionary conclusions can have a negative effect on accuracy.

☒ **Attempting to compare when commonality is absent.** Results obtained from one study might not always apply to other situations. Similarly, research with a certain population might not be consistent when the same research is conducted with another population.

☒ **Assuming a cause–effect relationship when one does not exist.** A company president might have been in office one year, and sales might have doubled. However, sales might have doubled in spite of the president rather than because of the president.

Failing to consider important factors. For example, although Eastman Kodak developed the digital camera in 1975, it didn't invest in the technology for fear it would undercut sales of its film business. Only when film's popularity began to wane in the mid-1990s in favor of digital photography did the company push into the digital market. But competitors entered the market faster and Kodak was never able to fully capitalize on the product it invented.[2]

Basing a conclusion on lack of evidence. "We have had no complaints about our present policy" does not mean that the policy is appropriate. Conversely, lack of evidence that a proposed project will succeed does not necessarily mean that it will fail.

Assuming constancy of human behavior. A survey conducted in March indicating 60% of the public favors one political party over the other might not have the same results if conducted in November. Because some people paid their bills late last year does not mean a company should refuse to sell to them next year, since reasons for slow payment might have been eliminated.

If you avoid common data-collection errors, you are more likely to collect valid and reliable data and reach sound conclusions. However, if you interpret valid and reliable data incorrectly, your conclusions will still *not* be sound.

Keep in mind the differences in meaning of some common research terms as you analyze your material and attempt to seek meaning from it. Most research reports include all three of the following items or sections:

Finding: A specific, measurable fact from a research study

Conclusion: Summation of major facts and evidence derived from findings

Recommendation: A suggested action based on your research

Consider the following examples of conclusions and recommendations generated by analyzing research findings:

Example 1

Finding: Fully 90% of managers responded that poor writing skills are the biggest communication problem in the workplace today.

Conclusion: Greater emphasis on the development of good writing skills is needed at all levels of education.

Recommendation: Schools need to ensure that more time is spent on writing instruction to ensure that employees have the requisite skills for the workplace.

Example 2

Finding: Only 20% of online customers rated our system as "Excellent," while nearly 40% checked "Needs Improvement."

Conclusion: Our online ordering system needs improvement.

Recommendation: Designers in charge of the online ordering system need to use the findings from our recent customer survey to improve the quality of the system.

STUDY TOOLS
CHAPTER 9

Located at back of the textbook

❑ Rip out Chapter Review Card

Located at www.cengagebrain.com

❑ Review Key Terms Flashcards (Print or Online)

❑ Download Audio Summaries for on-the-go review

❑ Complete Practice Quizzes to prepare for tests

❑ Play "Beat the Clock" to master concepts

❑ Complete the Crossword Puzzle to review key terms

❑ Watch the video about McDonaldson, a fictitious but all-too-realistic ad agency whose employees struggle with contemporary business communication issues.

ONE APPROACH.
70 UNIQUE SOLUTIONS.

CENGAGE
Learning™

www.cengage.com/4ltrpress

Managing Data and Using Graphics

OBJECTIVES

10-1 Communicate quantitative information effectively.

10-2 Apply principles of effectiveness and ethical responsibilities in the construction of graphic aids.

10-3 Select and design appropriate and meaningful graphics.

10-4 Integrate graphics within documents.

10-1 Communicating Quantitative Information

Before you can interpret quantitative data, the elements must be classified, summarized, and condensed into a manageable size. This condensed information is meaningful and can be used to answer your research questions. For example, assume that you have been given 400 completed questionnaires from a study of employee needs for financial planning. This large accumulation of data is overwhelming until you tabulate the responses for each questionnaire item by manually inputting or compiling responses received through an online survey or optically scanning the responses into a computer. Then you can apply appropriate statistical analysis techniques to the tabulated data.

The computer generates a report of the total responses for each possible answer to each item. For example, the tabulation of responses from each employee about his or her preferences for employee perks might appear like this:

More vacation time	198
Education reimbursement	102
Discount on data plan	63
Financial planning assistance	45
Incentives for healthy lifestyle choices	22
	430

The breakdown reduces 430 responses to a manageable set of information. The tabulation shows only five items, each with a specific number of responses from the total of 430 questionnaires. Because people tend to make comparisons during analysis, the totals are helpful. People generally want to know proportions or ratios, and these are best presented as percentage parts of the total. Thus the numbers converted to percentages are as follows:

Preferred Employee Perk	Number	Percentage
More vacation time	198	46
Education reimbursement	102	24
Discount on data plan	63	15
Financial planning assistance	45	10
Incentives for healthy lifestyle choices	22	5
	430	100

Now analyzing the data becomes relatively easy. Of the survey participants, 10% selected financial planning assistance while only 5% selected incentives for healthy choices. Other observations, depending on how exactly you intend to interpret percentages, could be that nearly half selected more vacation time. Combining data in two categories allows you to summarize that nearly three-quarters of employees selected more vacation time and education reimbursement.

When tabulating research results of people's opinions, likes, preferences, and other subjective items, rounding off statistics to fractions helps paint a clear picture for readers. In actuality, if the same group of people were asked this question again a day or two later, a few probably would have changed their minds. For example, an employee who had indicated a desire for more vacation time may have learned of the benefits of education reimbursement after talking with an acquaintance. The next day, the employee might indicate a preference for education reimbursement over more vacation time.

Fractions, ratios, and percentages are examples of **common language**. In effect, common language reduces difficult figures to the "common denominators" of language and ideas. Roth IRAs" is somewhat easy to understand, "26 percent prefer…" is even easier, and "approximately one out of four indicate a preference for traditional and Roth IRAs"

common language
reduces difficult figures to the common denominators of language and ideas

is even more understandable. Although "198 of 430 prefer more vacation time" is somewhat easy to understand, "46% prefer ..." is even easier, and "approximately one out of two indicate a preference for more vacation time" is even more understandable.

Common language also involves the use of indicators other than actual count or quantity. The Dow Jones Industrial Average provides a measure of stock market performance and is certainly easier to understand than the complete New York Stock Exchange figures. Similarly, oil is counted in barrels rather than in the quart or gallon sizes purchased by consumers. Because of inflation, dollars are not accurate items to use as comparisons from one year to another in certain areas; for example, automobile manufacturers use "automobile units" to represent production changes in the industry. The important thing for the report writer to remember is that reports are communication media, and everything possible should be done to make sure communication occurs effectively.

10-2 Using Graphics

Imagine trying to put in composition style all the information available in a financial statement. Several hundred pages might be necessary to explain material that could otherwise be contained in three or four pages of balance sheets and income statements. Even then, the reader would no doubt be thoroughly confused! To protect readers from being overwhelmed or simply bored with data, report writers can design visually appealing graphics that are appropriate for the data being presented. Data reported in a table, graph, or picture will make your written analysis clearer to the reader.

The term **graphics** is used in this chapter to refer to all types of illustrations used in written and spoken reports. The most commonly used graphics are tables, bar charts, line charts, pie charts, pictograms, maps, flowcharts, diagrams, and photographs.

10-2a Effective and Ethical Use of Graphics

The use of graphics with a written discussion serves three purposes: to clarify, to simplify, or to reinforce data. As you read this chapter, ask yourself if the discussion would be effective if the accompanying graphic figures were not included. Use the following questions to help you determine whether using a graphic element is appropriate and effective in a written or spoken report.

- **Is a graphic needed to clarify, reinforce, or emphasize a particular idea?** Or can the material be covered adequately in words rather than in visual ways? To maintain a reasonable balance between words and graphics, save graphics for data that are difficult to communicate in words alone.

Adapting Your Presentation for YouTube

YouTube is a great potential resource for a business and can be used to distribute your sales message or training material to a wide audience. The easily accessed Web site can be a great avenue for sharing business presentations; however, some adaptation is necessary for the best effect.

© iStockphoto.com/dem10

- **Keep it short.** The average viewing time for a YouTube clip is 2.5 minutes. If you must stay with a longer presentation format, divide it into several short segments posted as separate videos.
- **Make it loud and clear.** Use an external microphone rather than relying on one built into the camera. Your audio quality will be much improved.
- **Avoid bulleted PowerPoint slides.** Bullet points will appear blurry on YouTube and be next to impossible to read. Edit your content and change it to full-screen slides before uploading.

Viewers don't have the time or inclination to struggle through a long, poorly prepared video. Make sure your postings on social media sites are "online compatible."[1]

- **Does the graphic presentation contribute to the overall understanding of the idea under discussion?** Will the written or spoken text add meaning to the graphic display?
- **Is the graphic easily understood?** Does the graphic emphasize the key idea and spur the reader to think intelligently about this information? Follow these important design principles:
  - Avoid *chartjunk*. This term, coined by design expert Edward Tufte, describes decorative distractions that bury relevant data.[2] Extreme use of color, complicated symbols and art techniques, and unusual combinations of typefaces reduce the impact of the material presented.
  - Develop a consistent design for graphics. Arbitrary changes in the design of graphics (e.g., use of colors, typefaces, three-dimensional or flat designs) within a written or spoken report can be confusing as the receiver expects consistency in elements within a single report.
  - Write meaningful titles that reinforce the point you are making. For example, a receiver can interpret data faster when graphics use a talking title; that is, a title that interprets the data. Consider the usefulness of the following graphic titles for a customer service manager browsing through survey results in preparation for a meeting with top management:

    Descriptive Title: *Customer Complaints for First Quarter*

    Talking Title: *Customer Complaints Rise in First Quarter*

    The talking title saves the manager time in understanding the data and also ensures the accuracy of his interpretation, his recommendations, and the content of his presentation. Similarly, poor business decisions can be averted if graphic titles reveal key information. You will learn more about the appropriate use of descriptive and talking headings as you study the preparation of informational and analytical reports in Chapter 11.
- **Is the graphic honest?** Visual data can be distorted easily, leading the reader to form incorrect opinions about the data.
- **Can a graphic used in a presentation be seen by the entire audience?** Electronic presentations, flip charts, whiteboards, and overhead transparencies are the visual means most often used to accompany presentations.

The key to preparing effective graphics is selecting an appropriate graphic for the data and developing a clean, simple design that allows the reader or audience to quickly extract the needed information and meaning.

> WE REMEMBER MORE OF WHAT WE BOTH SEE *AND* HEAR THAN OF WHAT WE RECEIVE THROUGH ONLY ONE SENSORY CHANNEL. WHEN TEXT AND GRAPHICS ARE COMBINED, RETENTION GOES UP AN AVERAGE OF 42%.[3]

10-3 Types of Graphic Aids

Using powerful software programs, managers can perform data management functions discussed in this chapter to produce highly professional graphics. The information can be reproduced in a variety of ways for integrating into reports and for supporting highly effective presentations.

Selecting the graphic type that will depict data in the most effective manner is the first decision you must make. After identifying the idea you want your receiver to understand, you can choose to use a table, bar chart, line chart, pie chart, flowchart, organization chart, photographs, models, and so on. Use Figure 10-1 on the next page to help you choose the graphic type that matches the objective you hope to achieve.

Figures 10-2 through 10-8 on the following pages illustrate a variety of graphics commonly used in reports. The figures show acceptable variations in graphic design, including placement of the caption (figure number and title), inclusion or exclusion of grid lines, proper labeling of the axes, proper referencing of the source of data, and other features. When designing graphics, adhere to the requirements in your company policy manual or the style manual you are instructed to follow. Then be certain that you design graphics for a particular document or presentation consistently. When preparing a graphic for a slide show or mounted chart, remove the figure number and include the title only.

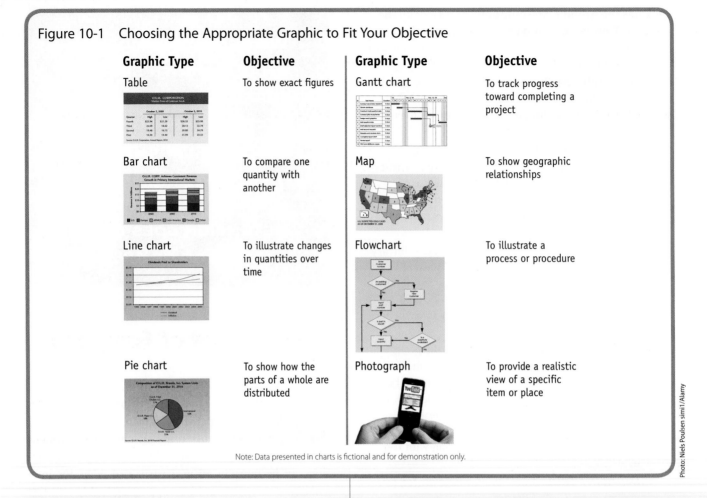

Figure 10-1   Choosing the Appropriate Graphic to Fit Your Objective

Graphic Type	Objective	Graphic Type	Objective
Table	To show exact figures	Gantt chart	To track progress toward completing a project
Bar chart	To compare one quantity with another	Map	To show geographic relationships
Line chart	To illustrate changes in quantities over time	Flowchart	To illustrate a process or procedure
Pie chart	To show how the parts of a whole are distributed	Photograph	To provide a realistic view of a specific item or place

Note: Data presented in charts is fictional and for demonstration only.

Photo: Niels Poulsen simi1/Alamy

10-3a **Tables**

A **table** presents data in columns and rows, which aid in clarifying large quantities of data in a small space. Proper labeling techniques make the content clear. Guidelines for preparing an effective table follow and are illustrated in Figure 10-2:

- **Number tables and all other graphics consecutively throughout the report.** This practice enables you to refer to "Figure 1" rather than to "the following table" or "the figure on the following page."

- **Give each table a title that is complete enough to clarify what is included without forcing the reader to review the table.** Table titles can be quite long as they can contain sources of data, numbers included in the table, and the subject, as shown in Figure 10-2. Titles should be written in either all capitals or upper and lower-case letters. Titles that extend beyond one line should be arranged on the page so that they are balanced.

table
a graphic that presents data in columns and rows, which aid in clarifying large quantities of data in a small space

bar chart
a graphic used to compare quantities

- **Label columns of data clearly enough to identify the items.** Usually, column headings are short and easily arranged. If, however, they happen to be lengthy, use some ingenuity in planning the arrangement.

- **Indent the second line of a label for the rows (horizontal items) two or three spaces.** Labels that are subdivisions of more comprehensive labels should be indented, as should summary labels such as "total."

- **Place a superscript symbol beside an entry that requires additional explanation, and include the explanatory note beneath the visual.**

- **Document the source of the data presented in a visual by adding a source note beneath the visual.** If more than one source was used to prepare a visual, use superscripts beside the various information references and provide the sources beneath the figure.

10-3b **Bar Charts**

A **bar chart** is an effective graphic for comparing quantities (see Figure 10-3 on page 174). The length of the bars, horizontal or vertical, indicates quantity.

Figure 10-2 Effective Table Layout, Identifying Information, Labels, and Source

A Summary of the Differences and Similarities Exhibited in Discourse Styles by the Three Leader Types

DISCOURSE ELEMENTS	DIRECTIVE LEADER	COOPERATIVE LEADER	COLLABORATIVE LEADER
Meaning of Questions	To direct members	To solicit participation	To frame the interaction and check for agreement
Links between Turns	Few	To acknowledge contribution	Some acknowledgment of contribution
Topic Shifts	Abrupt	Smooth	Smooth
Listening	Minimal	Active	Minimal
Simultaneous Speech	Interruptions	Few overlaps	Frequent cooperative overlaps

* Source: Walker, R., & Aritz, J. (In press). *Leadership Talk: A Discourse Approach to Leader Emergence.* New York, NY: Business Expert Press.

The vertical bars in Figure 10-3a (left) show changes in the number of subscribers to a popular mail movie-rental business. Because of the lengthy labels, horizontal bars are ideal for depicting the top objections to drinking water shown in Figure 10-3a (right). Variations of the simple bar chart make it useful for a variety of purposes:

- **Grouped bar charts** (also called *clustered bar charts*) are useful for comparing more than one quantity. Figure 10-3b shows changes in the average inflation-adjusted prices in three major housing markets.

- **Segmented bar charts** (also called *subdivided, stacked bar,* or *100% bar charts*) show how components contribute to a total figure. The segments in Figure 10-3c illustrate that sales outside of a company's three primary market areas (Japan, the United States, and Europe) are steadily becoming a large portion of the company's total sales.

- **Pictograms** use pictures or symbols to illustrate objects, concepts, or numerical values. A simple use of a pictogram is a picture of an envelope used to represent an email message. Pictograms are common in everyday life, such as on signs in public places or roads, whereas the term *icon* is specific to interfaces on computers or other electronic devices. An image of a house is used in Figure 10-3d to depict home sales in the United States over a 20-year period.

- The **Gantt chart**, another variation of the bar chart, is useful for tracking progress toward completing a series of events over time. The Gantt chart in Figure 10-3e, prepared using Microsoft Project, plots the output on the *y*-axis (activities involved in planning and implementing a research study) and the time (days planned to complete the activity) on the *x*-axis. This version of the Gantt chart not only schedules the important activities required to complete this research but also plots the *actual* progress of each activity along with the *planned* progress. Simple Gantt charts can be created using a spreadsheet program such as Microsoft Excel.

In addition to the suggestions for developing tables, here are further suggestions related to constructing bar charts:

- **Avoid visual distortion that could exaggerate the data.** Begin the quantitative axis at zero, divide the bars into equal increments, and use bars of equal width.

- **Position chronologically or in some other logical order.**

- **Use color to convey meaning.** For example, use variations in color to distinguish among the bars when the bars represent different data. Avoid large surfaces of bright colors that may be tiring to the audience and detract from the data.

- **Avoid fancy formatting such as 3D that makes values more difficult to distinguish.**

grouped bar chart
a graphic used for comparing more than one quantity (set of data) at each point along the *y*-axis (vertical) or *x*-axis (horizontal); also called a *clustered bar chart*

segmented bar chart
a graphic used to show how different facts (components) contribute to a total; also called a *subdivided, stacked bar,* or *100% bar chart*

pictogram
a graphic that uses pictures or symbols to illustrate objects, concepts, or numerical relationships

Gantt chart
a specific type of bar chart that is useful for tracking progress toward completing a series of events over time

Figure 10-3   Variety of Bar Chart Formats

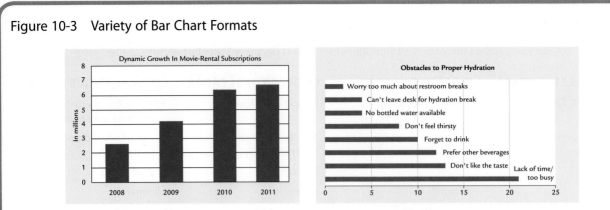

(a) Simple vertical bar chart with gridlines (left) and simple horizontal bar with data table and no gridlines (right)

(b) Grouped bar chart

(c) Segmented bar chart

(d) Pictograms: Poor example (left) and good example (right)

(e) Gantt chart

Note: Data presented in charts is fictional and for demonstration only.

Figure 10-4 Line Chart

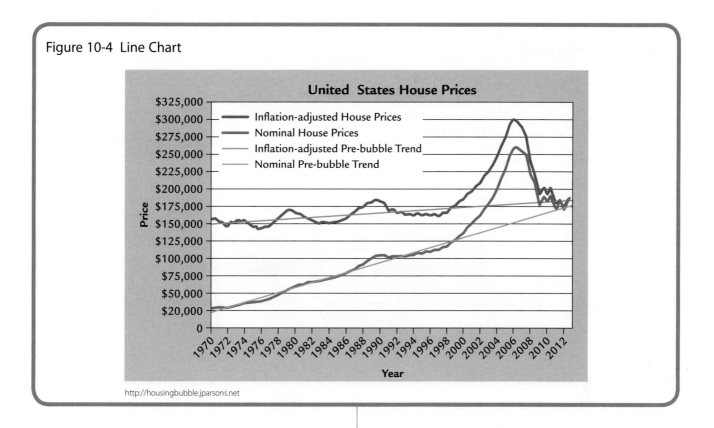

http://housingbubble.jparsons.net

- **Keep the labeling simple to reduce clutter and increase readability.** Exclude nonessential information such as data labels, gridlines, and explanatory notes if the meaning is understood. To determine labeling needs, consider the audience's use of the data. Omit actual amounts if a visual estimate is adequate for understanding the relationships presented in the chart. Include the data values above the bars or as a data table for an audience who expects specific data.

10-3c **Line Charts**

A **line chart** depicts changes in quantitative data over time and illustrates trends. The line chart shown in Figure 10-4 shows house prices in the United States from 1970 to 2012. When constructing line charts, keep these general guidelines in mind:

- **Use the vertical axis for amount and the horizontal axis for time.**
- **Begin the vertical axis at zero.**
- **Divide the vertical and horizontal scales into equal increments.** The vertical or quantity increments, however, need not be the same as the horizontal or time increments so that the line or lines drawn will have reasonable slopes. Unrealistic scales might produce startling slopes that could mislead readers.

An **area chart**, also called a *cumulative line chart* or a *surface chart*, is similar to a segmented bar chart because

it shows how different factors contribute to a total. An area chart is especially useful when you want to illustrate changes in components over time. For example, the area chart in Figure 10-5 illustrates the number of Olympic medals won by countries for all time. A reader can easily recognize the number of medals won by each country listed and how each compares. The cumulative total of medals is illustrated on the vertical axis of the chart. The amount of medals won by each country can be estimated by visual assessment.

10-3d **Pie Charts**

Pie charts, like segmented charts and area charts, show how the parts of a whole are distributed. Pie charts are effective for showing percentages (parts of a whole), but they are ineffective in showing quantitative totals or comparisons. Bars are used for those purposes. The pie chart in Figure 10-6 shows the percentage of taxable sales per county in North Carolina.

line chart
a graphic that depicts changes in quantitative data over time and illustrates trends

area chart
a graphic that shows how different factors contribute to a total; also referred to as a *cumulative line chart* or *surface chart*

pie chart
a graphic that shows how the parts of a whole are distributed

Figrue 10-5   Area Chart

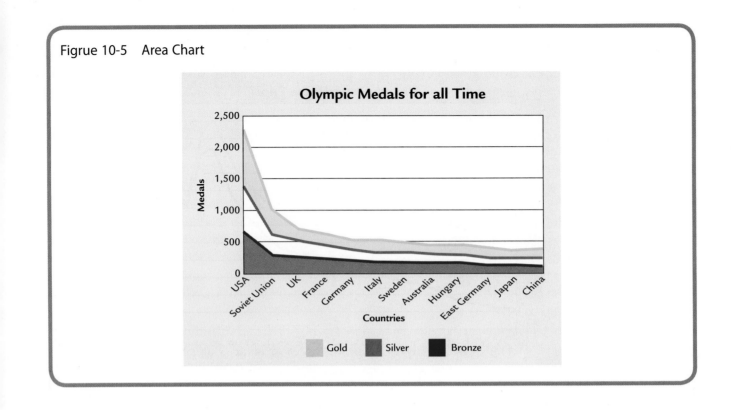

Olympic Medals for all Time

(Chart with y-axis labeled "Medals" ranging from 0 to 2,500; x-axis labeled "Countries" with USA, Soviet Union, UK, France, Germany, Italy, Sweden, Australia, Hungary, East Germany, Japan, China)

Legend: Gold, Silver, Bronze

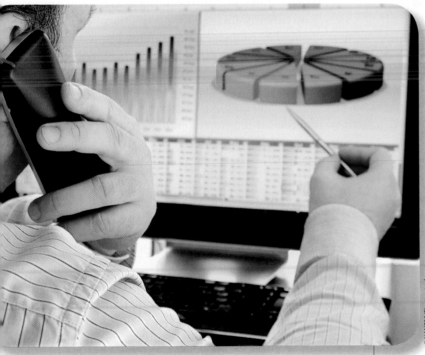

- **Label each slice and include information about the quantitative size (percentage, dollars, etc.) of each slice.** If you are unable to attractively place the appropriate labeling information beside each slice, use a legend to identify each slice.

- **Draw attention to one or more slices for desired emphasis.** Special effects include exploding the slice(s) to be emphasized (i.e. removing it from immediate contact with the pie) or displaying or printing only the slice(s) to be emphasized.

- **Avoid using 3D-type formatting that makes values more difficult to distinguish.**

Your software may limit your ability to follow rules explicitly, and the nature of the data or the presentation may require slight deviations. For example, if you intend to explode the largest pie slice, placing it in the 12 o'clock position may not be desirable because the slice is likely to intrude into the space occupied by a title positioned above the graphic.

10-3e Maps

A **map** shows geographic relationships. This graphic type is especially useful when a receiver may not be familiar with the geography discussed in a report. The

Here are some general guidelines for constructing pie charts:

- **Position the largest slice or the slice to be emphasized at the 12 o'clock position.** Working clockwise, place the other slices in descending order of size or some other logical order of presentation.

Figure 10-6 Pie Chart

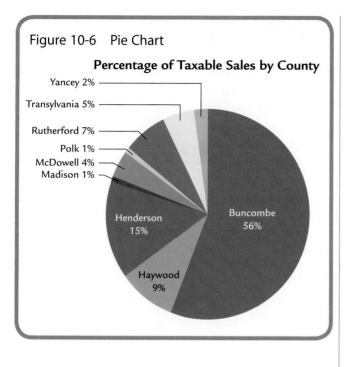

Percentage of Taxable Sales by County

- Yancey 2%
- Transylvania 5%
- Rutherford 7%
- Polk 1%
- McDowell 4%
- Madison 1%
- Henderson 15%
- Buncombe 56%
- Haywood 9%

map shown in Figure 10-7 shows the number of food animals by county in the United States. The map gives the information visually and thus eliminates the difficulty of explaining the information in words. In addition to being less confusing, a map is more concise and interesting than a written message.

map
a graphic that shows geographic relationships

flowchart
a step-by-step diagram of a procedure or a graphic depiction of a system or organization

10-3f Flowcharts

A **flowchart** is a step-by-step diagram of a procedure or a graphic depiction of a system or organization. A variety of problems can be resolved by using flowcharts to support written analyses. For example, most companies have procedure manuals to instruct employees

Figure 10-7 Map Conveying Statistical Data

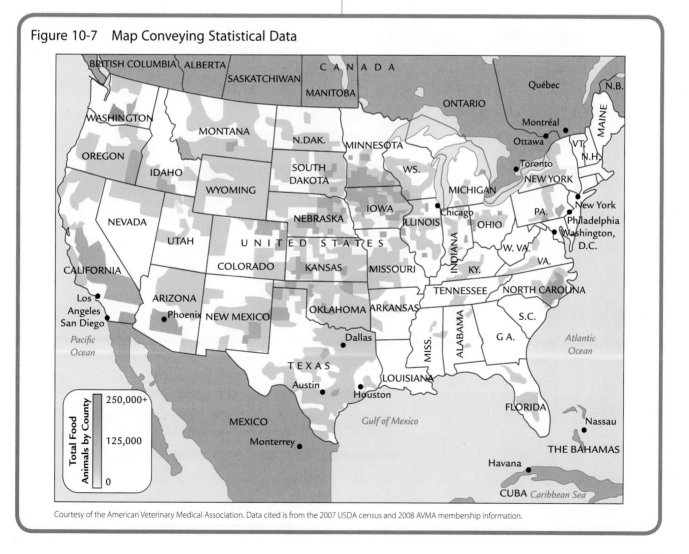

Courtesy of the American Veterinary Medical Association. Data cited is from the 2007 USDA census and 2008 AVMA membership information.

in certain work tasks. Including a flowchart with written instructions minimizes the chance of errors. The flowchart in Figure 10-8 illustrates the procedures for a guided brainstorming process in a series of simple steps. If this information had been presented only in a series of written steps, rely not only on the user's reading ability but also on his or her willingness to study the written procedures.

Organization charts, discussed in Chapter 1, are widely used to provide a picture of the authority structure and relationships within an organization. They provide employees with an idea of what their organization looks like in terms of the flow of authority and responsibility. When businesses change (because of new employees or reorganization of units and responsibilities), organization charts must be revised. Revisions to organizational charts are simple when prepared using word processing or graphics software.

10-3g Other Graphics

Other graphics, such as architectural plans, photographs, cartoons, blueprints, and lists of various kinds, may be included in reports. The availability of graphics

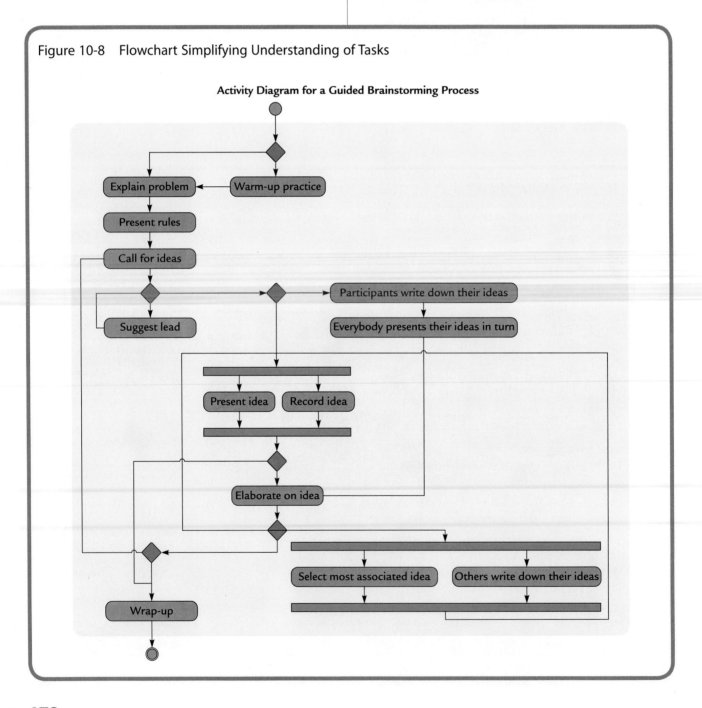

Figure 10-8   Flowchart Simplifying Understanding of Tasks

Activity Diagram for a Guided Brainstorming Process

Introducing Graphics in Text

The pattern for incorporating graphics in text is (1) introduce, (2) show, and (3) interpret. and analyze. The following range of examples, from poor to best, explain how to introduce graphic and tabular material.

		Example	Rationale
X	**Poor:**	Figure 1 shows preferences for shopping locations.	Poor because it tells the reader nothing more than would the title of the figure.
✓	**Acceptable:**	About two-thirds of the consumers preferred to shop in suburban areas rather than in the city (see Figure 1).	Acceptable because it interprets the data, but it places the figure reference in parentheses rather than integrating it into the sentence.
✓+	**Better:**	As shown in Figure 1, about two-thirds of the consumers preferred to shop in suburban areas rather than in the city.	Better than the previous examples but puts reference to the figure at the beginning, thus detracting from the interpretation of the data.
✓++	**Best:**	About two-thirds of the consumers preferred to shop in suburban areas rather than in the city, as shown in Figure 1.	Best for introducing figures because it talks about the graphic and also includes introductory phrasing, but only after stressing the main point.

and sophisticated drawing software facilitate inclusion of these more complex visuals in reports and spoken presentations. Photographs are used frequently in annual reports to help the general audience understand complex concepts and to make the documents more appealing to read. Frequently, you must include some graphic material in a report that would make the narrative discussion otherwise unwieldy. In this case, the material might be placed in an appendix and only referred to in the report.

10-4 Including Graphics in Text

Text and graphics are partners in the communication process. If graphics appear before readers have been informed, they will begin to study the graphics and draw their own inferences and conclusions. For this reason, always introduce a graphic in the text immediately before the graphic appears. A graphic that follows an introduction and brief explanation will supplement what has been said in the report. Additional interpretation and needed analysis should follow the graphic.

10-4a Positioning Graphics in Text

Ideally, a graphic should be integrated within the text material immediately after its introduction. A graphic that will not fit on the page where it is introduced should appear at the top of the following page. The previous page is filled with text that would have ideally

followed the graphic. In this chapter, figures are placed as closely as possible to their introductions in accordance with these suggestions. However, in some cases, several figures may be introduced on one page, making perfect placement difficult and sometimes impossible.

When interpreting and analyzing the graphic, avoid a mere restatement of what the graphic obviously shows. Instead, emphasize the main point you are making. Contrast the boring style of the following discussion of graphic data with the improved revision:

Obvious Restatement of Data:	When asked to identify the causes of ineffective meetings, 10% of employees blamed poor communication skills, 8% cited egocentric behavior by attendees, 7% attributed nonparticipation, and 6.5% said the discussion became sidetracked.
Emphasis on Main Point:	The most cited reason for ineffective meetings is poor communication skills, while issues related to poor interpersonal communication skills were also blamed.

Your analysis may include summary statements about the data, compare information in the figure to information obtained from other sources, or extend the shown data into reasonably supported speculative outcomes. Strive to transition naturally from the discussion of the graphic into the next point you wish to make.

CONSISTENCY COUNTS

Throughout the discussion of tables and graphs, the term *graphics* has been used to include all illustrations. Although your report may include tables, graphs, maps, and even photographs, you will find organizing easier and writing about the illustrations more effective if you label each item as a "Figure" followed by a number; then number the items consecutively.

Some report writers prefer to label tables consecutively as "Table 1," and so on, and graphs and charts consecutively in another sequence as "Graph 1," and so on. When this dual numbering system is used, readers of the report may become confused if they come upon a sentence that reads, "Evidence presented in Tables 3 and 4 and Graph 2 supports. . . ." Both writers and readers appreciate the single numbering system, which makes the sentence read, "Evidence presented in Figures 3, 4, and 5 supports. . . ."

STUDY TOOLS
CHAPTER 10

Located at back of the textbook

❏ Rip out Chapter Review Card

Located at www.cengagebrain.com

❏ Review Key Terms Flashcards (Print or Online)

❏ Download Audio Summaries for on-the-go review

❏ Complete Practice Quizzes to prepare for tests

❏ Play "Beat the Clock" to master concepts

❏ Complete the Crossword Puzzle to review key terms

❏ Watch the video about McDonaldson, a fictitious but all-too-realistic ad agency whose employees struggle with contemporary business communication issues.

4LTR Press solutions are designed for today's learners through the continuous feedback of students like you. Tell us what you think about BCOM6 and help us improve the learning experience for future students.

YOUR FEEDBACK MATTERS.

Organizing and Preparing Reports and Proposals

11-1 Parts of a Formal Report

Reports serve a variety of purposes; the type of report you prepare depends on the subject matter, the purpose of the report, and the readers' needs. The differences between a formal report and an informal report lie in the format and possibly in the writing style. At the short, informal end of the report continuum described in Chapter 9, a report could look exactly like a brief memorandum. At the long, formal extreme of the continuum, the report might include most or all of the parts shown in Figure 11-1 on page 184.

A business report rarely contains all of the parts shown but may include any combination of them. The preliminary parts and addenda are organizational items that support the body of a report. The body contains the report of the research and covers the four steps in the research process. The organization of the body of a report leads to the construction of the contents page.

Because individuals usually write to affect or influence others favorably, they often add report parts as the number of pages increases. When a report exceeds one or two pages, you might add a cover or title page. When the body of a report exceeds four or five pages, you might even add a finishing touch by placing the report in a binder or binding it in a professional manner. Reports frequently take on the characteristics of the formal end of the continuum simply by reason of length. First, note how the preliminary parts and addenda items shown in Figure 11-2 on page 185 increase in number as the report increases in length. Second, notice the order in which report parts appear in a complete report and the distribution of reports in print and electronic forms.

Memo and letter reports are often one page in length, but they can be expanded into several pages. As depicted, long reports may include some special pages that do not appear in short reports. The format you select—long or short, formal or informal—may help determine the supporting preliminary and addenda items to include.

To understand how each part of a formal report contributes to reader comprehension and ease of access to the information in the report, study the following explanations of each part shown in Figure 11-1. The three basic sections—preliminary parts, report text, and addenda—are combined to prepare a complete formal report.

11-1a Preliminary Parts of a Report

Preliminary parts are included to add formality to a report, emphasize report content, and aid the reader in locating information in the report quickly and in understanding the report more easily. These parts might include a half-title page, title page, authorization, transmittal, table of contents, table of figures, and executive summary. The most frequently used preliminary parts are described here.

Title Page

The title page includes the title, author, date, and often the name of the person or organization who requested the report. A title page is often added when opting for a formal report format rather than a memorandum or letter arrangement.

preliminary parts
report sections included to add formality to a report, emphasize report content, and aid the reader in locating information in the report quickly and in understanding the report more easily

Log onto www.cengagebrain.com for additional resources, including flashcards, games, self-quizzing for chapter review, grammar exercises, and more.

BCOM

Figure 11-1 Parts of a Formal Report: Preliminary Parts, Report Text, and Addenda

PRELIMINARY PARTS

Half-title page (Title Fly)	Title page	Authorization	Transmittal	Table of contents	Table of figures	Executive summary
Contains report title; adds formality.	Includes title, author, and date; adds formality.	Provides written authorization to complete report.	Presents report to reader and summarizes main points or analysis.	Provides overview of report and order in which information will be presented; contains headings and page numbers.	Includes number, title, and page number of tables and graphics.	Summarizes essential elements in report.

REPORT TEXT

Introduction	Body	Analysis
Orients reader to topic and previews major divisions.	Presents information collected.	Reviews main points presented in body and may include conclusions and recommendations.

ADDENDA

References	Appendix	Index
Includes alphabetical list of sources used in preparing report.	Contains supplementary information that supports report, but placing this information in report would make report bulky and unmanageable.	Includes alphabetical guide to subjects in report.

The selected title should be descriptive and comprehensive; its words should reflect the content of the report. Avoid short, vague titles or excessively long titles. Instead, use concise wording to identify the topic adequately. For example, a title such as "Marketing Survey: Internet Providers" leaves the reader confused when the title could have been "Internet Provider Preferences of Residents of St. Louis." To give some clues for writing a descriptive title, think of the "Five Ws": *Who*, *What*, *When*, *Where*, and *Why*. Avoid such phrases as "A Study of …," "A Critical Analysis of …," or "A Review of …".

Follow company procedures or a style manual to place the title attractively on the page. Arrange the title consistently on the half-title page, title page, and the first page of a report.

Table of Contents

The table of contents provides the reader with an analytical overview of the report and the order in which information is presented. Thus this preliminary part aids the reader in understanding the report and in locating a specific section of it. The list includes the name and location (beginning page number) of every report part except those that precede the contents page. Include the list of figures and the transmittal, executive summary, report headings, references, appendices, and index. Placing spaced periods (leaders) between the report part and the page numbers helps lead the reader's eyes to the appropriate page number.

Word-processing software simplifies the time-consuming, tedious task of preparing many of the preliminary and addenda report parts, including the table of contents. Because the software can generate these parts automatically, report writers can make last-minute changes to a report with updated preliminary and addenda parts.

Table of Figures

To aid the reader in locating a specific graphic in a report with many graphics, the writer might include a list of figures separate from the contents. The list should include a reference to each figure that appears in the report, identified by both figure number and name, along with the page number on which the figure

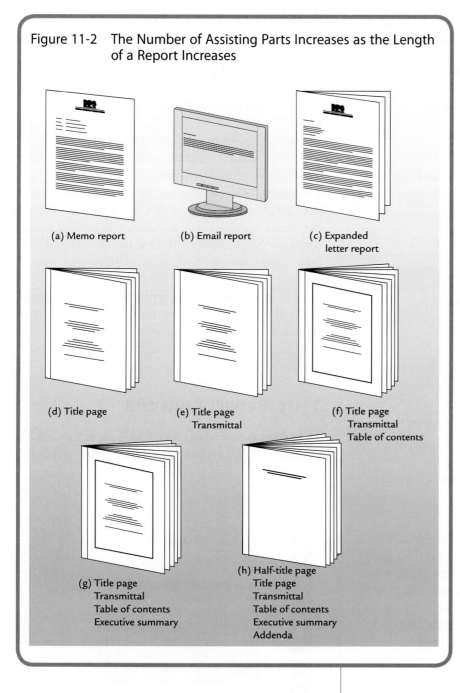

Figure 11-2   The Number of Assisting Parts Increases as the Length of a Report Increases

(a) Memo report

(b) Email report

(c) Expanded letter report

(d) Title page

(e) Title page
Transmittal

(f) Title page
Transmittal
Table of contents

(g) Title page
Transmittal
Table of contents
Executive summary

(h) Half-title page
Title page
Transmittal
Table of contents
Executive summary
Addenda

Typically, an executive summary is included to assist the reader in understanding a long, complex report. Because of the increased volume of information that managers must review, some managers require an executive summary regardless of the length and complexity of a report. The executive summary presents the report in miniature: the introduction, body, and summary as well as any conclusions and recommendations. Thus an executive summary should (1) introduce briefly the report and preview the major divisions, (2) summarize the major sections of the report, and (3) summarize the report summary and any conclusions and recommendations. Pay special attention to topic sentences and to concluding sentences in paragraphs or within sections of reports. This technique helps you write concise executive summaries based on major ideas and reduces the use of supporting details and background information.

To assist them in staying up-to-date professionally, busy executives frequently request assistants to prepare executive summaries of articles they do not have time to read and conferences and meetings they cannot attend. Many practitioner journals include an executive summary (abstract) of each article. The executive summary provides the gist of the article and alerts the executive to articles that should be read in detail. The executive summary is prepared with the needs of specific executive readers in mind. For instance, a technically oriented executive may require more detail, whereas a strategist may require more analysis. An executive summary should "boil down" a report to its barest essentials without making the overview

occurs. The contents and the figures can be combined on one page if both lists are brief. Word-processing software can be used to automatically generate the list of figures.

Executive Summary

The **executive summary** (also called the *abstract*, *overview*, or *précis*) summarizes the essential elements in an entire report. This overview simplifies the reader's understanding of a long report and is positioned before the first page of the report.

executive summary
short summary of the essential elements in an entire report; also called an *abstract, overview,* or *précis*

meaningless. Top executives should be able to glean enough information and understanding to feel confident making a decision.

Preliminary pages are numbered with small Roman numerals (i, ii, iii, etc.). Figure 11-1 provides more information about the purpose of each preliminary part.

11-1b Report Text

The report itself contains the introduction, body, summary, and any conclusions and recommendations. Report pages are numbered with Arabic numerals (1, 2, 3, etc.).

Introduction

The introduction orients the reader to the problem. It may include the following information:

- what the topic is
- why it is being reported on
- the scope and limitations of the research
- where the information came from
- an explanation of special terminology
- a preview of the major sections of the report to provide coherence and transitions:
  - how the topic is divided into parts
  - the order in which the parts will be presented

Body

The body, often called the heart of the report, presents the information collected and relates it to the problem. To increase readability and coherence, this section contains numerous headings to denote the various divisions within a report. Refer to the section titled "Organization of Formal Reports" in this chapter for an in-depth discussion of preparing the body.

Analysis

A good report ends with an analysis of what the reported information means or how it should be acted upon. An informational report ends with a brief summary that adds unity to a report by reviewing the main points presented in the body. A summary includes only material that is discussed in a report. Introducing a new idea in the summary may

suggest that the study was not completed adequately or that the writer did not plan the report well before beginning to write.

An **analytical report** is designed to solve a specific problem or answer research questions. It will end with an "analysis," which may include a summary of the major research findings, particularly if the report is lengthy. Reviewing the major findings prepares the reader for the conclusions, which are inferences the writer draws from the findings. If required by the person/organization authorizing the report, recommendations follow the conclusions. Recommendations present the writer's opinion on a possible course of action based on the conclusions. Review the examples of findings, conclusions, and recommendations presented in Chapter 9.

For a long report, the writer may place the summary, the conclusions, and the recommendations in three separate sections or in one section referred to as *analysis*. For shorter reports, all three sections are often combined.

11-1c Report Addenda

The **addenda** to a report may include materials used in the research that are not appropriate to be included in

analytical report
a type of report designed to solve a specific problem or answer research questions

addenda
may include all materials used in the research but not appropriate to be included in the report itself

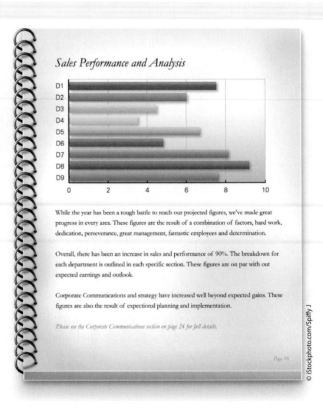

Sales Performance and Analysis

While the year has been a tough battle to reach our projected figures, we've made great progress in every area. These figures are the result of a combination of factors, hard work, dedication, perseverance, great management, fantastic employees and determination.

Overall, there has been an increase in sales and performance of 90%. The breakdown for each department is outlined in each specific section. These figures are on par with out expected earnings and outlook.

Corporate Communications and strategy have increased well beyond expected gains. These figures are also the result of expectional planning and implementation.

Please see the Corporate Communications section on page 24 for full details.

© iStockphoto.com/Spiffy J

the report itself. The three basic addenda parts are the references, appendices, and index. Addenda parts continue with the same page numbering system used in the body of the report.

References

The references (also called *works cited* or *bibliography*) section is an alphabetical listing of the sources used in preparing the report. Because the writer may be influenced by any information consulted, some reference manuals require all sources consulted to be included in the reference list. When the reference list includes sources not cited in the report, it is referred to as a *bibliography* or a list of *works consulted*. If a report includes endnotes rather than in-text parenthetical citations (author and date within the text), the endnotes precede the references. Using word-processing software to create footnotes and endnotes reduces much of the effort of preparing accurate documentation.

Appendix

An appendix contains supplementary information that supports the report but is not appropriate for inclusion in the report itself. This information may include questionnaires and accompanying transmittal letters, summary tabulations, verbatim comments from respondents, complex mathematical computations and formulas, legal documents, and a variety of items the writer presents to support the body of the report and the quality of the research. Placing supplementary material in an appendix helps prevent the report body from becoming excessively long.

If the report contains more than one appendix, label each with a capital letter and a title. For example, the two appendices (or appendixes) in a report could be identified as follows:

Appendix A: Employee Benefits Survey

Appendix B: Results of Employee Benefits Survey

Each item included in the appendix must be mentioned in the report. A reference within the report to the two appendices mentioned in the previous example might appear as follows:

The survey (Appendix A) was distributed to employees on May 4, 2014. The tabulated results (Appendix B) were delivered to management on June 1.

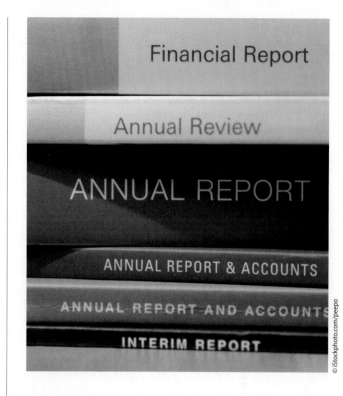

©iStockphoto.com/peepo

Index

The index is an alphabetical guide to the subject matter in a report. The subject and each page number on which the subject appears are listed. Word-processing software can generate the index automatically. Each time a new draft is prepared, a new index with revised terms and correct page numbers can be generated quickly and easily.

11-2 Organization of Formal Reports

The authors of certain types of publications known as tabloids typically have no valid documentation to support their claims, so they make up their own support. Hopefully, absolutely no one believes them. The purpose of such publications is to entertain, not to inform. The writer of a bona fide report, however, must do a much more convincing and thorough job of reporting.

11-2a Writing Convincing and Effective Reports

As discussed in Chapter 9, reports often require you to conduct research to find quotes, statistics, or ideas from others to back up the ideas presented. This support from outside sources serves to bolster the research as well as your credibility. Doing research and taking notes, however, are only parts of the process of putting together a well-documented, acceptable report. Careful organization and formatting ensure that the reader will understand and comprehend the information presented. While many companies have their own style manuals that give examples of acceptable formats for reports, this section presents some general organization guidelines.

Outlining and Sequencing

The content outline serves as a framework on which to build the report. In the development of the outline, the writer identifies the major and minor points that are to be covered and organizes them into a logical sequence. Outlining is an essential prerequisite to writing the report. The outline is a planning document and is thus subject to modification as the writer develops the report.

Developing an outline requires the writer to think about the information to be presented and how it can best be organized for the clear understanding of the reader. Assume, for instance, your firm must decide whether to develop its own wellness program or contract with an outside provider. You need to research the steps and costs associated with developing your own program and compare them to the cost and benefits of a packaged service. Your analysis along with your reasons and recommendations will be delivered in a **justification report**.

You gather all available information about wellness programs and wellness program providers and compare the two against a list of criteria created by management. Your final selection is to contract with a program provider. Why did you select it? What criteria served as decision guides? When you write the report, you will have to tell the reader—the one who will pay for the provider—how the selection was made so that he or she is "sold" on your conclusion.

If you organize your report so that you tell the reader everything about the two options—in-house program versus outside

justification report
a report that outlines comparative information clearly to the reader; used commonly when comparing items for purchase

© hfng/Shutterstock.com

provider—each in a separate section, the reader may have trouble making comparisons. Your content outline might look like this:

I. **Introduction**
    A. **The Problem**
    B. **The Method Used**
II. **In-house Program**
III. **Outside Provider**
IV. **Conclusion**

Note that this outline devotes two Roman numeral sections to the findings, one to the introduction that presents the problem and the method, and one to the conclusion. This division is appropriate because the most space must be devoted to the findings. However, the reader may have difficulty comparing the two options because the information is in two different places. Would discussing the differences in the options in the same section of the report be better? Would costs be compared more easily if they were all in the same section? Most reports should be divided into sections that reflect the criteria used rather than into sections devoted to the alternatives compared.

If you selected your service based on cost, quality, services available, and time to implement, these criteria rather than the wellness options themselves might serve as divisions of the findings. Then your content outline would appear this way:

I. **Introduction**
    A. **The Problem**
    B. **The Methods Used**
II. **Product Comparison**
    A. **Outside Provider Is Least Expensive**
    B. **Outside Provider Is Higher Quality**
    C. **Outside Provider Offers More Services**
    D. **Outside Provider Offers Faster Implementation**
III. **Conclusion: Outside Provider Is the Best Choice**

The outline now has three major sections, with the product comparison consisting of four subsections. When the report is prepared in this way, the features of each wellness approach (the evaluation criteria) are compared in the same section, and the reader is led logically to the conclusion.

Note the headings used in Sections II and III. These are called *talking headings* because they talk about the content of the section and even give a conclusion about the section. Adding page numbers after each outline item will convert the outline into a contents page. Interestingly, the headings justify the selection of an outside provider. As a result, a knowledgeable reader who has confidence in the researcher might be satisfied by reading only the content headings.

In addition to organizing findings for analytical reports by criteria, report writers can also use other organizational plans. When a report is informational and not analytical, you should use the most logical organization. A report on sales might be divided by geographic sales region, by product groups sold, by price range, or by time periods. A report on the development of a product might use chronological order. By visualizing the whole report first, you can then divide it into its major components and perhaps divide the major components into their parts.

When developing content outlines, some report writers believe that readers expect the beginning of the body to be an introduction, so they begin the outline with the first heading related to findings. In our example then, Section I would be "Product Comparison." Additionally, when they reach the contents page, readers may eliminate the Roman numeral or other outline symbols.

The research process consists of inductively arranged steps as shown in Figure 11-3: (1) Problem, (2) Method, (3) Findings, and

A FINAL CAUTION: BEWARE OF OVER-DIVIDING THE SECTIONS. TOO MANY DIVISIONS MIGHT MAKE THE REPORT APPEAR DISORGANIZED AND CHOPPY. ON THE OTHER HAND, TOO FEW DIVISIONS MIGHT CLOUD UNDERSTANDING FOR THE READER.

(4) Conclusion. Note how the four steps of research have been developed through headings in the Roman numeral outline and in a contents page for a report. When the report is organized in the same order, its users must read through the body to learn about the conclusions—generally the most important part of the report to users. To make the reader's job easier, report writers may organize the report deductively, with the conclusions at the beginning. This sequence is usually achieved by placing a synopsis or summary at the beginning:

I. **Conclusion Reported in the Synopsis**
II. **Body of the Report**
  A. **Problem**
  B. **Method**
  C. **Findings**
III. **Conclusion**

Figure 11-3   The Basic Outline Expands into a Contents Page

Problem
Method
Findings
Conclusion

CONTENTS

This arrangement permits the reader to get the primary message early and then to look for support in the body of the report. The deductive arrangement contributes to the repetitious nature of reports, but it also facilitates understanding.

Using Headings Effectively

Headings are signposts informing readers about what text is ahead. Headings take their positions from their relative importance in a complete outline. For example, in a Roman numeral outline, "I" is a first-level heading, "A" is a second-level heading, and "1" is a third-level heading:

I. **First-Level Heading**
    A. **Second-Level Heading**
    B. **Second-Level Heading**
        1. **Third-Level Heading**
        2. **Third-Level Heading**
II. **First-Level Heading**

Two important points about the use of headings also relate to outlines:

- **Because second-level headings are subdivisions of first-level headings, you should have at least two subdivisions (A and B).** Otherwise, the first-level heading cannot be divided—something divides into at least two parts or it is not divisible. Thus in an outline, you must have a "B" subsection if you have an "A" subsection following a Roman numeral, or you should have no subsections. The same logic applies to the use of third-level headings following second-level headings.

- **All headings of the same level must be treated consistently.** Consistent elements include the physical position on the page, appearance (type style, underline), and grammatical construction. For instance, if Point A is worded as a noun phrase, Point B should be worded in the same manner. Or if Point I is a complete sentence, Points II and III should also be worded as sentences.

The method illustrated in Figure 11-3 is typical but not universal. Always identify the format specified by the documentation style you are using and follow it consistently. Develop fourth- and fifth-level headings simply by using boldface, underline, and varying fonts. In short reports, however, organization rarely goes beyond third-level headings; thoughtful organization can limit excessive heading levels in formal reports.

11-3 Choosing a Writing Style for Formal Reports

As you might expect, the writing style of long, formal reports is more formal than that used in many other routine business documents. The following suggestions should be applied when writing a formal report:

- **Avoid first-person pronouns as a rule.** In formal reports, the use of *I* is generally unacceptable. Because of the objective nature of research, the fewer personal references you use the better. However, in some organizations the first person is acceptable. Certainly, writing is easier when you can use yourself as the subject of sentences.

- **Use active voice.** "Acceptance was received from the seller" might not be as effective as "The seller accepted the offer." Subjects that can be visualized are advantageous, but you should also attempt to use the things most important to the report as subjects. If "acceptance" were more important than "buyer," the writer should stay with the first version.

- **Use tense consistently.** Because you are writing about past actions, much of your report writing is in the past tense. However, when you call the reader's attention to the content of a graphic, remember that the graphic *shows* in the present tense, and use the future-tense verb if you want to mention that the study *will convince* the reader.

- **Avoid placing two headings consecutively without any intervening text.** For example, always write something following a first-level heading and before the initial second-level heading.

- **Use transition sentences to link sections of a report.** Because you are writing a report in parts, show the connection between those parts by using transition sentences. "Although some customers may like the new sales program, many will not like the changes" may be a sentence written at the end of a section stressing advantages and before a section stressing problems.

- **Use a variety of coherence techniques.** Just as transition sentences bind portions of a report together, certain coherence techniques bind sentences together: repeating a word, using a pronoun, or using a conjunction. If such devices are used, each sentence seems to be joined smoothly to the next. The following words and phrases keep you from making abrupt changes in thought:

Time Connectors	Contrast Connectors
at the same time	although
finally	despite
further	however
initially	in contrast
next	nevertheless
since	on the contrary
then	on the other hand
while	yet

Similarity Connectors	Cause-and-Effect Connectors
for instance/example	alternately
in the same way	because
just as	but
likewise	consequently
similarly	hence
thus	therefore

Other ways to improve transition include the following:

- **Use tabulations and enumerations.** When you have a series of items, bullet them or give each a number and list them consecutively. This list of writing suggestions is easier to understand because it contains bulleted items.

- **Define terms carefully.** When terms are not widely understood or have specific meanings in the study, define them. Definitions should be written in the term-family-differentiation sequence: "A dictionary (*term*) is a reference book (*family*) that contains a list of all words in a language (*point of difference*)." "A sophomore is a college student in the second year."

- **Check for variety.** In your first-draft stage, most of your attention should be directed toward presenting the right ideas and support. When reviewing the rough draft, you may discover certain portions with a monotonous sameness in sentence length or construction. Changes and improvements in writing style at this stage are easy and well worth the effort.

11-3a Enhancing Credibility

Readers are more likely to accept your research as valid and reliable if you have designed the research effectively and collected, interpreted, and presented the

Susan van Etten

The Annual Report. Of all the documents corporations publish, none receives as much attention as the annual report. Offering a valuable glimpse into the workings and financial performance of companies, these annual scorecards guide investors' decisions.

In addition to projecting profitability, many U.S. firms see the annual report as a vehicle for illuminating prevailing management philosophy, projecting corporate charisma, and humanizing themselves to the public.

data in an objective, unbiased manner. The following writing suggestions will enhance your credibility as a researcher:

- **Avoid emotional terms.** "The program was fantastic" doesn't convince anyone. However, "The program saw an increase of 18% over that of the previous year" does convince.

- **Identify assumptions.** Assumptions are things or conditions that are taken for granted. However, when you make an assumption, state that clearly. Statements such as, "Assuming all other factors remain the same …," inform the reader of important assumptions.

- **Label opinions.** Facts are preferred over opinion, but sometimes the opinion of a recognized professional is the closest thing to fact. "In the opinion of legal counsel …," lends conviction to the statement that follows and lends credence to the integrity of the writer.

- **Use documentation.** Citations and references (works cited) are evidence of the writer's scholarship and honesty. These methods acknowledge the use of secondary material in the research.

11-4 Short Reports

Short reports incorporate many of the same organizational strategies as long reports. However, most **short reports** include only the minimum supporting materials to achieve effective communication. Short reports focus on the body—problem, method, findings, and conclusion. In addition, short reports might incorporate any of the following features:

- personal writing style using first or second person
- contractions when they contribute to a natural style
- graphics to reinforce the written text
- headings and subheadings to partition portions of the body and to reflect organization
- memorandum, email, and letter formats when appropriate

11-4a Memorandum, Email, and Letter Reports

Short reports are often written in memorandum, email, or letter format. The memorandum report is directed to an organizational insider, as are most email reports. The letter report is directed to a reader outside the organization. Short reports to internal and external readers are illustrated in Figure 11-4 on the next page and Figure 11-5 on pages 194–195. The commentary in the right column will help you understand how effective writing principles are applied.

The memo report in Figure 11-4 communicates a weekly call log of a telephone sales department. The periodic report is formatted as a memorandum because it is prepared for personnel within the company and is a brief, informal report. An outside auditing firm presents an audit of a company's accounting department in the short report in Figure 11-5. A concise, professional email will serve as a transmittal for this one-page report sent to the client as an email attachment.

The report in Figure 11-6 on pages 196–199 is written deductively. Implementation of global virtual teams is described in an expanded letter report written by a consultant to a client (external audience). The consultant briefly describes the procedures used to analyze the problem, presents the findings in a logical sequence, and provides specific recommendations.

11-4b Form Reports

Form reports meet the demand for numerous, repetitive reports. College registration forms, applications for credit, airline tickets, and bank checks are examples of simple form reports. Form reports have the following benefits:

- When designed properly, form reports increase clerical accuracy by providing designated places for specific items.
- Forms save time by telling the preparer where to put each item and by preprinting common elements to eliminate the need for narrative writing.
- In addition to their advantages of accuracy and saving time, forms make tabulation of data relatively simple. The value of the form is uniformity.

Most form reports, such as a bank teller's cash sheet, are informational. At the end of the teller's work period, cash is counted and totals are entered in designated blanks. Cash reports from all tellers are then totaled to arrive at period totals and perhaps to be verified by computer records.

In addition to their informational purpose, form reports assist in analytical work. A residential appraisal report assists real estate appraisers in analyzing real property. With this information, the appraiser is able to determine the market value of a specific piece of property.

Many form reports are computer generated. For example, an automated hospital admission process expedites the repetitive patient reports that must be created. The admission clerk inputs the patient information using the carefully designed input screen. If the patient has been admitted previously, the patient's name, address, and telephone number are displayed automatically for the clerk to verify. When the clerk inputs the patient's date of birth, the computer calculates the patient's age, eliminating the need to ask a potentially sensitive question and ensuring accuracy when patients cannot remember their ages. All data are stored in a computer file and retrieved as needed to generate numerous reports required during a patient's stay, such as the admissions summary sheet, admissions report,

short reports
reports that include only the minimum supporting materials to achieve effective communication

form reports
reports that meet the demand for numerous, repetitive reports; include college registration forms, applications for credit, airline tickets, and bank checks

Figure 11-4   Short, Periodic Report in Memorandum Format

TO: Sally Landers, President
FROM: Denny Williams, Sales Manager
DATE: April 13, 2014
SUBJECT: Weekly Call Report

The call log for the week beginning April 7, 2014, shows that sales remained on track for the year with projected sales revenue for the week at $25,133. The week's number of calls and number of sales by salesperson is shown in the table below along with each person's average sales per week for the year.

Salesperson	Number of Calls	Number of Sales	Average Weekly Sales
Jackson	149	15	15
Tilly	138	14	12
Juarez	135	12	13
Smith	127	10	11
Lee	123	10	12

This week, we continued a promotion that gave subscribers six months of service at 50% off the regular price. This promotion has been in effect for two weeks. Although it may be too soon to judge, it does not appear that the promotion is having a significant effect in terms of increasing sales, as can be seen by the figures shown in the "Average Weekly Sales" column of the table.

We continue to employ five full-time salespeople. Current staffing levels are sufficient for the current sales volume.

We are continuing to look at ways that we might increase our marketing presence in the region. One suggestion offered by Dan Smith, one of our full-time salespersons, is to purchase pop-up advertising on a popular entertainment Web site, offering our 50% off promotion. Advertising costs have been a concern for the company, but I believe that the cost of pop-up advertising is significantly lower than that of traditional methods. Perhaps this is a topic we might add to our agenda for next week's planning meetings.

Attachment

Includes headings to serve formal report functions of transmittal and title page.

Uses deductive approach to present periodic report requested by management on weekly basis.

Uses table to highlight standard information; allows for easy update when preparing subsequent report.

Includes suggestion for improving marketing and sales.

Attaches information page that would be appendix item in a formal report.

Format Pointer
Uses memorandum format for brief periodic report prepared for personnel within company.

Figure 11-5   Audit Report in Short Report Format, Page 1

We have audited the financial statements of Global Equities Limited for the year ended 2014, which comprise the Profit and Loss Account, the Balance Sheet, the Statement of Total Recognized Gains and Losses, and the related notes.

This report is made solely to the company's members as a body in accordance with the requirements of the Companies Acts 1983 to 2012. Our audit work has been undertaken so that we might state to the company's members those matters that we are required to state to them in the audit report and for no other purpose. To the fullest extent permitted by law, we do not accept or assume responsibility to anyone other than the company or the company's members as a body for our audit work, for this report, or for the opinions we have formed.

RESPECTIVE RESPONSIBILITIES OF DIRECTORS AND AUDITORS
As described in the Statement of Directors' Responsibilities, the company's directors are responsible for the preparation of the financial statements in accordance with applicable law and the accounting standards issued by the Accounting Standards Board.

Our responsibility is to audit the financial statements in accordance with relevant legal and regulatory requirements and International Standards on Auditing.

We report to you our opinion as to whether the financial statements give a true and fair view in accordance with Generally Accepted Accounting Practice and are properly prepared in accordance with the Companies Acts 1983 to 2012. We also report to you whether in our opinion proper books of account have been kept by the company; whether, at the balance sheet date, there exists a financial situation requiring the convening of an extraordinary general meeting of the company; and whether the information given in the Directors' Report is consistent with the financial statements. In addition, we state whether we have obtained all the information and explanations necessary for the purposes of our audit and whether the company's Balance Sheet and its Profit and Loss Account are in agreement with the books of account.

We report to the shareholders if, in our opinion, any information specified by law regarding directors' remuneration and directors' transactions is not disclosed, and where practicable, include such information in our report.

We read the Directors' Report and consider the implications for our report if we become aware of any apparent misstatement within it.

BASIS OF AUDIT OPINION
We conducted our audit in accordance with International Standards on Auditing issued by the Auditing Practices Board. An audit includes examination, on a test basis, of evidence relevant to the amounts and disclosures in the financial statements. It also includes an assessment of the significant estimates and judgments made by the directors in the preparation of the financial statements, and of whether the accounting policies are appropriate to the company's circumstances, consistently applied and adequately disclosed.

We planned and performed our audit so as to obtain all the information and explanations that we considered necessary in order to provide us with sufficient evidence to give reasonable assurance that the financial statements are free from material misstatement, whether caused by fraud or other irregularity or error. In forming our opinion we also evaluated the overall adequacy of the presentation of information in the financial statements.

(continued on next page)

Figure 11-5   Audit Report in Short Report Format, Page 2

OPINION

In our opinion the financial statements give a true and fair view, in accordance with Generally Accepted Accounting Practice, of the state of the company's affairs as at July 1, 2014, and of its profit/(loss) for the year then ended and have been properly prepared in accordance with the Companies Acts 1983 to 2012.

We have obtained all the information and explanations we consider necessary for the purpose of our audit. In our opinion, proper books of account have been kept by the company. The financial statements are in agreement with the books of account.

In our opinion, the information given in the Directors' Report is consistent with the financial statements.

The net assets of the company, as stated in the balance sheet are more than half of the amount of its called up share capital and, in our opinion, on that basis there did not exist at July 1, 2014, a financial situation which, under section 40(1) of the Companies (Amendment) Act 1983, would require the convening of an extraordinary general meeting of the company.

Format Pointers
Uses short format for report prepared by outside consultant.

Uses email channel to transmit formatted document as attachment for quick, convenient delivery.

pharmacy profile, and even the addressograph used to stamp each page of the patient's record and the identification arm band.

Using the computer to prepare each report in the previous example leads to higher efficiency levels and minimizes errors because recurring data are entered only once. Preparing error-free form reports is a critical public relations tool because even minor clerical errors may cause patients or customers to question the organization's ability to deliver quality service. The "Check Your Communication" section on the Chapter 11 Review Card provides a comprehensive checklist for use in preparing effective reports.

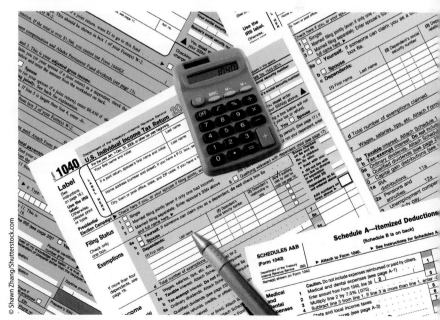

© Shawn Zhang/Shutterstock.com

The federal tax return is one of America's least-liked form reports.

Figure 11-6 Short Report in Expanded Letter Format, Page 1

January 23, 2014

Joseph Fergusson, President
TechPRO, Inc.
1660 Fremont Street
Austin, TX 77539

Dear Mr. Fergusson:

RECOMMENDATIONS FOR IMPLEMENTING GLOBAL VIRTUAL
TEAMS

Thank you for allowing us to assist you in outlining a plan for
successful implementation of virtual teams in a global environment
for TechPRO, Inc. This trend is gaining wide support throughout
the business community as more companies expand operations
internationally and as budgets for employee travel shrink.

Procedures

In preparing this report, a variety of resources were consulted, including
paper and online resources. Additionally, interviews were conducted
with decision makers from 25 organizations in the United States and
Europe that have used virtual teams. Their perceptions, along with
published research, led to the recommendations in this report. Published
resources, as well as telephone interviews, generally support the use of
well-managed virtual teams operating in a global environment.

Findings

Research revealed useful information concerning the unique challenges
faced by global virtual teams.

Challenges Faced by Global Virtual Teams

Virtual teams have various challenges, even when their membership
is homogeneous. Virtual teams can lack cohesion, members may
feel isolated, and coordination of work is more challenging. Special
leadership skills are required to manage the challenges of virtual teams.
An effective team leader must be able to skillfully leverage team talent,
include all members, provide the team with necessary information,
promote trust, encourage healthy discussions, and help manage conflict.
Unless teams can effectively deal with interpersonal communication
challenges, members quickly face burnout. Research indicates that
virtual team performance typically peaks and then declines after the
first year.

(Continued on next page)

Letterhead and letter address function as title page and transmittal.

Uses deductive approach to present main idea to president.

Provides research methods and sources to add credibility.

Uses centered heading to denote major division of body.

Uses transition sentence to move reader smoothly to minor section.

Uses side heading to denote minor section.

Uses bulleted list to emphasize important information.

Format Pointer
Uses subject line to introduce topic of letter report.

Figure 11-6 Short Report in Expanded Letter Format, Page 2

Joseph Fergusson
Page 2
January 23, 2014

Culturally heterogeneous groups have the potential for greater conflict than do groups in which members are culturally similar. Obviously, a certain degree of fluency in the common language used by the team is a requisite to effective communication. Beyond the basic language consideration, team members must recognize other challenges of cultural diversity and adapt their behavior accordingly. Recognition of cultural patterns and expectations and adaptations to spoken and written messages can improve virtual team interactions in global settings.

Recommendations for Effective Global Virtual Teams

Culturally diverse virtual teams do have a greater potential for conflict than do teams that are homogeneous and are able to meet face to face. While variations in beliefs, behaviors, and expectations occur within all cultural groups, certain generalities about a person based on his or her cultural group can be useful for others seeking better understanding. Given little or no other information about an individual's values and behaviors, culture provides a good first impression of that person.

Studies have found that experiences in cross-cultural interactions do serve to improve one's agilities to adapt in such situations. One advantage gained through experience is the overcoming of cultural stereotypes that often stand in the way of effective communication. Cross-cultural experience also leads to the establishment of norms that support interaction among individuals and to the development of mutual consideration for people.

Several studies have established that individuals who learn a foreign language also gain appropriate culturally determined behavior and are thus better able to adapt to specific characteristics of the other culture.

Some individuals are better suited than are others for membership in virtual teams comprised of members from different cultures due to their temperament and experiences. In addition to possessing strong technical skills, qualities that are important to successful membership in cross-cultural virtual teams include

- Flexibility and adaptability
- Strong interpersonal skills
- Ability to think both globally and locally
- Linguistic skills
- Listening (interpretive) skills
- Initiative
- Enthusiasm
- Consensus-building skills
- Patience and empathy
- Nonjudgmental attitude

(continued on next page)

Includes second page heading to show continuation; appears on plain matching paper.

Uses side heading and transition sentence to move reader smoothly to minor section.

Uses bulleted list to emphasize important information.

Uses bulleted list to emphasize important information.

Figure 11-6   Short Report in Expanded Letter Format, Page 3

Joseph Fergusson
Page 3
January 23, 2014

A primary goal of global virtual teams should be to harmonize differences between cultures so that normal business activity can occur. Some suggestions for building harmony include the following:

- Provide cross-cultural training to increase ability to identify and cope with potential conflicts.
- Select a skillful leader who can perceive and facilitate handling of potential cultural misunderstandings.
- Strive for transparency in all stages of activity, which aids in the development of trust.
- Set clear, specific agenda with no surprises that could be seen as hidden agendas.
- Encourage the use of questions to solicit input and check for understanding.

Uses bullets to highlight goals important to globally diverse teams.

Success in global virtual teams is largely dependent on the formation of a group culture that supersedes the individual cultural norms of the various members.

Summary

Combines summary with recommendation as is typical in short reports.

In the global business environment, the success of many organizations depends on the effective functioning of global virtual teams, and individuals possessing the specific skill set to be successful in global virtual teams are highly marketable to a wide variety of organizations. Obviously, teams cannot pay constant attention to cross-cultural differences. However, virtual teams whose members recognize, respect, and respond to cultural expectations for behavior enhance their prospects for achieving high levels of performance. Education about other cultures and experience in cross-cultural exchange will serve to strengthen team members' ability to interact effectively in cross-cultural virtual teams.

Closes with courteous offer to provide additional service.

Thank you for the opportunity to provide this information concerning global virtual team development. Please let us know how we can assist you further with this project or with other related matters.

Sincerely,

Patti Gelson
Patti Gelson, Consultant

Enclosure: Reading list

Includes enclosure notation to alert reader to enclosed reading list.

Format Pointer
Includes complimentary close and signature to comply with letter format.

(*Continued on next page*)

Figure 11-6 Short Report in Expanded Letter Format, Page 4

Joseph Fergusson
Page 4
January 23, 2014

Reading List

Adler, N. J., & Gundersen, A. (2008). *International dimensions of organizational behavior.* Boston: Kent.

Dunkel, A., & Meierewert, S. (2004). Cultural standards and their impact on teamwork: An empirical analysis of Austrian, German, Hungarian and Spanish culture differences. *Journal for East European Management Studies, 9,* 147–174.

Harzing, A. W., & Feely, A. J. (2008). The language barrier and its implications for HQ-subsidiary relationships. *Cross Cultural Management, 15*(1), 49–61.

Hawkes, J. (2010, March 12). Virtual teams need human touch. *Canadian HR Reporter, 20*(5), 16.

Hurn, B. F., & Jenkins, M. (2000). International peer group development. *Industrial and Commercial Training, 32*(4), 128–131.

Maznevski, M. L., & Peterson, M. F. (1997). Societal values, social interpretation, and multinational teams. In C. Grandrose (Ed.), *Cross-cultural workgroups.* Thousand Oaks, CA: Sage.

Nawati, D. A., & Craig, A. (2006, March). Behavioral adaptation within cross-cultural virtual teams. *IEEE Transactions, 49*(1), 44–56. doi:10.1109/TPC.2006.870459

Neyer, A., & Harzine, A. (2008). The impact of culture on interactions: Five lessons learned from the European Commission. *European Management Journal, 26*(5), 325–334. doi:10.1016/j.emj.2008.05.005

Thomas, D. C. (1999). Cultural diversity and work group effectiveness: An experimental study. *Journal of Cross-Cultural Psychology, 30*(2), 242–263.

Yang, K. S., & Bond, M. H. (1980). Ethnic affirmation by Chinese bilinguals. *Journal of Cross-Cultural Psychology, 11*(4), 411–425.

Format Pointers
Uses Readings List instead of References as the title to comply with employing company preference.

Includes alphabetical listing of all cited sources using APA 6th edition referencing style to comply with employing company preference.

Includes digital object identifier (DOI) for electronic resources when available.

11-5 Proposals

Managers prepare **internal proposals** to justify or recommend purchases or changes in the company; for instance, installing a new computer system, introducing telecommuting or other flexible work schedules, or reorganizing the company into work groups. An **external proposal**, as described in Chapter 9, is a written description of how one organization can meet the needs of another by, for example, providing products or services. Written to generate business, external proposals are a critical part of the successful operation of many companies.

Proposals may be solicited or unsolicited. **Solicited proposals** are invited and initiated when a potential customer or client submits exact specifications or needs in a bid request or a request for proposal, commonly referred to as an *RFP*.

internal proposals
proposals used by managers to justify or recommend purchases or changes in the company

external proposal
a proposal written to generate business; one organization describes how it can meet the needs of another by, for example, providing a product or service

Governmental agencies such as the Department of Education solicit proposals and place orders and contracts based on the most desirable proposal. The bid request or RFP describes a problem to be solved and invites respondents to describe their proposed solutions.

An **unsolicited proposal** is prepared by an individual or firm who sees a problem to be solved and submits a solution. For example, a business consultant is a regular customer of a family-owned retail store. On numerous occasions she has attempted to purchase an item that was out of stock. Recognizing that stock shortages decrease sales and profits, she prepares a proposal to assist the business in designing a computerized perpetual inventory with an automatic reordering system. For the business to accept the proposal, the consultant must convince the business that the resulting increase in sales and profits will more than offset the cost of the computer system and the consulting fee.

11-5a Proposal Structure

A proposal includes (1) details about the manner in which the problem will be solved and (2) the price to be charged or costs to be incurred. Often the proposal is a lengthy report designed to "sell" the prospective buyer on the ability of the bidder to perform. However, a simple price quotation also constitutes a proposal in response to a request for a price quotation.

The format of a proposal depends on the length of the proposal and the intended audience:

Format	Proposal Length and Intended Audience
Memo or email report	Short; remains within the organization
Letter report	Short; travels outside the organization
Formal report	Long; remains within the organization or travels outside the organization

Most work resulting from proposals is covered by a working agreement or contract to avoid discrepancies in the intents of the parties. In some cases, for example, users of outside consultants insist that each consultant be covered by a sizable general personal liability insurance policy that also insures the company. Many large firms and governmental organizations use highly structured procedures to ensure understanding of contract terms.

The following general parts, or variations of them, might appear as headings in a proposal: (1) Problem or Purpose, (2) Scope, (3) Methods or Procedures, (4) Materials and Equipment, (5) Qualifications, (6) Follow-Up and/or Evaluation, (7) Budget or Costs, (8) Summary, and (9) Addenda. In addition to these parts, a proposal might include preliminary report parts such as the title page, transmittal message, and contents, as well as addenda parts such as references, appendix, and index.

Problem and/or Purpose

Problem and purpose are often used as interchangeable terms in reports. Here is the introductory purpose statement, called "Project Description," in a proposal by a firm to construct a commercial building:

> *Project Description: EcoSystems, Inc., plans and constructs environmentally friendly buildings for commercial use. Through the use of sustainable building materials and energy-efficient designs, EcoSystems, Inc., helps organizations to decrease their energy "footprint" as well as decrease energy costs. EcoSystems, Inc., also retrofits existing structures to increase energy efficiency.*

Note how the heading "Project Description" has been used in place of "Purpose." In the following opening statement, "Problem" is used as the heading:

> *Problem: Employee training can be a significant cost to organizations in terms of salaries and lost productivity. This report will examine the benefits of using online training programs rather than staffing the function internally.*

The purpose of the proposal may be listed as a separate heading (in addition to "Problem") when the proposal intends to include objectives of a measurable nature. When you list objectives such as "To reduce overall expenses for maintenance by 10%," attempt to list measurable and attainable objectives, and list only enough to accomplish the purpose of selling your proposal. Many proposals are rejected simply because writers promise more than they can actually deliver.

Scope

When determining the scope of your proposal, you can place limits on what you propose to do or on what the

solicited proposals proposals generated when a potential buyer submits exact specifications or needs in a bid request

unsolicited proposal a proposal prepared by an individual or firm who sees a problem to be solved and proposes a solution material or equipment you sell can accomplish. The term *scope* need not necessarily be the only heading for this section. "Areas Served," "Limitations to the Study," and "Where (*specify topic*) Can Be Used," are examples of headings that describe the scope of a proposal. Here is a "Scope" section from a consulting firm's proposal to conduct a marketing study.

> *What the Study Will Cover: To assist MooGoo Yogurt in formulating a marketing strategy, Johns Consulting will provide an analysis of all competitors in the organic Greek-style yogurt market, including their sales, target market, and promotion and distribution methods. In addition, Johns will provide an analysis of the market potential for MooGoo's unique product given the competition, product trends, and the target market for the product. Finally, Johns will provide recommendations for distribution, promotion, and placement of MooGoo products based on its analysis.*

Another statement of scope might be as follows:

> *Scope: This report will examine employment trends in the past 10 years for medical technicians in the United States and will use that data to provide recommendations to Providence HealthCare to help it plan future staffing strategies.*

Methods and/or Procedures

The method(s) used to solve the problem or to conduct the business of the proposal should be spelled out in detail. In this section, simply think through all the steps necessary to meet the terms of the proposal and write them in sequence. When feasible, you should include a time schedule for implementation of the project.

Materials and Equipment

For large proposals, such as construction or research and development, indicate the nature and quantities of materials and equipment to be used. In some cases, several departments will contribute to this section. When materials and equipment constitute a major portion of the total cost, include prices. Much litigation arises when clients are charged for "cost overruns." When contracts are made on the basis of "cost plus XX%," the major costs of materials, equipment, and labor/personnel must be thoroughly described and documented.

Qualifications

Assuming your proposal is acceptable in terms of services to be performed or products to be supplied, your proposal must convince the potential buyer that you have the expertise to deliver what you have described and that you are a credible individual or company. Therefore, devote a section to presenting the specific qualifications and special expertise of the personnel involved in the proposal. You may include past records of the bidder and the recommendations of its past customers, and the proposed cost. Note how the brief biography of the principal member in the following excerpt from a proposal contributes to the credibility of the proposer:

> *Principals: Maria Vega has won the prestigious Wright award for her building designs, including those for the Weston Theater in Minneapolis and the Cincinnati Museum of Art. Larry Roberts has managed the planning and construction of dozens of municipal projects, including the St. Louis Justice Complex, Detroit Superior Court building, and the Michigan State Department of Education building.*

In another related section, the proposal might mention other work performed:

> *Major Clients: City governments in Minneapolis and Duluth, Minnesota; Detroit and Lansing, Michigan; St. Louis, Kansas City, and Springfield, Missouri; and Cincinnati, Columbus, and Dayton, Ohio; and state governments of Kentucky, Michigan, Minnesota, and Ohio. Personal references available on request.*

Follow-Up and/or Evaluation

Although your entire proposal is devoted to convincing the reader of its merit, clients are frequently concerned about what will happen when the proposed work or service is completed. Will you return to make certain your work is satisfactory? Can you adjust your method of research as times change?

If you propose to conduct a study, do not promise more than you can deliver. Not all funded research proves to be successful. If you propose to prepare a study in your firm's area of expertise, you may be more confident. A public accounting firm's proposal to audit a company's records need not be modest. The accountant follows certain audit functions that are prescribed by the profession. However, a proposal that involves providing psychological services probably warrants a thoughtful follow-up program to evaluate the service.

Budget or Costs

The budget or costs of the program should be detailed when materials, equipment, outside help, consultants, salaries, and travel are to be included. A simple proposal for service by one person might consist of a statement such as "15 hours at $200/hour, totaling $3,000, plus mileage and expenses estimated at $550." Present the budget or costs section after the main body of the proposal.

Summary

You might conclude the proposal with a summary. This summary may also be used as the initial section of the proposal if deductive sequence is desired.

Addenda

When supporting material is necessary to the proposal but would make it too bulky or detract from it, include the material as addenda items. A bibliography and an appendix are examples of addenda items. References used should appear in the bibliography or as footnotes. Maps, questionnaires, letters of recommendation, and similar materials are suitable appendix items.

A short, informal proposal that includes several of the parts previously discussed is shown in Figure 11-7 on the next two pages. This proposal consists of three major divisions: "Purpose," "Proposed Course of Instruction," and "Cost." The "Proposed Course of Instruction" section is divided into five minor divisions to facilitate understanding. Wanting to increase the chances of securing the contract, the writer made sure the proposal was highly professional and had the impact needed to get the reader's attention. To add to the overall effectiveness of the proposal, the writer incorporated appealing, but not distracting, page design features. Printing the proposal with a laser printer using fonts of varying sizes and styles resulted in a professional appearance and an appealing document. The reader's positive impression of the high standards exhibited in this targeted proposal is likely to influence his or her confidence in the writer's ability to present the proposed seminar.

11-5b Proposal Preparation

Writers have much flexibility in preparing proposals. When they find a particular pattern that seems to be successful, they no doubt will adopt it as their basic plan. The ultimate test of a proposal is its effectiveness in achieving its purpose. The task is to assemble the parts of a proposal in a way that persuades the reader to accept it.

As with most report writing, first prepare the pieces of information that you will assemble later as the "whole" report. Determine the parts to include, select one part that will be easy to prepare, prepare that part, and then go on to another. When you have completed the parts, you can arrange them in whatever order you like, incorporate the transitional items necessary to create coherence, and then put the proposal in finished form. Allow adequate time after completing the research and writing for proofreading and editing. Figures should be checked carefully for accuracy, since underreporting costs can lead to a financial loss if the proposal is accepted, and overreporting costs may lead to refusal of the proposal. If you fail to allow sufficient time for proposal completion, you may miss the required deadline for proposal submission.

If you become part of a collaborative writing team producing a proposal of major size, you will probably be responsible for writing only a small portion of the total proposal. For example, a proposal team of 16 executives, managers, and engineers might be required to prepare an 87-page proposal presenting a supplier's plan to supply parts to a military aircraft manufacturer. After the group brainstorms and plans the proposal, a project director delegates responsibility for the research and origination of particular sections of the proposal. Finally, one person compiles all the sections, creates many of the preliminary and addenda parts, and produces and distributes the final product.

Check figures carefully. Underreporting costs can lead to financial loss, and overreporting costs might lead to refusal of the proposal.

Figure 11-7   Short Proposal, Page 1

PROPOSAL FOR MANAGEMENT DEVELOPMENT SEMINAR: DEVELOPING LEADERSHIP SKILLS

for Worldwide Consumer Products, Inc.

by Lawford Miller, Management Consultant

August 24, 2014

Purpose

Because of its global market for consumer products, Worldwide Consumer Products, Inc., has managers dispersed across the globe in its 52 international locations. The proposed training course is designed to help your managers better understand how to demonstrate effective leadership while working as part of a globally diverse organization.

Proposed Course of Instruction

The training course will be delivered by Albert Prince, a seasoned consultant with more than 10 years of experience providing cross-cultural training in a corporate environment. The program will actively involve participants and facilitate personal application of our patented "Seven Steps to Becoming an Effective Leader" process. Participants will be videotaped as they apply the steps in the leader process and will receive copies of the tapes for their review.

Teaching/Learning Methods

This activity-oriented training program will involve response to videos, role playing, and case discussion. The trainer will act as a facilitator to assist each participant in assessing his or her leadership behaviors and expectations and planning effective strategies for improving overall effectiveness while working as a leader in a globally diverse organization.

Program Content

The following topics constitute the content core of the program:

- Challenges faced by leaders in globally diverse organizations
- Differences and similarities in cultural values, beliefs, and practices of global leaders
- Strategies for effectively leading a globally diverse department or teams

Learning Materials

The following materials will be provided to facilitate learning:

- Copies of current published articles on the importance and function of globally diverse teams
- Consultant-development workbook for each participant

(continued on next page)

- Describes problem and presents proposed plan as solution to problem.

- Uses headings to aid reader in understanding proposal's organization. Boldface font adds emphasis.

- Divides "Proposed Course of Instruction" into five minor divisions for easier comprehension. Describes course content, instructional method, and design in detail.

- Uses bulleted lists to highlight course components and learning materials.

Format Pointer
Incorporates page design features to enhance appeal and readability (e.g., headings styles including color; crisp, open fonts and wide line-spacing for easy onscreen reading or print copy; bulleted lists; and appealing table).

Figure 11-7   Short Proposal, Page 2

Worldwide Consumer Products, Inc.   August 24, 2014   Page 2

Length of Course

As requested by management, this course will consist of three 2-hour sessions; each session will be held on a selected day of the week for three consecutive weeks.

Number of Participants

The seminar will serve all 452 Worldwide Consumer Products' managers working in 52 international locations.

Cost

All teaching-learning materials will be provided by the consulting firm and include workbooks, videos, and video camera and recorder. Exact cost figures are as follows:

Workbooks and other materials for 452 participants	15,820.00
Equipment lease fees	15,600.00
Professional fees (6 hours' instruction @ $250/hour @ 52 locations)	78,000.00
Total	**$109,420.00**

Includes informational header to identify second page and client.

Itemizes costs so reader understands exactly how figure was calculated. Disclosing detailed breakdown gives reader confidence that cost is accurate.

STUDY TOOLS
CHAPTER 11

Located at back of the textbook
- ❏ **Rip out Chapter Review Card**

Located at www.cengagebrain.com
- ❏ **Review Key Terms Flashcards (Print or Online)**
- ❏ **Download Audio Summaries for on-the-go review**
- ❏ **Complete Practice Quizzes to prepare for tests**
- ❏ **Play "Beat the Clock" to master concepts**
- ❏ **Complete the Crossword Puzzle to review key terms**
- ❏ **Watch the video about McDonaldson, a fictitious but all-too-realistic ad agency whose employees struggle with contemporary business communication issues.**

Designing and Delivering Business Presentations

12-1 Planning an Effective Business Presentation

The simplicity of writing email and talking on the phone has deterred many workers from learning to communicate in front of people with authority and authenticity.[1] Being a skilled business communicator requires skill in both writing and speaking. A business presentation is an important means of exchanging information for decision making and policy development, relating the benefits of the services offered, and sharing our goals, values, and vision. Because multiple people receive the message at the same time and are able to provide immediate feedback for clarification, presentations can significantly reduce message distortion and misunderstanding.

Many of the presentations you give will be formal, with sufficient time allowed for planning and developing elaborate visual support. You might present information and recommendations to external audiences such as customers and clients whom you've never met or to an internal audience made up of coworkers and managers you know well. You can also expect to present some less formal presentations, often referred to as **oral briefings**. An oral briefing might entail a short update on a current project requested during a meeting without advance notice or a brief explanation in the hallway when your supervisor walks past. Sales representatives give oral briefings daily as they present short, informal pitches for new products and services.

Regardless of the formality of the presentation, the time given to prepare, the nature of the audience (friends or strangers), or the media used (live, distant, Web, or DVD delivery on demand), your success depends on your ability to think on your feet and speak confidently as you address audience needs. Understanding the purpose you hope to achieve through your presentation and conceptualizing your audience will enable you to organize the content in a way the audience can understand *and* accept.

12-1a Identify Your Purpose

Determining what you want to accomplish during a presentation is a fundamental principle of planning an effective presentation. Some speech coaches recommend completing the following vital sentence to lay the foundation for a successful presentation: "At the end of my presentation, the audience will _____." In his book *Do's and Taboos of Public Speaking*, Axtell provides two excellent mechanisms for condensing your presentation into a brief, achievable purpose that will direct you in identifying and supporting the major points:[2]

- Ask yourself, "What is my message?" Then, develop a phrase, a single thought, or a conclusion you want the audience to take with them from the presentation. This elementary statement will likely be the final sentence in your presentation—the basic message you want the audience to remember.

- Imagine a member of your audience has been asked to summarize your message. Ideally, you want to hear him or her describe your central purpose.

12-1b Know Your Audience

A common mistake for many presenters is to presume they know the audience without attempting to find out about them. If you expect to get results, you

oral briefings
informal presentations prepared and presented with little time for planning and developing

BCOM

© robootb/Shutterstock.com

must commit the time to know your audience and focus your presentation on them—from planning your speech to practicing its delivery.

As a general rule, audiences *do* want to be in tune with a speaker. Yet people listen to speeches about things of interest to them. "What's in it for me?" is the question most listeners ask. A speech about global warming to a farm group should address the farmers' problems, for example, and not focus on theories of global warming. Additionally, different strategies are needed for audiences who think and make decisions differently. For instance, different strategies are needed for making a successful presentation to sell software to a group of lawyers than to a group of doctors. Lawyers typically think quickly and are argumentative and decisive while doctors are often cautious, skeptical, and don't make quick purchasing decisions.[3]

To deliver a presentation that focuses on the wants and expectations of an audience, you must determine who they are, what motivates them, how they think, and how they make decisions. Helpful information you can obtain about most audiences includes ages, genders, occupations, educational levels, attitudes, values, broad and specific interests, and needs. In addition, you should also consider certain things about the occasion and location. Patriotic speeches to a group of military veterans will differ from speeches to a group of new recruits, just as Fourth of July speeches will differ from Veterans Day speeches. Seek answers to the following questions when you discuss your speaking engagement with someone representing the group or audience:

1. *Who* is the audience and *who* requested the presentation? General characteristics of the audience should be considered, as well as the extent of their knowledge and experience with the topic, attitude toward the topic and you as a credible speaker, anticipated response to the use of electronic media, and required or volunteer attendance.

2. *Why* is this topic important to the audience? What will the audience do with the information presented?

3. *What* environmental factors affect the presentation?
   - How many will be in the audience?
   - Will I be the only speaker? If not, where does my presentation fit in the program? What time of day?
   - How much time will I be permitted? Minimum? Maximum?
   - What are the seating arrangements? How far will the audience be from the speaker? Will a microphone or other equipment be available?

Answers to these questions reveal whether the speaking environment will be intimate or remote, whether the audience is likely to be receptive and alert or nonreceptive and tired, and whether you will need to use additional motivational or persuasive techniques.

12-2 Organizing the Content

With an understanding of the purpose of your business presentation—why you are giving it and what you hope to achieve—and a conception of the size, interest, and background of the audience, you are prepared to outline your presentation and identify appropriate content. First introduced by famous speech trainer Dale Carnegie and still recommended by speech experts today, the simple but effective presentation format includes an introduction, a body, and a closing. In the introduction, tell the audience what you are going to tell them; in the body, tell them; and in the closing, tell them what you told them.

Although this design might sound repetitive, it works quite well. The audience processes information verbally and cannot slow the speaker down when information is complex. Thus repetition aids the listener in processing the information that supports the speaker's purpose.

12-2a Introduction

What you say at the beginning sets the stage for your entire presentation and initiates your rapport with the audience. However, inexperienced speakers often settle for unoriginal and overused introductions, such as "My name is …, and my topic is …," or "It is a pleasure …," or negative statements, such as apologies for lack of preparation, boring delivery, or late arrival, that reduce the audience's desire to listen. An effective introduction accomplishes the following goals:

- **Captures attention and involves the audience.** Choose an attention-getter that is relevant to the subject and appropriate for the situation.

> ## Attention-Getting Techniques Might Include:
>
> - A shocking statement or startling statistic.
> - A quotation by an expert or well-known person.
> - A rhetorical or open-ended question that generates discussion from the audience.
> - An appropriate joke or humor.
> - A demonstration or dramatic presentation aid.
> - An anecdote or timely story from a business periodical.
> - A personal reference, compliment to the audience, or a reference to the occasion of the presentation.

To involve the audience directly, ask for a show of hands in response to a direct question, allow the audience time to think about the answer to a rhetorical question, or explain why the information is important and how it will benefit the listeners. Consider the following examples.

A speech to motivate women business owners might begin with a true story:

> **"I had a six-figure salary and vice president title, but I felt bored with my job. I had always loved challenges but the only ones I got were negative ones, dealing with difficult people and navigating outdated procedures. I couldn't sleep at night. All the negative challenges ended, though, when I finally got the courage to do what I love!"**

A report presenting a new product spin-off could introduce the subject and set the stage for the findings (inductive sequence) or the recommendation (deductive sequence).

© Seregam/Shutterstock.com

Inductive: While looking at options to increase our profitability, an employee task force recommended that we branch into digital publishing, leveraging our knowledge of the print industry.

Deductive: By branching into digital publishing, we can leverage our knowledge of the print industry and thereby increase revenues significantly.

- **Establishes rapport.** Initiate rapport with the listeners; convince them that you are concerned that they benefit from the presentation and that you are qualified to speak on the topic. You might share a personal story that relates to the topic but reveals something about yourself, or discuss your background or a specific experience with the topic being discussed.

- **Presents the purpose statement and previews the points that will be developed.** To maintain the interest you have captured, present your purpose statement directly so that the audience is certain to hear it. Use original statements and avoid clichés such as "My topic today is …," or "I'd like to talk with you about …."

> **"Communication skills are consistently identified as the key to management and organizational success. Our online certificate program will help you to enhance your professional communication skills better enabling you to vie for management positions in your organization."**

Next, preview the major points you will discuss in the order you will discuss them. For example, you might say, "First, I'll discuss …, then …, and finally …."

Revealing the presentation plan will help the audience understand how the parts of the body are tied together to support the purpose statement, thus increasing their understanding. For a long, complex presentation, you might display a presentation visual that lists the points in the order they will be covered. As you begin each major point, display a slide that contains that point and perhaps a related image. These section slides partition your presentation just as headings do in a written report, and thus move the listener more easily from one major point to the next.

12-2b Body

In a typical presentation of 20 to 30 minutes, limit your presentation to only a few major points (typically three to five) to combat time constraints and your audience's ability to concentrate and absorb. Making every statement in a presentation into a major point—something to be remembered—is impossible, unless the presentation lasts only 2 or 3 minutes.

Once you have selected your major points, locate your supporting material. You can use several techniques to ensure the audience understands your point and to reinforce it:

- **Provide support in a form that is easy to understand.** Three techniques will assist you in accomplishing this goal:

  1. **Use simple vocabulary and short sentences that the listener can understand easily and that sound conversational and interesting.** Spoken communication is more difficult to process than written communication; therefore, complex, varied vocabulary and long sentences often included in written documents are not effective in a presentation.

  2. **Avoid jargon or technical terms that the listeners might not understand.** Instead, use plain English that the audience can easily comprehend. Make your speech more interesting and memorable by using word pictures to make your points. Matt Hughes, a speech consultant, provides this example: "If your message is a warning of difficulties ahead, you might say: 'We're climbing a hill that's getting steeper, and there are rocks and potholes in the road.'"[4]

  3. **Use a familiar frame of reference.** Drawing analogies between new ideas and familiar ones is another technique for generating understanding. For example, noting that the U.S. blog-reading audience is already one-half the size of the newspaper-reading population helps clarify an abstract or complex concept. Saying that "infodumping" is the verbal equivalent of email spam explains well the expected consequences of overloading an audience with too many details.[5]

- **Provide relevant statistics.** Provide statistics or other quantitative measures to lend authority and credibility to your points. A word of warning: Do not overwhelm your audience with excessive statistics. Instead, round off numbers and use broad terms or word pictures that the listener can remember. Instead of "68.2%" say "more than two-thirds;" instead of "112% rise in production" say "our output more than doubled."

- **Use quotes from prominent people.** Comments made by other authorities are helpful in establishing credibility.

- **Use interesting anecdotes.** Audiences like and remember anecdotes or interesting stories that tie into the presentation and make strong emotional connections. In her book *Whoever Tells the Best Story Wins*, Annette Simmons stresses that when telling stories, the storyteller allows the audience to feel his or her presence and reveals a trace of humanity, which is vital for developing understanding, influence, and strong relationships with the audience. She encourages leaders to craft personal stories into specific, intentional messages that communicate values, vision, and important lessons.[6] While communicating their values, leaders communicate the values they expect from employees. As with jokes, be sure you can get straight to the point of a story.

- **Use jokes and humor appropriately.** A joke or humor can create a special bond between you and the audience, ease your approach to sensitive subjects, disarm a nonreceptive audience, or make your message easier to understand and remember. Plan your joke carefully so that you can (1) get the point across as quickly as possible, (2) deliver it in a conversational manner with interesting inflections and effective body movements, and (3) deliver the punch line effectively. If you cannot tell a joke well, use humor instead—amusing things that happened to you or someone you know, one-liners, or humorous quotations that relate to your presentation. Refrain from any humor that reflects negatively on race, color, religion, gender, age, culture, or other personal areas of sensitivity.

- **Use presentation visuals.** Presentation visuals, such as handouts, whiteboards, flip charts, transparencies, electronic presentations, and demonstrations, enhance the effectiveness of the presentation. Develop presentation visuals that will enable your audience to see, hear, and even experience your presentation.

- **Encourage audience involvement.** Skilled presenters involve their audiences through techniques such as asking reflective questioning, role playing, directing audience-centered activities, and incorporating current events or periodicals that tie directly to the message. One communications coach's advice for getting an audience "to sit up and listen" is to make the presentation contemporary by working Twitter, texting, video, and other technologies into the speech.[7]

12-2c Closing

The closing provides unity to your presentation by "telling the audience what you have already told them." The conclusion should be "your best line, your most dramatic point, your most profound thought, your most memorable bit of information, or your best anecdote."[8] Because listeners tend to remember what they hear last, use these final words strategically. Develop a closing that supports and refocuses the audience's attention on your purpose statement.

- **Commit the time and energy needed to develop a creative, memorable conclusion.** An audience is not impressed with endings such as "That's all I have" or "That's it." Useful concluding techniques include summarizing the main points that have been made in the presentation and using anecdotes, humor, and illustrations. When closing an analytical presentation, state your conclusion and support it with the highlights from your supporting evidence: "In summary, you should select our communication training program because it offers … ." In a persuasive presentation, the closing is often an urgent plea for the members of the audience to take some action or to look on the subject from a new point of view.

- **Tie the closing to the introduction to strengthen the unity of the presentation.** For example, you might answer the rhetorical question you asked in the opening, refer to and build on an anecdote included in the introduction, and so on. A unifying close to a speech to motivate women business owners might be, "Life is too short to spend it doing other people's work and paying the price with unhappiness. With appropriate planning, you can spend your days as I do, making a life you love."

- **Use transition words that clearly indicate you are moving from the body to the closing.** Attempt to develop original words rather than rely on standard statements such as "In closing" or "In conclusion."

- **Practice your closing until you can deliver it without stumbling.** Use your voice and gestures to communicate this important idea clearly, emphatically, and sincerely rather than fade out at the end as inexperienced speakers often do.

- **Smile and stand back to accept the audience's applause.** A solid closing does not require a "thank you"; instead, wait confidently for the audience's spontaneous applause to thank you for

a worthwhile presentation. Appear eager to begin a question-and-answer period or walk with assurance to your seat.

12-3 Designing Compelling Presentation Visuals

Speakers who use presentation visuals are considered better prepared and more interesting, and achieve their goals more often than speakers who do not use visuals. Presentation visuals support and clarify a speaker's ideas and help the audience visualize the message. A speaker using presentation visuals reaches the receiver with double impact—through the eyes and the ears—and achieves the results quoted in an ancient Chinese proverb: "Tell me, I'll forget. Show me, I'll remember. But involve me and I'll understand." Research studies confirm that using visuals enhances a presentation.

The effective use of presentation visuals provides several advantages:[9]

- clarifies and emphasizes important points
- increases retention from 14% to 38%
- reduces the time required to present a concept
- results in a speaker achieving goals 34% more often than when presentation visuals are not used
- increases occurrence of group consensus by 21% when presentation visuals are used in a meeting

12-3a Types of Presentation Visuals

A speaker must select the appropriate medium or combination of media to accomplish the purpose and to meet the needs of a specific audience. The most common presentation visuals are discussed in Figure 12-1.

12-3b Design of Presentation Visuals

Computer technology has raised the standards for presentation visuals; however, inexperienced designers often use too many visuals and make them overly complex and difficult to understand. Not only are live audiences subjected to "PowerPoint poisoning," but "docu-points"

Figure 12-1 Selecting an Appropriate Presentation Visual

VISUAL	ADVANTAGES	LIMITATIONS
HANDOUTS	• Provide detailed information that audience can examine closely • Extend a presentation by providing resources for later use • Reduce the need for note taking and aid in audience retention	• Can divert audience's attention from the speaker • Can be expensive
BOARDS AND FLIP CHARTS	• Facilitate interaction • Are easy to use • Are inexpensive if traditional units are used	• Require turning speaker's back to audience • Are cumbersome to transport and can be messy and not professional looking • Provide no hard copy and must be developed on-site if traditional units are used
OVERHEAD TRANSPARENCIES	• Are simple to prepare and use • Allow versatile use; can be prepared beforehand or while speaking • Are inexpensive and readily available	• Are not easily updated and are awkward to use • Require special acetate sheets and markers unless using a document camera • Pose potential for equipment failure
ELECTRONIC PRESENTATIONS	• Meet audience expectations of visual standards • Enhance professionalism and credibility of the speaker • Provide special effects to enhance retention, appeal, flexibility, and reuse	• Can lead to poor delivery if misused • Can be expensive and time-consuming • Can require highly developed skills • Pose technology failure and transportability challenges
35MM SLIDES	• Are highly professional • Depict real people and places • Show color and detail dramatically	• Require a darkened room • Create a formal environment not conducive to group interaction • Lack flexibility in presentation sequence
MODELS OR PHYSICAL OBJECTS	• Are useful to demonstrate an idea • Show dimensions • Can feel more immediate and provide clearer example than images	• Can compete with the speaker for attention • If model, can be expensive and time-consuming to build

are often sent when a different type of communication is called for. An "electability" PowerPoint slideshow sent by the 2008 Hillary Clinton Campaign to all House Democrats contained nine slides, 275 words, one table, three bar charts, and two pie charts. Such "docu-points" are usually less effective than a concise, well-designed handout or summary report.[10]

Your goal is to create an appealing, easy-to-read design that supports your main points without overwhelming the audience. Presentation visuals should possess the same degree of professionalism as your delivery and personal appearance. You can create dynamic and useful presentation visuals, including slides, handouts, and notes pages, by following these simple guidelines:

- **Limit the number of visual aids used in a single presentation.** While audiences value being able to "see" your points, they also welcome the variety provided by listening and the break from concentrating on visuals. Design compelling visuals that direct the audience's attention to major points and clarify or illustrate complex information. Use precise, vivid language that will involve the audience and enrich your message and delivery style.

- **Limit slide content to key ideas presented in as few words as possible.** Well-organized, crisp slide content enhances the audience's ability to grasp the speaker's meaning and find immediate value in the information. Good content also leads to an extemporaneous delivery rather than a speaker's monotonous reading of scripted slides. Short text lines are also easier for the eye to follow and open up the slide with appealing white space.

- **Develop only one major idea using targeted keywords the audience can scan quickly, understand, and remember.** Full sentences can be used for a direct quotation; otherwise, less is more. William Earnest, author of *Save Our Slides*, offers a cure for verbalitis: "PowerPoint is not a word processor"—it is a visual medium in which fewer words are always more.[11]

  - Keep type sizes large enough to read when projected and to discourage crowding slides with text. Strive for these font sizes: slide titles, 44 points; main bullets, 32 points; sub-bullets, 24 points. Do not use text smaller than 18 points, as it is unreadable when projected.

  - Limit slide titles and headings to four words and follow the 7 × 7 rule, which limits text to 7 lines per slide and 7 words per line. Eliminate articles (*a*, *an*, *the*), understood pronouns/possessives (*we*, *you*, *your*), simple verbs and infinitive beginnings (*are*, *to*), and repetitive phrasing.[12]

  - Develop powerful bulleted lists that are easy to follow and remember. For easy recall, limit the list to three to five main bullets, but absolutely no more than seven. To eliminate confusion and rereading, use bulleted lists that are grammatically parallel. One item appearing out of place weakens the emphasis given to each item and can distract audience attention from the message. Be certain each major point relates to the key concept presented in the slide title and each subpoint relates to its major point. Unless sequence is important, use bullets as they add less clutter and are easier to follow than numbers.

- **Choose an effective template and powerful images to reinforce ideas, illustrate complex ideas, and enliven boring content.** Images and shapes are more visually appealing and memorable than words, and they enable audiences to grasp information more easily. Today's audiences expect media-rich, dynamic visuals, not a speaker's dense crutch notes displayed on screen. Although photographs and clip art available in your presentation software gallery are acceptable, avoid images that are overused, outdated, grainy, and convey an unprofessional tone. Instead search for or create high-quality, professional images that convey the desired message and can project onscreen without distortion.

- **Choose an effective color scheme.** The colors you choose and the way you combine them determine the overall effectiveness of your presentation and add a personal touch to your work. Follow these simple rules to plan a nondistracting, complementary color scheme that has unity with the template graphics:

  - **Limit colors to no more than three colors on a slide, to avoid an overwhelming feel.**

  - **Begin by selecting a background color that conveys the appropriate formality and tone.** Choose cool colors (blue and green) in muted shades for formal presentations; choose warm colors (red, orange, and yellow) or brighter shades of cool colors for a less formal and perhaps trendy look. Think carefully about whether your color selection has a natural association with your topic or organization. For example, a presentation on environmentally friendly policies might incorporate colors naturally associated with nature and cleanliness (earth tones, white and blue); a presentation to Pepsi-Cola likely would be designed around the company colors of red, white, and blue.

  - **Choose complementary foreground (text) colors that have high contrast to the background to ensure readability.** To ensure high contrast, choose either dark text on a light background or light text on a dark background. For example, the often-used color scheme of yellow slide title text and white bulleted list with a blue background is a good choice because the colors are complementary and have high contrast. Choose a slightly brighter color for the slide title that distinguishes it from the color chosen for the bullet list.

Black text against a white background has the greatest contrast. A blue background with yellow text contrasts well, but a light blue background with white text would be difficult to read because of low contrast. Evaluate the readability of the following contrast variations.

| High-contrast options: | Dark text on a light background | Light text on dark background |
| Poor contract options: | White text on a light blue background | Bright text on a bright background |

Because the lower resolution of projectors can wash out colors and make them less vibrant than what is seen on a printed page or computer screen, choose options with very high—not minimally high—contrast. Project your presentation ahead of time in the room where you are to present so you can assess the color scheme. You can also double-check for readability and typographical errors at the same time.

- **Choose the accent colors that complement the color scheme.** Accent colors are used in small doses to draw attention to key elements: bullet markers; bars/slices in graphs, backgrounds (fills) of shapes and lines, selected text; or drawings that are color coded for emphasis. Avoid red and green when differentiating important points as almost 10% of the population is color impaired and cannot distinguish between red and green. The red and green bars in a graph would be seen as one large area.

- **Choose an appealing font that can be read onscreen easily.** Avoid delicate, decorative, or condensed choices that are difficult to read when projected. The clean, simple lines of a sans serif font, such as Calibri, Tahoma, or Verdana, are ideal for projecting on a large screen, newspaper headline, sign, or billboard. A *sans serif* font has no short cross-strokes, known as *serifs*, which provide extra detail that helps guide the eye on print media. Examples of serif fonts are Cambria, Times New Roman, and Garamond.

- **Follow these keyboarding rules for easy reading.** Use capital letters sparingly as they are difficult to read from a distance. Capitalize the first letter of important words in slide titles (initial caps) and the first letter of the first word and proper nouns in a bulleted list (sentence case). Omit hard-to-see punctuation at the end of bulleted lists and elsewhere, and avoid abbreviations and hyphenations that might cause confusion.

memorized presentation
a presentation in which a speaker writes out a speech, commits it to memory, and recites it verbatim

- **Reflect legal and ethical responsibility in the design of presentation visuals.** Like the graphics you developed in Chapter 10, presentation visuals should be uncluttered, easily understood, and depict information honestly.

- **Proofread the visual carefully following the same systematic procedures used for printed letters and reports and electronic communication.** Misspellings in visuals are embarrassing and diminish your credibility. Double-check to be certain that names of people, companies, and products are spelled correctly.

Figure 12-2 on the next page offers a review of slide design guidelines. The poor example (left) relies on text to convey the message, while the good example (right) illustrates the point.

12-3c Design Tips for Audience Handouts and Notes Pages

Audience handouts should add value for individual audience members; otherwise, the information can better be conveyed in a projected format for group benefit. An effective handout can help audience members remember your message, serve as a reference for later consideration or action, and encourage involvement when space is provided for note taking or response. You can prepare useful presenter notes on small index cards or on pages generated by electronic presentation software.

12-4 Refining Your Delivery

After you have organized your message, you must identify the appropriate delivery method, refine your vocal qualities, and practice your delivery.

12-4a Delivery Method

Four presentation methods can be used: memorized, scripted, impromptu, and extemporaneous. Impromptu and extemporaneous styles are generally more useful for business presentations.

Memorized presentations are written out ahead of time, memorized, and recited verbatim. Memorization has the greatest limitations of the speech styles. Speakers are almost totally unable to react to feedback, and the speaker who forgets a point and develops a

Figure 12-2   Designing Compelling Slides: Poor (left) and Good (right) Examples

Company Background

- Established in 2009
- Headquarters in Ann Arbor, Michigan
- 300 employees
- Annual sales of nearly $3 million

Headquarters of Triton Enterprises

The revised slide

- Includes short descriptive title that captures major idea of slide.
- Limits content to meet the 7 x 7 criteria.
- Recognizes the difference between a written communication channel and a visual one through enhanced use of visual elements and reduction of text.
- Takes advantage of SmartArt feature of Microsoft PowerPoint to increase visual appeal while reducing time needed for custom design creation.
- Uses a simple but appealing template with high-quality, relevant image that is large enough for audience to see and has not been overused.
- Uses high-contrast background and sans serif fonts to ensure legibility. Color choices are complementary and convey a professional tone.
- Uses initial caps in slide title, capitalizes the first word in bulleted list, and omits period at end of bulleted items.
- Has been proofread carefully to avoid misspellings that damage credibility.

mental block might lose the entire speech. Memorized speeches tend to sound monotonous, restrict natural body gestures and motions, and lack conviction. For short religious or fraternal rites, however, the memorized presentation is often impressive.

Manuscript, or *scripted*, **presentations** involve writing the speech word for word and reading it to the audience. For complex material and technical conference presentations, manuscript presentations ensure content coverage. Additionally, this style protects speakers against being misquoted (when accuracy is absolutely critical) and fits into exact time constraints, as in television or radio presentations. Speeches are sometimes read when time does not permit adequate preparation or when several different presentations are given in one day (e.g., the speaking demands of the president of the United States and other top-level executives). Manuscript presentations limit speaker–audience rapport, particularly when speakers keep their eyes and heads buried in their manuscripts. Teleprompters that project the manuscript out of view of the audience allow the speaker to appear to be speaking extemporaneously.

Impromptu presentations are frightening to many people because the speaker is called on without prior notice. Experienced speakers can easily analyze the request, organize supporting points from memory, and present a simple, logical response. In many cases, businesspeople can anticipate a request and be prepared to discuss a particular idea when requested (e.g., status report on an area of control at a team meeting). Because professionals are expected to present ideas and data spontaneously on demand, businesspeople must develop the ability to deliver impromptu presentations.

manuscript presentation
a presentation in which a speaker writes out the entire speech and reads it to the audience; also called a *scripted presentation*

impromptu presentation
a presentation in which a speaker is called on without prior notice

tone. You project your voice and convey feelings—even thoughts—by varying your vocal tones. Important factors of phonation are pitch, volume, and rate. These factors permit us to recognize other people's voices over the phone.

- **Pitch.** The highness or lowness of the voice is called pitch. Pleasant voices have medium or low pitch; however, a varied pitch pattern is desirable. The pitch of the voice rises and falls to reflect emotions; for example, fear and anger are reflected in a higher pitch; sadness, in a lower pitch. Lower pitches for both men and women are perceived as sounding more authoritative; higher pitches indicate less confidence and suggest pleading or whining. Techniques discussed later in this section can help you lower the pitch of your voice.

- **Volume.** The loudness of tones is referred to as volume. Generally, good voices are easily heard by everyone in the audience but are not too loud. Use variety to hold the audience's attention, emphasize words or ideas, and create a desired atmosphere (energetic, excited tone versus a dull, boring one).

- **Rate.** The speed at which words are spoken is called rate. Never speak so quickly that the audience cannot understand your message or so slowly that they are distracted or irritated. Vary the rate with the demands of the situation. For example, speak at a slower rate when presenting a complex concept or emphasizing an important idea. Pause to add emphasis to a key point or to transition to another major section of the presentation. Speak at a faster rate when presenting less important information or when reviewing.

Extemporaneous presentations are planned, prepared, and rehearsed but not written in detail. Brief notes prompt the speaker on the next point, but the words are chosen spontaneously as the speaker interacts with the audience and identifies this audience's specific needs. Extemporaneous presentations include natural body gestures, sound conversational, and can be delivered with conviction because the speaker is speaking "with" the listeners and not "to" them. The audience appreciates a warm, genuine communicator and will forgive an occasional stumble or groping for a word that occurs with an extemporaneous presentation.

12-4b Vocal Qualities

The sound of your voice is a powerful instrument used to deliver your message and to project your professional image. To maximize your vocal strengths, focus on three important qualities of speech: phonation, articulation, and pronunciation.

Phonation involves both the production and the variation of the speaker's vocal

An inherent problem related to speaking rate is verbal fillers—also called nonwords. Verbal fillers, such as *uhhh*, *ahhh*, *ummm*, and *errr*, are irritating to the audience and destroy your effectiveness. Many speakers fill space with their own verbal fillers; these include *you know, I mean, basically, like I said, okay,* and *as a matter of fact.* Because of the conversational style of impromptu and extemporaneous presentations, a speaker will naturally struggle for a word or idea from time to time. Become aware of verbal fillers you frequently use by critiquing a recording of yourself and then focus on replacing fillers with a three- to five-second pause. This brief gap between thoughts gives you an opportunity to think about what you want to say

extemporaneous presentation
a presentation in which a speaker plans, prepares, and rehearses but does not write everything down; brief notes prompt the speaker, but the exact words are chosen spontaneously as the speaker interacts with the audience and identifies its specific needs

phonation
the production and variation of a speaker's vocal tone

next and time for your audience to absorb your idea. Presenting an idea (sound bite) and then pausing briefly is an effective way to influence your audience positively. The listener will not notice the slight delay, and the absence of meaningless words will make you appear more confident and polished. Also avoid annoying speech habits, such as clearing your throat or coughing, that shift the audience's attention from the speech to the speaker.

The following activities will help you achieve good vocal qualities:

- **Breathe properly and relax.** Nervousness affects normal breathing patterns and is reflected in vocal tone and pitch. The better prepared you are, the better your phonation will be. Although relaxing might seem difficult to practice before a speech, a few deep breaths, just as swimmers take before diving, can help.

- **Listen to yourself.** A recording of your voice reveals much about pitch, intensity, and duration. Most people are amazed to find their voices are not quite what they had expected. "I never dreamed I sounded that bad" is a common reaction. Nasal twangs usually result from a failure to speak from the diaphragm, which involves taking in and letting out air through the larynx, where the vocal cords operate. High pitch can occur from the same cause, or it can be a product of speaking too fast or experiencing stage fright.

- **Develop flexibility.** A good speaking voice is somewhat musical, with words and sounds similar to notes in a musical scale. Read each of the following sentences aloud, and emphasize the *italicized* word in each. Even though the sentences are identical, emphasizing different words changes the meaning.

I am happy you are here.	*Maybe I'm the only happy one.*
I *am* happy you are here.	*I really am.*
I am *happy* you are here.	*Happy best describes my feeling.*
I am happy *you* are here.	*Yes, you especially.*
I am happy you *are* here.	*You may not be happy, but I am.*
I am happy you are *here*.	*Here and not somewhere else.*

Articulation involves smooth, fluent, and pleasant speech. It results from the way in which a speaker produces and joins sounds. Faulty articulation is often caused by not carefully forming individual sounds. Common examples include:

- dropping word endings—saying *workin'* for *working*

- running words together—saying *kinda* for *kind of*, *gonna* for *going to*

- imprecise enunciation—saying *dis* for *this*, *wid* for *with*, *dem* for *them*, *pin* for *pen*, or *pitcher* for *picture*

These examples should not be confused with *dialect*, which people informally call an *accent*. A dialect is a variation in pronunciation, usually of vowels, from one part of the country to another. Actually, everyone speaks a dialect; speech experts can often identify, even pinpoint, the section of the country from where a speaker comes. In the United States, common dialects are New England, New York, Southern, Texan, Midwestern, and so forth. Within each of these, minor dialects often arise regionally or from immigrant influence. The simple fact is that when people interact, they influence each other even down to speech sounds. Many prominent speakers have developed a rather universal dialect, known as Standard American Speech or American Broadcast English, that seems to be effective no matter who the audience is. This model for professional language is widely used by newscasters and announcers and is easily understood by those who speak English as a second language because they likely listened to this speech pattern on television as they learned the language.

You can improve the clarity of your voice, reduce strain and voice distortion, and increase your expressiveness by following these guidelines:

- **Stand up straight with your shoulders back, and breathe from your diaphragm rather than your chest.** If you are breathing correctly, you can then use your mouth and teeth to form sounds precisely. For example, vowels are always sounded with the mouth open and the tongue clear of the palate. Consonants are responsible primarily for the distinctness of speech and are formed by an interference with or stoppage of outgoing breath.

- **Focus on completing the endings of all words, not running words together, and enunciating words correctly.** To identify recurring enunciation errors, listen to a recording and seek feedback from others.

- **Obtain formal training to improve your speech.** Pursue a self-study program by purchasing recordings that help you reduce your dialect and move more closely to a universal dialect. You can also enroll in a diction course to improve your speech patterns or arrange for private lessons from a voice coach.

articulation
smooth, fluent, and pleasant speech

Pronunciation involves using principles of phonetics to create accurate sounds, rhythm, stress, and intonation. People might articulate perfectly but still mispronounce words. A dictionary provides the best source to review pronunciation. Two pronunciations are often given for a word, the first one being the desired pronunciation and the second an acceptable variation. An American adopting a pronunciation commonly used in England, such as *shedule* for *schedule* or *a-gane* for *again*, could be seen negatively. In some cases, leeway exists in pronunciation. The first choice for pronouncing *data* is to pronounce the first *a* long, as in *date*; but common usage is fast making pronunciation of the short *a* sound, as in *cat*, acceptable. Likewise, the preferred pronunciation of *often* is with a silent *t*. Good speakers use proper pronunciation and refer to the dictionary frequently in both pronunciation and vocabulary development.

When your voice qualities combine to make your messages pleasingly receptive, your primary concerns revolve around developing an effective delivery style.

12-4c Delivery Style

Speaking effectively is both an art and a skill. Careful planning and practice are essential for increasing speaking effectiveness.

Before the Presentation

Follow these guidelines when preparing for your presentation:

- **Prepare thoroughly.** You can expect a degree of nervousness as you anticipate speaking before a group. This natural tension is constructive because it increases your concentration and your energy and enhances your performance. However, even those seasoned to the spotlight can experience a debilitating case of the jitters. In spring 2013, New Kids on the Block singer Jonathan Knight walked offstage in the middle of a concert in New York, prompting him to tweet apologies about his anxiety.[13] Being well prepared is the surest way to control speech anxiety. Develop an outline for your presentation that supports your purpose and addresses the needs of your audience, and take advantage of every opportunity to gain speaking experience.

- **Prepare effective presentation support tools.** Follow the guidelines presented in the preceding section to select and design visuals, handouts, and notes pages appropriate for your audience and purpose. Additionally, develop a contingency plan in the event of technical difficulties with computer equipment, such as hard copies of the slides or a backup computer preloaded and ready. Arrive early so you can troubleshoot unexpected technological glitches. Despite your degree of planning, however, technical problems might occur during your presentation.

Figure 12-3 Causes for Communication Performance Gaps

- Lack of communication knowledge and skills
- Failing communication inhibits motivation
- Disconnect of organizational communication

Step 5: Causes for Communication Performance Gaps

Lack of communication knowledge and skills

Failing Communication Inhibits Motivation

Disconnect of organizational communication

© Yuri Arcurs/Shutterstock.com

"Never, never, never give a speech on a subject you don't believe in. You'll fail. On the other hand, if you prepare properly, know your material, and believe in it … your audience will not only hear but feel your message."
—John Davis, a successful speech coach[14]

Remain calm and correct them as quickly and professionally as you can. Take heart in the fact that Bill Gates's computer once crashed when he introduced a new version of Windows!

- **Practice, but do not rehearse.** Your goal is to become familiar with the key phrases on your note cards so that you can deliver the presentation naturally as if you are talking with the audience—not reciting the presentation or acting out a role. Avoid overpracticing, which can make your presentation sound mechanical and limit your ability to respond to the audience.

- **Practice the entire presentation.** This practice will allow you to identify (1) flaws in organization or unity, (2) long, complex sentences or ineffective expressions, and (3) "verbal potholes." Verbal potholes include word combinations that could cause you to stumble, words you have trouble pronouncing ("irrelevant" or "statistics"), and words that accentuate your dialect ("get" can sound like "git" regardless of the intention of a Southern speaker).

- **Spend additional time practicing the introduction and conclusion.** You will want to deliver these important parts with finesse while making a confident connection with the audience. A good closing leaves the audience in a good mood and can help overcome some possible weaknesses during the speech. Depending on the techniques used, consider memorizing significant brief statements to ensure their accuracy and impact (e.g., direct quotation, exact statistic, etc.).

- **Practice displaying presentation visuals so that your delivery appears effortless and seamless.** Your goal is to make the technology virtually transparent, positioned in the background to support *you* as the primary focus of the presentation. First, be sure you know basic commands for advancing through your presentation without displaying distracting menus. Develop skill in returning to a specific slide in the event of a computer glitch or an audience question.

- **Seek feedback on your performance to help you to polish your delivery and improve organization.** Critique your own performance by practicing in front of a mirror and evaluating a recording of your presentation. If possible, present to a small audience ahead of time for feedback and to minimize anxiety when presenting to the real audience.

© iStockphoto.com/alxpin

- **Request a lectern to hold your notes and to steady a shaky hand, at least until you gain some confidence and experience.** Keep in mind, though, that weaning yourself from the lectern will eliminate a physical barrier between you and the audience. Without the lectern, you will speak more naturally. If you are using a microphone, ask for a portable microphone so that you can move freely.

- **Request a proper introduction if the audience knows little about you.** An effective introduction will establish your credibility as a speaker on the subject and will make the audience eager to hear you. You can prepare your own introduction as professional speakers do, or you can provide concise, targeted information that answers these three questions: (1) Why is the subject relevant? (2) Who is the speaker? and (3) What credentials qualify the speaker to talk about the subject? Talk with the person introducing you to verify any information, especially the pronunciation of your name, and to review the format of the presentation (time limit, question-and-answer period, etc.). Be certain to thank the person who made the introduction as you begin your presentation. "Thank you for your kind introduction, Ms. Garcia," is adequate. Then follow with your own introduction to your presentation topic.

- **Dress appropriately to create a strong professional image and to bolster your self-confidence.** An audience's initial impression of your personal appearance, your clothing and grooming, affects their ability to accept you as a credible speaker. Because first impressions are difficult to overcome, take time to groom yourself immaculately and to select clothing that is appropriate for the speaking occasion and consistent with the audience's expectations.

- **Arrive early to become familiar with the setup of the room and to check the equipment.** Check the location of your chair, the lectern, the projection screen, light switches, and electrical outlets. Check the microphone and Internet connection and ensure that all equipment is in the appropriate place and working properly. Project your electronic presentation so you can adjust the color scheme to ensure maximum readability. Finally, identify the technician who will be responsible for resolving any technical problems that might occur during the presentation.

During the Presentation

The following are things you can do during your presentation to increase your effectiveness as a speaker:

- **Communicate confidence, warmth, and enthusiasm for the presentation and the time spent with the audience.** "Your listeners won't care how much you know until they know how much you care," is pertinent advice.[15]

  - **Exhibit a confident appearance with alert posture.** Stand tall with your shoulders back and your stomach tucked in. Stand in the "ready position"—no slouching, hunching over the lectern, or rocking. Keep weight forward with knees slightly flexed so you are ready to move easily rather than rooted rigidly in one spot, hiding behind the lectern.

  - **Smile genuinely throughout the presentation.** Pause as you take your place behind the lectern, and smile before you speak the first word. Smile as you finish your presentation and wait for the applause.

  - **Maintain steady eye contact with the audience in random places throughout the room.** Stay with one person approximately three to five seconds—long enough to finish a complete thought or sentence to convince the listener you are communicating individually with him or her. If the audience is large, select a few friendly faces and concentrate on speaking to them rather than to a sea of nondescript faces.

  - **Refine gestures to portray a relaxed, approachable appearance.** Vary hand motions to emphasize important points; otherwise, let hands fall naturally to your side. Practice using only one hand to make points unless you specifically need two hands, such as when drawing a figure or showing dimensions or location. Eliminate any nervous gestures that can distract the audience (e.g., clenching your hands in front of or behind your body, steepling your hands, placing your hands in your pockets, jingling keys or change, or playing with a ring or pen).

  - **Move from behind the lectern and toward the audience to reduce the barrier created between you and the audience.** You can stand to one side and casually present a relaxed pose beside the lectern. However, avoid methodically walking without a purpose.

- **Exercise strong vocal qualities.** Review the guidelines provided for using your voice to project confidence and credibility.

- **Watch your audience.** They will tell you how you are doing and whether you should shorten your speech. Be attentive to negative feedback in the form of talking, coughing, moving chairs, and other signs of discomfort.

- **Use your visuals effectively.** Many speakers will go to a great deal of effort to prepare good presentation visuals—and then not use them effectively. Inexperienced speakers often ignore the visual altogether or fall into the habit of simply nodding their heads toward the visual. Neither of these techniques is adequate for involving the audience with the visual. In fact, if the material is complex, the speaker is likely to lose the audience completely.

  - **Step to one side of the visual so the audience can see it.** Use a pointer if necessary. Direct your remarks to the audience, so that you can maintain eye contact and resist the temptation to look over your shoulder or turn your back to read the information from the screen behind you.

  - **Paraphrase the visual rather than reading it line for line.** To increase the quality of your delivery, develop a workable method of recording what you plan to say about each graphic.

- **Handle questions from the audience during the presentation.** Questions often disrupt carefully laid plans. At the same time, questions provide feedback, clarify points, and ensure understanding. When people ask questions that will be answered later in the presentation, say, "I believe the next slide will clarify that point; if not, we will come back to it." If the question can be answered quickly, you should do so while indicating that it will also be covered more later. Anticipate and prepare for questions that might be raised. You can generate presentation visuals pertaining to certain anticipated questions and display them only if the question is posed. An audience will appreciate your thorough and complete explanation and your ability to adjust your presentation to their needs—this strategy is much more professional than stumbling through an explanation or delaying the answer until the information is available. Speakers giving electronic presentations have ready access to enormous amounts of information that can be displayed instantly for audience discussion. Hyperlinks created within a presentation file will move a speaker instantaneously to a specific slide, another file, or an embedded music or video file.

- **Keep within the time limit.** Be prepared to complete the presentation within the allotted time. In many organizations, speakers have one or more rehearsals before delivering reports to a group such as a board of directors. These rehearsals, or dry runs, are made before other executives, and are critiqued, timed, revised, and rehearsed again. Presentation software makes rehearsing your timing as simple as clicking a button and advancing through the slides as you practice. By evaluating the total presentation time and the time spent on each slide, you can modify the presentation and rehearse it again until the presentation fits the time slot.

After the Presentation

How you handle the time following a presentation is as important as preparing for the presentation itself:

- **Be prepared for a question-and-answer period.** Encourage the audience to ask questions, recognizing an opportunity to ensure that your presentation meets audience needs. Paraphrasing the question allows you time to reflect on what was asked, ensures that everyone heard the question, and assures the questioner that he or she was understood. You can ask the questioner if your answer was adequate. Be courteous even to hostile questioners so you will maintain the respect of your audience. Stay in control of the time by announcing that you have time for one or two more questions, and then invite individual questions when the presentation is over.

- **Distribute handouts.** Distribute the handout when it is needed, rather than at the beginning of the presentation. Otherwise, the audience might read the handout while you are explaining background information needed to understand the written ideas. If you expect the audience to take notes directly on the handout or if the audience will need to refer to the handout immediately, distribute the handout at the beginning of the presentation or before it begins. To keep control of the audience's attention, be sure listeners know when they should be looking at the handout or listening to you. If the handout is intended as resource material only, post the handout to a Web page or place it on a table at the back of the room and at the front for those who come by to talk with you after the presentation.

12-5 Adapting to Alternate Delivery Situations

As you've learned, presenting a dynamic presentation that focuses on the audience's needs and expectations is the fundamental principle in presenting effectively. Along with the solid foundation you've set for spoken communication, you'll also need to adapt your presentation style to the ever-changing business environment and the special needs of culturally diverse audiences. Delivering team presentations and presenting in distance formats are other common situations you'll need to master.

12-5a Culturally Diverse Audiences

When speaking to a culturally diverse audience, you will want to be as natural as possible, while adjusting your message for important cultural variations. Using empathy, you can effectively focus on the listener as an individual rather than a stereotype of a specific culture. Be open and willing to learn, and you will reap the benefits of communicating effectively with people who possess a variety of strengths and creative abilities. Additionally, follow these suggestions for presenting to people from outside your own culture:

- **Speak simply.** Use simple English and short sentences. Avoid acronyms and expressions that can be confusing to nonnative English speakers—namely slang, jargon, figurative expressions, and sports analogies.

- **Avoid words that trigger negative emotional responses such as anger, fear, or suspicion.** Such "red flag" words vary among cultures; thus, try to anticipate audience reaction and choose your words carefully.

- **Enunciate each word precisely and speak somewhat slowly.** Clear, articulate speech is especially important when the audience is not familiar with various dialects and vocabulary. Avoid the temptation to speak in a loud voice, a habit considered rude in any culture and especially annoying to the Japanese, who perceive the normal tone of North Americans as too loud.

- **Be extremely cautious in the use of humor and jokes.** Cultures that prefer more formality might think you are not serious about your purpose or find your humor and jokes inappropriate. Asians, for instance, do not appreciate jokes about family members and the elderly.

- **Learn the culture's preferences for a direct or indirect presentation.** While North Americans tend

Tim Graham/Alamy

time conscious and who believe that personal relationships are the basis of business dealings (e.g., Asian, Latin American). When communicating with cultures that are not time driven, be patient with what you might consider time-consuming formalities and courtesies and lengthy decision-making styles when you would rather get right down to business or move to the next point. Recognize that the presentation might not begin on time or stay on a precise schedule. Allow additional time at the beginning of the presentation to establish rapport and credibility with the audience, and perhaps provide brief discussion periods devoted to building relationships during the presentation.

Be patient and attentive during long periods of silence; in many cultures people are inclined to stay silent unless they have something significant to say or if they are considering (not necessarily rejecting) an idea. In fact, some Japanese have asked how North Americans can think and talk at the same time. Understanding patterns of silence can help you feel more comfortable during these seemingly endless moments and less compelled to fill the gaps with unnecessary words or to make concessions before the other side has a chance to reply.

Other significant points of difference between cultures are the varying rules of business etiquette. Should you use the traditional American handshake or some other symbol of greeting? Is using the person's given name acceptable? What formal titles should be used with a surname? Can you introduce yourself, or must you have someone else who knows the other person introduce you? Are business cards critical, and what rules should you follow when presenting a business card? Should you have business cards that are printed in two languages?

Gift giving can be another confusing issue. When you believe a gift should be presented to your event host, investigate the appropriateness of gift giving, types of gifts considered appropriate or absolutely inappropriate, and colors of wrapping to be avoided in the speaker's culture. Liquor, for example, is an inappropriate gift in Arab countries.

Gaining competence in matters of etiquette will enable you to make a positive initial impression and concentrate on the presentation rather than agonizing over an awkward, embarrassing slip in protocol. Your audience will appreciate your willingness to learn and

to prefer directness, with the main idea presented first, people from many cultures, such as Japanese, Latin American, and Arabic, consider a straightforward approach tactless and rude.

- **Adapt to subtle differences in nonverbal communication.** The direct eye contact expected by most North Americans is not typical of Asian listeners who often keep their eyes lowered and avoid eye contact to show respect. Arab audiences might stare into your eyes in an attempt to "see into the window of the soul." Cultures also vary on personal space and degree of physical contact (slap on the back or arm around the other as signs of friendship).

- **Adapt your dress and presentation style to fit the formality of the culture.** Some cultures prefer a higher degree of formality than the casual style of North Americans. To accommodate, dress conservatively; strive to connect with the audience in a formal, reserved manner; and use highly professional visuals rather than jotting ideas on a flip chart.

- **Seek feedback to determine whether the audience is understanding your message.** Observe listeners carefully for signs of misunderstanding, restating ideas as necessary. Consider allowing time for questions after short segments of your presentation. Avoid asking "Is that clear?" or "Do you understand?" as these statements might elicit a "Yes" answer if the person perceives saying "No" to be a sign of incompetence.

Potential frustrations can also occur when presentations or meetings bring together North Americans, who see "time as money," with people of cultures who are not value their customs. Being sensitive to cultural issues and persistent in learning specific differences in customs and practices can minimize confusion and unnecessary embarrassment.

12-5b Team Presentations

Because much of the work in business today is done in teams, many presentations are planned and delivered by teams of presenters. Well-conducted team presentations give an organization an opportunity to showcase its brightest talent while capitalizing on each person's unique presentation skills. Email, collaborative software, and other technologies make it easy to develop, edit, review, and deliver impressive team presentations.

The potential payoff of many team presentations is quite high—perhaps a $200,000 contract or a million-dollar account. Yet, according to experts, team presentations fail primarily because presenters don't devote enough time and resources to develop and rehearse them.[16] Resist the sure-to-fail strategy of "winging" a team presentation rather than taking the time to do it correctly. Instead, adapt the skills you already possess in planning and delivering an individual presentation to ensure a successful team presentation. Follow these guidelines as you plan and prepare your team presentation:

- **Select a winning team.** Begin by choosing a leader who is well liked and respected by the team, is knowledgeable of the project, is well organized, and will follow through. Likewise, the leader should be committed to leading the team in the development of a cohesive strategy for the presentation as well as the delegation of specific responsibilities to individual members. Frank Carillo, president of Executive Communications Group, warns team presenters that a frequent problem with "divvying up" work into pieces is that the "pieces don't fit together well when they come back."[17] The core team members, along with management, should choose a balanced mix of individuals who each has something important to contribute to the team. Use these questions to guide team selection: What are this member's complementary strengths and style (e.g., technical expertise, personality traits, and presentation skills)? Can this member meet the expectations of the audience (e.g., a numbers person, technical person, person with an

A member of a winning team will have:
- Complementary strengths/style
- Ability to meet expectations
- Willingness to support team strategy
- Willingness to commit to schedule

© Andresr/Shutterstock.com

existing relationship with the audience)? Is this member willing to support the team strategy and commit to the schedule?[18]

- **Agree on the purpose and schedule.** The team as a whole should plan the presentation using the same process used for an individual presentation. Agreeing on the purpose to be achieved and selecting content that focuses on a specific audience will prevent the challenges caused by an individual's submitting off-target material. The quality of the presentation deteriorates when material must be redone hurriedly in the final days before the deadline or when unacceptable material is included just because the team worked so hard on it. Mapping out a complete presentation strategy can also minimize bickering among team members because of uneven workloads or unfavorable work assignments.

The team will also need to agree on a standard design for presentation visuals to ensure consistency in the visuals prepared by individual presenters. Assign a person to merge the various files, to edit for consistency in design elements and the use of jargon and specialized terminology, and to proofread carefully for grammatical accuracy.

Developing a rehearsal schedule ensures adequate time for preparation and practice. Many experts recommend five practice sessions to produce team presentations that are delivered with a unified look. Planning time in the schedule to present before a review team is especially useful for obtaining feedback on team continuity and adjustments needed to balance major discrepancies in the delivery styles of individual presenters.

- **Practice ahead of time.** The team must be well prepared, which will require several rehearsals. Each member must know what others will say to avoid repetition and to fit the time slot. The team must also work out logistical details such as where people will stand, who will run the slides, and when handouts will be distributed. A great deal of the rehearsal time for a team presentation should be spent planning and rehearsing appropriate verbal and physical transitions between team members. The transitions serve to introduce each part of the presentation and make the whole presentation cohesive. This continuity makes the team look polished and conveys team commitment.

Follow these suggestions for delivering seamless, impressive team presentations:

- **Decide who will open and conclude the presentation.** The team member who knows the audience and has established rapport is a logical choice for these two critical sections of a presentation. If no one knows the audience, select the member with the strongest presentation skills and personality traits for connecting well with strangers. This person will introduce all team members and give a brief description of the roles they will play in the presentation.

- **Build natural bridges between segments of the presentation and presenters.** A lead presenter must build a bridge from the points that have been made that will launch the following presenter smoothly into what he or she will discuss. If a lead presenter forgets to make the connection to the next section clear, the next person must summarize what's been said and then preview his or her section. These transitions might seem repetitive to a team that has been working extensively with the material; however, audiences require clear guideposts through longer team presentations. Also, courtesies such as maintaining eye contact, thanking the previous speaker, and clearing the presentation area for the next speaker communicate an important message that the presenters are in sync and work well together.

- **Deliver as a team.** You must present a unified look and communicate to the audience that you care about the team. Spend your time on the "sideline" paying close attention to the current presenter, monitoring the audience for feedback, and being ready to assist the presenter with equipment malfunctions, handouts, and so on. Avoid side conversations and reading notes, yawning, or coughing. To keep an audience engaged in a team presentation, Frank Carillo recommends that team members not presenting should focus on the presenter at least two-thirds of the time. "It may be the 27th time you've heard it, but for that audience it's the first time. Keep it fresh for the listeners."[19]

- **Field questions as a team.** Decide in advance who will field questions to avoid awkward stares and silence that erode the audience's confidence in your team. Normally, the person presenting a section is the logical person to field questions about that section. You can refer questions to team members who are more knowledgeable, but avoid pleading looks for someone else to rescue you. Rather, check visually to see if the person wants to respond and ask if he or she would like to add information. Tactfully contradict other presenters *only* when the presenter makes a mistake that will cause misunderstanding or confusion. While you should be ready to help presenters having difficulty, resist the urge to tack on your response to a presenter's response when the question has already been answered adequately.

12-5c Distance Presentations

Videoconferencing has been used for some time for large, high-exposure activities, such as quarterly executive staff presentations, companywide addresses, new product launches, and crisis management. The technology's lower cost, improved quality, and increased ease of use have opened videoconferencing to many settings.

Substantial cost savings from reduced travel is a compelling reason for companies to use videoconferencing. Threats of terrorism and contagious disease provide more reasons for companies to restrict business travel and look for alternative delivery methods. In addition, important communication benefits, such as the following, can be achieved with videoconferencing:[20]

- improving employee productivity by calling impromptu videoconferences to clear up issues
- involving more people in key decisions rather than limiting important discussions to those who are allowed to travel
- involving expertise critical to the mission, regardless of geographic boundaries
- creating a consistent corporate culture rather than depending on memos to describe company policy

Become proficient in delivering and participating through distance technology.

- improving employees' quality of life by reducing travel time that often cuts into personal time (e.g., Saturday night layovers for a reasonable airfare)

Internet conferencing, or *webcasting*, allows a company to conduct a presentation in real time over the Internet simultaneously with a conference telephone call. Because it runs on each participant's Internet browser, a presentation can reach hundreds of locations at once. While listening to the call, participants can go to a designated Web site and view slides or a PowerPoint presentation that is displayed in sync with the speaker's statements being heard on the phone. Participants key comments and questions in chat boxes or press a keypad system to respond to an audience poll, thus giving valuable feedback without interrupting the speaker.

Companies deliver live Web presentations on issues ranging from internal briefings on new developments and organizational and procedural changes to product strategy and training presentations. Ernst & Young uses Web presentations to announce organizational changes and has found it to be an effective alternative to memos and emails that weren't always remembered or understood. People most affected by an organizational change are able to interact with leaders announcing the change.

Follow these guidelines for adapting your presentation skills to videoconferences and Web presentations:

- **Determine whether a distance delivery method is appropriate for the presentation.** Is the presentation purpose suited to the technology? Can costs in time, money, and human energy be justified? Are key people willing and able to participate? For example, a videoconference for a formal presentation such as an important speech by the CEO to a number of locations justifies the major expense and brings attention to the importance of the message. Distance delivery formats are inappropriate for presentations that cover highly sensitive or confidential issues, for persuasive or problem-solving meetings where no relationship has been established among the participants, and whenever participants are unfamiliar with and perhaps unsupportive of the technology.

- **Establish rapport with the participants prior to the distance presentation.** If possible, meet with or phone participants beforehand to get to know them and gain insights about their attitudes. This rapport will enhance your ability to interpret subtle nonverbal cues and to cultivate the relationship further through the distance format. Emailing or faxing a short questionnaire or posting presentation slides with a request for questions is an excellent way to establish a connection with participants and to ensure that the presentation is tailored to audience needs. Some enterprising distance presenters engage participants in email discussions before the presentation and then use this dialogue to develop positive interaction during the presentation.

- **Become proficient in delivering and participating through distance technology.** Begin by becoming familiar with the equipment and the surroundings. Although technical support staff might be available to manage equipment and transmission tasks, your goal is to concentrate on the contribution you are to make and not your intimidation with the delivery method.

- **Concentrate on projecting positive nonverbal messages.** Keep a natural, friendly expression; relax and smile. Avoid the tendency to stare into the camera. Instead, look naturally at the entire audience as you would in a live presentation. Speak clearly with as much energy as you can. If a lag occurs between the video and audio transmission, adjust your timing to avoid interrupting other speakers. Use gestures to reinforce

Internet conferencing
a method of real-time conferencing that allows a company to conduct a presentation in real time over the Internet simultaneously with a conference telephone call; also called *webcasting*

points, but avoid fast or excessive motion that will appear blurry. Avoid side conversations, coughing, and clearing your throat, which could trigger voice-activated microphones. Pay close attention to other presenters to guard against easy distraction in a distance environment and to capture subtle nonverbal cues. You will need to judge the vocal tone of the person asking a question because you might not see faces.

- **Adjust camera settings to enhance communication.** Generally, adjust the camera so that all participants can be seen, but zoom in more closely on participants when you wish to clearly observe nonverbal language. Project a wide-angle shot of yourself during rapport-building comments at the presentation's beginning and zoom in to signal the start of the agenda or to emphasize an important point during the presentation. Some systems accommodate a split screen, but others allow participants to view either you or your presentation visuals only. You will want to switch the camera between a view of you and your visuals, depending on what is needed at the time.

- **Develop high-quality graphics appropriate for the particular distance format.** Even more than in a live presentation, you will need graphics to engage and maintain participants' attention. Graphics are a welcome variation to the "talking head"—you—displayed on the screen for long periods. Some

companies provide assistance from a webmaster or graphics support staff in preparing slide shows specifically for distance presentations. Also, e-conferencing companies will develop and post presentation slides and host live Web presentations including managing email messages and audience polling. Regardless of the support you receive, you should understand basic guidelines for preparing effective visuals for videoconferencing and Web presentations.

- **Videoconferences.** Readability of text will be a critical issue when displaying visuals during a videoconference because text becomes fuzzy when transmitted through compressed video. Select large, sturdy fonts and choose a color scheme that provides high contrast between the background and the text. Stay with a tested color scheme such as dark blue background, yellow title text, and white bulleted list text to ensure readability. Projecting your visuals ahead of time so you can adjust the color scheme, font selections, and other design elements is an especially good idea.

- **Web presentations.** In addition to considering overall appeal, clarity, and readability, Web presentations must be designed for minimal load time and compatibility with various computers. For your first presentation, consider using a Web template in your electronic presentations software and experiment with the appropriateness of other designs as you gain experience.

Stand-alone presentations designed specifically for Web delivery require unique design strategies to compensate for the absence of a speaker.[21]

- Consider posting text-based explanations in the notes view area or adding vocal narration.

- Develop interactive slide formats that allow viewers to navigate to the most useful information in your presentation. For example, design an agenda slide that includes hyperlinks to the first slide in each section of the presentation.

- Select simple, high-quality graphics that convey ideas effectively.

- Plan limited animation that focuses audience attention on specific ideas on the slide.

- Consider adding video if bandwidth is not an issue.

© iStockphoto.com/jamirae

STUDY TOOLS

CHAPTER 12

Located at back of the textbook

❑ Rip out Chapter Review Card

Located at www.cengagebrain.com

❑ Review Key Terms Flashcards (Print or Online)

❑ Download Audio Summaries for on-the-go review

❑ Complete Practice Quizzes to prepare for tests

❑ Play "Beat the Clock" to master concepts

❑ Complete the Crossword Puzzle to review key terms

❑ Watch the video about McDonaldson, a fictitious but all-too-realistic ad agency whose employees struggle with contemporary business communication issues.

Preparing Résumés and Application Messages

13-1 Preparing for the Job Search

Managing your career begins with recognizing that securing a new job is less important than assessing the impact of that job on your life. Work isn't something that happens from 8 a.m.–5 p.m., with life happening after 5 p.m. Life and work are interconnected, and true satisfaction comes from being able to fully express yourself in what you do. This means merging who you are—your values, emotions, capabilities, and desires—with the activities you perform on the job.[1]

An ideal job provides satisfaction at all of Maslow's need levels, from basic economic to self-actualizing needs. The right job for you will not be drudgery; the work itself will be satisfying and give you a sense of well-being. Synchronizing your work with your core beliefs and talents leads to enthusiasm and fulfillment. You will probably work 10,000 days of your life, not including time spent commuting and on other related activities. Why spend all this time doing something unfulfilling when you could just as easily spend it doing what you enjoy?

Your **résumé** is a vital communication tool that provides a basis for judgment about your capabilities on the job. In preparing this document, your major tasks will be gathering essential information about yourself and the job using traditional and electronic resources, planning and organizing the résumé to showcase your key qualifications, and adapting the résumé for various types of delivery. You will need to supplement your résumé with examples of your accomplishments and abilities. Finally, you'll prepare persuasive application messages appropriate for the delivery of your résumé.

13-1a Gathering Essential Information

The job search begins with research—collecting, compiling, and analyzing information—in order to assess your marketability. The research phase of the job search involves the steps shown in Figure 13-1 on the next page and are summarized as follows:

1. **Gather relevant information for decision making.** Complete a self-assessment to identify your own job-related qualifications, and an analysis of the career field that interests you and of a specific job in that field. Follow up with an interview of a career person in your field to acquire additional information.

2. **Prepare a company/job profile.** Compile the information you gathered into a format that allows you to compare your qualifications with the company and job requirements. This organized information will help you determine a possible match between you and the potential job.

3. **Identify unique selling points and specific support.** Determine several key qualifications and accomplishments that enhance your marketability. These are the key selling points you'll target in your résumé and later in a job interview.

13-1b Identifying Potential Career Opportunities

Plan to begin your job search for prospective employers months in advance. Waiting too long to begin and then hurrying through the job

résumé
a vital communication tool that provides a basis for judgment about a person's capabilities on the job

229

Figure 13-1 Process of Applying for a Job

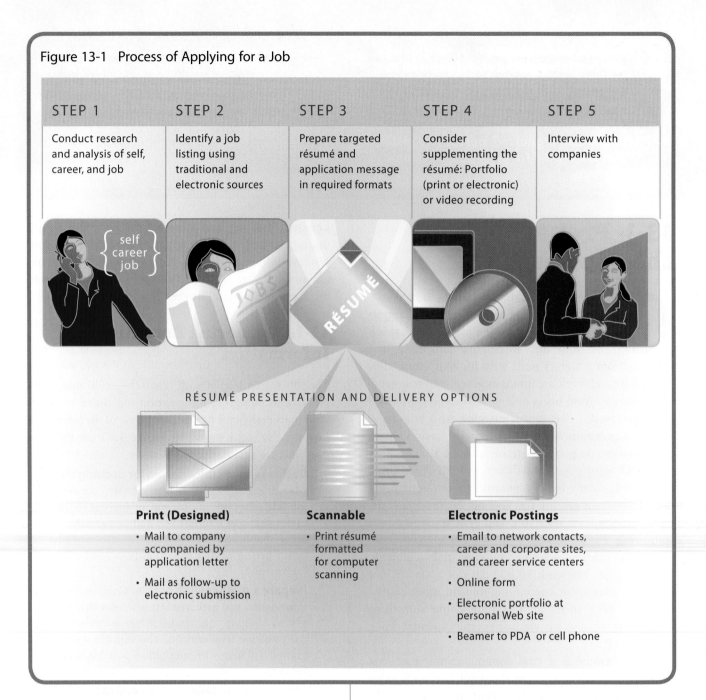

STEP 1	STEP 2	STEP 3	STEP 4	STEP 5
Conduct research and analysis of self, career, and job	Identify a job listing using traditional and electronic sources	Prepare targeted résumé and application message in required formats	Consider supplementing the résumé: Portfolio (print or electronic) or video recording	Interview with companies

RÉSUMÉ PRESENTATION AND DELIVERY OPTIONS

Print (Designed)
- Mail to company accompanied by application letter
- Mail as follow-up to electronic submission

Scannable
- Print résumé formatted for computer scanning

Electronic Postings
- Email to network contacts, career and corporate sites, and career service centers
- Online form
- Electronic portfolio at personal Web site
- Beamer to PDA or cell phone

search process could affect your ability to land a satisfying job.

Before you begin, take the time to develop an organized strategy for your search efforts. You might download a template such as Microsoft's job search log (**http://office.microsoft.com/en-us/templates/results.aspx?qu=job%20search%20log**) or invest in software such as Winway Résumé and Résumé Maker Deluxe to simplify the task of tracking your contacts. You'll need a record of the name, address, email address, and telephone number of each potential employer. Later, record the date of each job contact you make and receive

(along with what you learned from the contact), the name of the contact person, the date you sent a résumé, and so on.

Your search for potential career opportunities likely will involve traditional and electronic job search sources.

Using Traditional Sources

Traditional means of locating a job include printed sources, networks, career services centers, employers' offices, employment agencies and contractors, and professional organizations.

Printed Sources

Numerous printed sources are useful in identifying firms in need of employees. Responses to advertised positions in the employment sections of newspapers should be made as quickly as possible after the ad is circulated. If your résumé is received early and is impressive, you could get a favorable response before other applications are received. If an ad requests that responses be sent to a box number without giving a name, be cautious. The employer could be legitimate but does not want present employees to know about the ad or does not want applicants to phone or drop by. However, you have a right to be suspicious of someone who wants to remain obscure while learning everything you reveal in your résumé. Print job listings can also be found in company newsletters, industry directories, and trade and professional publications, which often are available on the Internet.

Networks

The majority of job openings are never advertised. Therefore, developing a network of contacts is often the most valuable source of information about jobs. Your network could include current and past employers, guest speakers in your classes or at student organization meetings, business contacts you met while interning or participating in shadowing or over-the-shoulder experiences, and so on. Let these individuals know the type of job you are seeking, and ask their advice for finding employment in today's competitive market.

Career Services Centers

You will want to register with your college's career services center at least three semesters before you graduate. Typically, the center has a Web site and a browsing room loaded with career information and job announcement bulletins. Career counseling is available at most career services centers, including workshops on résumé writing, interviewing, etiquette, mock interviews, "mocktail" parties for learning to mingle in pre interview social events, and more. Through the center, you can learn about job fairs at which you can meet prospective employers and schedule on-campus, phone, and video interviews with company recruiters.

Most career services centers use electronic tracking systems. Rather than submitting printed résumés, students input their résumés into a computer file following the specific requirements of the tracking system used by the college or university. A search of the résumé database generates an interview roster of the top applicants for a campus recruiter's needs. Some centers assist students in preparing electronic portfolios to supplement their résumés.

Employers' Offices

Employers who have not advertised their employment needs might respond favorably to a phone or personal inquiry. The receptionist might be able to provide useful information, direct you to someone with whom you can talk, or set up an appointment.

Employment Agencies and Contractors

City, county, state, and federal employment agencies provide free or inexpensive services. Some agencies offer online listings or phone recordings so that applicants can get information about job opportunities and procedures for using their services. The fee charged by private agencies is paid by either the employee or the employer and usually is based on the first month's salary and due within a few months. Some agencies specialize in finding high-level executives or specialists for major firms. Employment contractors specialize in providing temporary employees and might be able to place you in a position on a temporary basis until you find a full-time job.

Professional Organizations

Officers of professional organizations, through their contacts with members, can be good sources of information about job opportunities. Much job information is exchanged at meetings of professional associations. In addition to job listings in journals or organization Web sites, interviews are sometimes conducted at conference locations.

In addition to the professional growth that comes from membership in professional organizations, active participation is a good way to learn about jobs. Guest speakers share valuable information about the industry and its career and job opportunities. Employers are often favorably impressed when membership

© ALMAGAMI/Shutterstock.com

and experiences gained are included on the résumé and discussed during an interview. They are even more impressed if the applicant has been an officer in the organization, as it indicates leadership, community commitment, and willingness to serve without tangible reward, social acceptance, or high level of aspiration. By joining and actively participating in professional, social, and honorary organizations, you increase your opportunities to develop rapport with peers and professors and gain an edge over less-involved applicants.

Using Electronic Job Searches

An increasing number of companies and job hunters are using the Internet to assist in various stages of the job search process. Convenience, speed, and accessibility are all reasons for the popularity of electronic job searches among human resources managers. The cost of electronic recruiting is lower than traditional methods, and applicants, and employers can respond more quickly. Job seekers can use the Internet to complement rather than replace the traditional methods previously discussed.

Locating Career Guidance Information

According to one career consultant, "Most people in the old days could go into an organization [during a job interview] and not really know about it and hope for the best. Now, people can understand the organization before they even apply."[2] The Internet places at your fingertips a wealth of information that will prepare you for the job interview if you use it as a research tool. Suggestions follow for effectively using the career guidance information you can locate on the Internet:

- **Visit career sites for information related to various phases of the job search.** You'll find a wide range of timely discussions at career sites: planning a job search, finding a job you love, researching employers, working a career fair, crafting winning résumés and cover letters, negotiating a salary, and so on.

- **Visit corporate Web sites to learn about companies.** You can locate information online for targeting your résumé appropriately and to prepare for the job interview. Read mission statements or descriptions of services to see how the organization describes itself, and review the annual report and strategic plan to learn about the financial condition and predicted growth rates. Search for "What's New" or "News" sections promoting new developments, as well as career opportunities and job postings. Evaluating the development and professional nature of the Web

site will give you an impression of the organization. Supplement this information with independent sources to confirm the company's stability and status, as negative news likely will not be posted on the Web site.

- **Identify specific skills companies are seeking.** Study the job descriptions provided on corporate home pages and job sites to identify the skills required for the job and the latest industry buzzwords. Use this information to target your résumé to a specific job listing and to generate keywords for an electronic résumé.

- **Network electronically with prospective employers.** It's easy to network online by attending electronic job fairs, chatting with career counselors, participating in news groups and Listservs applicable to your field, and corresponding by email with contacts in companies. The value of these electronic networking experiences is to learn about an industry and career, seek valued opinions, and uncover potential job opportunities. By applying effective communication strategies for an online community, you can make a good impression, create rapport with employment contacts online, and polish your interviewing skills.

Identifying Job Listings

You can use the Internet to locate job opportunities in several ways:

- Look in the employment section of companies' corporate Web sites to see if they are advertising job openings.

- Search the electronic databases of job openings of third-party services.

- Access online job classifieds from daily and trade newspapers. CareerBuilder (**www.careerbuilder.com**) offers the classifieds of a number of major newspapers.

- Subscribe to a newsgroup through UseNext (http://www.usenext.com/?gclid=CJaU6Y3q37k CFUVk7AodUWMAe) that gives you access to jobs by geographic location and specific job categories.

- Subscribe to services such as America Online (http://www.aol.com/) that provide job search sites and services by keying "Career."

Online and printed sources will help you learn to search particular databases. The following general suggestions will help you get started:

- Input words and phrases that describe your skills rather than job titles because job titles vary by company.

- Use specific phrases such as "entry-level job" or "job in advertising" rather than "job search."

- Start with a wider job description term, such as "pharmaceutical sales jobs"; then narrow down to the specific subject, geographic region, state, and so forth.

- Don't limit yourself to one search engine; try several and bookmark interesting sites.

- Stay focused on your goal and don't get distracted as you go.

Searching for useful career sites among the hundreds available can be quite time consuming. CareerBuilder, JobCentral, and Monster.com are major career sites offering a wide array of information and services.

© NAN728/Shutterstock.com

Another name for "résumé" is "curriculum vitae" or "CV," which is Latin for "course of one's life."

13-2 Planning a Targeted Résumé

In order to match your interests and qualifications with available jobs, you'll need an effective résumé. To win a job interview in today's tight market where job seekers outnumber positions, you need more than a general résumé that documents your education and work history. The powerful wording of a **targeted résumé** reflects the requirements of a specific job listing that you have identified through traditional and electronic job search methods.

An employer typically scans résumés quickly looking for reasons to reject the applicant, schedule an interview, or place it in a stack for rereading. This initial scan and a second brief look for those who make the cut give little time to explain why you are the best person for the job. To grab an employer's attention, you must selectively choose *what to say*, *how to say it*, and *how to arrange it* on the page so that it can be read quickly but thoroughly. A concise, informative, easy-to-read summary of your relevant qualifications will demonstrate that you possess the straightforward communication skills demanded in today's information-intensive society.

The goal of the résumé is to get an interview, so ask yourself this question: "Does including this information increase my chances of getting an interview?"

If the answer is "Yes," include the information; if the answer is "No," omit the information and use the space to develop your qualifications. When selecting information to be included, you must also be cautious of the temptation to inflate your résumé to increase your chances of being hired.

13-2a Standard Parts of a Résumé

A winning résumé contains standard parts that are adapted to highlight key qualifications for a specific job. The sample résumés and in-depth explanation of each standard part provided in Figures 13-2 to 13-5 (see pages 242–247) will prepare you for creating a résumé that describes your qualifications best.

Identification

Your objective is to provide information that will allow the interviewer to reach you. Include your name, current address, phone number, and email address. Provide a clear, benign email address that reflects a positive impression (e.g., no "mustangsally"). You should also include your Web site address to provide access to more detailed information.

> **targeted résumé**
> a résumé that reflects the requirements of a specific job listing

To ensure that the interviewer can quickly locate the identification information, center it on the page or use graphic design elements to call attention to your name. You should include a permanent address (parent's or other relative's address) if you are interviewing when classes are not in session. Leave a clear, straightforward greeting on your phone that portrays you as a person serious about securing a job. Eliminate music, clever sayings, or background noise.

Job and/or Career Objective

Following the "Identification" section, state your job/career objective—the job you want. Interviewers can see quickly whether the job you seek matches the one they have to offer. A good job/career objective must be specific enough to be meaningful yet general enough to apply to a variety of jobs. The following example illustrates a general objective that has been revised to describe a specific job:

General Objective	Specific Objective
A challenging position that enables me to contribute to an organization's success.	Position where my creative Web design skills and ability to work under pressure will enable me to contribute to organizational success.
A position with a stable organization that provides an opportunity for development and career advancement.	Position where my accounting knowledge, attention to detail, and strong work ethic will enable me to contribute to a firm's financial success.

Some experts argue that a statement of your job or career objective can limit your job opportunities; your objective should be obvious from your qualifications. In general, however, making your objective clear at the beginning assures the interviewer that you have a definite career goal.

Career Summary

To survive the interviewer's 40-second scan, you must provide a compelling reason for a more thorough review of your résumé. Craft a persuasive introductory statement that quickly synthesizes your most transferable skills, accomplishments, and attributes, and place it in a section labeled "Summary" or "Professional Profile."

In this synopsis of your key qualifications, communicate why you should be hired. Your answer should evolve naturally from the career objective and focus on your ability to meet the needs of the

company you have identified from your extensive research. Combining the career objective with the career statement is an acceptable strategy as noted in the following examples:

Separate Objective and Career Summary

Objective: Position where my proven customer service skills and strong work habits will enable me to contribute to a growing company.
Career Summary: Six years of experience in telephone service center; promoted to team lead after two years and supervisor after four.

Combined Objective with Career Summary

Professional Profile: Entry-level position in investment banking or finance. Internship experience with two investment banking firms, where I prepared and delivered multiple sales presentations to potential high-volume clients.

Linked Objective and Career Summary

Profile: Position as sales representative in which demonstrated commission selling and hard work bring rewards.
Accomplishments:
- Three years' straight commission sales
- Average of $35,000–$55,000 a year in commissioned earnings
- Consistent success in development and growth of territories

A high-impact career summary, once considered optional, has become a standard section of résumés in today's fast-paced information age. Develop your résumé to skillfully target the requirements of a specific position; then compose a career summary sure to interest any interviewer who instantly sees an applicant with exactly the skills needed.

Qualifications

The "Qualifications" section varies depending on the information identified in the analysis of self, career, and job. This information is used to divide your qualifications into appropriate parts, label them appropriately, and arrange them in the best sequence. Usually, qualifications stem from your education and work experience (words that appear as headings in the résumé). Order these categories according to which you perceive as more impressive to the employer, with the more impressive category appearing first. For example, education is usually the chief qualification of a recent college graduate. However, a sales representative with related work experience might list experience first, particularly if the educational background is inadequate for the job sought.

Education

Beginning with the most recent, list the degree, major, school, and graduation date. Include a blank line between schools for easy reading. The interviewer will probably want to know first whether you have the appropriate degree, then the institution, and then other details. Recent or near college graduates should omit high school activities because that information is "old news." However, include high school activities if they provide a pertinent dimension to your qualifications. For example, having attended high school abroad is a definite advantage to an applicant seeking employment in an international firm. In addition, high school accomplishments could be relevant for freshmen or sophomores seeking cooperative education assignments, scholarships, or part-time jobs. Of course, this information will be replaced with college activities when the résumé is revised for subsequent jobs or other uses.

Include overall and major grade-point averages if they are B or better—but be prepared to discuss any omissions during an interview. Some recruiters recommend that every candidate include his or her grade-point average, since an omission might lead the reader to assume the worst. Honors and achievements that relate directly to education can be incorporated in this section or included in a separate section. Listing scholarships, appearance on academic lists, and initiation into honor societies is common; but consider also including business-relevant skills you've developed, including client projects, team building, and field experiences. If honors and achievements are included in the "Education" section, be sure to include plenty of white space or use bullets to highlight these points (see Figure 13-2 on page 242 and Figure 13-4 on page 244).

The "Education" section could also include a list of special skills and abilities such as foreign language and computer competency. A list of courses typically required in your field is unnecessary and occupies valuable space. However, you should include any courses, workshops, or educational experiences that are not usual requirements, such as internships, cooperative education semesters, "shadowing," and study abroad.

Work Experience

The "Work Experience" section provides information about your employment history. For each job held, list the job title, company name, dates of employment, primary responsibilities, and key accomplishments. The jobs can be listed in reverse chronological order (beginning with the most recent) or in order of job relatedness. Begin with the job that most obviously relates to the job being sought if you have gaps in your work history, if the job you are seeking is very different from the job you currently hold, or if you are just entering the job market and have little, if any, related work experience.

Arrange the order and format of information about each job (dates, job title, company, description, and accomplishments) so that the most important information is emphasized—but format all job information consistently. If you have held numerous jobs in a short time, embed dates of employment within the text rather than surround them with white space. Give related job experience added emphasis by listing it first or surrounding it with white space.

Employers are interested in how you can contribute to their bottom line, so a winning strategy involves concentrating on accomplishments and achievements. Begin with the job title and company name that provides basic information about your duties, and then craft powerful descriptions of the quality and scope of your performance. These bullet points will provide deeper insight into your capability, ambition, and personality and set you apart from other applicants who take the easy route of providing only a work history.

Return to the in-depth analysis you completed at the beginning of the job search process to recall insights as to how you can add immediate value to this company. Consider the following questions to spur your recognition of marketable skills from your education, work, and community experiences.[3]

My Marketable Skills

- How does my potential employer define success in the job for which I'm applying? How do I measure up?
- What is my potential employer's bottom line (money, attendance, sales, etc.)? When have I shown that I know how to address that bottom line?
- What project am I proud of that demonstrates I have the skill for my job objective?
- What technical or management skills do I have that indicate the level at which I perform?
- What problem did I solve, how did I solve it, and what were the results?

Because interviewers spend such a short time reading résumés, the style must be direct and simple. Therefore, a résumé should use crisp phrases to help employers see the value of the applicant's education and experiences. To save space and to emphasize what you have accomplished, use these stylistic techniques:

1. Omit pronouns referring to yourself (*I*, *me*, *my*).

2. Use subject-understood sentences.

3. Begin sentences with action verbs as shown in the following examples:

Instead of	Use
I had responsibility for developing sales materials.	**Developed sales materials, including brochures and Web site promotions.**
My duties included meeting with potential clients to review financial products.	**Met with potential clients and used interpersonal communication skills to sell a wide range of financial products.**
I was the treasurer of my fraternity and managed a charitable fund-raising event.	**Managed a $200,000-plus budget and organized a charitable fund-raising event that garnered $15,000, a 25 percent increase over previous year.**
I worked in retail sales, selling fashions and accessories.	**Named salesperson of the year for sales of more than $50,000.**
I was the president of the Student Marketing Association and a member of a winning case-competition team.	**Demonstrated excellent leadership skills as president of Student Marketing Association and collaborative teamwork skills as member of winning case-competition group.**

Action verbs are especially appropriate for résumés because employers are looking for people who will work. Note the subject-understood sentences in the right column of the previous example: action words used as first words provide emphasis.

The following list contains action verbs that are useful in résumés:

achieved	drafted	participated
analyzed	increased	planned
assisted	initiated	recruited
compiled	managed	streamlined
developed	organized	wrote

To avoid a tone of egotism, do not use too many adjectives or adverbs that seem overly strong. Plan to do some careful editing after writing your first draft.

Honors and Activities

Make a trial list of any other information that qualifies you for the job. Divide the list into appropriate divisions and then select an appropriate label. Your heading might be "Honors and Activities." You might include a section for "Activities," "Leadership Activities," or "Memberships," depending on the items listed. You might also include a separate section on "Military Service," "Civic Activities," "Volunteer Work," or "Interests." If you have only a few items under each category, use a more general term and combine the lists. If your list is lengthy, divide it into more than one category as interviewers prefer "bite-size" pieces that are easy to read and remember.

Resist the urge to include everything you have ever done; keep in mind that every item you add distracts from other information. Consider summarizing information that is relevant but does not merit several separate lines—for example, "Involved in art, drama, and choral groups." To decide whether to include certain information, ask these questions: How closely related is it to the job being sought? Does it provide job-related information that has not been presented elsewhere?

Personal Information

Because a résumé should contain primarily information that is relevant to an applicant's experience and qualifications, you must be selective when including personal information that is not related to the job you are seeking. The space could be used more effectively to include more about your qualifications or to add more white space. Personal information is commonly placed at the end of the résumé just above the "References" section

LIVING ONLINE?

Your Facebook or MySpace profile, photos, and "innermost" thoughts create a "shadow" résumé that may hurt your employment opportunities far into the future. A recent employer survey indicated that 44 percent of employers use social networking sites to examine the profiles of job candidates, and 39 percent have looked up the profile of a current employee.[4]

because it is less important than qualifications (education, experience, and activities).

Under the 1964 Civil Rights Act (and subsequent amendments) and the Americans with Disabilities Act (ADA), employers cannot make hiring decisions based on gender, age, marital status, religion, national origin, or disability. Employers prefer not to receive information about these protected areas because questions could be raised about whether the information was used in the hiring decision.

Follow these guidelines related to personal information:

- **Do not include personal information that could lead to discriminatory hiring.** Exclude height, weight, color of hair and eyes, and a personal photograph on the résumé.

- **Reveal ethnic background (and other personal information) only if it is job related.** For example, certain businesses might be actively seeking employees in certain ethnic groups because the ethnic background is a legitimate part of the job description. For such a business, ethnic information is useful and appreciated.

- **Include personal information (other than information covered by employment legislation) that will strengthen your résumé.** Select information that is related to the job you are seeking or that portrays you as a well-rounded, happy individual off the job. Include interests, hobbies, favorite sports, and willingness to relocate. You can also include the following topics if you have not covered them elsewhere in the résumé: spoken and written communication skills, computer competency, foreign language or computer skills, military service, community service, scholastic honors, job-related hobbies, and professional association memberships.

- **Consider whether personal information might be controversial.** For example, listing a sport that an interviewer might perceive to be overly time consuming or dangerous would be questionable. An applicant seeking a position with a religious or political organization could benefit from revealing a related affiliation.

References

Providing potential employers a list of references (people who have agreed to supply information about you when requested) complements your employment credentials. Listing names, addresses, phone numbers, and email addresses of people who can provide information about you adds credibility to the résumé. Employers, former employers, and college instructors are good possibilities. Friends, relatives, and neighbors are not (because of their perceived bias in your favor). Some career experts recommend including a peer to document your ability to work as a member of a team, an important job skill in today's team-oriented environment.[5] According to Bob Daugherty, who heads U.S. recruiting for PricewaterhouseCoopers, the best references are people who work for the organization you are looking to join.[6] You'll gain these employee referrals through strong relationships developed through proactive and professional networking through traditional and electronic means. Update your reference list often to be certain that your choices remain relevant and credible (e.g., none are deceased or dismissed for embezzlement).

References can be handled on the résumé in several ways. As the closing section of your résumé, you can provide a list of references, include a brief statement that references are available on request or from a career services center, or omit any statement regarding references assuming that references are not needed until after an interview. You can list references directly on the résumé if you have limited qualifications to include, if you know a company interviews applicants *after* references are contacted, or when you believe the names of your references will be recognizable in your career field. You could include a statement such as "For references … ," or "For additional information … ," and give the address of the career services center of your college or university, the job bank posting your credentials, or the URL of your electronic portfolio.

Withholding the names of references until they are requested prevents unnecessary or untimely requests going to your present employer. This action also conveys genuine courtesy to the references. Even the most enthusiastic references could become apathetic if required to provide recommendations to endless interviewers. For this same reason, be sure to communicate with your references regularly if your job search continues longer than expected. Suggestions for communicating with references are discussed in Chapter 14.

When preparing a separate list of references to be given after a successful interview, place the word *References* and your name in a visible position as shown in Figure 13-3 on page 243. Balance the list (name, address, phone number, and relationship of reference to applicant) attractively on the page, and use the same paper used for printing the résumé. Whether it is handed to the interviewer personally or mailed, the references page professionally complements your résumé. Confident that you have a good message, you are now ready to put it in writing—to construct a résumé that will impress an employer favorably.

chronological résumé
the traditional organizational format for résumés with headings that spotlight an applicant's education and experience

functional résumé
the organizational format for résumés that highlights an applicant's transferable skills

13-2b Types of Résumés

The general organization of all résumés is fairly standard: identification (name, address, phone number, and email address), job objective, qualifications, personal information, and references.

The primary organizational challenge is in dividing the qualifications section into parts, choosing labels for them, and arranging them in the best sequence. When you review your self-, career-, and job analyses data and career/job profile, you will recognize that your qualifications stem mainly from your education and your experience. Your task is to decide how to present these two categories of qualifications. Résumés usually are organized in one of three ways: reverse chronological order (most recent activity listed first), functional order (most important activity listed first), or a chrono-functional, which combines the chronological and functional orders as the name implies. To determine which organizational plan to use, draft your résumé in each.

Chronological Résumé

The **chronological résumé** is the traditional organizational format for résumés. Two headings normally appear in the portion that presents qualifications: "Education" and "Experience." Which one should appear first? Decide which one you think is more impressive to the employer, and put that one first. Within each section, the most recent information is presented first. Reverse chronological order is easier to use and is more common than functional order; however, it is not always more effective.

The chronological résumé is an especially effective format for applicants who have progressed up a clearly defined career ladder and want to move up another rung. Because the format emphasizes dates and job titles, the chronological résumé is less effective for applicants who have gaps in their work histories, are seeking jobs different from the job currently held, or are just entering the job market with little or no experience.[7]

If you choose the chronological format, look at the two headings from the employer's point of view, and reverse their positions if doing so is to your advantage. In the "Experience" section, jobs are listed in reverse-chronological order. Assuming you have progressed typically, your latest job is likely to be more closely related to the job being sought than the first job held. Placing the latest or current job first will give it the emphasis it deserves. Include beginning and ending dates for each job.

Functional Résumé

In a **functional résumé**, points of primary interest to employers—transferable skills—appear in major headings. These headings highlight what an applicant can *do* for the employer—functions that the applicant can perform well. Under each heading, an applicant could draw from educational and/or work-related experience to provide supporting evidence.

A functional résumé requires a complete analysis of self, career, and the job sought. Suppose, for example, that a person seeking a job as an assistant hospital administrator wants to emphasize qualifications by placing them in major headings. From the hospital's advertisement of the job and from accumulated job appraisal information, an applicant sees this job as both an administrative and a public-relations job. The job requires skill in communicating and knowledge of accounting and finance. Thus, headings in the "Qualifications" section of the résumé could be "Administration," "Public Relations," "Communication," and "Budgeting." Under "Public Relations," for example, an applicant could reveal that a public relations course was taken at State University, from which a degree is to be conferred in May, and that a sales job at ABC Store provided abundant opportunity to apply principles learned. With other headings receiving similar treatment, the qualifications portion reveals the significant aspects of education and experience.

Order of importance is the best sequence for functional headings. If you have prepared an accurate self- and job analysis, the selected headings will highlight points of special interest to the employer. Glancing at headings only, an employer can see that you understand the job's requirements and have the qualities needed for success.

Having done the thinking required for preparing a functional résumé, you are well prepared for a question that is commonly asked in interviews: "What can you do for us?" The answer is revealed in your major headings. They emphasize the functions you can perform and the special qualifications you have to offer.

If you consider yourself well qualified, a functional résumé is worth considering. If your education or experience is scant, a functional résumé could be best for you. Using "Education" and "Experience" as headings (as in a chronological résumé) works against your purpose if you have little to report under the headings; the format would emphasize the absence of education or experience.

Chrono-Functional Résumé

The **chrono-functional résumé** combines features of chronological and functional résumés. This format can

give quick assurance that educational and experience requirements are met and still use other headings that emphasize qualifications.

13-3 Preparing Résumés for Print and Electronic Delivery

Format requirements for résumés have changed significantly in recent years. Whether presented on paper or electronically, the arrangement of a résumé is just as important as the content. If the arrangement is unattractive, unappealing, or in poor taste, the message might never be read. Errors in keyboarding, spelling, and punctuation could be taken as evidence of a poor academic background, lack of respect for the employer, or carelessness. Recognize that résumés serve as your introduction to employers and indicate the quality of work you'll produce.

As in preparing other difficult documents, prepare a rough draft as quickly as you can and then revise as many times as needed to prepare an effective résumé that sells you. After you are confident with the résumé, ask at least two other people to check it for you. Carefully select people who are knowledgeable about résumé preparation and the job you are seeking and can suggest ways to present your qualifications more effectively. After you have incorporated those changes, ask a skillful proofreader to review the document.

To accommodate employers' preferences for the presentation and delivery of résumés, you'll need three versions of your résumé as shown in Figure 13-1: a designed résumé printed on paper, a scannable résumé to be read by a computer, and a designed résumé accessible through email and Web sites.

13-3a Preparing a Print (Designed) Résumé

Your print (designed) résumé is considered your primary marketing document, and appearance is critical. To win out among hundreds of competing résumés, it must look professional and reflect current formatting and production standards while maintaining a distinctive conservative tone.

chrono-functional résumé
a résumé that combines features of chronological and functional résumés

tone. Follow these guidelines for designing and producing a highly professional résumé:

- **Develop an appealing résumé format that highlights your key qualifications and distinguishes your résumé.** Use the power of your word processing software for style enhancements rather than settle for overused, inflexible templates. Study the example résumés in this chapter and models from other sources for ideas for enhancing the style, readability, and overall impact of the document. Then create a custom design that best highlights your key qualifications.

- **Format information for quick, easy reading.** To format your résumé so that it can be read at a glance, follow these guidelines:

  - Use attention-getting headings to partition major divisions, and add graphic lines and borders to separate sections of text.

  - Use an outline format when possible to list activities and events on separate lines, and include bullets to emphasize multiple points.

  - Use 10-point fonts or larger to avoid reader eye strain.

  - Use type styles and print attributes to emphasize key points. For example, to draw attention to the identification and headings, select a bold sans serif font (e.g., Calibri or Arial) slightly larger than the serif font (e.g., Cambria or Times New Roman) used for the remaining text. Capitalization, indention, and print enhancements (underline, italics, bold) are useful for adding emphasis. Limit the number of type styles and enhancements, however, so the page is clean and simple to read.

  - Include identification on each page of a multiple-page résumé. Place your name and a page number at the top of the second and successive pages with "Continued" at the bottom of the first page. The interviewer is reexposed to your name, and pages can be reassembled if separated.

- **Create an appealing output to produce top professional quality.**

  - Check for consistency throughout the résumé. Consistency in spacing, end punctuation, capitalization, appearance of headings, and sequencing of details within sections will communicate your eye for detail and commitment to high standards.

  - Balance the résumé attractively on the page with approximately equal margins. Allow generous white space so the résumé looks uncluttered and easy to read.

- **Consider adding a statement of your creativity and originality.** Be certain that your creativity will not be construed as gimmickry and distract from the content of the résumé. Demonstrating creativity is particularly useful for fields such as advertising, public relations, graphic design, and those requiring computer proficiency.

- Select paper of a standard size (8 1/2" by 11"), neutral color (white, buff, or gray), and high quality (preferably 24-pound, 100 percent cotton fiber). Consider using a mailing envelope large enough to accommodate the résumé without folding. The unfolded documents on the reader's desk will get favorable attention and will scan correctly if posted to an electronic database.

- Print with a laser printer that produces high-quality output. Position paper so the watermark is read across the sheet in the same direction as the printing.

Some employers insist that the "best" length for a résumé is one page, stating that long résumés are often ignored. However, general rules about length are more flexible. Most students and recent graduates can present all relevant résumé information on one page. However, as you gain experience, you might need two or more pages to format an informative, easy-to-read résumé. A résumé forced on one page will likely have narrow margins and large blocks of run-on text (multiple lines with no space to break them). This dense format is unappealing and complicates the interviewer's task of skimming quickly for key information.

The rule about length is simple: Be certain your résumé contains only relevant information presented as concisely as possible. A one-page résumé that includes irrelevant information is too long. A two-page résumé that omits relevant information is too short.

The résumés illustrated in Figures 13-2 and 13-4 (see pages 242 and 244) demonstrate the organizational principles for the chronological and functional résumés. A references page is illustrated in Figure 13-3 on page 243. Study the various layouts to decide on one that will highlight your key qualifications most effectively.

13-3b Preparing Electronic Résumé Submissions

To this point you have focused on the preparation of a print résumé. However, in the digital age of instant information, you'll use various online methods to apply for a job and present your qualifications to prospective employers.

The easiest and most common method of putting your résumé online is through emailing a résumé to a job bank for posting or to a networking contact who asked you to send a résumé. Many job banks, corporate sites, and career services centers require you to respond to specific openings by completing an online form or pasting your résumé into a designated section of the form. Frequently, you can input information directly on the Web site or download the form to be submitted by email, fax, or mail. You might also choose to post your résumé on your personal Web site as part of an electronic portfolio that showcases evidence of your qualifications. You could also develop a **beamer**, or *beamable résumé*, a quick version of your résumé designed in a format suitable for broadcasting on smartphones. Recruiting professionals predict that millions of these electronic résumés will be exchanged silently at conferences, business meetings, and power lunches, similar to exchanging business cards.[8]

Electronic submissions are quick and easy but present new challenges and many opportunities to jeopardize your employment chances and compromise your privacy. Just consider recent struggles you might have faced in dealing with viruses and unwelcomed emails, attempting to access nonworking links, and more. Before sending your résumé into cyberspace, follow these suggestions to ensure that your electronic submission is both professional and technically effective:

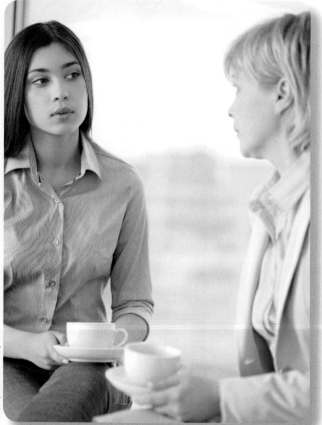

"The best references are people who work for the organization you are looking to join."
—*Bob Daugherty, U.S. Recruiting, PricewaterhouseCoopers*

- **Choose postings for your résumé with purpose.** Online résumé postings are not confidential. Once your résumé is online, anyone can read it, including your current employer. You might also begin to receive junk mail and cold calls from companies who see your résumé online; even more seriously, you could become a victim of identity theft. To protect your privacy online, limit personal information disclosed in the résumé and post only to sites with password protection allowing you to approve the release of your résumé to specific employers. Dating your electronic résumé will also prevent embarrassment should your employer find an old version of your résumé, which could occur as result of exchange of résumés between career sites and delays in updating postings.

  Protect your references' privacy by omitting their names when posting online. Withholding this information will prevent unwelcomed calls by recruiters and other inappropriate contacts and threats to privacy. Because technology allows broadcast of your résumé to all available positions on a career site, read postings carefully and apply only to those that match your qualifications. This action improves the efficiency of the job selection process for the company and the applicant and depicts fair, ethical behavior.

- **Don't hurry.** The speed, convenience, and informality of filling in online boxes or composing an email cover letter for an attached résumé can lead to sloppiness that reflects negatively on your abilities and attitude. Make sure every aspect of your electronic submission is top-notch just as you would for a print résumé. Provide all information exactly as requested, write concise, clear statements relevant to the job sought, and proofread carefully for grammatical and spelling errors. If you direct an employer to an electronic portfolio, devote necessary time to make it attractive, informative, and technically sound. Double-check your files to ensure they can be opened and retain an appealing format. Finally, read the posting carefully to learn how long your résumé will remain active, how to update it, and how to delete it from the site.

beamer
a quick version of a résumé designed in a format suitable for broadcasting on smartphones; also called a *beamable résumé*

Figure 13-2 GOOD :-) Chronological Résumé

Kathy Lawrence
159 Oak Tree Lane
Oklahoma City, OK 75009
410-755-4918
klawrence@gmail.com

OBJECTIVE Entry-level position in marketing that enables to put my knowledge of social media and excellent communication skills to work for a growing organization.

Includes email address that reflects professional image.

Reveals position sought and powerful summary of qualifications.

CAREER
SUMMARY Two marketing internships that enabled me to produce and deliver sales presentations to potential clients, and provided me opportunities to design social media marketing campaigns and work as part of creative team.

Positions education as top qualification for recent graduate. Includes high GPA.

EDUCATION Bachelor of Business Administration, emphasis in Marketing, **Oklahoma State University** expected graduation, May 2014
GPA 3.7 on a 4.0 scale

Edges out competition by expanding on related experience and work achievements.

RELATED
EXPERIENCE Marketing Intern, Thompson Creative Agency, Oklahoma City, OK June–August, 2013
- Prepared and delivered sales presentations to potential clients
- Developed time management, team building, and communication skills while working with creative marketing team
- Demonstrated ability to accept and respond to criticism, learn job tasks quickly, and perform duties with minimal supervision

Lists academic recognitions and highlights relevant skills.

Marketing Intern, TechWorld, Oklahoma City, OK June-August 2012
- Worked with team to develop social media marketing program
- Wrote blog entries on company web site and responded to customer posts
- Posted entries to company's Twitter feed

Format Pointers
Places name at top center for easy viewing (top right is also acceptable). Uses bold font to distinguish identification section and headings from remaining text.

Uses two-column format for easy location of specific sections.

LANGUAGES Native fluency in English
Fluent in Spanish

SKILLS Proficient in Microsoft Office Suite

Creates visual appeal through custom format rather than commonly used template, short readable sections focusing on targeted qualifications, and streamlined bulleted lists.

LEADERSHIP Alpha Psi Beta, 2010–2014
- Served as local chapter president
- Received commendation from chapter advisor

Diversity Considerations
Follows standard format and rules for résumés for application with U.S. company. Specific formats vary for specific countries and federal government.

Figure 13-3 **GOOD :-)** References Page

Kathy Lawrence
159 Oak Tree Lane
Oklahoma City, OK 75009
410-755-4918
klawrence@gmail.com

REFERENCES

Jack Lewis
President
Thompson Creative Agency
P.O. Box 1555
Oklahoma City, OK 75009
410-555-9000
jlewis@thompsoncreative.com
Relationship: Immediate supervisor during summer internship, 2013

Dr. Juanita Garcia, Professor
Marketing Department
Oklahoma State University
120 River Avenue, MKT 240
Oklahoma City, OK 75009
410-555-8956
jgarcia@osu.edu
Relationship: Academic adviser and professor for marketing courses

Leonard Owens
Marketing Manager
TechWorld
345 Sonora Way
Oklahoma City, OK 75009
410-555-3209
lowens@techworld.com
Relationship: Immediate supervisor during summer internship, 2012

Includes professor and immediate supervisors as references, but excludes friends, relatives, or clergy to avoid potential bias.

Includes for each reference full contact information, including email address if available, and relationship to job applicant.

Format Pointers
Prepares reference page at same time as résumé and makes available immediately after successful interview. Paper (color, texture, and size) and print type match résumé.

Balances references attractively.

- **Include your résumé in the format requested by the employer or job bank.** You could be instructed to send the résumé as an attachment to the message or include it in the body of an email message, known as an **inline résumé**. The inline résumé is becoming the preferred choice as fear of computer viruses and daily email overload prevent employers from opening attachments. Unless instructed to send your attachment in a specific format such as Word, save your résumé and cover letter in one file beginning with the cover letter as an ASCII or Rich Text Format file with line length limited to 65 characters and spacing. This plain text version, referred to as

inline résumé
a résumé included in the body of an email message

Figure 13-4 **GOOD** :-) Functional Résumé

Clare Thompson
432 Sierra Drive
Aurora, C) 87009
705-855-4491
cthompson@gmail.com

OBJECTIVE	Position in sales with advancement to marketing and promotion.
CAREER SUMMARY	• Degree in business administration with three years of part-time experience in sales. • Develop Web site promotion strategies for small-business clients. • Strong communication skills, particularly in the area of sales and customer service.
RELEVANT SKILLS	**MARKETING AND PROMOTIONS** • Worked as part of a team charged with developing Web site promotion strategies for a broad range of clients. • Designed promotional flyers for video game retailer and distributed to local business community and potential individual customers. • Worked as part of a team tasked with creating a marketing program for a small business in Marketing Fundamentals course. **TECHNOLOGY SKILLS** • Well-versed in use of Microsoft Office Suite, InDesign, and DreamWeaver. • Experienced in use of gaming programs and technology. • Designed and created Web sites for clients at a public relations and marketing firm. **COMMUNICATION** • Provided customer service to game enthusiasts by answering questions about gaming products and their functionality. • Worked with diverse group of students providing coaching as a volunteer math tutor for Aurora Elementary School. • Collaborated successfully with diverse groups as part of course requirements for business administration degree.
EMPLOYMENT HISTORY	Marketing Intern, Conway Associates, Summer 2014 Sales Associate, Mod Squad, 2013 to present (part-time)
EDUCATION	B.S., Business Administration, Northern Colorado College, Expected graduation May 2014
REFERENCES	Fred Conway, President, Conway Associates, 214 Desert Dr., Aurora, CO 89040, 852-203-5678. Tina Perkins, Manager, Mod Squad, 4506 Central Ave., Aurora, CO 89040, 852-334-2121. Dr. Freda Waring, Advisor, Business Administration, Northern Colorado College, P.O. Box 2340, Denver, CO 89040, 852-334-7073.

Includes clear objective and descriptive summary statements to grab attention and invite close reading.

Arranges qualifications into sections that emphasize applicant's relevant skills and accomplishments. Uses headings that show applicant knows what skills are needed to succeed in sales.

Uses employers' names and dates to match skills with work history.

Limits education and work history to quick overview of basic qualifications and accommodates employers' preference for chronological format.

Lists references for employer convenience and to strengthen résumé.

Format Pointers
Places name at top center where it can be easily seen.

Uses bold font to distinguish identification section and headings from remaining text.

Creates visual appeal with easy-to-read columnar format and balanced page arrangement.

a **text résumé**, removes formatting and lacks the appeal of your designed résumé; however, you can be confident that an employer can open the file and won't have to spend time "cleaning up" your résumé if it doesn't transmit correctly. For this reason, you'll also paste the text version of your résumé below your email message when sending an inline résumé.

As an added safeguard, send yourself and a couple of friends a copy of the résumé and see how it looks on different computers before sending it out to an employer. If you wish, follow up with a print résumé and cover letter on high-quality paper.

- **Include a keyword summary after the identification section.** You'll want to grab the employer's attention by placing the keywords on the first screen (within the first 24 lines of text). Providing this relevant information will motivate the employer to keep scrolling down to see how the keywords are supported rather than click to the next résumé.

- **Email a cover message to accompany an online résumé.** Some companies consider this cover email message to be prescreening for a job interview. Write a formal, grammatically correct message just as you would if you were sending an application letter in the mail.

Some print résumés become electronic files when they are scanned by the employer into an electronic database where they can be read and sorted by a computer. Companies of all sizes are using **electronic applicant-tracking systems** to increase efficiency of processing the volume of résumés received in a competitive market. Such systems store scanned résumés in an electronic database where they can be sorted by keywords with a resulting ranking of applicants. The system can also automatically prepare letters of rejection and interview offers and store the résumés of hired applicants for future promotion consideration.

When seeking a job with a company that scans résumés into an electronic database, you will need to submit a **scannable résumé** as well as a print résumé that will be read by a person. If you are unsure whether a company scans résumés, call and ask. If still in doubt, take the safe route and submit your résumé in both formats.

Formatting a Scannable Résumé

To ensure that the scanner can read your résumé accurately and clearly, you must prepare a plain résumé with no special formatting. Follow these guidelines to prepare an electronic résumé that can be scanned accurately:

- **Use popular, nondecorative typefaces.** Typefaces such as Cambria and Times New Roman are clear and distinct and will not lose clarity in scanning.

- **Use 10- to 14-point font.** Computers cannot read small, tight print well. With a larger font, your résumé may extend to two pages, but page length is not an issue because a computer is reading the résumé.

- **Do not include italics, underlining, open bullets, or graphic lines and boxes.** Use boldface or all capitals for emphasis. Italicized letters that touch and underlining that runs into the text result in a garbled scanned image. Design elements such as graphic lines, shading, and shadowing effects can confuse equipment. Use solid bullets (•) because an open bullet (□) could be read as an "o".

- **Use ample white space.** Use at least one-inch margins. Leave plenty of white space between the sections of a résumé so the computer recognizes the partitions.

- **Print on one side of white, standard-size paper with sharp laser print.** Colored and textured paper scans poorly, and the scanner can pick up dirty specks on a photocopy.

- **Use a traditional résumé format.** Complex layouts that simulate catalogs or newspaper columns can confuse scanners.

- **Do not fold or staple your résumé.** If you must fold it, do not do so on a line of text.

Making a Scannable Résumé Searchable

You have two concerns in preparing a scannable résumé. You want to (1) be certain information is presented in a manner the computer can read, and (2) maximize the number of "hits" your résumé receives in a computerized résumé search. Follow these guidelines for making your print résumé searchable:

- **Position your name as the first readable item on the page.** Follow with your address, phone number, fax

text résumé
a plain text (unformatted) version of a résumé

electronic applicant-tracking systems
systems that increase the efficiency of processing résumés by storing scanned résumés in an electronic database where they can be sorted by keywords with a resulting ranking of applicants

scannable résumé
a résumé formatted to ensure a scanner can accurately read and convert it into a digital format

number, and email below your name on separate lines.

- **Add powerful keywords in a separate section called "Keywords" or "Keyword Summary" that follows the identification.** To identify keywords, ask yourself what words best describe your qualifications. Make maximum use of industry jargon and standard, easily recognizable abbreviations (e.g., B.A., M.S.) in the keyword summary and the body of the résumé, as these buzzwords will likely be matches with the computer's keywords.

- **Format the keyword summary to maximize hits.** Capitalize the first letter of each word and separate each keyword with a period. Position keywords describing your most important qualifications first and move to the least important ones. Order is important because some systems stop scanning after the first 80 keywords. The usual order is (a) job title, occupation, or career field, (b) education, and (c) essential skills for a specific position. Be certain to include keywords that describe interpersonal traits, such as *adaptable, flexible, sensitive, team player, willing to travel, ethical, industrious, innovative, open minded,* and *detail oriented.*

- **Support your keywords with specific facts in the body of the résumé.** Use synonyms of your keywords in the body in the event the computer does not recognize the keyword (e.g., use *M.B.A.* in the keyword summary and *Master of Business Administration* in the body; use *presentation graphics software* in the keyword summary and a specific program in the body). One unfortunate applicant reported using "computer-assisted design" consistently throughout his résumé when the computer was searching for "CAD." Also, use a specific date of graduation in the education section. Some computer programs read two dates beside an institution to mean the applicant did not earn the degree (e.g., 2007–2011).

The scannable résumé Samuel Barkley prepared when seeking an entry-level computer Web development position appears in Figure 13-5. Note how he presents qualifications that correspond to the company/job profile posted at your companion Web site at **www.cengagebrain.com**. The scannable résumé is formatted for scanning into an electronic database to be matched with employer requirements.

professional portfolio
a portfolio presented in digital format and distributed to prospective employers via a Web site, CD/DVD, or other media; also called an *electronic portfolio* or *e-portfolio*

13-4 Supplementing a Résumé

Some candidates feel their career accomplishments are not appropriately captured in a standard résumé. Two additional tools for communicating your qualifications and abilities are the portfolio and the employment video.

13-4a Professional Portfolios

The **professional portfolio** (also called the *electronic portfolio* or *e-portfolio* when presented in a digital format) can be used to illustrate past activities, projects, and accomplishments. It is a collection of artifacts that demonstrate your communication, people, and technical skills. Although portfolios were once thought of as only for writers, artists, or photographers, they are now seen as appropriate for other fields of work when the applicant wants to showcase abilities.

Many portfolios are now presented in digital format, making the portfolio easier to organize and distribute to prospective employers via a Web site or burned to a CD or other media. With the availability of user-friendly software, college campuses are offering e-portfolio systems that aid students in reflecting on their experiences and producing e-portfolios. Just as students currently are not asked if they have an email account, predictions are that soon they will also be expected to have "a Web space that represents their learning and their assessment."[9]

A clear understanding of your audience's needs and your qualifications will allow you to develop a logical organizational structure for your portfolio. Some possible items to include are:

- sample speeches with digitized audio or video clips of the delivery
- performance appraisals
- awards
- certificates of completion
- reports, proposals, or written documents prepared for classes or on the job
- brochures or programs describing workshops attended
- commendation messages, records, or surveys showing client or customer satisfaction with service

After selecting the items for inclusion in your portfolio, select the appropriate software or binder you will use to showcase your accomplishments. Once you're

Figure 13-5 **GOOD :-)** Scannable Résumé

SAMUEL BARKLEY
742 Elm Street
Tuscaloosa, AL 24800
230-324-9044
Sbarkley@hotmail.com

Professional Profile
- Experience in web development, using HTML and Javascript
- Superior teamwork skills developed through involvement in academic group projects and student organizations
- Strong written and spoken communication skills
- Bachelor's of Science degree, Information Technology

Keywords
Entry-level computer web development position. Bachelor's degree in Information Technology. Professional internship. Team player. Strong written and spoken communication skills. Word Office Suite, HTML, Javascript

Education
B.S., Information Technology, Alabama State University, May 2014, GPA 3.6 Dean's List, 2010-2014

Related Employment
Intern, RodRat's Inc., Tuscaloosa, AL Summer 2013
- Developed web site for hot rod parts and accessories supplier
- Interviewed shop employees and customers to gather information about online needs
- Analyzed data from employee and customer interviews and prepared and delivered presentation to shop management on planned web-site design

Intern, Karen's Fashion Warehouse, Tuscaloosa, AL, Summer 2012
- Developed web site for local fashion retailer
- Researched web site design and functionality in the fashion retail industry
- Used research results to develop a plan for web site design and presented plan for approval to management

Honor's and Activities
- Dean's List (3.6 GPA or higher)
- Member, Society for Information Management
- Participant in annual Geek-a-Thon, 2010-2014

An attractive and fully formatted hard copy version of this document is available upon request.
Last revised 12/15/14

Positions name as first readable item.

Includes position sought and reason to hire in separate section.

Includes "Keyword Summary" section listing qualifications that match job description.

Edges out competition by expanding on related experience and work achievements.

Omits references to use space for additional qualifications; references furnished when requested.

Includes date of last revision to avoid confusion or embarrassment if résumé is accessed after hiring.

Format Pointers
Keeps résumé simple and readable by computer: ample white space especially between sections; easy-to-read font of 10 to 14 points; solid bullets; and no italics, underlining, or graphic lines or borders.

Mails cover letter and print résumé unfolded and unstapled in large envelope.

organized, you can add items that demonstrate you have the characteristics the employer is seeking. Maintain your portfolio even after you are hired because it can demonstrate your eligibility for promotion, salary increase, advanced training, or even justify why you should not be laid off.

For illustration purposes, take a look at Samuel Barkley's electronic portfolio shown in Figure 13-6

on this page that was created using a Microsoft Web template and posted to his personal Web site.

13-4b Employment Videos

A video recording can be used to extend the impact of the printed résumé visually. A video can capture your stage presence and ability to speak effectively and add a human dimension to the written process. Current technology enables applicants to embed video segments into **multimedia résumés** created with presentation software such as Camtasia Studio and sent to prospective employers on CD or DVD or posted on the applicant's personal Web site.

Figure 13-6 Electronic Portfolio Posted to an Applicant's Personal Web Site

© iStockphoto.com/mikkelwilliam

Video résumés, which job seekers post on sites such as YouTube, are the latest trend in developing creative job qualifications. You can learn some important lessons for your video project by taking a look at the abundance of good and bad examples already posted. If possible, solicit the help of someone with film experience and follow these simple suggestions for creating a visually enhanced résumé that is brief, showcases your key qualifications, and reflects your personality:[10]

- Keep your video simple with one stationary shot using a good camera and tripod. Avoid gimmicky effects and excessive panning that distract from the message.

- Use proper lighting, making sure that the employer can see your face. Avoid light behind you that casts shadows.

- Invest in a good quality microphone, and speak clearly and at an appropriate pace for easy listening.

- Choose clothing appropriate for the job you are seeking. Video yourself wearing different clothing, and watch the video to select the ideal choice. Avoid

clothing that gaps and bunches when you sit, as well as bright colors and close patterns that tend to vibrate when filmed.

- Edit your video to eliminate dead air and other imperfections that detract from a professional image.

Employment videos are more commonly used to obtain employment in career fields for which verbal delivery or visual performance is a key element. These fields include broadcasting and the visual and performing arts. The following guidelines apply when preparing an employment video:

- Be sure the video makes a professional appearance and is complimentary to you. A "home movie" quality recording will be a liability instead of an asset to your application.

- Avoid long "talking head" segments. Include segments that reflect you in a variety of activities; shots that include samples of your work are also desirable.

- Remember that visual media (such as photographs and videos) encourage the potential employer to focus on your physical characteristics and attributes, which might lead to undesired stereotyping and discrimination.

Be sure to advertise the availability of your portfolio and employment video to maximize its exposure. List your URL address in the identification section of your résumé. In your application letter, motivate the prospective employer to view your portfolio or video by describing the types of information included. Talk enthusiastically about the detailed supplementary information available during your job interview, and encourage the interviewer to view it when convenient. Note Thomas Kincaid's promotion of his e-portfolio when you read his application letter later in this chapter (see Figure 13-7 on the next page).

13-5 Composing Application Messages

When employers invite you to send either a print or electronic résumé, they expect you to include an **application message** (also known as a *cover message*).

Figure 13-7 **GOOD :-)** Example of an Application Letter

SAMUEL BARKLEY
742 Elm Street
Tuscaloosa, AL 24800
230-324-9044
Sbarkley@hotmail.com

January 18, 2014
Bernie Walters, Manager
Rettig Motorsports, Inc.
2332 Industrial Boulevard
Dallas, TX 44909

Dear Mr. Walters:

Dennis Riley of your human resources department told me at our university's career fair of a web developer opening in your technology department and recommended that I apply. Experience in retail web development, a degree in Information Technology, and excellent communication skills qualify me for this position.

I have developed web sites for two retail operations. Using HTML and Javascript, I designed online order systems for both businesses as well as redesigned their home pages to be more navigable by visitors. In both cases, I gathered information from users and industry sources to ensure that the designs included desired features and functionality.

My Information Technology degree from Alabama State University prepared me well to work in web development. In addition to foundational computer programming courses, I was able to complete courses in web site design as well as communication courses that enhanced my understanding of presentations, business writing, working in teams, and using digital technologies.

Please review the enclosed résumé for additional information about my work experience and education. You can also view examples of my web-design efforts by visiting www.rodrats.com and www.karensfashions.com. I look forward to talking with you about how my skills and experiences can benefit Rettig Motorsports.

Sincerely,

Samuel Barkley

Samuel Barkley

Enclosure

- Addresses letter to specific person using correct name and job title.

- Identifies how applicant learned of position, specific position sought, and background.

- Discusses how education relates to job requirements.

- Uses bulleted list to highlight qualifications corresponding to job requirements.

- Introduces résumé and Web site for additional information.

- Encourages employer to take action without sounding pushy or apologetic.

Format Pointers
Formats as formal business letter since message is accompanying print résumé.

Abbreviated email message including online résumé in ASCII or RTF format would be appropriate for electronic submission.

Uses same high-quality, standard size paper as for résumé in neutral color; includes writer's address and contact information.

A mailed paper résumé should be accompanied by an application letter. When a résumé is submitted electronically, the application "letter" can take the form of an email message. As you have learned, a résumé summarizes information related to the job's requirements and the applicant's qualifications. An application message complements a résumé by (1) introducing the applicant, (2) attracting interest to the résumé, and (3) interpreting the résumé in terms of employer benefits. When mailed, the application message is placed on top of the résumé so it can be read first by the employer.

Because it creates interest and points out employer benefits, the application message is persuasive and thus written inductively. It is designed to convince an employer that qualifications are adequate just as a sales message is designed to convince a buyer that a product will satisfy a need. Like sales messages, application messages can be either solicited or unsolicited. Job advertisements *solicit* applications. Unsolicited application messages have greater need for attention-getters; otherwise, solicited and unsolicited application messages are based on the same principles.

Unsolicited application messages are the same basic message (perhaps with slight modifications) sent to many prospective employers. By sending unsolicited messages, you increase your chances of locating potential openings and possibly alert employers to needs they had not previously identified for someone of your abilities. However, sending unsolicited messages has some disadvantages. Because the employer's specific needs are not known, the opening paragraph will likely be more general (less targeted to a specific position) than the opening paragraph in solicited messages. The process could also be time consuming.

Samuel Barkley wrote the letter in Figure 13-7 to accompany a chronological résumé he prepared after completing the company/job profile of a Web developer. The time Samuel devoted to analyzing the job, the company, and his qualifications was well spent.

13-5a Persuasive Organization

A persuasive message is designed to convince the reader to take action, which in this case is to read the résumé and invite you to an interview. Because an application message is persuasive, organize it as you would a sales message:

Sales Message	Application Message
Gets attention	Gets attention
Introduces product	Introduces qualifications
Presents evidence	Presents evidence
Encourages action	Encourages action
=	=
(sells a product, service, or idea)	(results in an interview)

Like a well-written sales message, a well-written application message uses a central selling feature as a theme. The central selling feature is introduced in the first or second paragraph and stressed in paragraphs that follow. Two to four paragraphs are normally sufficient for supporting evidence. Consider order of importance as a basis for their sequence, with the most significant aspects of your preparation coming first.

Gain the Receiver's Attention

To gain attention, begin the message by identifying the job sought and describing how your qualifications fit the job requirements. This information will provide instant confirmation that you are a qualified applicant for an open position. An employer who reads hundreds of application letters and résumés will appreciate this direct, concise approach.

For an announced job, you should indicate in the first paragraph how you learned of the position—for example, employee referral, customer referral, executive referral, newspaper advertising, or job fair. Your disclosure will confirm you are seeking an open job as well as facilitate evaluation of the company's recruiting practices. Note that the opening of the letter in Figure 13-7 indicates the applicant learned of the position through a referral from a company employee.

An opening for an unsolicited message must be more persuasive: you must convince the interviewer to continue to read your qualifications even though a job might not exist. As in the opening of a solicited message, indicate the type of position sought and your qualifications

unsolicited application message
an unrequested message sent to many prospective employers that contains the same basic message

but be more creative in gaining attention. The following paragraph uses the applicant's knowledge of recent company developments and an intense interest in the company's future to gain receiver attention.

> In the past three years, Johnson Foods has experienced phenomenal growth through various acquisitions, mergers, and market expansion. With this growth comes new opportunities, new customers, and the need for new team players to work in store management. While following the growth of Johnson Foods, I have become determined to join this exciting team and am eager to show you that my educational background, leadership abilities, and internship experience qualify me for the job.

Provide Evidence of Qualifications

For graduates entering the world of full-time work for the first time, educational backgrounds are usually more impressive than work histories. They can benefit from interpreting their educational experiences as meaningful, job-related experiences. An applicant for a human resources position should do more than merely report having taken courses in organizational behavior.

> In my business communication class, I could see specific application of principles encountered in my organizational behavior and marketing classes. Questions about leadership and motivation seemed to recur throughout the course: What really motivates people? Why do people fear change? How can those fears be overcome? What communication practices can be used to motivate people and help them accept change? The importance of the communication was a focus of many courses and my research report, "How to Get the Most from Others."

Your application message will not necessarily refer to information learned in a class. Recognizing that managers must be tactful (a point on which the person reading the message will surely agree), the applicant included some details of a class. That technique is basic in persuasion: do not just say a product or idea is good; say what makes it good. Do not just say that an educational or work experience was beneficial; say what made it so.

By making paragraphs long enough to include interpretation of experiences on the present or previous job, you show an employer that you are well prepared for your next job. For example, the following excerpt from an applicant whose only work experience was at a retail outlet is short and general:

> I have been the assistant manager at Fashion Flash for the past year and have helped supervise a team of five associates. I received high performance evaluations for my work as a leader.

Added details and interpretation could make the value of the work experience more convincing:

> As assistant manager at Fashion Flash, I have learned to listen to associates' concerns and make them feel valued by acting on their suggestions. I have trained associates in policies and procedures, and learned to reinforce those procedures for existing employees. I am able to preserve a good working relationship with my team even in sometimes difficult conversations.

The applicant has called attention to qualities that managers like to see in employees: willingness to listen, speed, accuracy, concern for clients or customers, a positive attitude, fairness, and tact. As a learning experience, the Fashion Flash job has taught or reinforced principles that the employer sees can be transferred to the job being sought.

In this section, you can discuss qualifications you have developed by participating in student organizations, student government, athletics, or community organizations. Be specific in describing gained skills that can be applied directly on the job—for example, organizational, leadership, spoken and written communication skills, and budgeting and financial management. You can also use your involvement as a channel for discussing important personal traits vital to the success of a business, such as interpersonal skills, motivation, imagination, responsibility, and team orientation.

> For the past year, I have served as treasurer for Alpha Chi Epsilon. In that duty, I have managed a $200,000 annual budget. By coordinating our yearly charitable fund-raising event, I have exercised leadership and organizational and communication skills.

Finally, end this section with an indirect reference to the résumé. If you refer to it in the first or second paragraph, readers might turn from the message at that point and look at the résumé. Avoid the obvious statement "Enclosed please find my résumé" or "A résumé is enclosed." Instead, refer indirectly to the résumé while restating your qualifications. The following sentence emphasizes that references can confirm applicant's qualifications:

References listed on the enclosed résumé would be glad to comment on my marketing education and experience.

Encourage Action

Once you have presented your qualifications and referred to your enclosed résumé, the next move is to encourage the receiver to extend an invitation for an interview. The goal is to introduce the idea of action without apologizing for doing so and without being demanding or "pushy." If the final paragraph (action closing) of your message is preceded by impressive paragraphs, you need not press hard for a response. Just mentioning the idea of a future discussion is probably sufficient. If you have significant related experience that you have developed as a central selling feature, mentioning this experience in the action closing adds unity and stresses your strongest qualification one last time. Forceful statements about *when* and *how* to respond are unnecessary and irritating. Avoid these frequently made errors:

- **Setting a date.** "May I have an appointment with you on January 15?" The date you name could be inconvenient; or even if it is convenient for the employer, your forwardness in setting it could be resented.
- **Expressing doubt.** "If you agree," "I hope you will," and "Should you decide" use subjunctive words that indicate lack of confidence.
- **Sounding apologetic.** "May I take some of your time" or "I know how busy you are" might seem considerate, but an apology is inappropriate when discussing ways you can contribute to a company.
- **Sounding overconfident.** "I will call you next week to set an appointment time that works for both of us." This statement is presumptuous and egotistical.
- **Giving permission to call.** "You may call me at 555-6543." By making the call sound like a

privilege ("may call") you could alienate the reader. Implied meaning: You are very selective about the calls you take, but the employer does qualify.

> ~~I hope you will …~~
>
> ~~I know how busy you are …~~
>
> ~~You may call me at 555-6543 …~~
>
> When a date and time can be arranged, I would like to talk with you.

The following sentences are possible closing sentences that refer to an invitation to interview. They are not intended as model sentences that should appear in your message. Because finding the right job is so important, you will be well rewarded for the time and thought you invest in original wording.

- **"When a date and time can be arranged, I would like to talk with you."** The statement does not indicate who will do the arranging, and the meeting place and the subject of the conversation are understood.
- **"I would appreciate an opportunity to discuss the marketing assistant's job with you."** The indirect reference to action is not forceful. However, if the applicant has impressive qualifications, the reader will want an interview and will not need to be pushed.
- **"I look forward to talking with you about how my skills and experiences can benefit Beck Restaurant Group."** The statement asks for the interview and re-emphasizes the applicant's strong qualifications.

13-5b General Writing Guidelines

An excellent application message might be the most difficult message you ever attempt to write. It's natural to feel uncomfortable writing about yourself; however, your confidence will increase as you study the wealth of model documents available through your career services center and other sources. The writing principles you've been introduced to in this chapter should help you write a thoughtful, original message that impresses the interviewer. Instead of standard verbiage included in dozens of models, your self-marketing connects *your* experiences to your future with a specific company and reflects *your* personality and values. The following writing techniques will help distinguish your application message from the competition:

- **Substitute fresh, original expressions that reflect contemporary language.** Overly casual expressions and overused statements will give your message a dull, unimaginative tone. Obvious ideas such as "This is an application," "I read your ad," and "I am writing to apply for," are sufficiently understood without making direct statements. With the application message *and* résumé in hand, a reader learns nothing from "I am enclosing my résumé for your review." Observe caution in choosing overused words such as *applicant, application, opening, position, vacancy,* and *interview.*

- **Avoid overuse of *I* and writer-focused statements.** Because the message is designed to sell your services, some use of *I* is natural and expected; but restrict the number of times *I* is used, especially as the first word in a paragraph. Focus on providing specific evidence that you can meet the company's needs. The employer is not interested in reading about your need to earn more income, to be closer to your work, to have more pleasant surroundings, or to gain greater advancement opportunities.

- **Avoid unconvincing generalizations that could sound boastful.** Self-confidence is commendable, but overconfidence (or worse still, just plain bragging) is objectionable. Overly strong adjectives, self-judgmental terms, and unsupported generalizations damage your credibility. Instead of labeling your performance as "superior" or "excellent," or describing yourself as "an efficient, technically skilled team player," give supporting facts that show the interviewer you can deliver on what you're selling.

- **Tailor the message to the employer's need.** To impress the interviewer that your message is not a generic one sent to everyone, provide requested information and communicate an understanding of the particular company, job requirements, and field.

- **Provide requested information.** Job listings often request certain information: "Must provide own transportation and be willing to travel. Give educational background, work experience, and salary expected." Discuss these points in your application message. Preferably, the question of salary is left until the interview, allowing you to focus your message on your contributions to the company—not what you want from the company (money). Discussion of salary isn't meaningful until after a mutually successful interview; however, if an ad requests a statement about it, the message should address it. You may give a minimum figure or range, indicate willingness to accept a figure that is customary for work of that type, or indicate a preference for discussing salary at the interview.

- **Communicate knowledge of the company, job requirements, and language of the field.** Your statements about a company's rapid expansion or competitive advantage show you really are interested in the company, read widely, do more than you are required to do, and gather information before making decisions. However, phrase these statements carefully to avoid the perception of insincere flattery. For example, referring to the employer as "*the* leader in the field," "*the* best in the business," or "a great company," could appear as an attempt to get a favorable decision as a reward for making a complimentary statement. To reflect your understanding of the job requirements, use indirect statements that are informative and tactful. Direct statements such as "The requirements of this job are …," presents information the employer presumes you already know; "An auditor should be able to …," and "Sales personnel should avoid …," sound like a lecture and could be perceived as condescending. Discussing experiences related to a specific job requirement or your preference for work that requires this skill reveals your understanding without a direct statement. Including terminology commonly used by the profession allows you to communicate clearly in terms the reader understands; it also saves space and implies your background in the field.

- **Focus on strengths and portray a positive attitude.** Concentrate on the positive aspects of your education or experience that have prepared you for the particular job. Apologizing for a shortcoming or admitting failure only weakens your case and raises questions about your self-esteem. Do not discuss your current employer's shortcomings. Regardless of how negatively you perceive your present employer, that perception has little to do with your prospective employer's needs. Also, if you speak negatively of your present employer, you could be perceived as someone who would do the same to the next employer.

13-5c Finishing Touches

The importance of professional formatting and careful proofreading of a print document is generally understood. However, proofing and formatting a "real" résumé and letter appears more important to some applicants than producing quality email submissions. Employers frequently voice concern with the sloppiness and unprofessional appearance and content of electronic submissions. To survive the skeptical eye of an interviewer scanning for ways to reject an applicant, allow yourself time to produce a professional-looking document regardless of the presentation or delivery option you've chosen. Include these steps in your finishing phase:

- Regardless of your delivery option, address your application letter or email message to the specific individual who is responsible for hiring for the position you are seeking rather than sending the document to the "Human Resources Department" or "To Whom It May Concern." If necessary, consult the company's annual report or Web site, or call the company to locate this information.

- Verify the correct spelling, job title, and address, and send a personalized message to the appropriate individual.

- Keep the message short and easy to read. A one-page letter is sufficient for most applications from students and graduates entering the job market.

- Apply visual enhancements learned previously to enhance the appeal and readability of the message and to draw attention to your strengths.

- Definitely keep the paragraphs short, and consider listing your top four or five achievements or other important ideas in a bulleted list.

- Use paper that matches the résumé (color, weight, texture, and size). The watermark should be readable across the sheet in the same direction as the printing. Since you're using plain paper, include your street address and city, state, and zip code above the date or formatted as a letterhead at the top of the page.

- Include "Enclosure" below the signature block to alert the employer that a résumé is enclosed. The proper letter format is shown in the example in Figure 13-7.

- Get opinions from qualified individuals, and make revisions where necessary.

In regard to preparing an application message for email submission, career experts recommend formatting it as a business letter with the complete address of the company exactly as presented in a letter sent by mail and a formal closing such as "Sincerely." To help people reach you, include a full signature block with your mailing and email addresses, and phone number(s). The recipient can easily contact you without opening your attachments. While seemingly unnecessary, the email address is useful when a recipient forwards your email to someone else who might want to reply to you but cannot see your email address. Exclude quotes from your signature block that could be misunderstood or offensive. Add an enclosure notation drawing attention to your résumé attachment provided as requested by the employer, such as "Résumé attached as Word document."

To compete with the high volumes of junk mail, daily messages, and fear of computer viruses, you must provide a motive for an interviewer to open an unexpected message from an unknown person. Messages with missing or vague subject lines might be ignored or deleted immediately. To bring attention to your message, include the name of the person referring you to the position directly in the subject line or mention your email is a follow-up to a conversation, for example, "RE: Follow-up: Résumé for ...." If the message is unsolicited, describe the specific value you can add to the company, for example, "Résumé for Forensics Accountant with Extensive ACL Skills." Stay away from tricks such as marking an email "urgent" or adding "re" to pass your message off as a reply to an earlier message.

Check any instructions provided by the prospective employer, and follow them precisely. Typically, however, you will want to send a complete letter and copy of your résumé by regular mail as a follow-up to the email submission. Figure 13-8 shows a sample application email an applicant sent after talking with a prospective employer at a career fair.

Figure 13-8　Example of Application Message Sent by Email

New Message

To: <dharris@newyorkbank.com>
From: sbarrett@netdoor.com
Subject: Career Fair Follow-up: Résumé for Samantha Barrett

Attachment: samantha_barrett.doc 📎

February 25, 2013

Donald Harris
Recruiter
New York Bank and Trust
1240 27th Avenue
New York, NY 03140-1000

Dear Mr. Harris:

It was a pleasure meeting you at the career fair this morning. The opportunities offered in commercial lending identify your company as a leader in today's financial products marketplace.

My experience and knowledge of banking and commercial lending enable me to be a valuable asset to your company:

- Knowledge of banking and commercial lending practices, necessary documentation, and consumer laws.
- Demonstrated commitment to delivering excellent customer service to customers and clients.
- Hardworking and achievement oriented as demonstrated by part-time employment throughout college, leadership, and maintenance of a 3.6 GPA.

After you have reviewed the attached résumé that you requested for additional information about my education and related work experience, please message me so we can discuss my joining New York Bank and Trust.

Sincerely,

Samantha Barrett
742 Elm Street
Brooklyn, NY 04800
430-324-9044
sbarrett@netdoor.com

Résumé text included in email below and attached as MS Word attachment.

Provides specific subject line that ensures message will be opened.

Email program automatically shows attached file containing resume.

Reveals how applicant learned of position and confirms knowledge of and interest in company.

Condenses persuasive application message to one screen. Avoids tendency to send impersonal message stating résumé is attached.

Introduces résumé and reminds interviewer that submission was requested.

Encourages employer to take action without sounding pushy or apologetic.

Includes email address in .sig file to simplify access to all contact information without opening attached résumé.

Includes enclosure notation pointing out that résumé is sent as required by the company.

Format Pointers
Formats as formal business letter with complete address exactly as done when job credentials are sent by mail. Complete letter and printed copy of résumé will be sent as follow-up to email.

STUDY TOOLS

CHAPTER 13

Located at back of the textbook

❏ **Rip out Chapter Review Card**

Located at www.cengagebrain.com

❏ **Review Key Terms Flashcards (Print or Online)**

❏ **Download Audio Summaries for on-the-go review**

❏ **Complete Practice Quizzes to prepare for tests**

❏ **Play "Beat the Clock" to master concepts**

❏ **Complete the Crossword Puzzle to review key terms**

❏ **Watch the video about McDonaldson, a fictitious but all-too-realistic ad agency whose employees struggle with contemporary business communication issues.**

Interviewing for a Job and Preparing Employment Messages

OBJECTIVES

14-1 Explain the nature of structured, unstructured, stress, group, and virtual interviews.

14-2 Explain the steps in the interview process.

14-3 Prepare effective answers to questions often asked in job interviews, including illegal interview questions.

14-4 Compose effective messages related to employment (including application, follow-up, thank-you, job-acceptance, job-refusal, resignation, and recommendation request messages).

14-1 Understanding Types of Employment Interviews

Most companies conduct various types of interviews before hiring a new employee. While the number and type of interviews vary among companies, applicants typically begin with a screening interview often completed by phone or videoconferencing, an in-depth interview, an on-site interview with multiple interviewers, and sometimes a stress interview. Depending on the goals of the interviewer, interviews follow a structured or an unstructured approach.

14-1a Structured Interviews

In a **structured interview** the interviewer follows a predetermined agenda, including a checklist of questions and statements designed to elicit necessary information and reactions from the interviewee. Because each applicant answers the same questions, the interviewer has comparable data to evaluate. A particular type of structured interview is the behavior-based interview, in which you are asked to give specific examples of occasions in which you demonstrated particular behaviors or skills. The interviewer already knows what skills, knowledge, and qualities successful candidates must possess. The examples you provide will indicate whether you possess them.[1]

Many companies are finding computer-assisted interviews to be a reliable and effective way to conduct screening interviews. Applicants use a computer to provide answers to a list of carefully selected questions. A computer-generated report provides standard, reliable information about each applicant that enables an interviewer to decide whether to invite the applicant for a second interview. The report flags any contradictory responses (e.g., an applicant indicated he was terminated for absenteeism but later indicated that he thought his former employer would give him an outstanding recommendation), highlights any potential problem areas (e.g., an applicant responded that she would remain on the job less than a year), and generates a list of structured interview questions for the interviewer to ask (e.g., "Todd, you said you feel your former employer would rate you average. Why don't you feel it would be higher?").

Research has shown that applicants prefer computer interviews to human interviews and that they respond more honestly to a computer, feeling less need to give polite, socially acceptable responses. Because expert computer systems can overcome some of the inherent problems with traditional face-to-face interviews, the overall quality of the selection process improves. Typical interviewer errors include talking too much, forgetting to ask important questions, being reluctant to ask sensitive or tough questions, forming unjustified negative first impressions, obtaining unreliable and illegal information that makes an applicant feel judged, and using interview data ineffectively.[2] Regardless of whether the interview is face-to-face or computer assisted, you will need to provide objective, truthful evidence of your qualifications as they relate to specific job requirements.

14-1b Unstructured Interviews

An **unstructured interview** is a freewheeling exchange and can shift from one subject to another, depending on the interests of the

structured interview
interview format generally used in the screening process in which the interviewer follows a predetermined agenda, including a checklist of items or a series of questions and statements designed to elicit the necessary information or interviewee reaction

unstructured interview
a freewheeling exchange that may shift from one subject to another, depending on the interests of the participants

BCOM

Yuri Arcurs/Fotolia LLC

14-1d Series Interviews

As organizations have increased emphasis on the team approach to management and problem solving, selecting employees who best fit their cultures and styles has become especially important. Involving key people in the organization in the candidate selection process has led to new interview styles. In a series interview, the candidate meets individually with a number of different interviewers. Each interviewer will likely ask questions from a differing perspective; for instance, a line manager might ask questions related to the applicant's knowledge of specific job tasks, while the vice president of operations might ask questions related to the applicant's career goals. Some questions will likely be asked more than once in the process. A popular trend in organizations that desire a broad range of input in the hiring decision but want to avoid the drawn-out nature of series interviews is to conduct group interviews.

14-1e Virtual Interviews

Technology is allowing much business activity, including job interviews, to be conducted virtually. Companies such as IBM, Microsoft, Nike, and Hallmark Cards save money and time by screening candidates through video interviews from remote locations. **Virtual interviews** help widen the applicant pool and decrease the cost of travel (since they can be conducted regardless of geography) and fill the position more quickly. The consensus is that the video interview is excellent for screening applicants, but a face-to-face interview is appropriate whenever possible for the important final interview.

Various companies have direct hookups with the career services centers of colleges and universities to interview students. These virtual interviews allow students to meet large companies whose representatives typically would not visit colleges with small applicant pools and to interview with companies whose representatives could not travel because of financial constraints or other reasons. Students simply sit in front of a camera, dial in, and interview with multiple interviewers; in some cases, several applicants are interviewed simultaneously. As you would imagine, some candidates who interview well in person can fail on camera or in a group conference call. Virtual interviewing is an excellent method for screening out candidates who are unable to communicate their competence, enthusiasm, and conviction in a technology-rich environment.

You should prepare for a virtual interview differently than you would for a traditional interview. First,

participants. Some experienced interviewers are able to make a structured interview seem unstructured. The goal of many unstructured interviews is to explore unknown areas to determine the applicant's ability to speak comfortably about a wide range of topics.

14-1c Stress Interviews

A **stress interview** is designed to place the interviewee in an anxiety-producing situation so an evaluation can be made of the interviewee's performance under stress. In all cases, interviewees should attempt to assess the nature of the interview quickly and adjust behavior accordingly. Understanding that interviewers sometimes deliberately create anxiety to assess your ability to perform under stress should help you handle such interviews more effectively. As the following discussion of different interviewer styles reveals, you can perform much better when you understand the interviewer's purpose.

stress interview
interview format designed to place the interviewee in an anxiety-producing situation so an evaluation of the interviewee's performance under stress may be made

virtual interview
interview conducted using videoconferencing technology

suggest a preliminary telephone conversation with the interviewer to establish rapport. Arrive early and acquaint yourself with the equipment; know how to adjust the volume and other camera functions for optimal performance after the interview begins. Second, concentrate on projecting strong nonverbal skills: speak clearly but do not slow down; be certain you are centered in the frame; sit straight; look up, not down; and use gestures and an enthusiastic voice to communicate energy and reinforce points while avoiding excessive motion that will appear blurry. Third, realize voices can be out of step with the pictures if there is a lag between the video and audio transmissions. You will need to adjust to the timing (e.g., slow down your voice) to avoid interrupting the interviewer.

14-2 Preparing for an Interview

College students frequently schedule on-campus interviews with representatives from various business organizations. Following the on-campus interviews, successful candidates often are invited for further interviews at the company location. The purpose of the second interview is to give executives and administrators other than the human resources interviewer an opportunity to appraise the candidate. Whether on campus or at the company location, interview methods and practices vary with the situation.

Pre-interview planning involves learning something about the company or organization, studying yourself, and making sure your appearance and mannerisms will not detract from the impression you hope to make.

14-2a Research the Company

Nothing can hurt a job candidate more than knowing little about the organization. No knowledge indicates insincerity, and the interviewer does not want to waste precious interview time providing candidates with information they should have considered long before. Preparation will also arm candidates with information needed to develop pertinent qualifications and point their stories to solve an employer's specific problems.

Companies that have publicly traded stock are required to publish annual reports that are available in school libraries or online. Be sure to read news items and blog posts, and sign up to receive news alerts from the prospective company for current company

information up until the day of the interview. Use social networking utilities such as LinkedIn and Hoovers.com to find profiles of company leaders and gain insights on the types of managers this company employs.

Employees of the company or other applicants who have interviewed might be of help to the interviewee. Employee reviews of selected companies, salaries, and sample interview questions are available online, and some universities share taped interviews with various company recruiters. Information about the company and the job sought pertinent in an interview includes the following:

Company Information

Be sure to research the following on the companies with which you interview:

- **Name.** Know, for example, that the publishing company Cengage Learning was so named to reflect the company's mission to be a "center of engagement" for its global customers.[3]
- **Status in the industry.** Know the company's share of the market, its *Fortune* 500 standing (if any), its sales, and its number of employees.
- **Latest stock market quote.** Be familiar with current market deviations and trends.
- **Recent news and developments.** Read current business periodicals, news, and blogs for special feature articles on the company, its new products, and its corporate leadership.
- **Scope of the company.** Is it local, national, or international?
- **Corporate officers.** Know the names of the chairperson, president, and chief executive officer.
- **Products and services.** Study the company's offerings, target markets, and innovative strategies.

Job Information

Be sure to know the following about the job you are seeking:

- **Job title.** Know the job titles of typical entry-level positions.
- **Job qualifications.** Understand the specific knowledge and skills desired.
- **Probable salary range.** Study salaries in comparable firms, as well as regional averages.
- **Career path of the job.** What opportunities for advancement are available?

14-2b Study Yourself

When you know something about the company, you will also know something about the kinds of jobs or training programs the company has to offer. Next, compare your qualifications to the company/job profile. This systematic comparison of your qualifications and job requirements helps you identify pertinent information (strengths or special abilities) to be included in your résumé. If you cannot see a relationship between you and the job or company, you might have difficulty demonstrating the interest or sincerity needed to sell yourself.

14-2c Plan Your Appearance

An employment interviewer once said she would not hire a job applicant who did not meet her *extremities* test: fingernails, shoes, and hair must be clean and well kept. This interviewer felt that if the candidate did not take care of those details, the candidate could not really be serious about, or fit into, her organization. Other important guidelines include avoiding heavy makeup

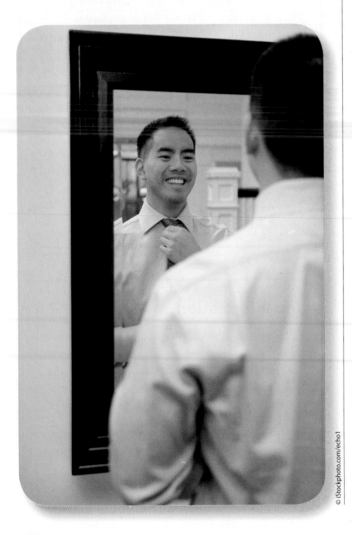

© iStockphoto.com/echo1

and large, excessive jewelry. Select conservative clothes, and be certain clothing is clean, unwrinkled, and properly fitted. Additionally, avoid smoking, drinking, or wearing heavy fragrance

You can locate a wealth of information on appropriate interview dress from numerous electronic and printed sources. Additionally, talk with professors in your field, professors of business etiquette and professional protocol, personnel at your career services center, and graduates who have recently acquired jobs in your field. Research the company dress code—real or implied—ahead of time. If you *look* and *dress* like the people who already work for the company, the interviewer will be able to visualize you working there.

14-2d Plan Your Time and Materials

One of the worst things you can do is be late for an interview. If something should happen to prevent your arriving on time, phone an apology. Another mistake is to miss the interview entirely. Plan your time so that you will arrive early and can unwind and review mentally the things you plan to accomplish. Be sure to bring a professional briefcase or notebook that contains everything you will need during the interview. These items might include copies of your résumé, a list of references and/or recommendations, a professional-looking pen, paper for taking notes, highlights of what you know about the company, a list of questions you plan to ask, and previous correspondence with the company.

14-2e Practice

The job interview could be the most important face-to-face interaction you ever have. You will be selling yourself in competition with others. How you listen and how you talk are characteristics the interviewer will be able to measure. Your actions, your mannerisms, and your appearance will combine to give the total picture of how you are perceived. Added to the marketable skills you have acquired from your education, experience, and activities, your interview performance can give a skilled interviewer an excellent picture of you. Practicing for an interview will prepare you to handle the nervousness that is natural when interviewing. However, do not memorize answers, as it will sound rehearsed and insincere. Instead, think carefully about how your accomplishments match the job requirements and practice communicating these ideas smoothly, confidently, and professionally.

Prepare for standard interview questions and other interview issues following suggestions provided later in this chapter. Once you are satisfied you have identified your key selling points, have a friend ask you interview questions you have developed and surprise you with others. Participate in mock interviews with someone in your career services center or with a friend, alternating roles as interviewer and interviewee. Then follow each practice interview with a constructive critique of your performance.

14-3 Conducting a Successful Interview

The way you handle an interview will vary somewhat depending on your stage in the hiring process. Regardless of whether you are being screened by a campus recruiter in person, by phone, or by videoconference, or have progressed to an on-site visit, an interview will have three parts: the opening formalities, an information exchange, and the closing.

14-3a The Opening Formalities

According to management consultant Dan Burns, most candidates don't realize that in the first 60 seconds, interviewers typically decide whether the candidate will be moved to the top of the list or dropped from consideration. Burns emphasizes that skills missing during the interview are important because he assumes these same deficiencies will carry over during employment.[4] Clearly, since the impression created during the first few seconds of an interview often determines the outcome, you cannot afford to take time to warm up in an interview. You must enter the door selling yourself!

Common courtesies and confident body language can contribute to a favorable first impression in the early moments when you have not yet had an opportunity to talk about your qualifications:

- **Use the interviewer's name, and pronounce it correctly.** Even if the interviewer calls you by your first name, always use the interviewer's surname unless specifically invited to do otherwise.

- **Apply a firm handshake.** Usually, the interviewer will initiate the handshake, although you may do so. In either case, apply a firm handshake. You do not want to leave the impression that you are weak or timid. At the same time, you do not want to overdo the firm grip and leave an impression of being overbearing.

© iStockphoto.com/michaeljung

Interviewers typically decide about a candidate in the first 60 seconds. You must enter the door selling yourself!

- **Wait for the interviewer to ask you to be seated.** If you aren't invited to sit, choose a chair across from or beside the interviewer's desk.

- **Maintain appropriate eye contact, and use your body language to convey confidence.** Sit erect and lean forward slightly to express interest. For a professional image, avoid slouching, chewing gum, and fidgeting.

- **Be conscious of nonverbal messages.** If the interviewer's eyes are glazing over, end your answer, but expand it if they are bright and the head is nodding vigorously. If the interviewer is from a different culture, be conscious of subtle differences in nonverbal communication that could affect the interviewer's perception of you. For example, a North American interviewer who sees eye contact as a sign of trust might perceive an Asian female who keeps her eyes lowered as a sign of respect to be uninterested or not listening.[5] Women should also be aware of typical "feminine behavior" during the interview. For instance, women nod more often than men when an interviewer speaks. Women are also likely to smile more and have a rising intonation at the end of sentences; such behaviors can convey a subservient attitude.[6]

Following the introductions, many interviewers will begin the conversation with nonbusiness talk to help you relax and to set the stage for the information exchange portion of the interview. Other interviewers bypass these casual remarks and move directly into the interview.

14-3b The Information Exchange

Much of the information about you will appear on your résumé or application form and is already available to the interviewer. Thus the interviewer most likely will seek to go beyond such facts as your education, work experience, and extracurricular activities. He or she will attempt to assess your general attitude toward work and the probability of your fitting successfully into the organization.

Presenting Your Qualifications

Your preparation pays off during the interview. Like a defense attorney ready to win a case, you are ready to present evidence that you should be hired. According to Joyce Kennedy and Thomas Morrow, leading career consultants, your case will have three major points: you must convince the interviewer that you (1) can do the job, (2) will do the job, and (3) will not stress out everyone else while doing the job.[7] That's an overwhelming task. Where do you begin? You learned during your study of persuasive writing that saying you're the best at what you do is not convincing. To convince an interviewer to allow you to continue to the next interview or to extend you a job offer, you must provide specific, concrete evidence that your qualifications match the job description and equip you to add immediate value to the company. Use the following guidelines to help you relate your skills and knowledge to the job:

- **List five or six key points that you want to emphasize.** You will probably want to present your education as a major asset. You should point out its relationship to the job sought. Even more important, the fact that you have succeeded in academics indicates that you have the ability and self-discipline to learn. Because most companies expect you to learn something on the job, your ability to learn and thus quickly become productive will be your greatest asset. Even lack of work experience can be an asset: you have acquired no bad work habits that you will have to unlearn.

- **Additionally, be sure to provide evidence of your interpersonal skills.** Communicate that you can get along with others and are sensitive to diversity.

- What did you do in college that helped you get along with others?

- Were you a member, an officer, or president of an organization? What did you accomplish? How did others perceive you? Were you a leader? How did your followers respond to your leadership style? To your commitment to ethical standards?

- Can you organize projects, motivate people to complete important goals, and deal with difficult people?

The extracurricular activities listed on your résumé give an indication of these traits, but how you talk about them in your interview helps demonstrate them. "I started as public relations vice president and was subsequently elected to higher office for four semesters, eventually becoming president," is a statement that proves your leadership qualities. If you can show your organization moved to greater heights, you will appear successful as well. You can also use questions about your extracurricular activities to show that you have broad, balanced interests rather than a single, time-consuming avocation that could lead to burnout and stress if carried to the job.

What are other skills that graduating students need to succeed in a cross-cultural, interdependent workforce? While academic performance is weighted more heavily for some types of jobs than others, the ability to juggle a complicated schedule is weighed heavily by many employers as an important job-success factor. Additionally, a UNESCO report of employer views revealed certain skills to be essential for workers in today's business climate as shown in Figure 14-1.[8]

Consider these general job-success traits and then use your knowledge of the job requirements and your own strengths to develop your "central selling features." These key points targeted to your audience are the central element of a winning argument: you are able and willing to become a contributing part of a high-performance team that will enhance the company's performance.

- **Be prepared to answer standard interview questions.** These questions are designed to show (a) why you want the job, (b) why you want to work for this organization, and (c) why the company should want you. Practice concise but fully developed answers that reflect your personality and your communication power. While one-word answers aren't adequate, long-winded answers can prevent interviewers from asking you other planned questions critical to making an informed decision.

- **Be prepared to answer behavioral questions.** These questions are designed to challenge you to provide evidence of your skills or the behaviors required

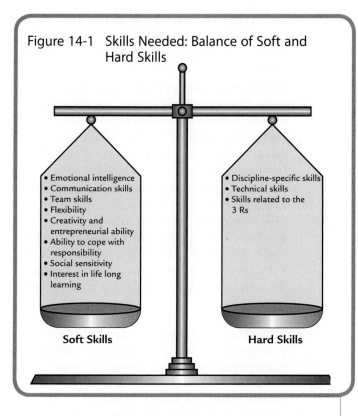

Figure 14-1 Skills Needed: Balance of Soft and Hard Skills

Soft Skills
- Emotional intelligence
- Communication skills
- Team skills
- Flexibility
- Creativity and entrepreneurial ability
- Ability to cope with responsibility
- Social sensitivity
- Interest in life long learning

Hard Skills
- Discipline-specific skills
- Technical skills
- Skills related to the 3 Rs

to perform the job. Rather than asking applicants how they feel about certain things, interviewers are finding that asking potential employees for specific examples to illustrate their answers is a more objective way to evaluate applicants' skills.

Behavioral questions include the following:

- Describe a time when you worked well under pressure, worked effectively with others, organized a major project, motivated and led others, solved a difficult problem, or used persuasion to convince someone to accept your idea.

- What was the most difficult problem you had to overcome in your last job (or an academic or extracurricular activity)? How did you cope with it? What lesson did you learn from the situation? Share a time you applied the lesson learned.

- Tell me about a time you had difficulty working with a supervisor or coworker (or professor or peer in a team in a class setting). How did you handle the situation?

- Describe something you have done that shows initiative and willingness to work or required you to think on your feet to solve a problem.

- How have your extracurricular activities, part-time work experience, or volunteer work prepared you for work in our company?

- Tell me about a time you hit a wall trying to push forward a great idea.

To prepare for answering behavioral questions, brainstorm to identify stories that illustrate how your qualifications fit the job requirements. These stories should show you applying the skills needed on the job. Career counselors recommend using the STAR method (Situation or Task/Action/Result) as a consistent format to help you present a complete answer to these open-ended questions. You first describe a situation or task you were involved in, the action you took, and finally the result of your effort.[9]

- **Be prepared to demonstrate logical thinking and creativity.** Many interviewers ask applicants to solve brain teasers and riddles, create art out of paper bags, and solve complex business problems. Some are asked to "do the job before we give it to you," for example, write a press release on the spot or field a tech-support call.[10] These techniques are used to gauge an applicant's ability to think quickly and creatively and observe an emotional response to an awkward situation. You cannot anticipate this type of interview question, but you can familiarize yourself with mind teasers that have been used. Most important, however, recognize the interviewer's purpose; relax, and do your best to showcase your logical reasoning, creativity, or your courage to even try.

- **Display a professional attitude.** First, communicate your sincere interest in the company; show that you are strongly interested in the company and not just taking an interview for practice. Reveal your knowledge of the company gained through reading published information, and refer to the people you have talked with about the working conditions, company achievements, and career paths.

  Second, focus on the satisfaction gained from contributing to a company rather than the benefits you will receive. What's important in a job goes beyond financial reward. All applicants are interested in a paycheck; any job satisfies that need— some will pay more, some less. Recognize that the paycheck is a part of the job and should not be your primary concern. Intrinsic rewards such as personal job satisfaction, the feeling of accomplishment, and making a contribution to society are ideas to discuss in the interview. You should like what you are doing and find a challenging job that will satisfy these needs.

- **Be prepared to discuss salary and benefits.** For most entry-level positions, the beginning salary is fixed. However, if you have work experience, excellent scholarship records, or added maturity, you might be able to obtain a higher salary. The interviewer should initiate the salary topic. What you should know is the general range for candidates with your qualifications so that your response to a question about how much you would expect is reasonable.

If you have other job offers, you are in a position to compare salaries, jobs, and companies. In this case, you might suggest to the interviewer that you would expect a competitive salary and that you have been offered X dollars by another firm. If salary has not been mentioned, and you really want to know about it, simply ask courteously how much the salary would be for someone with your qualifications. In any case, if you really believe the job offers the non-monetary benefits you seek, do not attempt to make salary a major issue.

- **Typically, an interviewer will introduce the subject of benefits without your asking about them.** In some cases, a discussion of total salary and "perks" is reserved for a follow-up interview. If nothing has been said about certain benefits, you should take the liberty of asking, particularly when an item is especially important to you.

- **Be knowledgeable of interview questions and information on your social networking sites that might lead to discriminatory hiring practices.** The Equal Employment Opportunity Commission (EEOC) and Fair Employment Practices Guidelines make it clear that an employer cannot legally discriminate against a job applicant on the basis of race, color, gender, age, religion, national origin, or disability. Interviewers must restrict questions to an applicant's ability to perform specific job-related functions essential to the job sought. Generally, the following topics should not be introduced:

  - *National origin and religion.* "You have an unusual accent; where were you born?" "What religious holidays will require you to miss work?"

  - *Age.* "I see you attended Central High School; what year did you graduate?" "Could you provide a copy of your birth certificate?"

  - *Disabilities, health conditions, and physical characteristics not reasonably related to the job.* "Do you have a disability that would interfere with your ability to perform the job? "Have you ever been injured on the

job?" "Have you ever been treated by a psychiatrist?" "How much alcohol do you consume each week?" "What prescription drugs are you currently taking?"

- *Marital status, spouse's employment, or dependents.* "Are you married?" "Who is going to care for your children if you work for us?" "Do you plan to have children?" "Is your spouse employed?" Additionally, employers may not ask the names or relationships of people with whom you live.

- *Arrests or criminal convictions that are not related to the job.* "Have you ever been arrested other than for traffic violations? If so, explain." Keep in mind that the arrest/conviction record of a person applying for a job as a law enforcement officer or a teacher could be highly relevant to the job, but the same information could be illegal for a person applying for a job as an engineer.

Since interviewers may ask illegal questions because of lack of training or an accidental slip, you must decide how to respond. You can refuse to answer and state the question is improper, though you risk offending the interviewer. A second option is to answer the inappropriate question, knowing it is illegal and unrelated to job requirements. A third approach is to provide a low-key response such as "How does this question relate to how I will do my job?" or to answer the legitimate concern that likely prompted the question. For example, an interviewer who asks, "Do you plan to have children?" is probably concerned about how long you might remain on the job. An answer to this concern would be, "I plan to pursue a career regardless of whether I decide to raise a family." If you can see no legitimate concern in a question, such as, "Do you own your home, rent, or live with parents?" answer, "I'm not sure how that question relates to the job. Can you explain?"[11]

Asking Questions of the Interviewer

Both the interviewer and interviewee want to know as much as possible about each other before making a commitment to hire. A good way to determine whether the job is right for you is to ask pertinent questions.

Good questions show the interviewer that you have initiative and are interested in making a well-informed decision. Responses can provide insight to job requirements that you can then show you possess. Therefore, be sure not to say, "I don't have any questions." Focus on questions that help you gain information about the company and the job that you could not learn from published sources or persons other than the interviewer. Respect the interviewer's time by avoiding questions that indicate you are unprepared (for example, questions about the company's scope, products/services, job requirements, or new developments). Avoid questions about salary, required overtime, and benefits that imply you are interested more in money and the effort required than in the contribution you can make.

14-3c The Closing

The interviewer will provide cues indicating that the interview is completed by rising or making a comment about the next step to be taken. At that point, do not prolong the interview needlessly. Simply rise, accept the handshake, thank the interviewer for the opportunity to meet, and close by saying you look forward to hearing from the company. The tact with which you close the interview can be almost as important as the first impression you made. Be enthusiastic. If you really want the job, you must ask for it.

Your ability to speak confidently and intelligently about your abilities will help you secure a desirable job. Effective interviewing skills will be just as valuable once you begin work. You will be involved in interviews with

your supervisor for various reasons: to seek advice or information about your work and working conditions, to receive informal feedback about your progress, to receive a deserved promotion, and to discuss other personnel matters. In addition, your supervisor will likely conduct a performance appraisal interview to evaluate your performance. This formal interview typically occurs annually on the anniversary of your start of employment.

14-4 Preparing Other Employment Messages

Preparing a winning résumé and application letter is an important first step in a job search. To expedite your job search, you will need to prepare other employment messages. For example, you might complete an application form, send a follow-up message to a company that does not respond to your résumé, send a thank-you message after an interview, accept a job offer, reject other job offers, and communicate with references. A career change will require a carefully written resignation letter.

14-4a Application Forms

Before beginning a new job, you will almost certainly complete the employer's application and employment forms. Some application forms, especially for applicants who apply for jobs with a high level of responsibility, are very long. They can actually appear to be tests in which applicants give their answers to hypothetical questions and write defenses for their answers. Increasing numbers of companies are designing employment forms as mechanisms for acquiring information about a candidate that often is not included in the résumé. Application forms also ensure consistency in the information received from each candidate and can prevent decisions based on illegal topics which might be presented in a résumé.

14-4b Follow-Up Messages

When an application message and résumé do not elicit a response, a follow-up message might bring results. Sent a few weeks after the original message, it includes a reminder that an application for a certain job is on file, presents additional education or experience accumulated and its relationship to the job, and closes with a reference to desired action. In addition to conveying new information, follow-up messages indicate persistence (a quality that impresses some employers). Figure 14-2 shows a good example of a follow-up letter.

14-4c Thank-You Messages

What purposes are served in sending a thank-you message, even though you expressed thanks in person after the interview or a discussion with a special employer at a career fair? After a job interview, a written message of appreciation is a professional courtesy and enhances your image within the organization. To be effective, it must be sent promptly. For maximum impact, send a thank-you message the day of the interview or the following day. Even if during the interview you decided you do not want the job or you and the interviewer mutually agreed that the job is not for you, a thank-you message is appropriate. As a matter of fact, if you've made a positive impression, interviewers might forward your résumé to others who are seeking qualified applicants.

The medium you choose for sending this message depends on the intended audience. If the company you've interviewed with prefers a traditional style, send a letter in complete business format on high-quality paper that matches your résumé and application letter. If the company has communicated with you extensively by email, follow the pattern and send a professional

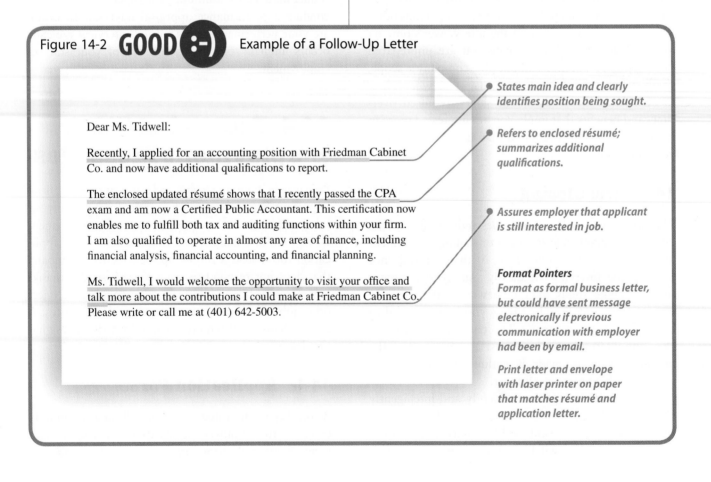

Figure 14-2 **GOOD :-)** Example of a Follow-Up Letter

Dear Ms. Tidwell:

Recently, I applied for an accounting position with Friedman Cabinet Co. and now have additional qualifications to report.

The enclosed updated résumé shows that I recently passed the CPA exam and am now a Certified Public Accountant. This certification now enables me to fulfill both tax and auditing functions within your firm. I am also qualified to operate in almost any area of finance, including financial analysis, financial accounting, and financial planning.

Ms. Tidwell, I would welcome the opportunity to visit your office and talk more about the contributions I could make at Friedman Cabinet Co. Please write or call me at (401) 642-5003.

• *States main idea and clearly identifies position being sought.*

• *Refers to enclosed résumé; summarizes additional qualifications.*

• *Assures employer that applicant is still interested in job.*

Format Pointers
Format as formal business letter, but could have sent message electronically if previous communication with employer had been by email.

Print letter and envelope with laser printer on paper that matches résumé and application letter.

email that can be read in a timely manner. Choosing to send an email rather than slower mail delivery can give you a competitive edge over other candidates whose mailed letters arrive several days later than yours.

After an interview has gone well and you think a job offer is a possibility, include these ideas in the message of appreciation: express gratitude, identify the specific job applied for, refer to some point discussed in the interview (the strength of the interview), and close by making some reference to the expected call or message that conveys the employer's decision. The tone of this business message should remain professional regardless of the personal relationship you might have developed with the interviewer and the informality encouraged by email. The message could be read by many others once it is placed in your personnel file as you complete annual appraisals and compete for promotions. Specific points to cover are outlined in Figure 14-3.

The résumé, application letter, and thank-you message should be stored in a computer file and adapted for submission to other firms when needed. Develop a database for keeping a record of the dates on which documents and résumés were sent to certain firms and answers were received, names of people talked with, facts conveyed, and so on. When an interviewer calls,

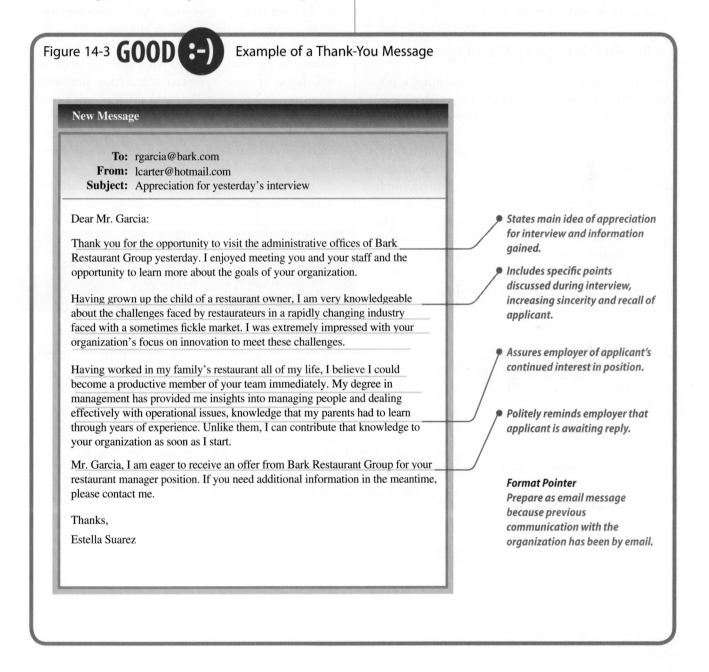

Figure 14-3 **GOOD :-)** Example of a Thank-You Message

New Message

To: rgarcia@bark.com
From: lcarter@hotmail.com
Subject: Appreciation for yesterday's interview

Dear Mr. Garcia:

Thank you for the opportunity to visit the administrative offices of Bark Restaurant Group yesterday. I enjoyed meeting you and your staff and the opportunity to learn more about the goals of your organization.

Having grown up the child of a restaurant owner, I am very knowledgeable about the challenges faced by restaurateurs in a rapidly changing industry faced with a sometimes fickle market. I was extremely impressed with your organization's focus on innovation to meet these challenges.

Having worked in my family's restaurant all of my life, I believe I could become a productive member of your team immediately. My degree in management has provided me insights into managing people and dealing effectively with operational issues, knowledge that my parents had to learn through years of experience. Unlike them, I can contribute that knowledge to your organization as soon as I start.

Mr. Garcia, I am eager to receive an offer from Bark Restaurant Group for your restaurant manager position. If you need additional information in the meantime, please contact me.

Thanks,
Estella Suarez

States main idea of appreciation for interview and information gained.

Includes specific points discussed during interview, increasing sincerity and recall of applicant.

Assures employer of applicant's continued interest in position.

Politely reminds employer that applicant is awaiting reply.

Format Pointer
Prepare as email message because previous communication with the organization has been by email.

you can retrieve and view that company's record while you are talking with the interviewer.

14-4d Job-Acceptance Messages

A job offer may be extended either by phone or in writing. If a job offer is extended over the phone, request that the company send a written confirmation of the job offer. The confirmation should include the job title, salary, benefits, starting date, and anything else negotiated.

Often, companies require a written acceptance of a job offer. Note the deductive sequence of the message shown in Figure 14-4: acceptance, details, and closing (confirms the report-for-work date).

14-4e Job-Refusal Messages

Like other messages that convey unpleasant news, job-refusal messages are written inductively—with a beginning that reveals the nature of the subject, explanations that lead to a refusal, the refusal, and a pleasant ending. Of course, certain reasons (even though valid in your mind) are better left unsaid, such as questionable company goals or methods of operation, negative attitude of present employees, possible bankruptcy, unsatisfactory working conditions, and so on. The applicant who prefers not to be specific about the reason for turning down a job might write this explanation: *After thoughtfully considering job offers received this week, I have decided to accept a job in the finance department of a commercial bank.*

You might want to be more specific about your reasons for refusal when you have a positive attitude toward the company or believe you will want to reapply at some later date. The letter excerpt in Figure 14-5 includes the reasons for refusal.

14-4f Resignation Messages

Resigning from a job requires effective communication skills. You might be allowed to give your notice in person or be required to write a formal resignation. Your supervisor will inform you of the company's policy. Regardless of whether the resignation is given orally or in writing, show empathy for your employer by giving enough time to allow the employer to find a replacement. Because your employer has had confidence in you, has benefited from your services, and will have to seek a replacement, your impending departure *is* bad news. As such, the message is written inductively. It calls attention to your job, gives your reasons for leaving it, conveys the resignation, and closes on a positive note. A written resignation is shown in Figure 14-6.

A resignation is not an appropriate instrument for telling managers how a business should be operated.

RESIST THE URGE to vent, rant, or tell your boss how to run the business. It's not professional IN A RESIGNATION LETTER.

Figure 14-4 **GOOD :-)** Example of a Job-Acceptance Message

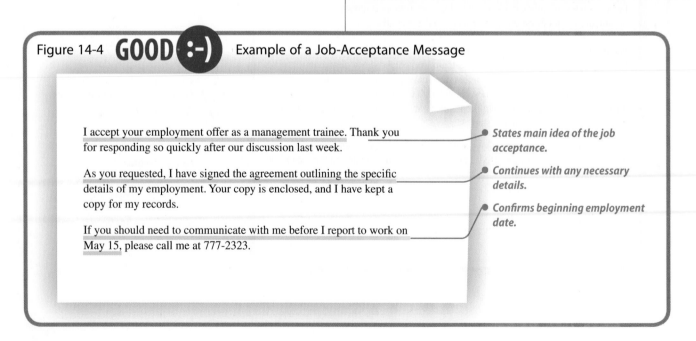

I accept your employment offer as a management trainee. Thank you for responding so quickly after our discussion last week.

→ *States main idea of the job acceptance.*

As you requested, I have signed the agreement outlining the specific details of my employment. Your copy is enclosed, and I have kept a copy for my records.

→ *Continues with any necessary details.*

If you should need to communicate with me before I report to work on May 15, please call me at 777-2323.

→ *Confirms beginning employment date.*

Figure 14-5 GOOD :-) Example of a Job-Refusal Message

I appreciate your spending time with me discussing the marketing position at Software Applications, Inc.

○ *Begins with neutral but related idea to buffer bad news.*

Your candid comments about my background and opportunities for marketers in your firm were especially helpful. Having received several job offers, I am now convinced that a career that would enable me to work in a sales team is more consistent with my interests and goals. Today, I am accepting a job in the sales department of Hawaiian Organic Products, Inc.

○ *Presents reasons diplomatically that lead to refusal.*

Thank you for your confidence demonstrated by the job offer. When I receive reports of Software App's continued success, I will think of the dedicated people who work for the company.

○ *Ends message on positive note that anticipates future association with company.*

Figure 14-6 GOOD :-) Example of a Resignation Message

SUBJECT: PLEASURE OF SERVING MOFFIT AND MOFFIT

My job as an administrative assistant for the past four years has been a rewarding experience. It has taught me much about the law, including the importance of communicating well with clients and of excellent research skills, as well as the reward that results from the hard work involved in winning a case.

○ *Begins with appreciative comments to buffer bad news.*

○ *Presents reasons that lead to main idea, the resignation.*

My experience at Moffit and Moffit has validated my interest in pursuing a career in the legal field. Now that I have completed my degree in Business Administration, that goal is becoming a reality, as I have been accepted to Occidental College's School of Law, beginning August 21. If satisfactory with you, I would like August 1 to be my last day in my position here.

○ *States resignation, including additional details.*

Thank you for the support and confidence you placed in me and all that I have learned from you about the legal field. As I continue my education, I will always recall how my position at Moffit and Moffit led me to my career choice.

○ *Conveys genuine appreciation for experience gained and ends on cordial note.*

Harshly worded statements could result in immediate termination or cause human relations problems during your remaining working days. If you can do so sincerely, recall positive experiences you had with the company. Doing so will leave a lasting record of your goodwill, making it likely that your supervisor will give you a good recommendation in the future.

14-4g Recommendation Requests

Companies seek information from references at various stages. Some prefer talking with references prior to an interview, and others, after a successful interview. Specific actions on your part will ensure that your references are treated with common courtesy and that references are prepared for the employer's call.

- **Remind the reference that he or she had previously agreed to supply information about you.** Identify the job for which you are applying, give a complete address to which the message is to be sent, and indicate a date by which the prospective employer needs the message. By sharing information about job requirements and reporting recent job-related experiences, you can assist the reference in writing an effective message. Indicate your gratitude,

but do not apologize for making the request. The reference has already agreed to write on your behalf and will likely take pleasure in assisting a deserving person.

- **Alert the reference of imminent requests for information, especially if considerable time has elapsed since the applicant and reference have last seen each other.** Enclosing a recent résumé and providing any other pertinent information (e.g., name change) will enable the reference to write a message that is specific and convincing. To ensure on-target job references, politely explain the types of information you perceive relevant to the job sought: specific job skills, work ethic, attitude and demeanor toward work, leadership style, and so on. If the job search becomes longer than anticipated, a follow-up message to references explaining the delay and expressing gratitude for their efforts is appropriate.

- **Send a sincere, original thank-you message after a position has been accepted.** This thoughtful gesture will build a positive relationship with a person who might continue to be important to your career. The message in Figure 14-7 is brief and avoids clichés and exaggerated expressions of praise but instead gives specific examples of the importance of the reference's recommendation.

Figure 14-7 **GOOD :-)** Example of a Thank-You Message to a Reference

Thank you so much for the letter of recommendation you prepared for my application to the Teaching America organization. I learned today that I have been hired and will begin work next month.

States main idea of appreciation for recommendation. Informs reference of success in locating job.

Because the position is in fund-raising, I believe your comments about my customer service skills as demonstrated at Cardinal Printing helped my case. Ms. Worther, who will be my manager, said that she found it notable that you were impressed enough with my skills to provide such a detailed recommendation, even though I left Cardinal two years ago.

Communicates sincere appreciation for assistance; uses specific examples and avoids exaggeration, unlike the general recommendations he frequently receives.

Dan, I appreciate your helping me secure my first career position in fund-raising at a nonprofit organization. Thanks, too, for all that you taught me about putting the customer first. I will keep you updated about how I am faring in the world of not-for-profits.

Restates main idea and anticipates continued relationship; is original and sincere.

STUDY TOOLS

CHAPTER 14

Located at back of the textbook

❑ **Rip out Chapter Review Card**

Located at www.cengagebrain.com

❑ **Review Key Terms Flashcards (Print or Online)**

❑ **Download Audio Summaries for on-the-go review**

❑ **Complete Practice Quizzes to prepare for tests**

❑ **Play "Beat the Clock" to master concepts**

❑ **Complete the Crossword Puzzle to review key terms**

❑ **Watch the video about McDonaldson, a fictitious but all-too-realistic ad agency whose employees struggle with contemporary business communication issues.**

Polishing your language skills will aid you in preparing error-free documents that reflect positively on you and your company. This text appendix is an abbreviated review that focuses on common problems frequently encountered by business writers and offers a quick "refreshing" of key skills.

GRAMMAR

Sentence Structure

1. **Rely mainly on sentences that follow the normal subject-verb-complement sequence for clarity and easy reading.**

   <u>Jennifer</u> and <u>I</u> <u>withdrew</u> for two <u>reasons</u>.
     (subject)   (verb)   (complement)

Original	Better
There are two <u>reasons</u> for our withdrawal.	Two <u>reasons</u> for our withdrawal are ....
	<u>Jennifer and I</u> withdrew for two reasons.
<u>It</u> is necessary that we withdraw.	<u>We</u> must withdraw.
<u>Here</u> is a copy of my résumé.	The enclosed <u>résumé</u> outlines ....

   There, *it*, and *here* are *expletives*—filler words that have no real meaning in the sentence.

2. **Put pronouns, adverbs, phrases, and clauses near the words they modify.**

Incorrect	Correct
Angie put a new type of gel in her hair, <u>which</u> she had just purchased.	Angie put a new type of <u>gel</u>, <u>which</u> she had just purchased, in her hair.
He works <u>only</u> in the call center during peak periods.	He works in the call center <u>only</u> during peak periods.
The clerk stood near the fax machine <u>wearing a denim skirt</u>.	The clerk <u>wearing a denim skirt</u> stood near the fax machine.

3. **Do not separate subject and predicate unnecessarily.**

Incorrect	Clear
<u>She</u>, hoping to receive a bonus, <u>worked</u> rapidly.	Hoping to receive a bonus, <u>she</u> <u>worked</u> rapidly.

4. **Place an introductory phrase near the subject of the independent clause it modifies.** Otherwise, the phrase dangles. To correct the dangling phrase, change the subject of the independent clause, or make the phrase into a dependent clause by assigning it a subject.

Incorrect	Correct
<u>When</u> a young boy, <u>my</u> <u>mother</u> insisted I learn a second language.	<u>When I was a young boy</u>, my mother insisted I learn a second language.
[Implies that the mother was once a young boy.]	
<u>Working</u> at full speed every morning, <u>fatigue</u> overtakes me in the afternoon.	<u>Working</u> at full speed every morning, <u>I</u> become tired in the afternoon.
[Implies that "fatigue" was working at full speed.]	<u>Because I work</u> at full speed every morning, <u>fatigue</u> overtakes me in the afternoon.
<u>To function</u> properly, <u>you</u> must oil the machine every hour.	<u>If the equipment</u> is to function properly, <u>you</u> must oil it every hour.
[Implies that if "you" are "to function properly," the machine must be oiled hourly.]	<u>To function properly</u>, the <u>equipment</u> must be oiled every hour.

5. Express related ideas in similar grammatical form (use parallel construction).

Incorrect	Correct
The machine operator made three resolutions: (1) to be punctual, (2) following instructions carefully, and third, the reduction of waste.	The machine operator made three resolutions: to be punctual, to follow instructions carefully, and to reduce waste.
The human resources manager is concerned with the selection of the right worker, providing appropriate orientation and the worker's progress.	The human resources manager is concerned with selecting the right worker, providing appropriate orientation, and evaluating the worker's progress.

6. Do not end a sentence with a needless preposition.

Where is the new sushi bar to be located (not *located at*)?

The applicant did not tell us where he was going (not *going to*).

End a sentence with a preposition if for some reason the preposition needs emphasis.

I am not concerned with what he is paying for. I am concerned with what he is paying with.

The prospect has everything—a goal to work toward, a house to live in, and an income to live on.

7. Avoid split infinitives. Two words are required to express an infinitive: *to* plus a *verb*. The two words belong together. An infinitive is split when another word is placed between the two.

Incorrect	Correct
The superintendent used to occasionally visit the offices.	The superintendent used to visit the offices occasionally.
I plan to briefly summarize the report.	I plan to summarize the report briefly.

EXERCISE 1

Identify the weakness in each sentence, and write an improved version.

1. It is essential that you learn to design spreadsheets that make financial information meaningful to users.

2. There are many online tools available that build relationships with customers.

3. I am submitting an employee testimonial to the company Web site, which I first posted to a presentation blog.

4. More companies are videoconferencing because of the need to significantly reduce travel costs.

5. To operate efficiently, you must perform periodic maintenance on your computer.

6. Planned store improvements include widening the aisles, improved lighting, and lower shelves for a sophisticated feel.

Pronoun Reference

1. Make a pronoun agree in number with its antecedent (the specific noun for which a pronoun stands).

   a. Use a plural pronoun when it represents two or more singular antecedents connected by *and*.

      The secretary and the treasurer will take their vacations.

      ["The" before "treasurer" indicates that the sentence is about two people.]

      The secretary and treasurer will take his vacation.

      [Omitting "the" before "treasurer" indicates that the sentence is about one person who has two sets of responsibilities.]

   b. Parenthetical remarks (remarks that can be omitted without destroying the basic meaning of the sentence) that appear between the pronoun and its antecedent have no effect on the form of the pronoun.

      President Ritter, not the managers, is responsible for his strategic goals.

      [Because "his" refers to President Ritter and not to "managers," "his" is used instead of "their."]

   c. Use a singular pronoun with *each*, *everyone*, *no*, and their variations.

      Each student and each team member will perform his or her own data collection.

      Everyone is responsible for her or his work.

   d. Use a singular pronoun when two or more singular antecedents are connected by *or* or *nor*.

      Neither Brandon nor Will can complete his work.

      Ask either Mallory or Suzanne about her in-service training.

e. Use pronouns that agree in number with the intended meaning of collective nouns.

The <u>team</u> has been asked for <u>its</u> contributions. ["Team" is thought of as a unit; the singular "its" is appropriate.]

The <u>team</u> have been asked for <u>their</u> contributions. ["Team" is thought of as more than one individual; the plural "their" is appropriate.]

2. **Place relative pronouns as near their antecedents as possible for clear understanding.** A relative pronoun joins a dependent clause to its antecedent.

Ambiguous	Clear
The <u>members</u> were given receipts <u>who</u> have paid.	The <u>members</u> <u>who</u> have paid were given receipts.
The agreement will enable you to pay <u>whichever</u> is lower, <u>6 percent or $50</u>.	The agreement will enable you to pay <u>6 percent or $50</u>, <u>whichever</u> is lower.

Restate a noun instead of risking a *vague* pronoun reference.

Vague	Clear
The officer captured the suspect even though <u>he</u> was unarmed.	The officer captured the suspect even though <u>the officer</u> was unarmed.

3. **Do not use a pronoun by itself to refer to a phrase, clause, sentence, or paragraph.** A pronoun should stand for a noun, and that noun should appear in the writing.

Incorrect	Correct
He expects to take all available accounting courses and obtain a position in a public accounting firm. <u>This</u> appeals to him.	He expects to take all available accounting courses and obtain a position in a public accounting firm. <u>This plan</u> appeals to him.

EXERCISE 2

In each of the sentences below, choose the correct word in parentheses.

1. Conversation skills and good listening (affect, affects) a leader's effectiveness.

2. Each sales rep (was, were) trained to encourage customers to buy more than one size or color since shipping is free.

3. The production manager, not the controller, presented (her, their) strongly opposing views.

4. Neither Stephen nor Lydia (was, were) recognized for their contribution.

5. The company restructured (its, their) recreation event to avoid a frivolous perception.

6. The committee will present (its, their) recommendation at the next staff meeting.

7. Jenna forgot to retain her receipts; (this, this oversight) caused a delay in reimbursement.

Pronoun Case

1. **Use the correct case of pronouns.** *Case* tells whether a pronoun is used as the subject of a sentence or as an object in it.

a. Use nominative-case pronouns (also known as subjective-case pronouns) (*I, he, she, they, we, you, it, who*) as subjects of a sentence or clause.

<u>You</u> and <u>I</u> must collaborate. ["You" and "I" are subjects of the verb "collaborate."]

Those <u>who</u> work will be paid. ["Who" is the subject of the dependent clause "who work."]

b. Use objective-case pronouns (*me, him, her, them, us, you, it, whom*) as objects of verbs and prepositions.

His mother texted <u>him</u> about the family emergency. ["Him" is the object of the verb "texted."]

The customer feedback survey was sent to the project manager and <u>them</u>. ["Them" is the object of the preposition "to."]

To <u>whom</u> should we send the analysis? ["Whom" is the object of the preposition "to."]

TIP: Restate a subordinate clause introduced by *who* or *whom* to determine the appropriate pronoun.

She is the type of manager <u>whom</u> we can promote. [Restating "whom we can promote" as "We can promote her (whom)" clarifies that "whom" is the object.]

She is the type of manager <u>who</u> can be promoted. [Restating "who can be promoted" as "She (who) can be promoted" clarifies that "who" is the subject.]

TIP: Change a question to a statement to determine the correct form of a pronoun.

<u>Whom</u> did you call? [You did call *whom*.]

<u>Whom</u> did you select for the position? [You did select *whom* for the position.]

c. Use the nominative case when forms of the linking verb *be* require a pronoun to complete the meaning.

It was <u>he</u> who received credit for the sale.

It is <u>she</u> who deserves the award.

["It was he" may to some people sound just as distracting as the incorrect "It was him." Express the ideas in a different way to avoid the error and an expletive beginning.]

He was the one who received credit for the sale.

She deserves the award.

d. Use the possessive form of a pronoun before a gerund (a verb used as a noun).

We were delighted at <u>his</u> (not *him*) assuming a leadership role.

["Assuming a leadership role" is used here as a noun. "His" in this sentence serves the same purpose it serves in "We are delighted at his initiative."]

EXERCISE 3

In each of the sentences below, choose the correct pronoun in parentheses.

1. The professor agreed to award (we, us) partial credit for the confusing question.

2. Stacey requested that tasks be divided equally between Addison and (her, she).

3. It was (her, she) (who, whom) recommended revising the company's technology policy to include social networking sites.

4. The manager seemed unaware of (him, his) inability to relate to younger employees.

5. Emma is a leader in (who, whom) we have great confidence.

Verb Agreement

1. **Make subjects agree with verbs.**

   a. Ignore intervening phrases that have no effect on the verb used.

   Good material <u>and</u> fast delivery <u>are</u> (not *is*) essential.

   <u>You</u>, not the carrier, <u>are</u> (not *is*) responsible for the damage. [Intervening phrase, "not the carrier," does not affect the verb used.]

   The <u>attitude</u> of these investors <u>is</u> (not *are*) a deep concern. [The subject is "attitude"; "of these investors" is a phrase coming between the subject and the verb.]

   b. Use a verb that agrees with the noun closer to the verb when *or* or *nor* connects two subjects.

   Only one or two <u>questions</u> <u>are</u> (not *is*) necessary.

   Several paint brushes or one paint <u>roller</u> <u>is</u> (not *are*) necessary.

   c. Use singular verbs with plural nouns that have a singular meaning or are thought of as singular units.

The <u>news</u> <u>is</u> good.	**<u>Economics</u> is a required course.**
Twenty <u>dollars</u> <u>is</u> too much.	**Ten <u>minutes</u> <u>is</u> sufficient time.**

   d. Use a singular verb for titles of articles, firm names, and slogans.

   "Etiquette in the Age of Social Media" <u>is</u> an interesting article.

   Forestieri and Chaudrue <u>is</u> the oldest firm in the city.

   "Eat Smart for Hearts" <u>is</u> a campaign slogan directed at better nutrition for senior adults.

2. **Choose verbs that agree in person with their subjects.** *Person* indicates whether the subject is (1) speaking, (2) being spoken to, or (3) being spoken about.

First person:	**I am, we are.** [Writer or speaker]
Second person:	**You are.** [Receiver of message]
Third person:	**He is, she is, they are.** [Person being discussed]

   She <u>doesn't</u> (not *don't*) eat well or exercise regularly.

   They <u>don't</u> recognize the value of strong networking skills.

Verb Tense and Mood

1. **Use the appropriate verb tense.** *Tense* indicates time. Tense can be either simple or compound.

   Simple tenses:

Present:	**I <u>see</u> you.** [Tells what is happening now.]
Past:	**I <u>saw</u> you.** [Tells what has already happened.]
Future:	**I <u>will</u> <u>see</u> you.** [Tells what is yet to happen.]

Compound tenses:

Present perfect: I <u>have</u> <u>seen</u> you. [Tells of past action that extends to the present.]

Past perfect: I <u>had</u> <u>seen</u> you. [Tells of past action that was finished before another past action.]

Future perfect: I <u>will</u> <u>have</u> <u>seen</u> you. [Tells of action that will be finished before a future time.]

a. Use present tense when something was and still is true.

> The speaker reminded us that Rhode Island <u>is</u> (not *was*) smaller than Wisconsin.
>
> The consultant's name <u>is</u> (not *was*) Ryan Abrams.

b. Avoid unnecessary shifts in tense.

> The carrier <u>brought</u> (not *brings*) my package but <u>left</u> without asking me to sign for it.

Verbs that appear in the same sentence are not required to be in the same tense.

> The contract that <u>was prepared</u> yesterday <u>will</u> be <u>signed</u> tomorrow.

2. **Use subjunctive mood to express situations that are untrue or highly unlikely.** Be sure to use *were* for the present tense of *to be* to indicate the subjunctive mood. Use *was* when the statement could be true.

> I wish the story <u>were</u> (not *was*) true.
>
> If I <u>were</u> (not *was*) you, I would try again.

EXERCISE 4

In each of the sentences below, choose the correct verb in parentheses.

1. Only one of the free smartphone applications (has, have) value to me.
2. Taxpayers, not the government, (are, is) held accountable for paying the national debt.
3. Neither the manager nor the employees (was, were) aware of the policy change.
4. Both Josh and Krystal (was, were) notified of the impending layoffs.
5. The news from the rescue mission (is, are) encouraging.
6. *Good to Great* (has, have) been placed in the company library.
7. The sales manager announced that Portsmouth, South Carolina, (is, was) the site for the annual sales meeting.
8. Tylor (don't, doesn't) expect preferential treatment.
9. The client studied the financial analysis for a minute and (starts, started) asking questions.
10. If the applicant (was, were) experienced with databases, she would have been hired.

Adjectives and Adverbs

1. **Use an adjective to modify a noun or pronoun and an adverb to modify a verb, an adjective, or another adverb.**

Adjective: Bryan gave an <u>impressive</u> sales pitch.

Adverb: The new employee looked <u>enthusiastically</u> at the sales prospect. [The adverb "enthusiastically" modifies the verb "looked."]

   The team leader was <u>really</u> visionary. [The adverb "really" modifies the adjective "visionary."]

   Worker A progressed <u>relatively</u> <u>faster</u> than did Worker B. [The adverb "relatively" modifies the adverb "faster."]

2. **Use an adjective after a linking verb when the modifier refers to the subject instead of to the verb.** [A linking verb connects a subject to the rest of the sentence. "He is old." "She seems sincere."]

> The man entering the building looked <u>suspicious</u>. [The adjective "suspicious" refers to "man," not to "looked."]

3. **Use comparatives (to compare two) and superlatives (to compare three or more) carefully.**

> She is the <u>faster</u> (not *fastest*) of the two workers.
>
> Edwin is the <u>better</u> (not *best*) writer of the two team members.

Exclude a person or thing from a group with which that person or thing is being compared.

> He is more observant than <u>anyone else</u> (not *anyone*) in his department. [As a member of his department, he cannot be more observant than himself.]
>
> "The X-60 is newer than <u>any other machine</u> (not *any machine*) in the plant." [The X-60 cannot be newer than itself.]

PUNCTUATION

Commas

1. **Use a comma**

   a. Between coordinate clauses joined by *and*, *but*, *for*, *or*, and *nor*.

      He wanted to pay his bills on time, but he did not have the money.

   b. To separate introductory clauses and certain phrases from independent clauses. Sentences that begin with dependent clauses (often with words such as *if*, *as*, *since*, *because*, *although*, and *when*) almost always need a comma. Prepositional phrases and verbal phrases with five or more words require commas.

Dependent clause:	**If you can postpone your departure, the research team will be able to finalize its proposal submission.** [The comma separates the introductory dependent clause from the independent clause.]
Infinitive:	**To get the full benefit of our insurance plan, complete and return the enclosed card.** [A verb preceded by "to" ("to get").]
Participial:	**Believing that her earnings would continue to increase, she requested a higher credit card limit.**

      [A verb form used as an adjective: "believing" modifies the dependent clause "she requested."]

Prepositional phrase:	**Within the next few days, you will receive written confirmation of this transaction.** [Comma needed because the phrase contains five words.] **Under the circumstances we think you are justified.** [Comma omitted because the phrase contains fewer than five words and the sentence is clear without the comma.]

   c. To separate three or more words in a series.

      You must choose between gray, green, purple, and white. [Without the comma after "purple," no one can tell for sure whether four choices are available, the last of which is "white," or whether three choices are available, the last of which is "purple and white."]

      You must choose between purple and white, gray, and green. [Choice is restricted to three, the first of which is "purple and white."]

   d. Between two or more independent adjectives that modify the same noun.

      New employees are given a long, difficult examination. [Both "long" and "difficult" modify "examination."]

      We want quick, factual news. [Both "quick" and "factual" modify "news."]

      Do not place a comma between two adjectives when the second adjective modifies the adjective and noun as a unit.

      The supervisor is an excellent team player. ["Excellent" modifies the noun phrase "team player."]

   e. To separate a nonrestrictive clause (a clause that is not essential to the basic meaning of the sentence) from the rest of the sentence.

      Kent Murray, who is head of customer resource management, has selected Century Consulting to oversee the product launch. [The parenthetical remark is not essential to the meaning of the sentence.]

The man **who is head of customer resource management** has selected Century Consulting to oversee the product launch. [Commas are not needed, because "who is head of customer resource management" is essential to the meaning of the sentence.]

f.   To set off or separate dates, addresses, geographical names, degrees, and long numbers:

On **July 2, 2013,** Jason Kennedy made the final payment. [Before and after the year in month-day-year format]

I saw him in **Tahoe City, California,** on the 12th of October. [Before and after the name of a state when the name of a city precedes it]

Jesse Marler, President [Between the printed name and the title on the same line beneath a signature or in a letter address]

Tristan A. Highfield
President of Academic Affairs [No comma is used if the title is on a separate line.]

g.   To separate parenthetical expressions or other elements interrupting the flow from the rest of the sentence.

Ms. Watson, **speaking on behalf of the entire department,** accepted the proposal. [Set off a parenthetical expression]

Cole, I believe you have earned a vacation. [After a direct address]

Yes, you can count on me. [After the words *No* and *Yes* when they introduce a statement]

Arun Ramage, **former president of the Jackson Institute,** spoke to the group. [Set off appositives when neutral emphasis is desired]

The job requires experience, **not formal education.** [Between contrasted elements]

EXERCISE 6
Insert needed commas. Write "correct" if you find no errors.

1. The employee who is featured in our latest television commercial is active in the community theatre.
2. Emoticons which are created by keying combinations of symbols to produce "sideway faces" communicate emotion in electronic messages.
3. Sean Cohen a new member of the board remained silent during the long bitter debate.
4. Top social networking sites include Facebook MySpace and Flickr.
5. The entire population was surveyed but three responses were unusable.
6. If you tag websites in a social bookmarking site you can locate them easily for later use.
7. To qualify for the position applicants must have technology certification.
8. We should be spending less money not more.
9. On May 9 2013 the company's Twitter site was launched.
10. Yes the president approved a team-building event to replace our annual golf outing.

Semicolons and Colons

1. **Use a semicolon**

a.   To join the independent clauses in a compound sentence when a conjunction is omitted.

Your voice counts; email us with your ideas and concerns.

b.   To join the independent clauses in a compound-complex sentence.

As indicated earlier, we prefer delivery on Saturday morning at four o'clock; but Friday night at ten o'clock will be satisfactory.

We prefer delivery on Saturday morning at four o'clock; but, if the arrangement is more convenient for you, Friday night at ten o'clock will be satisfactory.

c.   Before an adverbial conjunction. Use a comma after the adverbial conjunction.

Adverbial conjunction:	The shipment arrived too late for our weekend sale; therefore, we are returning the shipment to you.

Other frequently used adverbial conjunctions are *however, otherwise, consequently,* and *nevertheless.*

d.   Before words used to introduce enumerations or explanations that follow an independent clause.

Enumeration with commas:	Many factors affect the direction of the stock market; namely, interest rates, economic growth, and employment rates.

Explanation forming a complete thought:	We have plans for improvement; <u>for example</u>, we intend …. The engine has been "knocking"; <u>that is</u>, the gas in the cylinders explodes before the pistons complete their upward strokes.

NOTE: The following exceptions require a comma to introduce the enumeration or explanation:

Enumeration without commas:	Several Web 2.0 tools are available, <u>for example</u>, blogs and wikis. [A comma, not a semicolon, is used because the enumeration contains no commas.]
Explanation forming an incomplete thought:	A trend is to replace expensive employee networking events with purposeful recreation, for instance, community service events. [A comma, not a semicolon, is used because the explanation is not a complete thought.]

e. In a series that contains commas.

   Some of our workers have worked overtime this week: Smith, 6 hours; Hardin, 3; Cantrell, 10; and McGowan, 11.

2. **Use a colon**

   a. After a complete thought that introduces a list of items. Use a colon following both direct and indirect introductions of lists.

Direct introduction:	The following three factors influenced our decision: an expanded market, an inexpensive source of raw materials, and a ready source of labor. [The word "following" clearly introduces a list.]
Indirect introduction:	The carpet is available in three colors: green, burgundy, and blue.

Do not use a colon after an introductory statement that ends with a preposition or a verb (*are, is, were, include*). The list that follows the preposition or verb finishes the sentence.

Incomplete sentence:	We need to (1) expand our market, (2) locate an inexpensive source of materials, and (3) find a ready source of labor. [A colon does not follow "to", because the words preceding the list are not a complete sentence.]

   b. To stress an appositive (a noun that renames the preceding noun) at the end of a sentence.

   A majority of white collar criminals report that a single factor led to their crimes: pressure to achieve revenue targets.

   Our progress is due to the efforts of one person: Brooke Keating.

EXERCISE 7

Insert semicolons, colons, and commas where needed, and delete them where they are unnecessary. Write "correct" if you find no errors.

1. Some privacy concerns have become less important in recent years, however, most people feel extremely vulnerable to privacy invasion.

2. The following agents received bonuses Barnes, $750, Shelley, $800, and Jackson, $950.

3. Employees were notified today of the plant closing they received two weeks' severance pay.

4. This paint does have some disadvantages for example a lengthy drying time.

5. Soon after the applications are received, a team of judges will evaluate them, but the award recipients will not be announced until January 15.

6. The program has one shortcoming: flexibility.

7. The new bakery will offer: frozen yogurt, candies, and baked goods.

8. We are enthusiastic about the plan because: (1) it is least expensive, (2) its legality is unquestioned, and (3) it can be implemented quickly.

Apostrophes

1. **Use an apostrophe to form possessives.**

   a. Add an apostrophe and *s* (*'s*) to form the posessive case of a singular noun or a plural noun that does not end with a pronounced *s*.

Singular noun:	<u>Jenna's</u> position
	<u>firm's</u> assets
	<u>employee's</u> benefits

Plural noun without	<u>men's</u> clothing
a pronounced *s***:**	<u>children's</u> games
	<u>deer's</u> antlers

   b. Add only an apostrophe to form the possessive of a singular or plural noun that ends with a pronounced *s*.

Singular noun with	<u>Niagara Falls'</u> site
pronounced *s***:**	<u>Ms. Jenkins's</u> interview

Plural noun with	two <u>managers'</u> decision
pronounced *s***:**	six <u>months'</u> wages

   Exception: An apostrophe and *s* (*'s*) can be added to singular nouns ending in a pronounced *s* if an additional *s* sound is pronounced easily.

Singular noun with	<u>boss's</u> decision
additional *s* **sound:**	<u>class's</u> party
	<u>Jones's</u> invitation

   c. Use an apostrophe with the possessives of nouns that refer to time (minutes, hours, days, weeks, months, and years) or distance in a possessive manner.

eight <u>hours'</u> pay	two <u>weeks'</u> notice
<u>today's</u> global economy	ten <u>years'</u> experience
a <u>stone's</u> throw	a <u>yard's</u> length

   EXERCISE 8

   Correct the possessives.

   1. The new hires confidence was crushed by the managers harsh tone.
   2. This companies mission statement has been revised since it's recent merger.
   3. Employees who are retained may be asked to accept a reduction of one weeks pay.
   4. Vendors' have submitted sealed bids for the construction contract that will be opened in two week's.
   5. Younger workers must appreciate older employees extensive company knowledge.

Hyphens

1. **Use a hyphen**

   a. Between the words in a compound adjective. (A *compound adjective* is a group of adjectives appearing together and used as a single word to describe a noun.)

An <u>eye-catching</u> device	**A <u>two-thirds</u> interest**

   Do not hyphenate a compound adjective in the following cases:

   (1) When the compound adjective follows a noun.

   A design that is <u>eye catching</u>.

   Today's consumers are <u>convenience driven</u>.

   NOTE: Some compound adjectives that are familiar hyphenated words or phrases remain hyphenated when they follow a noun.

   The news release was <u>up-to-date</u>.

   For jobs that are <u>part-time</u>, ...

   (2) An expression made up of an adverb that ends in *ly* and an adjective is not a compound adjective and does not require a hyphen.

   <u>commonly accepted</u> principle

   <u>widely quoted</u> authority

   (3) A simple fraction and a percentage.

Simple fraction:	<u>Two thirds</u> of the respondents
Percentage:	<u>15 percent</u> sales increase

   b. To prevent misinterpretation.

   <u>Recover</u> a chair [To obtain possession of a chair once more]

   <u>Re-cover</u> a chair [To cover a chair again]

   <u>Eight inch</u> blades [Eight blades, each of which is an inch long]

   <u>Eight-inch</u> blades [Blades eight inches long]

Quotation Marks and Italics

1. **Use quotation marks**

   a. To enclose direct quotations.

Single-sentence quotation:	**The supervisor said, "We will make progress."**
Interrupted quotation:	**"We will make progress," the supervisor said, "even though we have to work overtime."**
Multiple-sentence quotation:	**The manager said, "Have a seat, Seth. Please wait a moment while I complete this email."** [Place quotation marks before the first word and after the last word of a multiple-sentence quotation.]
Quotation within quotation:	**The budget director said, "Believe me when I say 'A penny saved is a penny earned' is the best advice I ever had."** [Use single quotation marks to enclose a quotation that appears within a quotation.]

   b. To enclose titles of songs, magazine and newspaper articles, lecture titles, and themes within text.

   "Candle in the Wind"   "Making an Impact"

   The chapter, "Online Presence," ....

   c. To enclose a definition of a defined term. Italicize the defined word.

   The term *downsizing* is used to refer to "the planned reduction in the number of employees."

   d. To enclose words used in humor, a word used when a different word would be more appropriate, slang expressions that need to be emphasized or clarified for the reader, or nicknames. These words can also be shown in italics.

Humor/ different word:	**Our "football" team ....** [Hints that the team appears to be playing something other than football.]
	Our football "team" .... [Hints that "collection of individual players" would be more descriptive than "team."]
	... out for "lunch." [Hints that the reason for being out is something other than lunch.]
Slang:	**The "tipping point" in the planned reorganization is securing support of union management.**
Nicknames:	**And now for some comments by Robert "Bob" Johnson.**

2. **Use italics**

   a. To mention words, letters, numbers, and phrases within a sentence.

   He had difficulty learning to spell *recommendation.*

   b. To emphasize a word that is not sufficiently emphasized by other means.

   Our goal is to hire the *right* person, not necessarily the most experienced candidate.

   c. To indicate the titles of books, magazines, and newspapers.

   Creating a Culture of Excellence

   The New York Times

   Reader's Digest

Dashes, Parentheses, and Periods

1. **Use a dash**

   a. To place emphasis on appositives.

      His answer—the correct answer—was based on years of experience.

      Compare the price—$125—with the cost of a single repair job.

   b. When appositives contain commas.

      Their scores—Chloe, 21; Tairus, 20; and Drew, 19—were the highest in a group of 300.

   c. When a parenthetical remark consists of an abrupt change in thought.

      The committee decided—you may think it's a joke, but it isn't—that the resolution should be adopted.

      NOTE: Use an em dash (not two hyphens) to form a dash in computer-generated copy.

2. **Use parentheses for explanatory material that could be left out.**

   Three of our employees (Kristen Hubbard, Alex Russo, and Mark Coghlan) took their vacations in August.

   All our employees (believe it or not) have perfect attendance records.

3. Use a period after declarative and imperative sentences and courteous requests.

   We will attend. [Declarative sentence]

   Complete this report. [Imperative sentence]

   Will you please complete the report today. [Courteous request is a question but does not require a verbal answer with requested action]

Number Usage

1. **Use figures**

   a. In most business writing because figures provide deserved emphasis and are easy for readers to locate if they need to reread for critical points. Regardless of whether a number has one digit or many, use figures to express dates, sums of money, mixed numbers and decimals, distance, dimension, cubic capacity, percentage, weights, temperatures, and chapter and page numbers.

May 10, 2013	**165 pounds**
$9 million	**Chapter 3, page 29**

      5 percent (use % in a table)

      more than 200 applicants (or two hundred) [an approximation]

   b. With ordinals (*th, st, rd, nd*) only when the number precedes the month.

      The meeting is to be held on June 21.

      The meeting is to be held on the 21st of June.

   c. With ciphers but without decimals when presenting even-dollar figures, even if the figure appears in a sentence with another figure that includes dollars and cents.

      Miranda paid $70 for the cabinet.

      Miranda paid $99.95 for the table and $70 for the cabinet.

d. Numbers that represent time when a.m. or p.m. is used. Words or figures may be used with o'clock.

Please meet me at 10:15 p.m.

Please be there at ten o'clock (or 10 o'clock).

Omit the colon when expressing times of day that include hours but not minutes, even if the time appears in a sentence with another time that includes minutes.

The award program began at 6:30 p.m. with a reception at 7 p.m.

2. Spell out

a. Numbers if they are used as the first word of a sentence.

Thirty-two people attended.

b. Numbers one through nine if no larger number appears in the same sentence.

Only three auditors worked at the client's office.

Send 5 officers and 37 members.

c. The first number in two consecutive numbers that act as adjectives modifying the same noun; write the second number in figures. If the first number cannot be expressed in one or two words, place it in figures also.

The package required four 44-cent stamps. [A hyphen joins the second number with the word that follows it, thus forming a compound adjective that describes the noun "stamps."]

We shipped 250 180-horsepower engines today. [Figures are used because neither number can be expressed in one or two words.]

EXERCISE 12
Correct the number usage in the following sentences taken from a letter or a report.

1. The question was answered by sixty-one percent of the respondents.

2. The meeting is scheduled for 10:00 a.m. on February 3rd.

3. These 3 figures appeared on the expense account: $21.95, $30.00, and $35.14.

4. The purchasing manager ordered 50 4-GB hard drives.

5. 21 members voted in favor of the $2,000,000 proposal.

6. Approximately one hundred respondents requested a copy of the results.

7. Mix two quarts of white with 13 quarts of brown.

8. Examine the cost projections on page eight.

CAPITALIZATION

Capitalize

1. **Proper nouns (words that name a particular person, place, or thing) and adjectives derived from proper nouns.** Capitalize the names of persons, places, geographic areas, days of the week, months of the year, holidays, deities, specific events, and other specific names.

Proper nouns	Common nouns
Jessica Moore	An applicant for the management position
Bonita Lakes	A land development
Centre Park Mall	A new shopping center
Veteran's Day	A federal holiday
Information Age	A period of time
Proper adjectives:	Irish potatoes, Roman shades, Swiss army knife, Chinese executives, British accent, Southern dialect

Do not capitalize the name of the seasons unless they are personified.

Old Man Winter

2. **The principal words in the titles of books, magazines, newspapers, articles, compact discs, movies, plays, television series, songs, and poems.**

The Carrot Principle [Book]

"**Smart Moves for New Leaders**" [Article]

Time [Magazine]

The White Album [Compact disc]

3. **The names of academic courses that are numbered, are specific course titles, or contain proper nouns.** Capitalize degrees used after a person's name and specific academic sessions.

Addison Malone is enrolled in classes in <u>French</u>, <u>mathematics</u>, <u>science</u>, and <u>English</u>.

Students entering the <u>MBA</u> program must complete <u>Accounting 6093</u> and <u>Finance 5133</u>.

Allison Ward, <u>M.S.</u>, will teach <u>International Marketing</u> during <u>Spring Semester</u> 2013.

Professor O'Donnell earned a <u>master's</u> degree in business from Harvard.

4. Titles that precede a name.

Mr. Ronald Moxley	Editor Deeden
Dr. Lauren Zolna	President Lopez
Uncle Ian	Professor Copley

Do not capitalize titles appearing alone or following a name unless they appear in addresses.

The <u>manager</u> approved the proposal submitted by the <u>editorial assistant</u>.

Jon Sharma, <u>executive vice president</u>, is responsible for that account.

Clint has taken the position formerly held by his <u>father</u>.

Address all correspondence to Colonel Michael Anderson, <u>Department Head</u>, 109 Crescent Avenue, Baltimore, MD 21208.

5. The main words in a division or department name if the official or specific name is known or the name is used in a return address, a letter address, or a signature block.

Official or specific name known:	Return the completed questionnaire to the <u>Public Relations Department</u> by March 15.
Official or specific name unknown:	Employees in your information systems division are invited ….
Return or letter address, signature block:	Mr. Blake Cain, <u>Manager</u>, <u>Public Relations Department</u>

6. Most nouns followed by numbers (except in page, paragraph, line, size, and verse references).

Policy No. 8746826	Exhibit A	Chapter 7
page 97, paragraph 2	Figure 3-5	Model L-379
Flight 340, Gate 22	size 8, Style 319 jacket	

7. The first word of a direct quotation.

The placement officer warned, "Those with offensive email habits may be the first to lose their jobs during layoffs."

Do not capitalize the first word in the last part of an interrupted quotation or the first word in an indirect quotation.

"We will proceed," he said, "with the utmost caution." [Interrupted quotation]

He said that the report must be submitted by the end of the week. [Indirect quotation]

8. The first word following a colon when a formal statement or question follows.

Here is an important rule for report writers: Plan your work and work your plan.

Each sales staff should ask this question: Do I really look like a representative of my firm?

EXERCISE 13

Copy each of the following sentences, making essential changes in capitalization.

1. The first question professor Burney asked me during interviewing 101 was "why do you want to work for us?"

2. The remodeling will give the store a more sophisticated feel according to the Public Relations Director.

3. As the Summer Season arrives, gas prices are expected to rise.

4. We recently purchased digital juice, an excellent source of copyright-free animated images.

5. Thomas Frieden, Director of the Centers for Disease Control, is the agency's key communicator.

WORDS FREQUENTLY MISUSED

These words are frequently misused. If you're not certain of meaning or usage, check a dictionary or style guide.

1. Accept, except
2. Advice, advise
3. Affect, effect
4. Among, between
5. Amount, number
6. Capital, capitol
7. Cite, sight, site
8. Complement, compliment
9. Continual, continuous
10. Credible, creditable
11. Council, counsel
12. Different from, different than
13. Each other, one another
14. Eminent, imminent
15. Envelop, envelope
16. Farther, further
17. Fewer, less
18. Formally, formerly

19. Infer, imply

20. Its, it's

21. Lead, led

22. Lose, loose

23. Media, medium

24. Personal, personnel

25. Principal, principle

26. Reason is, because

27. Stationary, stationery

28. That, which

29. Their, there, they're

30. To, too, two

EXERCISE 14

Select the correct word or phrase in parentheses.

1. What (affect, effect) will the change have on us?

2. The consultant plans to (advice, advise) the company to eliminate the fourth shift for at least three months.

3. The (amount, number) of complaints from customers declined with the addition of online chat.

4. The (cite, sight, site) of the new 24/7 fitness center is being debated.

5. I consider your remark a (compliment, complement); I agree that the granite countertops (compliment, complement) the deep, earthy tones in the room.

6. The three panelists were constantly interrupting (each other, one another).

7. Generally staple merchandise is placed (farther, further) from the cashier than impulse items.

8. Limit your discussion to five or (fewer, less) points.

9. I (infer, imply) from Avanti's comments to the press that the merger will occur.

10. The hurricane seems to be (losing loosing) (its, it's) force, which is (different from, different than) predictions.

11. The chemical engineer (lead, led) the research team's investigation to eliminate (lead, led) from gas emissions.

12. Employees may handle (personal, personnel) business during e-breaks beginning next week.

13. Customer perception is the (principal, principle) reason for the change.

14. (Their, There, They're) planning to complete (their, there, they're) strategic plan this week.

15. The (to, too, two) external auditors expect us (to, too, two) complete (to, too, two) many unnecessary reports.

SOLUTIONS TO EXERCISES

Exercise 1—Sentence Structure

1. You must learn to design spreadsheets that make financial information meaningful to users.

2. Many online tools are available that build relationships with customers.

3. I am submitting an employee testimonial, which I first posted to a presentations blog, to the company Web site.

4. More companies are videoconferencing because of the need to reduce travel costs significantly.

5. You must perform periodic maintenance on your computer to keep it operating efficiently. [The introductory phrase dangles.]

6. Planned store improvements include widening the aisles, improving lighting, and lowering shelves for a sophisticated feel.

   Planned store improvements include widened aisles, improved lighting, and lowered shelves for a sophisticated feel.

Exercise 2—Pronoun Reference

1. affect
2. was
3. her
4. was
5. its
6. its
7. this oversight

Exercise 3—Pronoun Case

1. us
2. her
3. she; who
4. his
5. whom

Exercise 4—Verb Agreement, Tense, and Mood

1. has
2. are
3. were
4. were
5. is
6. has
7. is
8. doesn't
9. started
10. were

Exercise 5—Adjectives and Adverbs

1. infrequently
2. impatiently
3. quickly
4. best
5. any other

Exercise 6—Commas

1. Correct
2. Emoticons, which are created by keying combinations of symbols to produce "sideway faces," communicate emotion in electronic messages.
3. Sean Cohen, a new member of the board, remained silent during the long, bitter debate.
4. Top social networking sites include Facebook, MySpace, and Flickr.
5. The entire population was surveyed, but three responses were unusable.
6. If you tag websites in a social bookmarking site, you can locate them easily for later use.
7. To qualify for the position, applicants must have technology certification.
8. We should be spending less money, not more.
9. On May 9, 2013, the company's Twitter site was launched.
10. Yes, the president approved a team building event to replace our annual golf outing.

Exercise 7—Semicolons and Colons

1. Some privacy concerns have become less important in recent years; however, most people feel extremely vulnerable to privacy invasion.
2. The following agents received bonuses: Barnes, $750; Shelley, $800; and Jackson, $950.
3. Employees were notified today of the plant closing; they received two weeks' severance pay.
4. This paint does have some disadvantages, for example, a lengthy drying time.
5. Soon after the applications are received, a team of judges will evaluate them; but the award recipients will not be announced until January 15.
6. Correct
7. The new bakery will offer frozen yogurt, candies, and baked goods.

8. We are enthusiastic about the plan because (1) it is least expensive, (2) its legality is unquestioned, and (3) it can be implemented quickly.

Exercise 8—Apostrophes

1. hire's; manager's
2. company's; its
3. week's
4. Vendors; weeks
5. employees'

Exercise 9—Hyphens

1. Web-based; denial-of-service attack
2. State-of-the-art; timely business
3. Correct
4. two-thirds; 5 percent
5. one half; highly educated

Exercise 10—Quotation Marks and Italics

1. Cynthia Cooper's *Extraordinary Circumstances* is required reading in some forensic accounting classes. [Italicizes a book title]
2. The article "How to Persuade People to Say Yes" appeared in the May 2009 issue of *Training Journal*. [Encloses the name of an article in quotation marks and italicizes the title of a journal]
3. The consultant's "accomplishments" are summarized on her opening blog page. [Uses quotation marks to introduce doubt about whether *accomplishments* is the right label; her undertakings may have been of little significance]
4. Connie said, "I want to participate in a volunteer program that serves such a worthy cause." [Uses quotations marks in a direct quotation]
5. The term *flame* is online jargon for "a heated, sarcastic, sometimes abusive message or posting to a discussion group." [Italicizes a defined term and encloses the definition in quotes]
6. Limit random "tweets," but focus on ideas and issues that are interesting and relevant. [Uses quotation marks to emphasize or clarify a word for the reader]

Exercise 11—Dashes, Parentheses, and Periods

1. Additional consultants—programmers and analysts—were hired to complete the computer conversion.

2. The dividend will be raised to 15 cents a share (approved by the Board of Directors on December 1, 2013).

3. Would you link this YouTube video to my slide show. [Uses a period to follow courteous request that requires no verbal response]

Exercise 12—Number Usage

1. The question was answered by 61 percent of the respondents.

2. The meeting is scheduled for 10 a.m. on February 3.

3. These three figures appeared on the expense account: $21.95, $30, and $35.14.

4. The purchasing manager ordered fifty 4-GB Flash drives.

5. Twenty-one members voted in favor of the $2 million proposal.

6. Approximately 100 respondents requested a copy of the results. [Approximations above nine that can be expressed in one or two words may be written in either figures or words, but figures are more emphatic.]

7. Mix 2 quarts of white with 13 quarts of brown.

8. Examine the cost projections on page 8.

Exercise 13—Capitalization

1. The first question Professor Burney asked me during Interviewing 101 was "Why do you want to work for us?"

2. The remodeling will give the store a more sophisticated feel according to the public relations director.

3. As the summer season arrives, gas prices are expected to rise.

4. We recently purchased Digital Juice, an excellent source of copyright-free animated images.

5. Thomas Frieden, director of the Centers for Disease Control, is the agency's key communicator.

Exercise 14—Words Frequently Misused

1. effect
2. advise
3. number
4. site
5. compliment; complement
6. one another
7. farther
8. fewer
9. infer
10. losing; its; different from
11. led; lead
12. personal
13. principal
14. They're; their
15. two; to; too

References

Chapter 1

1. Koncz, A. (2007, March 15). Employers cite communication skills, honesty/integrity as key for job candidates. National Association of Colleges and Employers. Retrieved from www.naceweb.org/press/display.asp?year=2007&prid=254.
2. Best workplace for companies with more than 1,000 employees. (2013, April 10). *The Globe and Mail*. Retrieved from www.theglobeandmail.com/partners/advgreatplacestowork0413/best-workplace-for-companies-with-more-than-1000-employees/article10934650/.
3. Tapscott, D. (2008, December 8). Supervising Net Gen. *Business Week Online*, 5. Retrieved from Business Source Complete database.
4. Slayton, M. (1980). *Common sense & everyday ethics*. Washington, DC: Ethics Resource Center.
5. Slayton, M. (1991, May–June). Perspectives. *Ethics Journal*. Washington, DC: Ethics Resource Center.
6. A gift or a bribe? (2002, September). *State Legislatures*, 2(8), 9.
7. Mathison, D. L. (1988). Business ethics cases and decision models: A call for relevancy in the classroom. *Journal of Business Ethics*, 10, 781.
8. Jelly Belly Candy Company: Expanding internationally. (2007). *Talent Management*. Retrieved from http:// www.talentmgt.com/departments/application/54/.
9. Pelletier, B. (2012, January 28). Puma's intercultural gaffe. *Gestion des Risques Interculturels*. Retrieved from http:// gestion-des-risques-interculturels.com/risques/puma-s-intercultural-gaffe/
10. Mason, R. O. (1986). Four ethical issues of the information age. In Dejoie, R., Fowler, G., & Paradice, D. (1991) *Ethical issues in information systems* (pp. 46–55). Boston: Boyd & Fraser.
11. Felts, C. (1995). Taking the mystery out of self-directed work teams. *Industrial Management*, 37(2), 21–26.
12. Miller, B. K., & Butler, J. B. (1996, November/December). Teams in the workplace. *New Accountant*, 18–24.
13. Ray, D., & Bronstein, H. (1995). *Teaming up*. New York: McGraw Hill.
14. The trouble with teams. (1995, January 14). *Economist*, 61.
15. Frohman, M. A. (1995, April 3). Do teams . . . but do them right. *IndustryWeek*, 21–24.
16. Zuidema, K. R., & Kleiner, B. H. (1994). New developments in developing self-directed work groups. *Management Decision*, 32(8), 57–63.
17. Barry, D. (1991). Managing the baseless team: Lessons in distributed leadership. *Organizational Dynamics*, 20(1), 31–47.

Chapter 2

1. Interpersonal intelligence. (2009). *My Personality*. Retrieved from www.mypersonality.info/multiple-intelligences/interpersonal/.
2. Galpin, T. (1995, April). Pruning the grapevine. *Training & Development*, 49(4), 28+.
3. Hersey, P., & Blanchard, K. H. (1982). *Management of organizational behavior: Utilizing human resources* (4th ed.). Englewood Cliffs, NJ: Prentice-Hall.
4. Felts, C. (1995). Taking the mystery out of self-directed work teams. *Industrial Management*, 37(2), 21–26.
5. Mehrabian, A. (1971). *Silent messages*. Belmont, CA: Wadsworth.
6. Tapscott, D. (2008, December 8). Supervising Net Gen. *Business Week Online*, 5. Retrieved from Business Source Complete database.
7. Gratton, L. (2012, June 19). Working together when apart. *Wall Street Journal*. Retrieved from http://online.wsj.com/article/SB118165895540732559.html.
8. Lehman, C., & DuFrene, D. Communication in Virtual Teams, Enrichment Module. Retrieved from www.cengagesites.com/academic/assets/sites/4004/Communicating%20in%20Virtual%20Teams_word%20format.pdf
9. Zuidema, K. R., & Kleiner, B. H. (1994, October). Self-directed work groups gain popularity. *Business Credit*, 21–26.
10. Hunt, V. D. (1993). *Managing for quality: Integrating quality and business strategy* (p. 121). Homewood, IL: Business One Irwin.
11. Chaney, L. H., & Lyden, J. A. (1998, May). Managing meetings to manage your image. *Supervision*, 59(5), 13–15.
12. Munter, M. (1998, June). Meeting technology: From low-tech to high-tech. *Business Communication Quarterly*, 61(2), 80–87.
13. Ibid.

Chapter 3

1. Canavor, N., & Meirowitz, C. (2005). Good corporate writing: Why it matters, and what to do; Poor corporate writing—in press releases, ads, brochures, web sites and more—is costing companies credibility and revenues. Here's how to put the focus back on clear communication. *Communication World*, 22(4), 30(4).
2. Schein, E. H. (1992). *Organizational culture and leadership*. San Francisco, CA: Jossey-Bass Publishers.
3. Boreham, N. & Morgan, C. (2004). A socio-cultural analysis of organizational learning. Oxford Review of Education 30, 307–325.
4. Stallard, M. L. (2011, January 21). Has SAS Institute's goodnight cracked the code on corporate culture? Insights on Leadership and Employee Engagement. Retrieved from http://www.michaelleestallard.com/has-sas-institutes-goodnight-cracked-the-code-on-corporate-culture.
5. Dennett, J. T. (1988, September). Not to say is better than to say: How rhetorical structure reflects cultural context in Japanese-English technical writing. *IEEE Transactions on Professional Communication*, 31(3), 116–119. doi: 10.1109/47.7816.
6. Jury sent message with huge reward in Vioxx drug case. (2005, August 24). *Gainesville Times*. Retrieved from http://gainesvillelegals.com/news/stories/20050824/opinion/8060.shtml.
7. Zetter, K. (2010, March 9). Lifelock dinged $12 million for deceptive business practices. Wired. Retrieved from www.wired.com/threatlevel/2010/03/lifelock-accused-of-running-con-operation/.
8. Enserink, M. (2012, October 2). Diederik Stapel under investigation by Dutch prosecutors. *Science Insider*. Retrieved from http://news.sciencemag.org/people-events/2012/10/diederik-stapel-under-investigation-dutch-prosecutors.
9. Another worker pays the price for fabricating resume. (2007, April 28). Retrieved from http://www.eweek.com/c/a/IT-Management/Another-Worker-Pays-the-Price-for-Fabricating-Resume/.
10. Telushkin, J. (1997). Avoid words that hurt. *USA Today*, 74.
11. Mellor, W. (2011, January 26). McDonald's no match for KFC in China as Colonel rules fast food." *Bloomberg*. Retrieved from www.bloomberg.com/news/2011-01-26/mcdonald-s-no-match-for-kfc-in-china-where-colonel-sanders-rules-fast-food.html

Chapter 4

1. Charlton, J. (Ed.) (1985). *The writer's quotation book*. Stamford, CT: Ray Freeman.
2. Is email making bosses ruder? (2005). *European Business Forum*, 21, 72.
3. Rindegard, J. (1999). Use clear writing to show you mean business. *InfoWorld*, 21(47), 78.
4. Dyrud, M. A. (1996). Teaching by example: Suggestions for assignment design. *Business Communication Quarterly*, 59(3), 67–70.
5. Redish, J. C. (1993). Understanding readers. In C. M. Barnum & S. Carliner (Eds.), *Techniques for technical communicators*. New York: Prentice Hall.
6. Ibid.
7. Stout, David. (2009, March) Obama Apologizes for Quip About Disabled People, *The New York Times* website, http://www.nytimes.com/2009/03/21/us/politics/21special.html?_r=0.
8. Wrong number. (1995). *Central New Jersey Business*, 8(13), 3.
9. Neuwirth, R. (1998). Error message: To err is human, but darn expensive. *Editor & Publisher*, 131(29), 4.

10. UCSD sends acceptance email to wrong list. (2009, April 2). Eschool News. Retrieved from http://www .eschoolnews.com/news /around-the-web/index.cfm?i=58045.

Chapter 5

1. Hear no evil, see no evil: Business e-mail overtakes the telephone. (2007, August 20). *Network*. Retrieved from www.networkworld .com/community/node/18555.
2. Silverman, D. (2009, April 14). Words at work: How to revise an email so that people will read it. Retrieved from http://blogs.hbr .org/2009/04/how-to-revise-an-email-so-that/.
3. Silverman, D. (2009, April 14). Words at work: Is your email businesslike—or brusque? Retrieved from http://blogs.hbr.org/2009/05 /is-your-email-businesslike-or/.
4. New technology makes work harder. (1999, June 1). *BBC News*. Retrieved from http://news .bbc.co.uk/2/hi/science/nature/357993.stm.
5. Lacy, S. (2006, January 6). IM security one tough sell. *BusinessWeek Online*, 11.
6. Knapp, L. (2007, January 20). Switching to texting has pluses, minuses: Getting started. *The Seattle Times*, p. E6. Retrieved from General Business File database.
7. McGrath, C. (2006, January 22). The pleasures of the text. *The New York Times*, p. 15.
8. Knapp, L. (2007, January 20). Switching to texting has pluses, minuses: Getting started. *The Seattle Times*, p. E6. Retrieved from General Business File database.
9. Electronic Privacy Information Center. (2008, September 15). Public opinion on privacy. Retrieved from www.epic .org/privacy/survey.
10. 9th circuit rules on text-message privacy. (2008, July 15). *Law.com*. Retrieved from www.law.com/jsp/legaltechnology /pubArticleLT .jsp?id=1202422970200.
11. Brown, P. B. (2005, December 31). Resolved: I will take good advice. *The New York Times*. Retrieved from http://www.nytimes .com/2005/12/31/business/31offline.html.
12. Mabrey, V., Scott, D. W., & Foster, M. (2008, March 24). Charges filed in Detroit mayor scandal. *ABC News*. Retrieved from http://abcnews.go.com/print?id=4355795.
13. Varchaver, N. (2003). The perils of e-mail. *Fortune*, 147(3), 96+.
14. Ibid.
15. Downer, K. (2008). A great website in five steps. *Third Sector*, 9.
16. Tierney, J. (2007, April). Ignore universal web design at your own peril. *Multichannel Merchant*, 8.
17. Huettner, B. (2008, January 19). Web accessibility basics. *Professional Communication Society*. Retrieved from http://pcs.ieee.org /web-accessibility-basics/.
18. McAlpine, R. (2001). *Web word wizardry: A guide to writing for the Web and intranet*. Berkeley, CA: Ten Speed Press.
19. Strategy (2010). Social media in business: Fortune 100 statistics. Retrieved July 10, 2012 from http://misterthebodeau.preposterous.com /istrategy-2010-blog-archive-social-media-in-b
20. Fichter, D. (2001, November/December). Zooming in: Writing content for intranets. *Online*, 25(6), 80+.
21. Weblog. (2005). *Loosely coupled*. Retrieved from www.looselycoupled.com/glossary /weblog.
22. Quible, Z. K. (2005). Blogs and written business communication courses: A perfect union. *Journal of Education for Business*, 80(6), 327–332.
23. Jones, D. (2005, May 10). CEOs refuse to get tangled up in messy blogs. *USA Today*. Retrieved from Academic Search Premier database.
24. DeBare, I. (2005, May 5). Tips for effective use of blogs in business. *San Francisco Chronicle*, p. C6.
25. Hutchins, J. P. (2005, November 14). Beyond the water cooler. *Computerworld*, 39(46), 45–46.
26. How to write for the web. (2008, March 26). *The Online Journalism Review*. Retrieved from www.ojr.org/ojr/wiki/writing.
27. Goodnoe, E. (2005, August 8). How to use wikis for business. *Information Week*. Retrieved from www.informationweek.com /how-to-use-wikis-for-business/167600331.
28. Johnson, C. Y. (2008, July 7). Hurry up, the customer has a complaint: As blogs expand the reach of a single voice, firms monitor the Internet looking for the dissatisfied. *The Boston Globe*. Retrieved from www.Boston.com.
29. How to get the most out of voice mail (2000, February). *The CPA Journal*, 70(2), 11.
30. Leland, K., & Bailey, K. (1999). *Customer service for dummies* (2nd ed.). New York: Wiley.
31. Berkley, S. (2003, July). Help stamp out bad voicemail! *The Voice Coach Newsletter*. Retrieved from www.greatvoice.com/archive_ vc/archiveindex_vc.html.
32. McCarthy, M. L. (1999, October). Email, voicemail and the Internet: How employers can avoid getting cut by the double-edged sword of technology. *Business Credit*, 100(9), 44+.
33. Krotz, J. L. (2008). Cell phone etiquette: 10 dos and don'ts. *Microsoft Business*. Retrieved from www.microsoft.com/business/en-us /resources/technology/communications /cell-phone-etiquette-10-dos-and-donts .aspx?fbid=_g8-71HEDNA.
34. Cell phone etiquette (2001, March). *Office Solutions*, 18(3), 13.
35. Coustan, D., & Strickland, J. (n.d.). How smartphones work: The future of smartphones. Retrieved from http://electronics .howstuffworks.com/smartphone.htm.
36. Schaer, M. (2013, June 27). Tomfoolery introduces anchor, a Facebook for the workplace." *The Christian Science Monitor*. Retrieved from www.csmonitor.com/ Innovation/2013/0627/Tomfoolery-introduces-Anchor-a-Facebook-for-the-workplace.

Chapter 6

1. Williamson, M. (2008, June 11). Twittering the Internet. *TechnologyStory.com*. Retrieved from http://www.technologystory .com/2008/06/11/twittering-the-internet.

Chapter 7

1. Swisher, K. (2007, October 15). AOL layoffs letter from CEO Randy Falco. *All Things Digital*. Retrieved from http://allthingsd.com/20071015 /aol-layoffs-letter-from-randy-falco/.
2. Ethical workforce reflects honest management. (2008, June). *Internal Auditor*, 18–19.
3. Advice from the pros on the best way to deliver bad news. (2003, February). *IOMA's Report on Customer Relationship Management*, 5–6.
4. Purina on pet food recall 4-26-07. (2007). American Kennel Club. Retrieved from http://clubs.akc.org/brit/NEWS/07 .PurinaPetFoodRecall.htm.
5. Workers get better at bearing bad news. (2005, October 11). *Personnel Today*, 46.
6. Expert offers advice about how to lay off employees. (2008, October 9). *Immediate Care Business*. Retrieved from http://www .immediatecarebusiness.com/hotnews/laying-off-employees.html.

Chapter 8

1. Cody, S. (1906). *Success in letter writing: Business and social* (pp. 122–126). Chicago: A. C. McClurg.
2. Lotus Cars. Retrieved July 28, 2013, from www.lotuscars.com/gb/our-cars/current-range /elise-range.
3. Apple. Retrieved July 28, 2013, from www .apple.com/ipad/why-ipad-retina/.
4. http://home.mcafee.com/Store/PackageDetail .aspx?pkgid=275.
5. Sinclair, B. (2003, July 20). Handle client complaints. *The Web design business kit*. Retrieved from http:// www.sitepoint.com /article/handle -client-complaints/.

Chapter 9

1. Grimes, B. (2003, May 6). Fooling Google. *PC Magazine*, 22(8), 74.
2. McIntyre, Douglas A., Ashley C. Allen, Samuel Weigley, and Michael B. Sauter. (October 17, 2012). The worst business decisions of all time. *24/7 Wall St*. Retrieved from http://247wallst.com/special-report/2012/10/17/the-worst-business-decisions-of-all-time/3/.

Chapter 10

1. Gallo, C. (2008, December 10). Making YouTube work for your business. *Business Week Online*. Retrieved from www.businessweek.com/stories/2008-12-09 /making-youtube-work-for-your-businessbusinessweek-business-news-stock-market-and-financial-advice.
2. Martin, M. H. (1997, November 27). The man who makes sense of numbers. *Fortune*, 273–275.
3. Simons, T. (2004). The multimedia paradox. *Presentations*, 18(9), 24–25.

Chapter 11

No endnotes.

Chapter 12

1. Kalytiak, T. (2008, October). Overcoming speaking anxiety: Toastmasters sculpt shy speakers into outstanding orators. *Alaska Business Monthly*. Retrieved from http://www.akbizmag.com.

2. Axtell, R. E. (1992). *Do's and taboos of public speaking: How to get those butterflies flying in formation.* New York: John Wiley.

3. Britz, J. D. (1999, October). You can't catch a marlin with a meatball. *Presentations, 13*(10), A1–22.

4. Hughes, M. (1990). Tricks of the speechwriter's trade. *Management Review, 9*(11), 56–58.

5. Sommerville, J. (2003). Presentation tip: Stop the verbal spam. *About.com: Entrepreneurs.* Retrieved from http://entrepreneurs.about.com/cs/marketing/a/infodumping.htm.

6. Simmons, A. (2007). *Whoever tells the best story wins: How to use your own stories to communicate with power and impact.* New York: Amacon.

7. Gallo, Carmine. (2009, April 8). Making your presentations relevant. *Business Week Online,* 15.

8. Axtell, R. E. (1992). *Do's and taboos of public speaking: How to get those butterflies flying in formation.* New York: John Wiley.

9. Decker, B. (1992). *You've got to be believed to be heard.* New York: St. Martin's Press.

10. Hillary Campaign sends "docu-point" to House Dems. (2008, May 10). *Presentation Zen.* Retrieved from http://www.presentationzen.com/presentationzen/2008/05/hillary-campaig.html.

11. Earnest, W. (2007). *Save our slides: PowerPoint design that works.* Dubuque, IA: Kendall/Hunt.

12. Ibid.

13. Boardman, Madeline. (2013, April 5). New Kids on the Block Concert as Jonathan Knight Walks off the Stage. *Huffington Post.* Retrieved from www.huffingtonpost.com/2013/04/05/new-kids-on-the-block-concert-jonathan-knight_n_3019572.html?utm_hp_ref=entertainment"\t "_hplink

14. Axtell, R. E. (1992). *Do's and taboos of public speaking: How to get those butterflies flying in formation.* New York: John Wiley.

15. Decker, B. (1992). *You've got to be believed to be heard.* (p. 137). New York: St. Martin's Press.

16. Hanke, J. (1998, January). Presenting as a team. *Presentations, 12*(1), 74–82.

17. Ibid.

18. Ibid.

19. Ibid.

20. Davids, M. (1999). Smiling for the camera. *Journal of Business Strategy, 20*(3), 20–24.

21. Turner, C. (1998, February). Become a web presenter! (Really it's not that hard). *Presentations, 12*(2), 26–27.

Chapter 13

1. Jackson, T. (2003). Find a job you love and success will follow. Career Journal (*The Wall Street Journal*). Retrieved from www.careerjournaleurope.com/jobhunting/strategies/20030415-jackson.html.

2. Riley, M. F. (2009). *The Riley guide: Employment opportunities and job resources on the Internet.* Retrieved from http://www.rileyguide.com.

3. Ireland. S. (2002, July–August). A résumé that works. *Searcher, 10*(7), 98(12).

4. Elefant, C. (2008, March 11). Do employers using Facebook for background checks face legal risks? *Legal Blog Watch.* Retrieved from http://legalblogwatch.typepad.com/legal_blog_watch/2008/03/do-employers- us.html.

5. Harshbarger, C. (2003). You're out! *Strategic Finance, 84*(11), 46(4).

6. Garone, E. (2009, March 18). Do references really matter? *WSJ.com*: Careers Q&A. Retrieved from http://online.wsj.com/article/SB123672074032087901.html.

7. Are you using the wrong résumé? (2009). *Careerbuilder.com.* Retrieved from http://www.careerbuilder.com/Article/CB-998-Cover-Letters-and-Resumes-Are-You-Using-the-Wrong-R%C3%A9sum%C3%A9/.

8. Résumés you don't see every day. (2006). Retrieved from http:// www.dummies.com/WileyCDA/ DummiesArticle/id-1610.html.

9. Young, J. (2002). "E-portfolios" could give students a new sense of their accomplishments. *Chronicle of Higher Education, 48*(26), 31–32.

10. Sipper, R. A. (2007, October 15). Tips for creating a YouTube video résumé. Retrieved from http://www.associatedcontent.com/article/414702/tips_for_creating_a_youtube_video_resume.html?cat=3.

Chapter 14

1. Vogt, P. (2006). Acing behavioral interviews. *CareerJournal.com.* Retrieved from www.careerjournaleurope.com/jobhunting/interviewing/19980129-vogt.html

2. Marion, L. C. (1997, January 11). Companies tap keyboards to interview applicants. *The News and Observer,* p. B5.

3. Thomson Learning announces name change to Cengage Learning. (2007, October). High Beam Research. Retrieved from www.highbeam.com/doc/1G1-168632242.html (pay to view)

4. Burns, D. (2009). *The first 60 seconds: Win the job interview before it begins.* Naperville, IL: Sourcebooks.

5. Lai, P., & Wong, I. (2000). The clash of cultures in the job interview. *Journal of Language for International Business, 11*(1), 31–40.

6. Austin, N. K. (1996, March). The new job interview. *Working Woman,* 23–24.

7. Kennedy, J. L., & Morrow, T. J. (1994). *Electronic résumé revolution: Create a winning résumé for the new world of job seeking.* New York: John Wiley.

8. Kleiman, P. (2003, May). Armed for a multitude of tasks. *The Times Higher Education Supplement,* p. 4.

9. MIT Career Development Center (2008, September 16). STAR method: *Behavioral interviewing.* Retrieved from www.lpnet.org/site/programs/docs/STAR%20MethodHandout.pdf.

10. Stern, L. (2005, January 17). The tough new job hunt. *Newsweek,* 73–74.

11. Interviews: Handling illegal interview questions. *JobWeb.* Retrieved from http://www.jobweb.org/interviews.aspx?id=1343.

neutral-news messages
  deductive or direct sequence of, 89–90
  defined, 89
newspapers, 154
nonverbal communication, 23–25
  channel selection in, 40–41
  kinesic messages, 24
  metacommunication, 23
  understanding, 24–25
norm, 29
normative survey research, 156
norming, 30, 31
note-taking, 158
null hypothesis, 152

O

Obama, Barack, 65
objectivity in sales messages, 135–136
observational studies, 156
O'Leary, George, 46
oral briefings, 207
oral presentation, 42
orders
  acknowledgment message, 101
  online order confirmation, 102
  routine messages about, 101–104
organizational chart, 31
organizational communication, 4–8
  communication flow in, 4–8
  defined, 4
  levels of, 8
organizational culture
  characteristics of, 38–39
  defined, 37
organizational development (OD), 22
organizational news messages, negative, 123, 124–127
  breaking bad news, 124–125
  crisis, 126–127
  examples of, 125–126
outcome orientation, 38
outdated expressions, 60
outlining
  benefits of, 188–190
  defined, 47
  formal report, 188–190
overhead transparencies, 212

P

paragraphs
  closing, in bad-news messages, 115, 116
  coherence to link ideas in, 54–55
  deductive, 54
  inductive, 54
  introductory, in bad-news messages, 111–112
  length of, 55–56
  topic sentences in, 53
  unified, 55
paraphrase method, 158
Parker, Dorothy, 56
passive voice, 51–52, 63

Peohlman, Eric T., 46
people orientation, 38
performing, 30, 31
periodicals, 154
periodic report, 150
Perrella, James E., 10
personal interviews, 160
personal space requirements, 14
persuasion
  AIDA in, 130
  defined, 129
  strategies, 129–131
persuasive claims, 94
persuasive messages, 129–146
  action in, desired, 130
  idea in, 129–130, 132, 133
  inductive approach to, 130
  persuasion strategies in, 129–131
  persuasive requests, 140–145
  planning, 129–130
  product in, 129–130, 132, 133
  receiver of, 130, 132
  sales messages, 131–140
  service in, 129–130, 132, 133
  writing, principles in, 130–131
persuasive organization, 251–253
  encourage action, 253
  evidence of qualifications, 252–253
  gain receiver's attention, 251–252
persuasive requests, 140–145
claim messages, 141
  defined, 97
  for favors, 141, 142, 144
  for information, 143
  within organization, 143, 144, 145
phonation, 216–217
physical context, 39
pictogram, 173, 174
pie charts, 175, 176–177
pitch, 216
plagiarism, 159, 161, 163
positive group roles, 30
positive news, 90
preliminary parts, 183–186
  executive summary, 185–186
  table of contents, 184
  table of figures, 184, 185
  title page, 183, 184
presentation visuals
  design of, 211, 212–214
  effective use of, 211
  handouts, 212, 214, 221
  legal and ethical responsibility in, 214
  note pages, 214
  selecting, 212
  slides, 215
  types of, 211
price resistance and sales messages, 136–137
primary research, 156–157
  experimental research, 156
  normative survey research, 156
  observational studies, 156
  reliability, 157

sampling, 156–157
  validity, 157
printed sources
  in job search, 231
  in research, 154
privacy in electronic communication, 79–80
problem-solving process, 151–153
  documenting procedures in, 153
  hypothesis in, 152
  problem statement in, 151
  recognizing and defining the problem, 151–153
  scope of problem, limiting, 152
  statement of purpose in, 151
  terms defined clearly in, 153
problem statement, 151
procedural messages, 104–106
procedures, 153
product development team, 30
profanity, 60
professional organizations, 231–232
pronunciation, 218
proofreading. See revising and proofreading
proposal, 199–204
  addenda, 202
  budget or costs in, 201–202
  defined, 151
  example of, 203–204
  external, 199
  follow-up and/or evaluation in, 201
  internal, 199
  materials and equipment in, 201
  methods and/or procedures in, 201
  preparation of, 202
  problem and/or purpose in, 200
  qualifications in, 201
  scope of, 200–201
  solicited, 199–200
  structure of, 200–202
  summary, 202
  unsolicited, 200
proxemics, 14
Publication Manual of the American Psychological Association, 163, 164
public communication, 8

Q

quality assurance team, 30
question-and-answer period, 221
questionnaires, 159, 160–161, 162

R

racial bias, 67
range, 164
ranking scales, 160–161
rate, 216–217
readability, 57–60
  improving, 57–60
  measures, 57–58

visual enhancements to improve, 58–60
recommendation requests, 272
record keeper, 30
redundancy, 61–62
references
  citations, 164
  in formal report, 187
  methods for source notes, 163–164
research sources, 154–155
relaxation, 217
reliability, 157
repetition to emphasize ideas, 53
report, 149–166. See also formal report; proposal; short report
  characteristics of, 149–151
  conclusions, 164–166
  data, collecting and organizing, 157–164
  formality continuum, 150
  information, collecting, 153–157
  problem-solving process, 151–153
  procedures section, 153
  process, overview of, 165
  proposal, 151
  terms, 153
  types of, 149–151
reporter, 30
report formality continuum, 150
request refusal, 115–116, 117, 118, 119
requests, persuasive. See persuasive requests
requests for proposals (RFPs), 151
resale, 95
research methods, 153–157
  primary research, 156–157
  secondary research, 153–156
resignation messages, 270, 271–272
résumé, 233–256. See also résumé parts; résumé supplements; résumé types
  application messages, 249–256
  defined, 229
  delivery of, 239–246
  electronic, 240–241
  electronic applicant-tracking systems, 245
  planning, 233–239
  print, 239–240
  references page, 243
  targeted, 233–239
résumé parts, 233–239
  career summary, 234
  education, 235
  honors and activities, 236
  identification, 233–234
  job and/or career objective, 234
  personal information, 236–237
  qualifications, 235–236
  references, 237–238
  work experience, 235–236

Rough Draft of a Letter (excerpt)

April 1, 2014

Fax Transmission

Louisa Fox, Marketing Manager
Learner Consumer Products Group
2304 Pike Market Street
Seattle, ~~Washington~~ WA 90322

Dear Ms. Fochs:

Are you looking for help developing your organization's social media platform? . . . improve your retail marketing? . . . plan your external communication program? . . . enhance your mass advertising strategy? Then you need the services of the full-service brand engagement firm Souther and Associates to develop an integrated media plan that ensures your company's continued success.

With Souther and Associates full-service capabilities, you will receive support in all of the following areas:

- Social media. Leverage the millions of conversations taking place through the use of social media by taking advantage of our four-step approach. It ~~which~~ tracks conversations and dialogue; extracts insights from consumer conversations; interacts with key influences, brand advocates, and detractors; and measures consumer sentiment, advocacy, and engagement.
- Retail marketing. Engage consumers away from the noise and competing advertising, and reach them on an intimate, meaningful, and locally relevant level that will help you to drive trial, traffic, and sales.
- Communication planning. Build preference for your brand by translating emotional insights into high impact brand strategy and innovation. Our experts bypass consumers' rational thinking with tools and techniques that are reactive and observational. Then, we integrate these emotional insights with your brand's functional benefits to create the foundation for lasting behavior change.
- Influence marketing. Mass advertising still plays an important role in branding, but these days, credibility is especially important, and who is more credible than a trusted professional? We identify professionals to give your products that powerful endorsement.

~~Interested customers can~~ visit www.souther.com today and check out the list of consulting services we provide and read real-life stories from past clients about how we increased brand awareness for them. If you contact us before May 15, you will also receive a free assessment of your current marketing program from our proprietary MarketLab analysis tool. Our team is ready to assist you in improving the impact of your marketing programs today. Please call me at 509-788-1302 to make an appointment with a consultant.

Sincerely,

Frank Forester

Frank Forester
Engagement Director

Enclosure

Annotations:

- Adds mailing notation.
- Uses two-letter state abbreviation.
- Corrects spelling of name.
- Adds smooth transition to next paragraph.
- Bullet list for emphasis and conciseness.
- Divides into two sentences to enhance readability.
- Recasts from receiver's viewpoint.
- Includes specific action ending.

Errors Undetectable by Spell-Check

Verify spelling of names.

Correct proofreading grammatical error.

Check correctness of word substitutions, such as "to" for "too" and "your" for "you."

Improving Readability Through Cautious Use of a Grammar and Style Checker

Step 1: Evaluate and respond to advice given for grammar and style errors detected.

Step 2: Use counts, averages, and readability indexes as guides for adjusting writing level appropriately.

Spelling and Grammar: English (U.S.) [?] [X]

Subject-Verb Agreement:

I did not begin my presentation until everyone were in their places.

Ignore Once
Ignore Rule
Next Sentence

Suggestions:

was

Change
Explain...

☑ Check grammar

Options... | Undo | Cancel

Readability Statistics [?] [X]

Counts
Words	358
Characters	2,142
Paragraphs	10
Sentences	43

Averages
Sentences per Paragraph	2.3
Words per Sentence	18.3
Characters per Word	5.8

Readability
Passive Sentences	0%
Flesch Reading Ease	25.7
Flesch-Kincaid Grade Level	14.2

OK

Improving Your Writing with the Computer

Hone your computer skills to spend more time writing and less time formatting.

☑ Draft in a font style and size easily read on-screen; postpone formatting until the revision is done.

☑ Use the *find* and *go to* commands to search and make changes.

☑ Learn time-saving keyboard shortcuts for frequently used commands such as *copy* and *cut*. Customize software so that you can access these commands easily.

☑ Use automatic numbering to arrange numerical or alphabetical lists and to ensure accuracy.

☑ Save time by using built-in styles such as cover pages, headers/footers, list and table formats, text boxes, and graphical effects.

☑ Save frequently used text such as a letterhead or your signature line so you can insert it with a single click.

☑ Use the *citations and bibliography* command to format references and the *document styles* feature to automatically generate a content page and index.

Use formatting features to create an organized and polished appearance.

☑ Add spacing between lines and paragraphs, and use crisp, open fonts such as Calibri for a contemporary look that is easy to read on-screen.

☑ Apply color-infused document themes and built-in styles to reflect a consistent brand identity.

Use proofing features to locate errors.

☑ Use the spell-checker frequently as you draft and revise. Be aware that the spell-checker will not identify miskeyings (*than* for *then*), commonly misused words, homophones (*principle, principal*), omitted words, missing or out-of-order enumerations, and content errors.

☑ Use grammar check to provide feedback on usage, reading level, comprehension factors, and other errors and weaknesses that cannot be detected electronically.

☑ Use a thesaurus only when you can recognize the precise meaning needed.

Email Format

New Message

To: Tom Bowls <tbowls@computersolutions.com>
From: Jennifer Reagan <jreagan@lauder.com>
Subject: Laptop Repair or Replacement Needed

Includes descriptive subject line.

Mr. Bowls,

Please repair or send us a replacement for the laptop computer listed on the attached sales agreement. It has a faulty cooling fan. You should receive the computer tomorrow via overnight freight.

The computer was purchased six months ago under our agreement with your company to provide our salespeople with laptops. The computers are covered by a 12-month warranty for faulty parts replacement. I spoke with your sales manager, Tom Wilkins, this morning and he instructed me to contact you for extradited service.

Our salesperson Maria Rodriguez eagerly awaits the return of her laptop. Our salespeople are highly dependent on their computers because they spend so much time on the road.

Thanks,

Jennifer Reagan

Purchasing Manager

Includes signature file that identifies writer.

Format Pointers

Includes single-spaced, unindented paragraphs and short lines for complete screen display.

Uses mixed case for easy reading.

Keeps format simple for quick download and compatibility.

Email Format

While certain email formats are standard, some degree of flexibility exists in formatting email messages. Primarily, be certain your message is easy to read and represents the standards of formality that your company has set. The following guidelines and the model email illustrated above will assist you in formatting professional email messages:

- *Include an appropriate salutation and closing.* You might write "Dear" and the person's name or simply the person's first name when messaging someone for the first time. Casual expressions such as "Hi" and "Later" are appropriate for personal messages but not serious business email. A closing of "Sincerely" is considered quite formal for email messages; instead, a simple closing such as "Best wishes" or "Thank you" provides a courteous end to your message.
- *Include a signature file at the end of the message.* The signature file (known as a .sig file) contains a few lines of text that include your full name and title, mailing address, telephone number, and any other information you want people to know about you. You might include a clever quote that you update frequently.
- *Format for easy readability.* Follow these suggestions:
  - Limit each message to one screen to minimize scrolling. If you need more space, consider a short email message with a lengthier message attached as a word processing file. Be certain the recipient can receive and read the attachment.
  - Limit the line length to 60 characters so that the entire line is displayed on the monitor without scrolling.

- Use short, unindented paragraphs. Separate paragraphs with an extra space.
- Use mixed case for easy reading. Typing in all capital letters is perceived as shouting in email and considered rude online behavior.
- Emphasize a word or phrase by surrounding it with quotation marks or keying in uppercase letters.
- ***Use emoticons or email abbreviations in moderation when you believe the receiver will understand and approve.*** ***Emoticons,*** created by keying combinations of symbols to produce "sideways" faces, are a shorthand way of lightening the mood, adding emotion to email messages, and attempting to compensate for nonverbal cues lost in one-way communication:

:-)	smiling, indicates humor or sarcasm	%-(	confused
:-(	frowning, indicates sadness or anger	:-0	surprised

Alternately, you might put a "g" (for grin) or "smile" in parentheses after something that is obviously meant as tongue-in-cheek to help carry the intended message to the receiver. Abbreviations for commonly used phrases save space and avoid unnecessary keying. Popular ones include BCNU (be seeing you), BTW (by the way), FYI (for your information), FWIW (for what it's worth), HTH (hope this helps), IMHO (in my humble opinion), and LOL (laugh out loud).

Some email users feel strongly that emoticons and abbreviations are childish or inappropriate for serious email and decrease productivity when the receiver must take time for deciphering. Before using them, be certain the receiver will understand them and that the formality of the message and your relationship with the receiver justify this type of informal exchange. Then use only in moderation to punctuate your message.

GOOD :-) Good Example of an Email Message

New Message

To: Linda Roberts, Loan Officer

From: Juan Alvarez, Director of Loan Compliance

Subject: New Policies Affect Loans to Real-Estate Investors

Linda,

Please be aware of the new policies regarding mortgages to real-estate investors.

Loans can no longer be made to mortgage applicants who already have four or more outstanding mortgages. Because of the problems caused by the sub-prime lending situation, we are required to limit our exposure to mortgage debt. Applicants who have four or more active mortgages are now considered too risky because of a potential lack of liquidity in their current asset portfolio.

You will find this latest policy change attached to this message. Please come by my office if you have additional questions after reading the attached policy statement.

Regards,

Juan

Provides subject line that is meaningful to reader and writer.

Includes salutation and closing to personalize message.

Format Pointer

Composes short, concise message limited to one idea and one screen.

GOOD :-) Good Example of an Apology

New Message

To: Allen Melton <amelton@meltonpr.com>

cc:

Subject: Yesterday's Advertising Presentation

Allen:

Please accept my apology for the inconvenience you experienced yesterday because of the unavailability of computer equipment. Fortunately, you saved the day with your backup transparencies and gave an effective presentation on the new advertising campaign.

The next time you make a presentation at our company, I'll be sure to schedule the LGI room. This room has the latest technology to support multimedia presentations. Just call and let me know the date.

Later,

Thomas Lee Raferty
Administrative Assistant

States the apology briefly without providing an overly specific description of the error.

Reports measures taken to avoid repetition of such incidents, which strengthens the credibility of the apology.

Closes with a positive statement.

Format Pointers

Limits the message to a single idea—the apology.

Composes a short, concise message that fits on one screen.

Includes a salutation and closing to personalize the message.

New Message

To: Ellen Meyer <emeyer@techno.com>
cc: Martha Riggins <mriggins@techno.com>
Subject: Appreciation for Outstanding Contribution

Ellen,

Thank you for spearheading the initiative to improve interpersonal communication within the office and for arranging for the training sessions to achieve that goal. It was a big commitment on your part in addition to your regular duties.

Your efforts are already paying off. I have observed the techniques we learned in the training sessions being used in the department on several occasions already. In times of uncertainty, anxiety can often spill over into people's professional lives, so the seminar was very timely in helping to ensure a collaborative and civil workplace where everyone is treated respectfully.

You have proven yourself a dedicated and insightful employee, a true asset to the continued success of our organization.

Best regards,
Martha

Extends appreciation for employee's efforts to improve departmental communication.

Provides specific evidence of worth of experience without exaggerating or using overly strong language or mechanical statements.

Assures writer of tangible benefits to be gained from the training session.

Format Pointers

Uses short lines, mixed case; omits special formatting such as emoticons and email abbreviations for improved readability.

Developing the Components of a Bad-News Message

The current subprime mortgage situation and its subsequent effects on the economy have provided an opportunity to better educate loan seekers about the types of financial risk they might safely assume. For this reason, mortgage seekers may be restricted in the number of mortgage loans they might hold.

As part of the effort to help loan seekers reduce their financial risk, banks now limit the number of mortgages a person might judiciously hold to no more than four. Because of current sluggishness in the housing market, house sellers now have more difficulty selling homes in a timely manner, making such assets much less liquid. If a mortgage holder gets into trouble, he/she will have less ability to resell the property and recover the loan amount. This puts the mortgage holder and the lender at greater financial risk.

In order to secure an additional mortgage, you must first pay off one of your current mortgages. Alternately, our affiliated real estate brokers are available to help you sell one of your properties so that you might secure another. Please call me at 213-555-3400 to discuss these services.

Begins with statement with which both can agree. Sets stage for reasons for bad news.

Reveals subject of message and transitions into reasons.

Provides rule and clearly applies rule to situation.

States refusal positively and clearly using complex sentence and positive language.

Includes counterproposal as alternative.

Closes with sales promotion for other services, inferring a continuing business relationship.

Note the closing paragraph is a positive, forward-looking statement that includes sales promotion of other services the mortgage firm and its affiliated real estate brokers can offer.

Good Example of a Claim Denial

June 14, 2014

Lindsey Tucker
Snowcap Limited
1905 Southhaven Street
Santa Fe, NM 87501-7313

Dear Ms. Tucker:

Restocking of Returned Merchandise

The HighFly skis you stocked this past season are skillfully crafted and made from the most innovative materials available. Maintaining a wide selection of quality skiing products is an excellent strategy for developing customer loyalty and maximizing your sales.

Our refund policies provide you the opportunity to keep a fully stocked inventory at the lowest possible cost. You receive full refunds for merchandise returned within 10 days of receipt. For unsold merchandise returned after the primary selling season, a modest 15 percent restocking fee is charged to cover our costs of holding this merchandise until next season. The credit applied to your account for $2,069.75 covers merchandise you returned at the end of February.

While relaxing from another great skiing season, take a look at our new HighFly skis and other items available in the enclosed catalog for the 2015 season. You can save 10 percent by ordering premium ski products before May 10.

Sincerely,

Galen Fondren

Galen Fondren
Credit Manager
Enclosure: Catalog

Begins with a statement with which the reader can agree to get the message off to a good start.

Presents a clear explanation for the additional charge.

Shifts emphasis away from the refusal by presenting sales promotion on other services.

Format Pointer
Illustrates block format—all lines begin at the left margin.

GOOD :-) Good Example of a Persuasive Claim

Palmdale Galleria
3109 Overlook Drive / Palmdale, CA 93550
P: (661) 555-2130 \ F: (661) 555-3129

October 27, 2013

Samantha Reynolds
Senior Architect
Primera Design
3400 Wilshire Boulevard
Los Angeles, CA 90052-3674

Dear Samantha:

When Palmdale Galleria selected your firm to redesign our retail space, we were impressed by the work that you had done in a number of hotels and mall properties in Las Vegas and other upscale developments throughout the country. We were most impressed with the fantasy world that you created for the Insight Hotel's shopping galleria, a space that attended to every aspect of the consumer's shopping experience, including sight, sound, smell, taste, and sensation, through the implementation of the latest technological and design advances.

In our meeting with your creative team, we asked for attention to the visual design, the entertainment elements, and the creation of an ambiance that addressed all aspects of the consumers' sensual experience. After reviewing the initial plan for our redesign, we find the degree of incorporation of entertainment and sensual experiences for consumers to be disappointing. The redesign incorporates the latest trends in architectural design but needs more attention to entertainment features, including spaces for "street" entertainers, mini-concerts, and amusement park rides, including bungee jumping, etc. We also expected a more complete integration of water features, such as fountains, waterfalls, and streams, with the associated opportunities for entertainment, such as a simulated river rafting experience. In the tropical forest region of the mall, we hoped to have a better integration of spaces for zoo animals and an apparatus to create the "smells" and "sounds" of the jungle. Consumers no longer go to malls to simply shop but to want to be transported to a world of leisure, pampering, and entertainment, one that appeals to all of their senses.

With Primera Design's reputation for creative productions, we are confident the redesign plan for the Palmdale Galleria will be revised to incorporate these elements. Please let us know if you would like to meet to discuss and clarify any of the design issues raised here. Because of the importance of this project, I am at your disposal. Please call me at 444-1920 to schedule a meeting.

Sincerely,

Martinique Cole

Martinique Cole
General Manager
Palmdale Galleria

Seeks attention by giving sincere compliment that reveals subject of message.

Continues central appeal— commitment to creative redesign—while providing needed details.

Presents reasoning that leads to request and subtle reminder of central appeal.

Connects specific request with firm's commitment to develop a creative redesign.

Legal and Ethical Consideration
Uses letter rather than less formal email format to emphasize importance of these differences regarding contractual agreement.

Down-Home Restaurants

83 South Pass Road • Chattanooga TN 37426-2723 • (423) 555-5320

March 15, 2013

Mrs. Joyce Smith
976 Thompson Road
Crossville, TN 38555-0976

Dear Mrs. Smith:

Meeting you and touring the building on your property last week was a pleasure. That little building provided me with a fascinating glimpse of the past. You must have found it convenient using the building as a big "attic," storing all your canned goods and old farm implements over the years.

As the manager of the Down-Home Barbeque in Mena, I am constantly looking for items to build and display in our restaurants. Our restaurants are constructed of weathered wood to create a genuine rustic atmosphere, which we think complements our "down-home" menu.

As I toured your building, I couldn't help but notice some of the unique items inside and the old weathered boards hanging outside. The wood from the building and its contents would enable us to build and furnish a new restaurant in Clarksville and refurbish our Jackson location. Marc Lane, owner of Down-Home Restaurants, has asked me to extend you the offer explained in the enclosed proposal.

Naturally, no amount of money can compensate you for a building that holds so many memories for you. However, we would be happy to purchase the entire contents of the building, excluding any special items of sentimental value that you may want to keep.

Although the thought of selling the building may sadden you, think of the "second life" that the old farm equipment, dishes, washboards, seed bags, and weathered boards would have in our restaurants. People who would otherwise never see such Americana will have the opportunity to learn a little about its rich past.

After you have reviewed the proposal, please call me at 555-3253 to discuss our offer to display your treasures in our restaurants.

Sincerely,

Karla Ash

Karla Ash, Manager
Chattanooga Store
Enclosure

Opens with a compliment that introduces an appeal to the owner's pride in the old property.

Introduces the writer's interest in acquiring property and continues the primary appeal (desire to preserve the past).

Offsets reluctance to sell by acknowledging the sentimental value and suggesting options.

Stresses benefits of selling property in terms of the primary appeal.

Connects the specific request for action with the reward for saying "Yes."

Format Pointers
Illustrates modified block format—the date and closing lines (complimentary close and signature block) begin at the horizontal center.

Uses mixed punctuation—a colon follows the salutation, and a comma follows the complimentary close.

Uses an enclosure notation to alert the reader that something is included.

Example of an Effective Questionnaire

- Uses variety of items to elicit different types of responses.
- Uses clear, concise language to minimize confusion.
- Provides clear instructions for answering each item.

1. Rank the following new vehicle purchase factors in order of their importance to you.

		1	2	3	4	5	6
a.	Price	○	○	○	○	○	○
b.	Overall performance	○	○	○	○	○	○
c.	Reliability	○	○	○	○	○	○
d.	Comfort	○	○	○	○	○	○
e.	Driving enjoyment	○	○	○	○	○	○
f.	Safety record	○	○	○	○	○	○
g.	Fuel economy	○	○	○	○	○	○
h.	Other (specify) [_____▼]	○	○	○	○	○	○

2. **Which of the following is the single most important purchase factor that you feel needs more attention by today's car makers? (Please select only one.)**

- Provides additional lines to allow for individual opinions.

- ○ Price
- ○ Overall performance
- ○ Reliability
- ○ Comfort
- ○ Safety record
- ○ Fuel economy
- ○ Other (specify) [_____▼]

- Provides even number of rating choices to eliminate "fence" responses.

3. **Would you purchase this vehicle again?**

Definitely not 1	Probably not 2	I'm not sure 3	Only if improved 4	Probably would 5	Definitely yes 6
○	○	○	○	○	○

4. **How would you rate your overall purchase satisfaction?**

Very unsatisfied 1	Somewhat dissatisfied 2	Neutral 3	Somewhat satisfied 4	Satisfied 5	Very satisfied 6
○	○	○	○	○	○

- Asks for easily recalled information.

5. **Indicate your age group:**

- ○ 20–29
- ○ 30–39
- ○ 40–49
- ○ 50–59
- ○ 60–69
- ○ 70 years and over

- Provides non-overlapping categories of response and open-ended final category.

6. **Indicate how many vehicles you have previously purchased.**

- ○ None
- ○ 1–3
- ○ 4–6
- ○ 7–10
- ○ More than 10

Format Pointers

Provides adequate space for answering open-ended item.

Keeps length as short as possible while meeting survey objectives.

Includes instructions for submitting completed questionnaire.

7. **What could the car maker do to enhance your satisfaction with your new car purchase?**

[_____▲
_____
_____▼]

Thanks for your participation. Click to submit your questionnaire.

[Submit]

SAMPLE REPORT AND REFERENCES PAGES IN APA (6TH EDITION) STYLE

Culturally diverse virtual teams do have a greater potential for conflict than do teams that are homogeneous and are able to meet face to face ("Collaborative Teams," 2008). While variations in beliefs, behaviors, and expectations occur within all cultural groups, certain generalities about one based on his or her cultural group can be useful for others seeking better understanding. "Given little or no other information about an individual's values and behaviours, culture provides a good first impression of that person" (Maznevski & Peterson, 1997, p. 37).

Neyer and Harzing (2008) found that experiences in cross-cultural interactions do serve to improve one's abilities to adapt in such situations. One advantage gained through experience is the overcoming of cultural stereotypes which often stand in the way of effective communication (Williams & O'Reilly, 1998). Cross-cultural experience also leads to the establishment of norms that support interaction among individuals and to the development of mutual consideration for others (Neyer & Harzing, 2008). Studies have established that individuals who learn a foreign language also gain appropriate culturally determined behavior and are thus better able to adapt to specific characteristics of the other culture (Harzing & Feely, 2008).

In addition to possessing strong technical skills, qualities that are important to successful membership on cross-cultural virtual teams include the following (Adler, 1991; Hurn & Jenkins, 2000):

- Flexibility and adaptability
- Strong interpersonal skills
- Ability to think both globally and locally
- Linguistic skills

References

Adler, N. J. (1991). *International dimensions of organizational behavior*. Boston: PWS Kent.

Collaborative teams. (2008, June). *Bulletpoint, 152*, 3–5.

Hurn, B. F., & Jenkins, M. (2000). International peer group development. *Industrial and Commercial Training, 32*(4), 128–131. doi: 10.1108/00197850010372205

Maznevski, M. L. & Peterson, M. F. (1997). Societal values, social interpretation, and multinational teams. In C. Granrose (Ed.), *Cross-cultural workgroups* (pp. 27–29). Thousand Oaks, CA: Sage.

Neyer, A., & Harzine, A. (2008). The impact of culture on interactions: Five lessons learned from the European Commission. *European Management Journal, 26*(5), 325–334. doi: 10.1016/j.emj .2008.05.005

Williams, K. Y., & O'Reilly, C. A. (1998). Demography and diversity in organizations. In B. M. Staw & R. M. Sutton (Eds.), *Research in organizational behavior* (pp. 77–140). Stamford, CT: JAI.

Choosing the Appropriate Graphic to Fit Your Objective

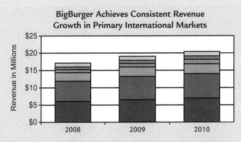

KoffeeKup Corporation Market Price of Common Stock				
	October 2, 2012		October 2, 2013	
Quarter	High	Low	High	Low
Fourth	$23.94	$21.29	$26.35	$23.08
Third	22.09	18.62	28.13	22.78
Second	19.48	16.15	30.80	24.79
First	16.50	14.40	31.94	23.53

Source: KoffeeKup Corporation, Annual Report, 2013

Graphic Type and Objective

Table—To show exact figures

BigBurger Achieves Consistent Revenue Growth in Primary International Markets

Revenue in Millions

■ U.S. ■ Europe ☐ APMEA ☐ Latin America ■ Canada ☐ Other

Bar chart—To compare one quantity with another

Dividends Paid to Shareholders

— Dividend
— Inflation

Line Chart—To illustrate changes in quantities over time

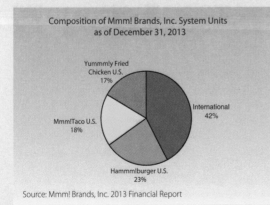

Composition of Mmm! Brands, Inc. System Units
as of December 31, 2013

Yummmly Fried Chicken U.S. 17%

International 42%

Mmm!Taco U.S. 18%

Hammm!burger U.S. 23%

Source: Mmm! Brands, Inc. 2013 Financial Report

Pie Chart—To show how the parts of a whole are distributed

Graphic Type and Objective

Gantt chart—To track progress toward completing a project

ID	Task Name	Duration	'04	Feb. 3, '04	Feb. 10, '04	Feb
			T W T F S	S M T W T F S	S M T W T F S	S
1	Conduct secondary research	3 days				
2	Obtain database	2 days				
3	Construct mail questionnaire	5 days				
4	Conduct pilot study/revise	3 days				
5	Design mock graphics	3 days				
6	Mail questionnaire	2 days				
7	Draft selected report sections	4 days				
8	Mail second requests	2 days				
9	Tabulate and analyze data	5 days				
10	Complete report draft	4 days				
11	Revise report	5 days				

Map—To show geographic relationships

U.S. SUSPECTED SARS

Flowchart—To illustrate a process or procedure

Photograph—To provide a realistic view of a specific item or place

GOOD :-) Short, Periodic Report in Memorandum Format

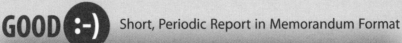

ETO Industries

233 State Boulvard
Kansas City, MO 64123-7600

TO: Candice Russell, Director, Human Resources
FROM: Tim Johnson, Manager, In-House Exercise Program
DATE: January 1, 2014
SUBJECT: Annual Report on In-House Exercise Program

The in-house exercise center has made significant gains in the past year. Data related to participation in our programs and current staffing follow:

Enrollment: 506 employees, up from 384 at end of 2013
Staff: One full-time trainer/manager and two part-time trainers

Our goal for the coming year is to increase our enrollment in the in-house exercise programs another 10 percent. We also have plans to create a nutrition program that will be rolled out next month. If that program is successful initially, we may need to hire a certified nutritionist. This person might also be used part-time in the company cafeteria to improve the nutritional value of the lunches and snacks provided there.

Employees report overall satisfaction with the quality of the current program. At the end of 2013, we asked program participants to complete a questionnaire. Eighty-eight percent indicated that they were very satisfied or extremely satisfied with our program. The most frequently mentioned suggestion for improvement was the extension of hours until 7 p.m. This change would allow employees to work late and still take advantage of the exercise facility. A copy of the questionnaire is provided for your review.

Call me should you wish to discuss the nutritional program, extended service hours, or any other aspects of this report.

Attachment

Includes header to serve formal report functions of transmittal and title page.

Includes horizontal line to add interest and separate transmittal from body of memo.

Uses deductive approach to present this periodic report requested by management on an annual basis.

Uses headings to highlight standard information; allows for easy update when preparing subsequent report.

Includes primary data from survey completed by program participants.

Attaches material to memorandum, which would be an appendix item in formal report.

Format Pointer
Uses memorandum format for brief periodic report prepared for personnel within company.

CommPlus Consultants, Inc.

101 MAIN STREET, SUITE 203
ST. LOUIS, MO 54011
800-555-3000

January 10, 2014

John Simpson
Franklin Associates
345 Plum Street
St. Louis, MO 54002

Dear Mr. Simpson:

The communication audit of Franklin Associates' external communication program has been completed. You will find a brief summary of our findings and conclusions and recommendations below.

FINDINGS

Findings from our audit can be found below:

1. Franklin Associates is a consultant to the oil and gas industry. It is a well-established business with a 100-year history. Its branding is well-recognized, but in recent years, it has been surpassed by several new entrants who have marketed themselves as innovative and using the latest technologies. This has created a challenge for Franklin Associates in terms of its external branding.
2. Franklin's major external stakeholders include its clients, the media, investors, government agencies, competitors, and the public. In terms of its clients, Franklin has focused its marketing efforts on the largest oil and gas producers. Because there are so few, this has created some competitive challenges for Franklin.
3. Franklin's most common methods for communicating its corporate message includes press releases; a company Web site; and personal communications with its clients through use of written, oral and electronic media.

CONCLUSIONS AND RECOMMENDATIONS

The following recommendations are made:

1. Continue advertising and service promotion at current levels but with some changes that help you better reach mid-sized clients and increase your market share.
2. Update the design for your company logo, and roll out a campaign that introduces this new image to current and prospective customers.
3. Develop a plan for shaping public opinion on issues important to Franklin Associates. As a consultant for the oil industry, it is important to show that your organization is interested in addressing global climate issues.

Thank you for the opportunity to assist you in reviewing your external communication program. We are also available to help you in completing the final step in the audit process: Create, refine, and test new messages with the appropriate stakeholders. If you are interested in continuing our consulting relationship in order to develop an implementation plan, please call me at 415-640-9001.

Sincerely,

Louise Parker

Louise Parker
Chief Auditor

Letterhead and letter address function as title page and transmittal.

Introduces overall topic and leads into procedures and findings.

Uses side heading to denote beginning of body.

Closes with appreciation for business and offer to answer questions.

Format Pointers
Uses letter format for short report prepared by outside consultant.

Includes reference initials of typist, who did not write message.

Selecting an Appropriate Presentation Visual

VISUAL	ADVANTAGES	LIMITATIONS
HANDOUTS	• Provide detailed information that audience can examine closely • Extend a presentation by providing resources for later use • Reduce the need for note taking and aid in audience retention	• Can divert audience's attention from the speaker • Can be expensive
BOARDS AND FLIPCHARTS	• Facilitate interaction • Are easy to use • Are inexpensive if traditional units are used	• Require turning speaker's back to audience • Are cumbersome to transport, can be messy and not professional looking • Provide no hard copy and must be developed on-site if traditional units are used
OVERHEAD TRANSPARENCIES	• Are simple to prepare and use • Allow versatile use; prepare beforehand or while speaking • Are inexpensive and readily available	• Are not easily updated and are awkward to use • Must have special acetate sheets and markers unless using a document camera • Pose potential for equipment failure
ELECTRONIC PRESENTATIONS	• Meet audience expectations of visual standards • Enhance professionalism and credibility of the speaker • Provide special effects to enhance retention, appeal, flexibility, and reuse	• Can lead to poor delivery if misused • Can be expensive, require highly developed skills, and are time-consuming • Pose technology failure and transportability challenges
35MM SLIDES	• Are highly professional • Depict real people and places	• Require a darkened room • Creates a formal environment not conducive to group interaction • Lacks flexibility in presentation sequence
MODELS OR PHYSICAL OBJECTS	• Are useful to demonstrate an idea	• Can compete with the speaker for attention

Writing Effective Slide Content: Poor (left) and Good (right) Examples

The revised slide

- Includes a descriptive title that captures major idea of slide, in this case, the value of humor.
- Omits items unrelated to value of humor. Specifically, "important element in any presentation" is a verbal transition and not needed on a slide; "shouldn't embarrass people" and related subpoints will appear on a separate slide focusing on tips for using humor.
- Collapses remaining content into a few memorable points that use parallel structure for clarity and grammatical accuracy (singular action verbs).
- Proofreads carefully to avoid misspellings that damage credibility, such as "conflect" in original slide.

Engaging Conceptual Slide Design: Poor (left) and Good (right) Examples

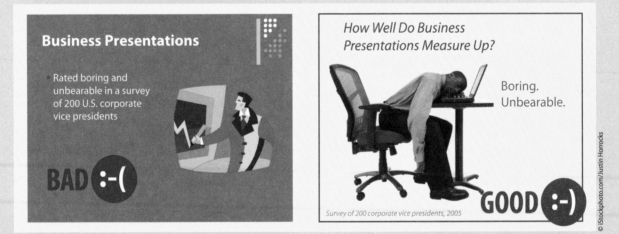

The revised slide

- Uses descriptive title that captures central idea of dissatisfaction with typical business presentation.
- Selects images that imply intended message—ineffectiveness of business presenters; enlarges images for slide appeal and balance.
- Trims text to emphasize central idea and eliminates bullet, as bulleted list should have at least two items.
- Moves source to less prominent slide position to add credibility to research data while keeping focus on central idea.

GOOD :-) Chronological Résumé

JOSEPH PRIESTLEY
89 Lincoln Street
Santa Fe, NM 78285-9063
512 555-9823
jpriestley@hotmail.com

- Includes email address that reflects professional image.

- Highlights professional skills.

Professional Profile

- Technical proficiency in ERP systems, ACL, database, and spreadsheet software.
- Hands-on experience in accounting gained through internship with well-regarded local firm.
- Excellent interpersonal communication and teamwork skills developed through course projects and active involvement in student organizations.
- Ability to manage time effectively, excellent work ethic, and dedication to high-quality work as demonstrated by part-time work to finance my education and 3.87 GPA.

- Positions education as top qualification for recent graduate. Includes high GPA (B or better).

- Edges out competition reflecting related experience and work achievements.

EDUCATION

B.B.A., Accounting,
University of New Mexico, May 2014, GPA 3.87
- Dean's List, 2010–2014
- Deanna D. Darling Academic Scholarship

RELATED EXPERIENCE

Intern, Gerald and Associates, CPAs, Santa Fe, NM
June–August 2013
- Shadowed auditor and helped write numerous auditing reports for corporate clients.
- Created and maintained spreadsheets and databases, containing client audit information.
- Worked with audit teams to hone communication skills and developed phone skills necessary to effectively interact with professional clientele.

- Uses separate section to emphasize language proficiencies listed in job requirements.

- Emphasizes activities that reflect service attitude, high level of responsibility, and people-oriented experiences.

OTHER EXPERIENCE

- Server, Bubba's BBQ, Santa Fe, NM 2011–2013
- Stockperson, University of New Mexico Bookstore, Santa Fe, NM 2010–2011

LANGUAGES

- **Fluent in English**
- **Conversational Spanish**

LEADERSHIP ACTIVITIES

Beta Alpha Psi, honorary accounting society, 2012–2014, chapter president, 2012–2013
Chess Team, 2010–2014, president, 2013–2014

Format Pointers

Places name at top center, where it can be easily seen when employers place it in file drawer (top right is also acceptable).

Creates visual appeal through custom format rather than commonly used template, short readable sections focusing on targeted qualifications, and streamlined bulleted lists.

GOOD :-) Functional Résumé

Clarence Foster
715 Armadillo Circle
San Antonio, TX 78710-0715
(512) 555-1396
cfoster@hotmail.com

Position in retail clothing sales with advancement to sales management. **OBJECTIVE**

CUSTOMER SERVICE

- Processed customer financial transactions within assigned limits and established guidelines.
- Provided excellent customer service in completing transactions efficiently and in a friendly, professional manner.
- Met sales and referral goals by identifying and selling financial products and services beneficial to the customer needs.
- Identified fraudulent activity to prevent potential losses to the bank.

SALES

- Provided quality customer service to store patrons.
- Handled cash transactions and daily receipt balances.
- Usually surpassed weekly goal of opening new credit accounts.
- Employee of the month.

COMMUNICATION SKILLS AND WORK ETHIC

- Ability to communicate effectively over the phone and in person.
- Ability to work well unsupervised.
- Experience working on team projects both at work and in courses.
- Report consistently and promptly when scheduled for work.

COMPUTER SKILLS

Proficient in spreadsheet and word processing software.

Sales Associate, Claremont Department Store, 2012–Present **EMPLOYMENT HISTORY**

Customer Service Associate, Union Bank, 2011–2012

B.S., Marketing, Claremont State College, Expected graduation, May 2013 **EDUCATION**

Clare Randall, Sales Manager, Claremont Department Store, 435 Main Street, Claremont, TX 78009, (818) 555-2345 **REFERENCES**

Daniel Shore, Professor, Marketing Department, Claremont State College, 890 Alamo Street, San Antonio, TX 87003, (803) 555-8907

Lisa Cox, Senior Teller, Union Bank, 900 Main Street, Claremont, TX 87303, (818) 555-1234

Includes clear objective statement to grab attention and invite close reading.

Uses headings that show applicant knows what skills are needed to succeed in sales.

Arranges qualifications into sections that emphasize applicant's relevant skills and accomplishments.

Uses employers' names and dates to match skills with work history.

Lists references for employer convenience and to strengthen résumé.

Format Pointers
Creates visual appeal with easy- to-read columnar format and balanced page arrangement.

Places name at top center, where it can be easily seen.

Uses bold font to distinguish identification section and headings from remaining text.

Lists education and work history as quick overview of basic qualifications and to accommodate employers' preference for chronological format.

GOOD :-) Example of a Follow-Up Letter

Dear Mr. Wagner:

Thank you for taking the time to meet with me today to discuss the position of Financial Planning Analyst with Carson Fine Foods.

During our discussion, you stated that you're looking for an organized and outgoing candidate to join your team. Through my previous work and life experience, I gained organizational and customer development skills and learned how to meet goals through teamwork. In my position with Biotech Inc., I communicated with internal and external customers and assisted in efficiency and customer relations for the Fraud Detection program. I am confident that my skills and background will make me an asset as a Financial Planning Analyst with Carson Fine Foods.

I am eager to discuss this opportunity with you further. Please let me know what additional information I can provide you and your colleagues in order to secure this position and begin working for your organization.

- States main idea and clearly identifies position being sought.

- Assures employer that applicant is still interested in job.

Format Pointers
Formats as formal business letter but could have sent message electronically if previous communication with employer had been by email.

Prints letter and envelope with laser printer on paper that matches résumé and application letter.

 GOOD :-) Example of a Thank-You Message to a Reference

Thank you so much for the letter of recommendation you prepared for my application to law school. I learned today that I have been accepted by Cleveland University for the fall semester.

Because of the rigor of that law program, I believe your comments about my work ethic, dedication to high-quality work, and willingness to seek out feedback for improvement carried a great deal of weight. The dean commented that she was impressed with the detailed evidence and examples you provided to support your statements, unlike the general recommendations she often receives.

Dr. Kenney, I appreciate your helping me secure a seat in a highly competitive academic discipline with such a well-regarded law program. Thanks for the recommendation and your outstanding instruction. I will keep you informed about my law school experience and hope to stop by your office next time I am in town to catch up.

- States main idea of appreciation for recommendation. Informs reference of success in acceptance to academic program.

- Communicates sincere appreciation for assistance; uses specific examples and avoids exaggeration.

- Restates main idea and anticipates continued relationship; is original and sincere.

Example of a Thank-You Message

New Message

To: wrfann@viking.com
From: mperkins@hotmail.com
Subject: Appreciation for Plant Interview

Dear Mr. Fann:

Thank you for the opportunity to visit Viking Range for a plant interview yesterday. I enjoyed meeting you and appreciated the complete tour of the operation and the opportunity to learn about the exciting research efforts underway at Viking.

Viking's success in developing higher quality products than its competitors after such a short time in the refrigeration market is impressive. Additionally, I was impressed with the many friendly, enthusiastic employees who were willing to share with me their knowledge and commitment to Viking.

After visiting your plant on Thursday, I am confident that my interest and previous experience in research and development at the DIAL labs in Starkville would allow me to contribute to Viking's important research efforts in the refrigeration area. I would also gain valuable real-world experience needed to enhance the mechanical engineering degree I'm pursuing at Mississippi State.

Mr. Fann, I am eager to receive an offer from Viking for the co-op position. If you need additional information in the meantime, please contact me.

Thanks,

Matt Perkins

- States main idea of appreciation for interview and information gained.
- Includes specific points discussed during interview, increasing sincerity and recall of applicant.
- Assures employer of continued interest in position.
- Politely reminds employer that applicant is awaiting reply.

Format Pointer

Prepared as email message because previous communication with the company has been by email.

GOOD :-) **Example of a Job-Refusal Message**

I appreciate your spending time with me discussing the sales associate position.

Your feedback regarding my fit for your organization and the opportunities available to me were particularly valuable. Having received offers in both sales and marketing, I feel that a career in the latter field better suits my personality and long-term career goals. Today, I am accepting an entry-level marketing position with Fashion Trends, Inc.

Thank you for your confidence demonstrated by the job offer. When I hear about Marasol's continued success, I will think of the dedicated people who work for the company.

- Begins with neutral but related idea to buffer bad news.
- Presents reasons diplomatically that lead to refusal.
- Ends message on positive note that anticipates future association with company.

BCOM'S READER-FRIENDLY DESIGN AND COMPREHENSIVE COVERAGE ENSURE SUCCESS

As in previous editions, *BCOM 6e* models the concise, coherent writing style demanded in business today. Revisions in *BCOM 6e* apply cognitive theory principles to maximize learning and minimize the mental effort needed to process information.

In response to feedback, the authors have made the following changes to this edition:

Chapter 1
- Updated example in the Informal Communication Network section
- Updated example in the Diversity Challenges section

Chapter 2
- Updated example in virtual teams box

Chapter 3
- Updated example in Organizational Culture section
- Updated example in sample message box
- Updated example of sender-centered and receiver-centered messages
- Updated examples in Communicate Ethically and Responsibly section
- Updated example in Meeting Diverse Audiences' Needs box

Chapter 4
- Updated examples of passive and active voice
- Updated examples in Emphasize Important Ideas section
- Revised Figure 4-2
- Revised examples in Enumerations section
- Revised examples in Enumerated and Bulleted Lists section
- Revised examples in Communicate Concisely section
- Revised examples in Project a Positive, Tactful Tone section
- Revised examples in Use a Connotative Tone Cautiously section
- Revised example in Use Specific Language Appropriately section
- Revised Figure 4-4

Chapter 5
- Revised Figure 5-1
- Revised Figure 5-2
- Updated iPhone for Work box

Chapter 6
- Revised Figure 6-2
- Revised To Express Thanks for Gift box
- Revised example in Appreciation Messages section
- Revised Figure 6-4
- Revised Figure 6-5
- Revised Figure 6-6
- Revised Figure 6-7
- Revised Figure 6-12
- Revised Figure 6-13
- Revised Dear Title Last Name box

Chapter 7
- Revised Figure 7-2
- Revised Figure 7-3
- Revised Figure 7-4
- Revised Figure 7-5
- Revised Figure 7-7
- Revised Figure 7-10
- Revised Figure 7-11

Chapter 8
- Updated example in Focus on a Central Selling Feature section
- Updated examples in Be Action Oriented section
- Updated example in Stress a Central Selling Point section
- Revised Figure 8-4
- Revised Figure 8-5
- Revised Figure 8-6
- Revised Figure 8-7
- Revised Figure 8-8
- Revised Figure 8-9

Chapter 9
- Revised Here Are the Limits box
- Revised example in Developing an Effective Survey Instrument section
- Updated examples in Interpreting the Data section

Chapter 10
- Updated examples in Communicating Quantitative Information section
- Updated example in Using Graphics section
- Revised Figure 10-2
- Revised Figure 10-4
- Revised Figure 10-6
- Revised Figure 10-8

Chapter 11
- Revised example in Appendix section
- Revised examples in Outlining and Sequencing section
- Revised Figure 11-3
- Revised Figure 11-4
- Revised Figure 11-6
- Revised example in Scope section

Chapter 12
- Revised examples in Introduction section
- Revised example in Closing section
- Revised Figure 12-2
- Updated example in Before the Presentation section

Chapter 13
- Updated examples in Jobs and/or Career Objective section
- Revised Figure 13-2
- Revised Figure 13-3
- Revised Figure 13-5
- Revised Figure 13-6
- Revised Figure 13-7

Chapter 14
- Revised Figure 14-2
- Revised Figure 14-3
- Revised Figure 14-5
- Revised Figure 14-6
- Revised Figure 14-7

To help you prepare, we've created a Prep Card for each chapter.

PREPCARD CHAPTER 1 ESTABLISHING A FRAMEWORK FOR BUSINESS COMMUNICATION

KEY CONCEPTS

Understanding what communication is and how it occurs is central to successful transactions in the workplace. Business communication does not take place in a vacuum but is impacted by various external forces, including legal and ethical constraints, diversity challenges, changing technology, and team environment.

CONCEPTUAL FIGURES AND TABLES

Figure 1-1 The Transactional Proc
Figure 1-2 Flow of Information
Figure 1-3 Levels of Commun
Figure 1-4 Factors Influencing Bu
Figure 1-5 Four Dimensions of Bu

> This column lists the Figures and Tables in the chapter as well as a number of key Lecture Slides from the PowerPoint slide set.

LEARNING OBJECTIVES

1-1 Define communication and describe the value of communication in business.

1-2 Expl

> For quick reference, this column lists the Learning Objectives that will be met in the chapter and presents a chapter outline with page references

1-3 Disc

1-4 Explain how legal and ethical constraints, diversity challenges, changing

KEY TERMS

Chronemics 14
Diversity skills 13
Downward communication 6
Ethics 10
Ethnocentrism 13
External messages 8
Formal communication network 5
Horizontal (o al) communication 8

> Key terms from the chapter are listed here in alphabetical order for quick reference.

Proxemics 14
Stakeholders 9
Stereotypes 13
Synergy 16
Team 16
Telecommuting 15
Upward communication 7

ASSIGNMENTS AND ACTIVITIES

Read

1. Ask students to read the following
article about predicted communic
trends: Communication technolog
the future. (2009). *Technology Awa*
Available at **www.technology**
.org/future_technology/
Communication_Technology_in
the_Future.html. Have students
break into small groups and discuss the
following:

Write

2. Direct students to take the team player quiz at **www.quintcareers.com/ team_player_quiz.html** and write a brief paper about their team orientation and how being a team player may affect their career success. **(Obj. 4)**

Think

3. Have students research a scandal in the business or popular press using campus resources. Assign students to read the article and respond to questions a–c. **(Obj. 4)**

    a. Who are the stakeholders in the case? What does each stand to gain or lose, depending on your decision?

    b. How does the situation described in the case relate to the four-dimension model shown in Figure 1-4?

    c. What factors might influence your decision as the manager in the case?

> To push your students to think critically about the material, or to add an experiential, applied element to your course, each card offers a variety of in-class or homework assignments organized according to essential business communication skills: reading, writing, thinking, speaking, and collaborating.

DIGGING DEEPER

Ask students to respond to the following discussion questions.

1. What aspect of cultural diversity do you feel will impact you most in your career: international, intercultural, intergenerational, or gender? Explain your answer, including how you plan to deal with the challenge.

2. Lack of Internet access is causing some nations to be classified as information "have nots." What international communication problems could result?

3. Considering the four strategic forces discussed, how is business communication today different from that of 30 years ago? In what ways is it easier? In what ways is it more difficult?

KEY CONCEPTS

Understanding what communication is and how it occurs is central to successful transactions in the workplace. Business communication does not take place in a vacuum but is impacted by various external forces, including legal and ethical constraints, diversity challenges, changing technology, and team environment.

CONCEPTUAL FIGURES AND TABLES

Figure 1-1   The Transactional Process Model of Communication
Figure 1-2   Flow of Information within an Organization
Figure 1-3   Levels of Communication
Figure 1-4   Factors Influencing Business Communication
Figure 1-5   Four Dimensions of Business Behavior

POWERPOINT HIGHLIGHTS

Lecture Presentation

Slide 5   Communication Channels
Slide 12   Contextual Forces Influencing Business Communication
Slide 15   Four Dimensions of Business Behavior
Slide 17   Diversity Challenges
Slide 20   Impacts of Technology

Resource Presentation

The Instructor Manual contains a menu of resource slides you can integrate into your lecture presentation. Select from a variety of slides with examples, short quizzes, activities, and supplemental information to customize your lecture slide deck to meet the needs of your students and your course.

LEARNING OBJECTIVES

1-1   Define communication and describe the value of communication in business.

1-2   Explain the communication process model and the ultimate objective of the communication process.

1-3   Discuss how information flows in an organization.

1-4   Explain how legal and ethical constraints, diversity challenges, changing technology, and team environment act as contextual forces that influence the process of business communication.

CHAPTER OUTLINE

ASSIGNMENTS AND ACTIVITIES

Read

1. Ask students to read the following article about predicted communication trends: Future Work Skills (2011). Available at **http://cdn.theatlantic.com/static /front/docs/sponsored/phoenix /future_work_skills_2020.pdf.** Have students break into small groups and discuss the following:

   a. What communication trends are predicted in the workplace? Are any of these surprising? Why?

   b. Which trends are likely to impact your chosen career field most significantly? In what ways?

   c. How do the predicted trends relate to the four strategic forces presented in this chapter?

   d. Select one of the communication means discussed in the article. Share your findings in a short class presentation. **(Obj. 1–4)**

Write

2. Direct students to take the team player quiz at **www.quintcareers.com /team_player_quiz.html** and write a brief paper about their team orientation and how being a team player may affect their career success. **(Obj. 4)**

Think

3. Have students research a scandal in the business or popular press using campus resources. Assign students to read the article and respond to questions a–c. **(Obj. 4)**

   a. Who are the stakeholders in the case? What does each stand to gain or lose, depending on your decision?

   b. How does the situation described in the case relate to the four-dimension model shown in Figure 1-4?

   c. What factors might influence your decision as the manager in the case?

Speak

4. Have students assemble in groups of three, interview an international student at your institution, and generate a list of English words that have no equivalents in his or her language. Your students should also find out about nonverbal communication that may differ from that used in American culture. Students can share their findings in a short presentation to the class. **(Obj. 4)**

Collaborate

5. Assign students to get into groups, and discuss experiences in which "communication failure" was blamed for problems that occurred in their work, academic, or personal interactions. Instruct students to generate three to five additional ways communication can fail, and give suggestions for correcting them. Groups can share their results with the case in a short presentation. **(Obj. 1 & 2)**

DIGGING DEEPER

Ask students to respond to the following discussion questions.

1. What aspect of cultural diversity do you feel will impact you most in your career: international, intercultural, intergenerational, or gender? Explain your answer, including how you plan to deal with the challenge.

2. Lack of Internet access is causing some nations to be classified as information "have nots." What international communication problems could result?

3. Considering the four strategic forces discussed, how is business communication today different from that of 30 years ago? In what ways is it easier? In what ways is it more difficult?

KEY CONCEPTS

Behavioral theories form the conceptual basis for business communication. Nonverbal communication, listening, and group communication are essential interpersonal skills for success in today's organizations. A team is a group with a clear identity and a high level of member commitment. Groups and teams communicate via both traditional and electronic meetings, which must be managed successfully to ensure that organizational goals are met.

CONCEPTUAL FIGURES AND TABLES

Figure 2-1   The Johari Window
Figure 2-2   Organizational Chart with Hierarchical and Team Structures
Figure 2-3   Sample Formal Generic Agenda for Meetings

POWERPOINT HIGHLIGHTS

Lecture Presentation

Slide 9   Nonverbal Communication Conveys Added Meaning
Slide 13   Understanding Nonverbal Messages
Slide 14   Effective Listeners . . .
Slide 16   Characteristics of Effective Groups
Slide 20   Suggestions for Effective Meetings

Resource Presentation

The Instructor Manual contains a menu of resource slides you can integrate into your lecture presentation. Select from a variety of slides with examples, short quizzes, activities, and supplemental information to customize your lecture slide deck to meet the needs of your students and your course.

LEARNING OBJECTIVES

2-1 Explain how behavioral theories about human needs, trust and disclosure, and motivation relate to business communication.

2-2 Describe the role of nonverbal messages in communication.

2-3 Identify aspects of effective listening.

2-4 Identify factors affecting group and team communication.

2-5 Discuss aspects of effective meeting management.

CHAPTER OUTLINE

KEY TERMS

ASSIGNMENTS AND ACTIVITIES

Read

1. Have students read the following article, which describes the importance of team development activities: Linley, A. (2008, January 29). Our top ten team building exercises. *Ezine*. Available at **http://ezinearticles.com/?Our-Top-Ten-Team-Building-Exercises&id5955336.**

   Ask students to form small groups in which they should discuss the shift in corporate team building over the past two or more years and the value gained from various types of team-building activities. Students should brainstorm ways that they believe these approaches could be used to boost the effectiveness of teams in an academic setting and the projected results. Afterward, they should share their ideas with the class in a short presentation. **(Obj. 1 & 4)**

2. Have students read the following article, which gives useful suggestions ensuring that nonverbal behavior communicates the intended message: Shephard, L. C. (2007, May 1). Reading body language can offer insight to HR pros. *Employee Benefit News*. Available from Business Source Complete database.

   Instruct students to expand the list of recommended and nonverbal messages and the interpretations mentioned in the article. They should then share their list with the class, complete with demonstrations, in an informal presentation. **(Obj. 2)**

Write

3. Assign students to keep a journal over a period of two to five days that records events involving metacommunication. Describe how each incident influences the understanding of the verbal message involved. **(Obj. 4)**

Think

4. Ask students to consider a distance learning conference or course in which they have participated. How were nonverbal communication, listening, and other factors different from what they have experienced in traditional class settings? How do their experiences relate to the conducting of electronic meetings? **(Obj. 2, 3, & 5)**

Speak

5. Have students locate one or more articles from a database or the Internet that discuss nonverbal communication in various cultures. Assign them to create a list of examples of body language and behaviors that have different meanings among cultures. Then lead the class in a discussion of how ignorance of these differences might affect interpersonal communication. **(Obj. 2)**

Collaborate

6. Assign students to groups of three to five, and have each team visit the website of the Institute for Performance Culture at **http://teaming-up.com.** The groups should take the survey that can be found in the Free Resources menu tab, under "Your team's performance blind spots?" Some of the items may not relate to the short-term project team but will provide students with ideas of issues faced in real-world work teams. After taking the survey, each group should discuss the evaluation report produced from the survey. Have each group send the instructor an email summarizing what the team survey revealed and how they will use the information to improve team performance. **(Obj. 4)**

DIGGING DEEPER

Ask students to respond to the following discussion questions.

1. How can managers use Maslow's need levels, the Johari Window, and the management theories of McGregor and Hersey and Blanchard to improve communication with employees?

2. How do effective conversation and listening impact a business' overall success?

3. Why do some teams never reach the highest stage of team development? What can be done to overcome the obstacles to peak team performance?

PREPCARD

CHAPTER 3 PLANNING SPOKEN AND WRITTEN MESSAGES

KEY CONCEPTS

Effective spoken and written communication involves a process of careful analysis, planning, adaptation, and organization that precedes the actual creation of the message. Chapter 3 focuses on these essential steps of preparation: (1) determining the purpose of the message and an appropriate channel, (2) envisioning the audience, (3) adapting the message to the audience, and (4) organizing the message.

CONCEPTUAL FIGURES AND TABLES

Figure 3-1   Process for Planning and Preparing Spoken and Written Messages
Figure 3-2   Use of Communication Media
Figure 3-3   Process of Selecting an Outline for a Spoken or Written Message

POWERPOINT HIGHLIGHTS

Lecture Presentation

Slide 3   Step 1: Consider the Applicable Contextual Forces
Slide 5   Step 2: Determine the Purpose and Select an Appropriate Channel and Medium
Slide 7   Step 3: Envision the Audience
Slide 9   Step 4: Adapt the Message to the Audience's Needs and Concerns
Slide 10   Cultivating the "You Attitude"

Resource Presentation

The Instructor Manual contains a menu of resource slides you can integrate into your lecture presentation. Select from a variety of slides with examples, short quizzes, activities, and supplemental information to customize your lecture slide deck to meet the needs of your students and your course.

LEARNING OBJECTIVES

3-1 Consider contextual forces that may affect whether, how, to whom, and when a message is sent.

3-2 Identify the purpose of the message and the appropriate channel and medium.

3-3 Develop clear perceptions of the audience to enhance the impact and persuasiveness of the message, improve goodwill, and establish and maintain the credibility of the communicator.

3-4 Apply tactics for adapting messages to the audience, including those for communicating ethically and responsibly.

3-5 Recognize the importance of organization when planning the first draft.

CHAPTER OUTLINE

ASSIGNMENTS AND ACTIVITIES

Read

1. Ask students to conduct an online search to identify strategies companies have adopted to raise their employees' awareness of diversity in the workplace. The students should, in chart form, summarize the indexes they used to locate articles, the companies they read about, and the successful strategies that companies used to promote diversity. **(Obj. 2 & 3)**

Write

2. Assign students to conduct research on social networking sites such as Twitter. They can begin with the following article: Graham, J. (2008, July 21). Twitter took off from simple "tweet" success. *USA Today*. Available from LexisNexis Academic database.

   Once students complete their research, assign the following activities:

   a. Compile a list of advantages and disadvantages of this communication medium, including examples of how two businesses have used this social networking site.

   b. Register at Twitter (or use your existing account) and exchange messages with a small group of students in the class. Prepare an engaging flyer describing efficient use of Twitter that will be distributed to staff as an attachment to an email. **(Obj. 1 & 2)**

Think

3. Ask students to compile a list of the advantages and disadvantages of email, as well as recommended uses and precautions for its use, after reading the following article: Seckler S., & Toomey, R. (2005, December 18). Commentary: E-mail: Career opportunities and pitfalls in workplace communication. *The Daily Record* (Kansas City, MO). Available from LexisNexis Academic database. **(Obj. 1)**

4. Divide the class into a number of small groups in which they should discuss a specific situation in work or educational experience that illustrates the negative effects of an individual who did not consider the impact of his or her message on the receiver.

Speak

5. Have students generate a list of phrases and nonverbal expressions peculiar to their culture that groups from another culture might not understand. Ask them to identify any conflict situations that could arise from the misinterpretation of the collectively understood terms. Have them also consider how group norms play a part in the understanding of collective culture. If time allows, assign each student to select one item from his or her list as the topic for a five-minute presentation to the class. **(Obj. 2)**

Collaborate

6. Explain to students that however experienced businesses are at writing formal business documents, such as press releases, advertising, and financial reports, creating an online brand or authentic voice through an online blog provides a new challenge for many business communicators. To learn more, have students locate the following articles, which are available from Lexis-Nexis database:

   Cardis, P. (2008, October). Blogging for business. *Professional Builder*.

   Get caught in the net. (2007, May 31). *Financial Advisor*.

   How to write a better blog. (July 2007). *Business World* (Weekender).

   After reading the articles, students should work in small teams to prepare an engaging flier describing efficient blog communication that will be distributed to staff as an attachment to an email message. **(Obj. 1 & 2)**

DIGGING DEEPER

Ask students to respond to the following discussion questions.

1. What is empathy and how does it affect business communication? How are empathy and sympathy different?

2. Explain what is meant by writing to *express* and not to *impress*.

3. How can you ensure quality in a collaboratively written document? Perhaps someone on your team makes unnecessary additions or questionable edits such as revising to make the document "sound more professional" while sacrificing clarity. What would you do?

KEY CONCEPTS

Chapter 4 focuses on preparing a first draft and on revising and proofreading for accuracy and desired impact. Such communication is carefully drafted and proofread for correct sentence structure, emphasis on important ideas, coherent paragraphs, and easy readability. After a review of the writing process in Chapters 3 and 4 (and the Grammar and Usage Appendix), students will prepare letters, memos, and a variety of electronic messages (email, instant, and text messages, blogs, and other web communications) and business reports and presentations.

CONCEPTUAL FIGURES AND TABLES

Figure 4-1   Process for Planning and Preparing Spoken and Written Messages
Figure 4-2   Contrast the Readability and Appeal of Bulky (left) versus Broken (right) Text
Figure 4-3   Improving Readability Through Cautious Use of a Grammar and Style Checker
Figure 4-4   Rough Draft of a Letter (excerpt)

POWERPOINT HIGHLIGHTS

Lecture Presentation

Slide 3   Process for Planning and Preparing Spoken and Written Messages
Slide 4   Step 6: Prepare the First Draft
Slide 8   Factors Affecting Readability
Slide 11   Step 7: Revise for Style and Tone
Slide 16   Proofreading Procedures

Resource Presentation

The Instructor Manual contains a menu of resource slides you can integrate into your lecture presentation. Select from a variety of slides with examples, short quizzes, activities, and supplemental information to customize your lecture slide deck to meet the needs of your students and your course.

LEARNING OBJECTIVES

4-1 Apply techniques for developing effective sentences and unified and coherent paragraphs.

4-2 Prepare visually appealing documents that grab the audience's attention and increase comprehension.

4-3 Identify factors affecting readability and revise messages to improve readability.

4-4 Revise and proofread a message for content, organization, style, and tone; mechanics; and format and layout.

CHAPTER OUTLINE

KEY TERMS

ASSIGNMENTS AND ACTIVITIES

Read

1. Have students locate the following article that offers tips on writing powerful business messages: Jolley, D. A. (2009). Clear and compelling messages: The foundation for effective communication. *Public Relations Tactics.* Available from Business Source Complete database. After they've read the article, ask students to respond to the following questions:

   a. What are the "Master P's"?

   b. Explain what the writer means by a "memorable quote." Could you foresee exceptions to the use of this approach for all business messages? Provide examples.

   c. What is the role of rehearsing in ensuring clear and compelling messages? **(Obj. 1–4)**

Write

2. Have students conduct an online search related to recent developments in speech (voice-recognition) technology. Students should prepare a brief written report providing information such as (a) current status of speech technology as a viable business application, including challenges that have hampered past developments; (b) examples of leading speech technology applications with related results; and (c) projections for future development of this technology. **(Obj. 1)**

Think

3. Ask students to complete the business usage quiz at **http://businesswriting .com/tests/commonusage.html.** Then have students assess their understanding of 26 common business writing problems. Once they have reviewed the feedback provided for each question, students should compile a list of areas in which they need improvement. Have students email their score to you, along with their plan for improvement. **(Obj. 1–4)**

4. Have students access the Plain Language website at **www.plainlanguage.gov/ examples/index.cfm**, view a variety of documents revised for easy reading following Plain English principles, and then select the "Before and After Comparisons" link. Once students have reviewed the examples posted under the "Using Visual Explanations to Convey Information More Clearly" section, they should complete the following activities:

   a. Have students prepare a brief paper explaining how applying plain English principles improved the readability of these documents. Ask them to suggest revisions to further improve the documents.

   b. Have students develop a new example (from a document they received in the past or one provided by you) that could be added to this site as a "before and after comparison." Ask them to place their two documents on a slide and be prepared to summarize their changes and explain how they improved the impact of the document. **(Obj. 3)**

Speak

5. Jon Warshawsky, coauthor of *Why Business People Speak Like Idiots*, was interviewed by Martha Barnette, who is host of *A Way with Words*, a program that airs on National Public Radio. In the interview, Jon says that many executives might feel "it's dangerous to have an original thought," which often leads to the use of a series of words they think they have to use to be seen as smart. Martha refers to this tendency as *corporate speak*. Please refer to

http://www.mcmcse.com/articles /corporatespeak.shtml to see a glossary of terms and phrases used in corporate America. Assign the following activities:

   a. Ask students to conduct an interview in person, by phone, or online with an executive in the student's chosen career field. Students should ask the executive whether corporate speak is a noticeable problem in the work environment, to identify common examples of corporate speak, and for advice related to communicating effectively in their career field.

   b. Ask students to make a short presentation to the class about how to avoid corporate speak and communicate effectively in their chosen career field. Alternately, students could make a video presentation and post it electronically for class access. **(Obj. 1, 2, & 4)**

DIGGING DEEPER

Ask students to respond to the following discussion questions.

1. What habits hinder your success or enjoyment of writing? Identify ways to overcome them.

2. How does online writing challenge a writer's effort to develop a seamless, coherent document?

3. Why do some writers rush through the proofreading phase of message development?

KEY CONCEPTS

A full chapter is devoted to the preparation of electronic communications—not only because of popular use in organizations but also because of their particular characteristics as informal but powerful forms of communication. Emphasis is given to email, instant and text messaging, Web communications (Web pages, wikis, and weblogs), and voice and wireless communication. Legal and ethical issues related to the use of technology are also discussed.

CONCEPTUAL FIGURES AND TABLES

Figure 5-1   Good Example of an Email Message
Figure 5-2   Good Example of an Instant Message
Figure 5-3   Levels of Formality Required by Various Technologies

POWERPOINT HIGHLIGHTS

Lecture Presentation

Slide 3   Guidelines for Preparing Email Messages
Slide 5   Email Fundamentals
Slide 9   Instant Messaging
Slide 12   Electronic Messages and the Law
Slide 21   Making a Professional Impression with Voice Mail
Slide 24   Cell Phone Communication

Resource Presentation

The Instructor Manual contains a menu of resource slides you can integrate into your lecture presentation. Select from a variety of slides with examples, short quizzes, activities, and supplemental information to customize your lecture slide deck to meet the needs of your students and your course.

LEARNING OBJECTIVES

5-1   Discuss the effective use of email, instant messaging, and text messaging in business communication.

5-2   Explain principles for writing effectively for the Web.

5-3   Discuss the effective use of voice and wireless technologies in business communication.

5-4   Consider legal and ethical implications associated with the use of communication technology.

CHAPTER OUTLINE

ASSIGNMENTS AND ACTIVITIES

Read

1. Have students conduct an electronic search to locate an article that deals with the successful use of electronic communication in a company or organization. They should prepare an abstract of the article that includes the following parts: (1) article citation, (2) name of organization/company, (3) brief description of the communication technique and situation, and (4) outcome(s) of the successful communication. As an alternative to locating an article, propose that students write about a successful communication situation in the organization/company for which they work. **(Obj. 1–4)**

Write

2. For the first part of this activity, have students read the following article, which discusses strategies for making Web information accessible to those who cannot access information in various ways: Tierney J. (2007, April 1). Ignore universal web design at your peril. *Multichannel Merchant*, p. 8. Available at **http://multichannelmerchant.com /ecommerce/ignore_universal_web/**

   After reading the article, ask students to visit a corporate website of their choice. Assign them to evaluate the accessibility of information on that site to viewers who are physically challenged.

   Students should imagine that they are an employee of that company and send an email to the instructor with recommendations for making the information on the site more accessible. **(Obj. 2)**

Think

3. Ask students to locate a company example of both a well written and a poorly written email message. Students should analyze the strengths and weaknesses of each document and be prepared to discuss their analyses in class. **(Obj. 1)**

Speak

4. In today's world, initial contact with a person is often via the telephone, so those important first impressions are dependent on practicing proper telephone etiquette. Ask students to make a list of ideas for increasing levels of telephone courtesy to build image and trust. Have them prepare a brief presentation providing suggestions for placing calls, answering calls, and taking telephone messages. **(Obj. 3)**

Collaborate

5. Assign students to small groups and ask them to share incidents of inappropriate cell phone behavior they have experienced in a school, work, or public setting. Ask them to explain how each incident affected the individuals involved. They should also discuss etiquette rules they believe are critical for courteous, productive cell phone use. Are some etiquette rules appropriate for business calls but not for personal calls or vice versa? Finally, each group should prepare a brief presentation on the dos and don'ts of cell phone usage. **(Obj. 3)**

DIGGING DEEPER

Ask students to respond to the following discussion questions.

1. Describe three business communication situations in which a technology channel would be inappropriate for exchanging information. Explain your choices.

2. How does a communicator balance the equally important goals of communicating efficiently and building team camaraderie?

3. How is Web communication different from other forms of business communication? How is it similar?

KEY CONCEPTS

Good-news and neutral-news messages are included together in this chapter because the outlines for these communications are both deductive. Strategies and examples are presented for the creation of good-news messages, appreciation messages, routine claims and requests, routine messages about orders and credit, and procedural messages. Strategies for the use of form documents and for adapting messages sent to international audiences are also presented.

CONCEPTUAL FIGURES AND TABLES

MODEL DOCUMENT FIGURES

POWERPOINT HIGHLIGHTS

Lecture Presentation

Resource Presentation

The Instructor Manual contains a menu of resource slides you can integrate into your lecture presentation. Select from a variety of slides with examples, short quizzes, activities, and supplemental information to customize your lecture slide deck to meet the needs of your students and your course.

LEARNING OBJECTIVES

6-1 Describe the deductive outline for good and neutral news and its adaptations for specific situations and for international audiences.

6-2 Prepare messages that convey good news, including thank-you and appreciation messages.

6-3 Write messages presenting routine claims and requests and favorable responses to them.

6-4 Write messages acknowledging customer orders, providing credit information, and extending credit.

6-5 Prepare procedural messages that ensure clear and consistent application.

CHAPTER OUTLINE

ASSIGNMENTS AND ACTIVITIES

Read

1. Assign students to conduct an electronic search to locate an article that deals with successful communication in a company or organization. Have them prepare an abstract of the article that includes the following parts: (1) article citation, (2) name of organization/company, (3) brief description of communication technique/situation, and (4) outcome(s) of the successful communication. As an alternative to locating an article, students could also write about a successful communication situation in the organization or company for which they work. **(Obj. 1–5)**

Write

2. Give students the following scenario and have them prepare the exercise listed. As the marketing manager for Pacific Golf Supply Co. (PGS), you have just approved a credit account for Highland Lake Golf Club, a new golf course in northern California. Send Jordan Martin, the golf pro at the club, a letter stating that you have approved a $25,000 initial credit line. PGS offers its customers 2/10, n/30 payment terms and charges interest at an 18 percent annual rate on overdue accounts. Each quarter, PGS reviews its outstanding accounts and offers an increase in its credit line to any customer with a current account. The letter should confirm that the initial order of golf balls, clubs, and accessories has been shipped via UPS ground, with an expected delivery time of 10 days. Encourage Kevin to use his remaining $12,400 credit line

to invest in quality display units. Explain that experience demonstrates that sales increase by 25 percent when the product is displayed using your display units.

Exercise

Write the credit approval/order acknowledgement letter to Jordan at 2500 Country Club Drive, Klamath, CA 95548-1200. **(Obj. 1 & 4)**

Think

3. Have students find an example of both a well written and a poorly written good-news or routine memo, email message, or letter; analyze the strengths and weaknesses of each document; and prepare to discuss them in class. **(Obj. 1–5)**

Speak

4. Assign students to obtain a copy of a business letter written by someone from another culture and to identify the major differences between this letter and a traditional U.S. letter. Their report should include information about cultural differences that might be reflected in the message style. Ask students to create a visual of their letter and share their analysis with the class. **(Obj. 1)**

Collaborate

5. Many companies naively rely on a file of form letters composed to fit almost any conceivable situation in order to protect against potentially poor writing and to get messages out as quickly as possible. While these form letters may form the basis for routine communication, they often miss the mark.

   Have students read and discuss the form letter that the National Mentoring Partnership sent to organizations who mentor **www.theregister .co.uk/2008/03/15/apple_iphone _developer_form_letter/.** After reading the letter, divide the class into groups of three or four. Each group should identify an organization and a form letter that it might send to customers or clients. Using the team's knowledge and Internet resources to research the organization, the group should write the form letter and include an incentive for the reader to follow the letter's request. **(Obj. 1–5)**

DIGGING DEEPER

Ask students to respond to the following discussion questions.

1. What criteria should be used in determining whether a good- or neutral-news message would best be communicated on paper, electronically, or verbally?

2. What considerations should be given to a message recipient's culture when planning a good-news or neutral-news message?

3. What role does goodwill play in composing effective deductive messages?

KEY CONCEPTS

Bad-news messages typically require an inductive strategy. Situations covered include sharing bad news, refusing a request, denying a claim, refusing an order, denying credit, delivering constructive criticism, and communicating negative organizational news. The construction of bad-news messages involves more delicate human relations issues than good news and neutral messages.

CONCEPTUAL FIGURES AND TABLES

Figure 7-1   Inductive Outline Used in Bad-News Messages Sent in Written, Electronic, or Spoken Form

MODEL DOCUMENT FIGURES

Figure 7-2   Developing the Components of a Bad-News Message
Figure 7-3   Good Example of a Refusal for a Favor
Figure 7-4   Poor Example of a Refusal to an Employee's Request
Figure 7-5   Good Example of a Refusal to an Employee's Request
Figure 7-6   Poor Example of a Claim Denial
Figure 7-7   Good Example of a Claim Denial
Figure 7-8   Poor Example of a Constructive Criticism
Figure 7-9   Good Example of a Constructive Criticism
Figure 7-10 Poor Example of a Message Announcing Negative Organizational News
Figure 7-11 Good Example of a Message Announcing Negative Organizational News

POWERPOINT HIGHLIGHTS

Lecture Presentation
Slide 6   Advantages of the Inductive Outline
Slide 17   Techniques for Closing Positively
Slide 32   Sharing Negative Organizational News

LEARNING OBJECTIVES

7-1 Explain the steps in the inductive outline, and understand its use for specific situations.

7-2 Discuss strategies for developing the five components of a bad-news message.

7-3 Prepare messages refusing requests and claims.

7-4 Prepare messages handling problems with customers' orders and denying credit.

7-5 Prepare messages providing constructive criticism, communicating negative organizational news, and responding to crises.

CHAPTER OUTLINE

ASSIGNMENTS AND ACTIVITIES

Read

1. Have students conduct an electronic search to locate an article that deals with successful negative communication in a company or organization. Assign them to prepare an abstract of the article that includes the following parts: (1) article citation, (2) name of organization/company, (3) brief description of communication technique/situation, and (4) outcome(s) of the successful communication. Students should present their abstract in a memo and give a short presentation in class. **(Obj. 1–5)**

Think

2. Instruct students to refer to a recent political or business event in which bad news was shared and prepare a written critique that includes (1) an assessment of the effectiveness of the message and the manner in which it was delivered, (2) an analysis of the results, and (3) a summary of what students learned from their analysis. **(Obj. 1, 2, & 5)**

Write

3. Give students the following scenario and have them complete the related exercises. **(Obj. 1, 2, & 4)**

   HGA Electronics is replacing its fleet of 100 automobiles used by its field representatives. As the regional corporate sales representative for the automobile manufacturer, you notice that HGA Electronics has not ordered sound system upgrades to accommodate mp3 players and smartphones that will enhance the employees' driving experience.

Exercises

1. Search the Internet to identify other options that you believe employers should consider for company vehicles.

2. Write an email to Joanny Gayle, the buyer at HGA Electronics, suggesting that she add these options to the automobiles that she's already ordered.

Speak

4. Give students the following scenario and have them complete the related exercise. (Obj. 3)

   Gulf South Communications Corporation has purchased a significant number of season tickets to the Riverside Community Theatre since its inaugural season in 1979. Gulf South distributes the tickets to special customers, vendors, and employees to foster goodwill and promote the company. Because of the financial crisis in the telecommunications industry, Gulf South's management has regrettably been forced to eliminate all noncritical expenditures. As a supervisor in the human resources department, you have been asked by management to inform Steve Cafferty, the business manager of the theatre, that Gulf South will not purchase season tickets this year. Because the loss of your long-time support will be a hard blow to the theatre, you decide to break the news to Steve over lunch at his favorite restaurant.

Exercise

Ask students to develop a script of the conversation they will have with Steve conveying the company's disappointing decision.

Collaborate

5. Despite the benefits of online brainstorming, waves are being generated as companies and individuals become victims of negative postings. The widespread electronic distribution of unflattering and possibly slanderous comments, often posted anonymously, is a major concern to many. Ask students to learn more about the negative effects of being "zapped in cyberspace" by reading the following articles: **(Obj. 1–5)**

   Valiquette, L. (2006). The dangerous myth of online invulnerability, *Ottawa Business Journal*, 11(23), p. 6. Available from Business Source Complete database.

   McCormick, J. B. & Rudlin, D. A. (2002). Zapped in cyberspace; as use of the Internet increases, so does the risk that people will post defamatory statements on message boards and in chat rooms. Here's how defamation law, which originated in medieval times, can be used in the 21st century.

Trial Magazine. Available at **http://www.highbeam.com /doc/1G1-84549980.html**

After they've completed the reading, assign students to prepare a presentation that (a) summarizes the advantages and disadvantages of online discussions and (b) provides a checklist for writing an effective reply to an online posting calling for constructive criticism of a company or individual.

After the presentations, have students visit the web site that allows students at your college/university to post faculty evaluations and select three to five postings for a professor(s) of their choice. Using their evaluation checklist, students should critique the postings, placing them in rank order of effectiveness. Then have students make a brief team presentation to the class about their analysis that includes a visual illustrating an example of a poorly written and a well-written posting. Be sure to remind students to omit all identification from the evaluations.

DIGGING DEEPER

Ask students to respond to the following discussion questions.

1. Explain the rationale and significance of this statement: Saying "no" is not difficult; the challenge is to do so while protecting goodwill.

2. Common channels for delivering business messages include written, electronic, and face-to-face means. What criteria would you use in selecting the appropriate channel for delivering bad news?

3. How might standard practices for internal and external communication change when a company is facing uncertain times (e.g., an economic recession, bankruptcy proceedings, and so on)?

KEY CONCEPTS

The persuasive principles presented in Chapter 8 have applications in face-to-face business relationships as well as in written messages. The ability to persuade is useful to a variety of life circumstances in which students will need to motivate action, such as selling a product, a service, or their abilities; gaining acceptance of an idea; or collecting money. Various types of persuasive writing situations are covered.

CONCEPTUAL FIGURES AND TABLES

Figure 8-1   Inductive Outline Used in Persuasive Messages Sent in Written, Electronic, or Spoken Form

MODEL DOCUMENT FIGURES

Figure 8-2   Poor Example of a Sales Message Promoting a Product
Figure 8-3   Good Example of a Sales Message Promoting a Service
Figure 8-4   Good Example of a Sales Message Promoting a Product
Figure 8-5   Poor Example of a Persuasive Claim
Figure 8-6   Good Example of a Persuasive Claim
Figure 8-7   Poor Example of a Persuasive Request (Asking a Favor)
Figure 8-8   Good Example of a Persuasive Request (Asking a Favor)
Figure 8-9   Good Example of a Persuasive Memo

POWERPOINT HIGHLIGHTS

Lecture Presentation

Slide 3   Persuasive Message: Plan Before You Write
Slide 5   Inductive Outline Used for Persuasive Messages
Slide 7   Apply Sound Writing Principles
Slide 12   Ways to Convince Customers
Slide 14   Motivating Action

Resource Presentation

The Instructor Manual contains a menu of resource slides you can integrate into your lecture presentation. Select from a variety of slides with examples, short quizzes, activities, and supplemental information to customize your lecture slide deck to meet the needs of your students and your course.

LEARNING OBJECTIVES

8-1 Develop effective outlines and appeals for messages that persuade.

8-2 Write effective sales messages.

8-3 Write effective persuasive requests (making a claim or asking for a favor or information) and persuasion within an organization.

CHAPTER OUTLINE

ASSIGNMENTS AND ACTIVITIES

Read

1. Assign students to conduct an electronic search to locate an article that deals with the successful use of persuasive communication in a company or organization. Ask them to prepare an abstract of the article that includes the following: (1) article citation, (2) name of the organization or company, (3) a brief description of the communication technique or situation, and (4) the outcome(s) of the successful communication. As an alternative to locating an article, provide the option of writing about successful communication situations in the organizations or companies in which students work.
   (Obj. 1–3)

Write

2. Provide students with the scenario below, and assign the accompanying exercise.

   You recently paid $250 to Keller & Jenkins for adding a provision in your will to establish a scholarship endowment at your alma mater. While eating lunch in a crowded restaurant, Abigail Kemp, a clerk at Keller & Jenkins, stopped by your table to commend you on your planned generosity. Although no harm was intended, you were placed in the uncomfortable position of explaining the clerk's comments to your lunch guests. Keller & Jenkins provides its clients with a bill of rights that clearly states that client information will be kept strictly confidential.

Exercise

1. Write a letter to H. Daniel Keller, the lawyer who performed the legal work for you. Inform him of the situation and seek a full refund for the legal services.

Think

3. Wyndham Vacation Resorts is continually expanding the selection of resorts available to its FairShare Plus members. One expansion method is to establish an alliance with an existing, independent resort, enabling FairShare Plus members to use their points to vacation there. Wyndham Vacation Resorts has even extended the "resort" concept by establishing an alliance with Carnival Cruise Lines.

   Ask students to use the Internet or print resources to identify a potential association location. Students should assume that Wyndham Vacation Resorts has just established an alliance with the resort. Ask them to write the script of a voice mail message that Wyndham Vacation Resorts could leave for its FairShare Plus members, which invites them to visit the new location.
   (Obj. 1 & 2)

Speak

4. Have students form groups of two; then have each group select a tangible item from a collection that you have prepared beforehand (include items such as a cell phone, stapler, pen, backpack, t-shirt, etc). After each group has selected an item, have students complete the following exercises.
   (Obj. 1 & 2)

Exercises

1. Designate one member of the team as the buyer and one as the seller. The seller will present a compelling sales pitch for the item to the buyer focusing on an appropriate central appeal and convincing evidence. Following the sales pitch, the buyer will give friendly feedback for making the pitch more convincing. Next, have students reverse roles, but this time have the buyer sell himself/herself as a potential employee of the company that makes the item. Again, students should share friendly feedback for improving the presentation and in addition discuss differences they encountered in selling a product versus promoting themselves. Students should be prepared to share their experiences with the class.

2. Ask students to use the experience gained from the previous activity to deliver a one- to two-minute sales pitch on a pet project or idea they genuinely support. Students should choose at least three points that prove their case.

Collaborate

5. Divide the class into groups of three to four students; then give them the following scenario and ask them to complete the related exercise.
   (Obj. 1 & 3)

   Despite having written what you consider an outstanding business proposal, you have not been successful in persuading any regional banks to finance the new venture. While attending a fund-raising dinner for a local charity, you had the good fortune to meet B. Stephen Richardson, a successful entrepreneur who you believed to be interested in your idea. He gave you his business card stating, "Let me know if I can ever lend a helping hand." More important, you interpreted his nonverbal cues as clear interest in financing the project.

Exercises

1. In your groups, identify a retail business you believe would be successful in your community. Assuming you have written a business proposal, write a cover letter to B. Stephen Richardson seeking his financial support of the project. The letter should include a brief summary of the proposed business and your justification for its potential success.

2. Assuming you receive financing for the project, design a company logo that will serve as the centerpiece for advertising campaigns and developing consumer recognition. Be certain that your logo has a contemporary look and portrays the essence of your brand. Be prepared to present your recommended logo to the class in a brief presentation.

DIGGING DEEPER

Ask students to respond to the following discussion questions.

1. Where does one cross the line between being persuasive and being coercive or overbearing?

2. How might a persuasive approach need to be modified when dealing with persons of other cultures?

KEY CONCEPTS

After having studied informal communications including letters, memos, and electronic communication, students seem to understand the objective and formal nature of reports simply because of the contrast. Chapter 9 follows a sequence that begins with report characteristics and then covers the four steps in problem solving. Methods of research are presented, with considerable attention given to sampling and designing survey instruments used in normative surveys. Information is included for locating both printed and electronic sources of information.

CONCEPTUAL FIGURES AND TABLES

Figure 9-1   Report Formality Continuum
Figure 9-2   The General Upward Flow of Reports
Figure 9-3   Useful Reference Sources
Figure 9-4   A Sample Computer Data Search Using an Online Database
Figure 9-5   Selecting an Appropriate Data Collection Method
Figure 9-7   The Report Process

MODEL DOCUMENT FIGURE

Figure 9-6   Example of an Effective Questionnaire

POWERPOINT HIGHLIGHTS

Lecture Presentation

Slide 4   Formal–Informal Report Continuum
Slide 12   Types of Sources
Slide 13   Objectives of Secondary Research
Slide 16   Reasons for Accurate, Complete Documentation
Slide 18   Common Errors in Data Interpretation

Resource Presentation

The Instructor Manual contains a menu of resource slides you can integrate into your lecture presentation. Select from a variety of slides with examples, short quizzes, activities, and supplemental information to customize your lecture slide deck to meet the needs of your students and your course.

LEARNING OBJECTIVES

9-1 Identify the characteristics of a report and the various classifications of business reports.

9-2 Apply steps in the problem-solving process and methods for solving a problem.

9-3 Use appropriate printed, electronic, and primary sources of information.

9-4 Demonstrate appropriate methods of collecting, organizing, and referencing information.

9-5 Explain techniques for the logical analysis and interpretation of data.

CHAPTER OUTLINE

ASSIGNMENTS AND ACTIVITIES

Read

1. Have students use an online database to locate and read an article related to challenges associated with experimental research. What legal and ethical challenges do researchers face when conducting experimental research with human subjects? How can they be managed? (Obj. 4)

Write

2. A focus group is a form of qualitative research in which a group of people are asked about their attitudes toward a product, service, concept, advertisement, idea, or packaging. Questions are asked in an interactive group setting where participants are free to talk with other group members. For marketers, focus groups are an important tool for acquiring feedback regarding product development, such as product name, features, and packaging. Information from the focus group can provide invaluable insight about the potential market acceptance of a product.

Ask students to select an existing product that could be improved and to write five questions that could be asked of a focus group to elicit needed responses for the improvement of the product. Next, students should ask several people to serve as a focus group, selecting participants who are knowledgeable about the product you have selected. After conducting the focus group with the questions they have prepared, students are to prepare reports of their findings and present them to the class. (Obj. 1–5)

Think

3. Have students prepare a one-page description of their plans to solve the problem for one of the following research studies. Use the following headings for the problem: (1) Statement of the Problem, (2) Research Method and Sources of Information, (3) Nature of Data to Be Gathered and Analyzed, (4) Hypothesis or Hypotheses to Be Proved or Disproved (if feasible). Here are some ideas to get students started:

- Investigate a problem occurring on your campus (e.g., declining enrollment in some majors, increasing tuition, delayed financial aid payments, high cost of textbooks, or closed classes) or in a job or student organization position you hold.

- Superior Foods, Inc., is considering adding organic versions of its frozen vegetables in an effort to establish itself as a leader in this fast-growing market. To increase its available supply of organic produce, management recognizes the need to assist local growers in adopting organic farming methods. The first step in this process is to recruit experts in organic farming to design and implement training.

- Rainbow Pool and Spas initiated a Web site to provide answers to frequently asked questions and product-update information. Customer response has been outstanding, freeing up the company's toll-free telephone lines for calls about more technical, nonrecurring problems—a primary goal of the service. As marketing

manager, you are considering the possibility of starting a corporate blog and a microblogging site on Twitter to strengthen your relationship and communication with customers.

- As branch manager of a bank, you are faced with the task in a sagging economy of reassuring customers of the solvency of your institution. Your current strategies for casting a positive light on negative performance indicators don't seem to be effective.

- For the first time, Greenwood Consulting Group held an all-company retreat that included customer service training, team-building sessions, and numerous social activities. Eight months following the conference, neither customer service nor employee morale seem to have had any noticeable improvement, and you must decide whether to schedule the retreat for the coming year. (Obj. 1–5)

Speak

4. Have students locate an article using either printed or electronic sources that addresses a problem that has occurred for some organization when it failed to realize that research findings that were true for one country or culture were not accurate for another. Ask each student to make a brief presentation to the class about his or her findings. (Obj. 4 & 5)

Collaborate

5. Organize students into groups of three or four, and have each group design a survey instrument for one of the scenarios in the Think section above. (Obj. 4)

DIGGING DEEPER

Ask students to respond to the following discussion questions.

1. How has the process of research changed in recent years? How have the changes been both beneficial and detrimental?

2. What communication skills should an effective researcher possess?

PREPCARD

CHAPTER 10 MANAGING DATA AND USING GRAPHICS

KEY CONCEPTS

To ensure that communication is effective, the elements of quantitative data must be classified, summarized, and condensed into a manageable size, then interpreted and written in common language. Readers remember information they gain from pictures or graphs longer than they remember the text they read. In this chapter, you will find tips for creating effective and ethical charts, descriptions of acceptable types of graphics, and methods for integrating graphics into text.

CONCEPTUAL FIGURES AND TABLES

Figure 10-1 Choosing the Appropriate Graphic to Fit Your Objective

MODEL DOCUMENT FIGURES

Figure 10-2 Effective Table Layout, Identifying Information, Labels, and Source
Figure 10-3 Variety of Bar Chart Formats
Figure 10-4 Line Chart
Figure 10-5 Area Chart
Figure 10-6 Pie Chart
Figure 10-7 Map Conveying Statistical Data
Figure 10-8 Flowchart Simplifying Understanding of Tasks

POWERPOINT HIGHLIGHTS

Lecture Presentation

Slide 2   Communicating Quantitative Information
Slide 3   Using Graphics Effectively and Ethically
Slide 4   Types of Graphic Aids
Slide 5   Preparing Effective Tables
Slide 13   Using Graphics in Text

Resource Presentation

The Instructor Manual contains a menu of resource slides you can integrate into your lecture presentation. Select from a variety of slides with examples, short quizzes, activities, and supplemental information to customize your lecture slide deck to meet the needs of your students and your course.

LEARNING OBJECTIVES

10-1 Communicate quantitative information effectively.

10-2 Apply principles of effectiveness and ethical responsibilities in the construction of graphic aids.

10-3 Select and design appropriate and meaningful graphics.

10-4 Integrate graphics within documents.

CHAPTER OUTLINE

ASSIGNMENTS AND ACTIVITIES

Read

1. Business professionals are responsible for communicating quantitative information, but many are unfamiliar with the design practices that make them effective. Have students read the following articles that discuss design strategies for effective charts and graphs:

   Royston, R. A. (2007, November/December). Book review: Show me the numbers: Designing tables and graphs to enlighten. *The Value Examiner*, 11–14. Available from Business Source Complete database.

   Jorge Cameos' Charts. (2008, October). 14 Misconceptions about charts and graphs. Available from **http://www.excelcharts.com/blog/misconceptions-charts-graphs/**

   After reading the articles, ask students to select three design techniques from these readings that were not covered in this chapter. Students should be prepared to share their insights with the class. **(Obj. 1–3)**

Write

2. Have each student prepare a table that shows the total revenue Scottsdale Fitness earned from membership fees for a fiscal period. Fees were collected by type of membership: single, $25; double, $40; family, $50; corporate, $22.50; senior $20. Scottsdale Fitness has 1,439 single memberships, 642 double, 543 family, 3,465 corporate, and 786 senior memberships. **(Obj. 2–4)**

3. Ask each student to prepare a pie chart that shows the percentage of operating income the Walt Disney Company generated in the following categories during 2010: media networks (56.2%), parks and resorts (22.4%), studio entertainment (12.9%), and consumer products (8.5%). Each student should write a descriptive or talking title that interprets the data depicted in the chart and then write a sentence to introduce the graphic and emphasize its most important idea(s). **(Obj. 2–4)**

Think

4. Have students clip a pictogram from *USA Today* and share it with groups in class. Ask them to discuss the effectiveness of the symbols used and the ethical presentation of the data. **(Obj. 1–3)**

5. Assign students to create graphics that would most effectively aid a human resources manager in identifying potential areas for employees' personal enrichment. Each student should write a descriptive or a talking title that interprets the data depicted in the table below, and each should also write a sentence that introduces the table and emphasizes its most important ideas. **(Obj. 2–4)**

Speak

6. Ask each student to locate a recent annual report of a company of his or her choice. They should prepare short summaries of effective graphic elements they observe; these could include photos, charts, and graphs, as well as the use of color, fonts, positioning, and spacing. In their summaries, students should describe how the graphic elements reflect the message each company wishes to convey. In addition, have each student identify a graphic that violates design principles and revise the graphic incorporating his or her suggestion. In their summaries, have students include the revised graphics and a list of their suggestions for improving it. **(Obj. 2–4)**

Interest by Age Group
January 2013

Age Group	Identity Security	Wireless Networking	Digital Photography	Online Investing
21–35	87	35	45	23
36–50	74	55	54	56
51–65	22	18	67	88

Collaborate

7. A movie theater must determine the genre of the films to show on each screen during its 7:00, 9:00, and midnight show times. A G-rated animated film historically sells 60 percent of the available seats at 7:00 and only 25 percent of the available seats at 9:00. Theaters usually consider 80 percent capacity to be sold out.

   Ask students to play the role of a work group at a software company developing a management information system targeted specifically to movie theaters. Using hypothetical data, they should create the reports the system should generate to enable theaters to manage their screens efficiently. For example, given a limited number of screens, a theater may elect to show an animated film on two screens at 7:00 but switch one of the screens to an action film at 9:00. **(Obj. 1–3)**

DIGGING DEEPER

Ask students to respond to the following discussion questions.

1. A poorly designed electronic slideshow can detract from the effectiveness of your presentation. Compose a list of blunders to avoid in designing effective slideshows.
2. How much is "too much" when considering the use of graphics in a business document?

KEY CONCEPTS

The structure and the preparation of various types of reports are presented including formal reports, letter reports, memorandum reports, and proposals. The problem-solving, research-based orientation of reports is emphasized for each of the various types.

CONCEPTUAL FIGURES AND TABLES

Figure 11-1 Parts of a Formal Report: Preliminary Parts, Report Text, and Addenda
Figure 11-2 The Number of Assisting Parts Increases as the Length of a Report Increases
Figure 11-3 The Basic Outline Expands into a Contents Page

MODEL DOCUMENT FIGURES

Figure 11-4 Short, Periodic Report in Memorandum Format
Figure 11-5 Audit Report in Short Report Format
Figure 11-6 Short Report in Expanded Letter Format, Pages 1–4
Figure 11-7 Short Proposal, Pages 1 and 2

POWERPOINT HIGHLIGHTS

Lecture Presentation

Slide 3   Parts of a Formal Report
Slide 6   Developing a Report Outline
Slide 13 Choosing an Effective Writing Style
Slide 19 Structure of a Proposal
Slide 20 Process for Preparing Proposals

Resource Presentation

The Instructor Manual contains a menu of resource slides you can integrate into your lecture presentation. Select from a variety of slides with examples, short quizzes, activities, and supplemental information to customize your lecture slide deck to meet the needs of your students and your course.

LEARNING OBJECTIVES

11-1 Identify the parts of a formal report and the contribution each part makes to the report's overall effectiveness.

11-2 Organize report findings.

11-3 Prepare effective formal reports using an acceptable format and writing style.

11-4 Prepare effective short reports in memorandum, email, and letter formats.

11-5 Prepare effective proposals for a variety of purposes.

CHAPTER OUTLINE

ASSIGNMENTS AND ACTIVITIES

Read

1. Have students use the selection of databases to which the campus library subscribes to find three articles on firewalls as a means to secure a company's intranet. Students should mark the main points of each article and create a bibliographic citation for each. **(Obj. 2 & 4)**

Write

2. Instruct students to visit a computer lab on your campus. Through observation and interviews, each student should prepare an audit report of the lab's offerings. They should include the following items in their reports: (1) the types of equipment available (e.g., PCs, Macs, mainframe terminals), (2) the quantity of each type, and (3) the operating systems and applications software available (products, versions). Require students to attach a table that summarizes their analyses and submit their work as letter reports. **(Obj. 4)**

Think

3. Assign students to attend a professional meeting of a campus or community organization and take notes on the program presented, the issues discussed, and so on. Students should submit a short report summarizing the events of the meeting and include a section that describes the benefits that might be derived from membership in that organization. **(Obj. 2 & 4)**

Speak

4. Ask each student to obtain a copy of a report prepared by an organization and analyze each of the following elements of the report:

a. Purpose

b. Intended audience

c. Degree of formality

d. Use of graphic support

e. Parts included (see Figure 11-1)

f. Referencing method

Extend the research by having each student make a brief presentation to the class about his or her findings. **(Obj. 1 & 2)**

Collaborate

5. Divide the class into small groups of three or four students each. Present the scenario below and then give them the related exercise. **(Obj. 4 & 6)**

Your team plans to open a business establishment in your city. Do you obtain a franchise or start your own independent restaurant? Select a franchise opportunity and research it. Include in your findings the initial investment cost, start-up expenses, franchise requirements and fees, and success and failure rate.

Exercise

Using the information on team writing, prepare a report that compares the options of franchising versus independent ownership. Make a recommendation as to the more desirable action to take.

6. Provide students with detailed instructions for completing a long or short report or proposal in teams.

a. Ask students to send you weekly progress reports via email. The reports should contain the following information about each meeting held during the week: date, place, and duration of the meeting, members present; report of work accomplished since last meeting; brief description of work accomplished during the current meeting; and work allocated to be completed before the next meeting.

b. About midway through the preparation of their reports, ask each student to send you an email message containing an evaluation of each member of his or her group. Students should assign a percentage indicating the contribution each member has made to the group. The total percentages awarded should equal 100 percent. Each student should also write a brief statement justifying the rating assigned to each member, along with specific, verifiable evidence.

c. Once the reports are completed, have each student email you a debriefing memo that describes his or her perceptions about the team's performance.

DIGGING DEEPER

Ask students to respond to the following discussion questions.

1. How do diversity considerations impact the choices made in report style and format?

2. Considering general trends in society toward more informality in many situations, how might the style of reports be impacted?

KEY CONCEPTS

In today's environment, delivering a successful business report involves not only making an effective spoken presentation but incorporating appropriate visuals as well. The chapter emphasizes timeless techniques of spoken delivery as well as visual and graphic design principles. Because the ability to give presentations using alternate delivery situations is important in today's workplace, the chapter covers strategies for responding to a culturally diverse audience and effective team and distance presentations.

CONCEPTUAL FIGURES AND TABLES

Figure 12-1   Selecting an Appropriate Presentation Visual
Figure 12-2   Designing Compelling Slides

POWERPOINT HIGHLIGHTS

Lecture Presentation

Slide 3   Preparing an Effective Presentation
Slide 6   Organizing Your Presentation
Slide 8   An Effective Introduction . . .
Slide 9   Crafting an Effective Body
Slide 11   Crafting an Effective Closing
Slide 22   Speaking to Culturally Diverse Audiences

Resource Presentation

The Instructor Manual contains a menu of resource slides you can integrate into your lecture presentation. Select from a variety of slides with examples, short quizzes, activities, and supplemental information to customize your lecture slide deck to meet the needs of your students and your course.

LEARNING OBJECTIVES

12-1   Plan a business presentation that accomplishes the speaker's goals and meets the audience's needs.

12-2   Organize and develop the three parts of an effective presentation.

12-3   Select, design, and use presentation visuals effectively.

12-4   Deliver speeches with increasing confidence.

12-5   Discuss strategies for presenting in alternate delivery situations such as culturally diverse audiences, teams, and distance presentations.

CHAPTER OUTLINE

ASSIGNMENTS AND ACTIVITIES

Read

1. Assign students to read the following article, which offers suggestions for developing business presentations for an international audience: St. Amant K. R. (2005, May). Presentations for international audiences, *Intercom*, 13–15. Available from Business Source Complete Database.

   After they've read the article, have students prepare a grid that compares presentation practices appropriate for audiences of the same culture as compared to international audiences. They should research further as necessary to complete the informational comparison. **(Obj. 1–5)**

Write

2. Have students read the presentation code of ethics for professional communicators and a related article: International Association of Business Communicators (IABC): IABC code of ethics for professional communicators. Available at **www.iabc.com/about /code.htm**; Zielinski, D. (2002, August 10). The presenter's pledge: Do presenters need a code of conduct? *Presentations, 16* (8), 24+. Available at **http://www .trainingmag.com/article/ presenters-pledge**.

   After they've read the articles, ask students to consider the ethical challenges presenters face and the behavioral guideposts presented in these readings. Have them write their own presenter's pledge to ensure honesty and integrity in their professional presentations. Students should also be prepared to explain to the rest of the class their rationale for the actions included. **(Obj. 1–5)**

Think

3. Assign students to evaluate the speaking skill of a well-known television newscaster, political figure, or a recognized speaker on your campus. Propose students locate a Webcast or podcast of their most admired CEO or company spokesperson at the company Web site or at the *Wall Street Journal online* or *BusinessWeek Online*. What are the strengths and weaknesses? Students can use the "Check Your Communication" checklist on their Review Cards to direct their attention to the various components of effective speaking. Ask each student to draft a proposal offering suggestions for improving the person's spoken communication skills, including paying special attention to vocal qualities, audience eye contact, audience rapport, and organization. **(Obj. 1–5)**

Speak

4. Provide students with specific instructions for presenting a proposal to management. Each student should select a topic from the following list of suggested proposals topics or use them as a springboard for other in-house presentations. **(Obj. 1–5)**

   a. Proposal to develop a policy that provides up to five paid days annually for volunteer work.

   b. Proposal to implement an in-house recycling program.

   c. Proposal to a local business to enhance the customer experience without increasing costs.

   d. Proposal to the board of directors to forge a strategic alliance with another company. Choose two likely companies and present the concept and the benefits that could be derived for each company.

   e. Proposal to extend your company's domestic retail market into an international market of your choice.

   f. Proposal to management for creating a joint venture with another company to offer a business-to-business (B2B) exchange for online commerce and supply-chain services.

      Choose two feasible companies that could take advantage of the benefits of supply-chain management (e.g., HomebuildersXchange links suppliers, distributors, and trade contractors and builders to bring efficiencies to every participant in the construction process).

Collaborate

5. Divide the class into small groups and ask each student to present a one- to two-minute presentation to his or her group explaining a key concept or new development in his or her career field. You should offer a brief period of time for preparation; however, the purpose of the activity is to prepare for impromptu spoken presentations. After all presentations are given, ask each group to briefly discuss the strengths and weaknesses of each presentation and provide each member with a few specific suggestions for improvement in delivering an impromptu presentation. **(Obj. 1, 2, 4, & 5)**

DIGGING DEEPER

Ask students to respond to the following discussion questions.

1. What is the single most important piece of advice you would give for making an effective business presentation?

2. With current advancements in technology, how has the business presenter's role been simplified? How has it become more difficult?

3. How does the advice "communicate a lot, using as little as possible" relate to the design of presentation visuals? Provide an example to support your point.

KEY CONCEPTS

Chapter 13 aids students in seeing the need for career planning, gathering information for inclusion on a résumé, and arranging the information on paper or for electronic distribution. Additionally, students learn to use traditional and electronic means to identify career opportunities and prospective employers to whom the résumé might be sent. The chapter discusses principles for writing a persuasive résumé using appropriate organizational patterns, and it explores alternate delivery options for résumés, including text formats, scannable versions, electronic postings, and YouTube video résumés. The chapter also presents techniques for writing effective application messages.

CONCEPTUAL FIGURES AND TABLES

Figure 13-1   Process of Applying for a Job

MODEL DOCUMENT FIGURES

Figure 13-2   Chronological Résumé
Figure 13-3   References Page
Figure 13-4   Functional Résumé
Figure 13-5   Scannable Résumé
Figure 13-6   Electronic Portfolio Posted to an Applicant's Personal Web Site
Figure 13-7   Example of an Application Letter
Figure 13-8   Example of Application Message Sent by Email

POWERPOINT HIGHLIGHTS

Lecture Presentation

Slide 3   Process of Applying for a Job
Slide 6   Standard Résumé Parts
Slide 7   Preparing a Print (Designed) Résumé
Slide 11   Preparing a Scannable Résumé
Slide 12   Making a Résumé Search Friendly
Slide 16   Preparing Effective Application Messages

Resource Presentation

The Instructor Manual contains a menu of resource slides you can integrate into your lecture presentation. Select from a variety of slides with examples, short quizzes, activities, and supplemental information to customize your lecture slide deck to meet the needs of your students and your course.

LEARNING OBJECTIVES

13-1 Prepare for employment by considering relevant information about yourself as it relates to job requirements.

13-2 Identify career opportunities using traditional and electronic methods.

13-3 Prepare an organized, persuasive résumé that is adapted for print and electronic postings.

13-4 Use employment tools other than the résumé that can enhance employability.

13-5 Write an application message that effectively introduces an accompanying print (designed) or electronic résumé.

CHAPTER OUTLINE

ASSIGNMENTS AND ACTIVITIES

Read

1. Have students watch the YouTube video that provides résumé tips entitled "How to Write a Great Resume and Cover Letter" created by Harvard Extension. Available at **www.youtube.com /watch?v=PAthQKLhBTs** Afterward, ask students to prepare their own résumés for a job posting in their preferred career field. **(Obj. 3 & 4)**

Write

2. Tell students to imagine a networking contact asked them to email their résumés for a potential opening in his firm. Each student should prepare an abbreviated version of an application letter and email to you the application message with an inline résumé positioned below the letter. Remind students to use a subject line that stands out in an overloaded mailbox as an expected message from a known person. **(Obj. 5)**

Think

3. Ask students to exchange résumés with another class member. Each should critique the document's effectiveness using the guidelines and examples provided in the chapter. Ask students to send their critiques to their partners via email. The emails should contain their overall impressions of the résumés and specific suggestions for improving them. **(Obj. 3)**

Speak

4. Have each student prepare a class presentation that will showcase his or her employment strengths. They may need to assemble a series of materials in a career portfolio. Suggest they emphasize preparation, experiences, and skills that have prepared them for their ideal career positions. **(Obj. 3–5)**

Collaborate

5. Divide the class into small groups, and ask each one to assume the role of a student organization that is initiating an online monthly recruiting newsletter for the organization's Web site. The vision is to create a fresh, personalized approach to career information specifically related to the needs of the members of the organization and the current competitive market. Each newsletter will include at least one article addressing specific job search skills, highlights of special recruiting events and previews of upcoming events, and an interview providing insights from an employer, returning co-op students, campus recruiters, etc. Students should prepare a one-page issue of the newsletter, after which they should email a copy to you and distribute it to the rest of the class. **(Obj. 1–5)**

DIGGING DEEPER

Ask students to respond to the following discussion questions.

1. Explain the rise in popularity of the "Career Summary" section on résumés. How else have résumés changed in recent years?

2. Is it possible for a candidate to "try too hard" when preparing a résumé? Explain your answer.

KEY CONCEPTS

Because it is probably the type of interview most familiar and of most concern to students, the employment interview receives primary emphasis in Chapter 14. Additionally, employment interviews are a logical continuation of the résumé and application-message topics in Chapter 13. Students are exposed to traditional interviews, as well as more contemporary techniques including computer-assisted, stress, series, and virtual interviews. The chapter gives special attention to preparation for interviews, interview behavior and feedback techniques (paraphrasing and questioning), and dress and grooming.

CONCEPTUAL FIGURES AND TABLES

Figure 14-1 Skills Needed: Balance of Soft and Hard Skills

MODEL DOCUMENT FIGURES

Figure 14-2 Example of a Follow-Up Letter
Figure 14-3 Example of a Thank-You Message
Figure 14-4 Example of a Job-Acceptance Message
Figure 14-5 Example of a Job-Refusal Message
Figure 14-6 Example of a Resignation Message
Figure 14-7 Example of a Thank-You Message to a Reference

POWERPOINT HIGHLIGHTS

Lecture Presentation

Slide 4   Preparing for an Interview
Slide 9   Exchanging Information
Slide 10   Standard Interview Questions
Slide 13   Sample Interviewee Questions
Slide 16   Other Employment Messages

Resource Presentation

The Instructor Manual contains a menu of resource slides you can integrate into your lecture presentation. Select from a variety of slides with examples, short quizzes, activities, and supplemental information to customize your lecture slide deck to meet the needs of your students and your course.

LEARNING OBJECTIVES

14-1 Explain the nature of structured, unstructured, stress, group, and virtual interviews.

14-2 Explain the steps in the interview process.

14-3 Prepare effective answers to questions often asked in job interviews, including illegal interview questions.

14-4 Compose effective messages related to employment (including application, follow-up, thank-you, job-acceptance, job-refusal, resignation, and recommendation request messages).

CHAPTER OUTLINE

KEY TERMS

ASSIGNMENTS AND ACTIVITIES

Read

1. Each year, many workers from every career field find themselves out of work. The process of becoming reemployed can be stressful, to say the least. Have students locate the following article that presents strategies for surviving a job termination and successfully becoming re-employed: Lim, F. (2007, March 28). What to do after job termination. Ezine Articles. Available at **http://ezinearticles.com/?What-to-Do-After-Job-Termination&id=506760**.

   Using the information in the article, ask students to develop checklists of strategies for locating and landing a desirable job. They should also add additional strategies of their own and submit the checklists to you. **(Obj. 1–4)**

Write

2. Ask students to assume that they have each applied for a position earlier in the class term. They should assume one of the following about the position: (a) it is an immediate part-time job, (b) it is a full-time job for next summer, (c) it is a cooperative education assignment or internship, or (d) it is a full-time job that begins immediately after graduation. Students should write follow-up letters to their applications, with special mention of the courses they have completed this term. **(Obj. 4)**

Think

3. Ask students, either in small groups or individually, to research a company of their choice. As a guide for their research, they should use the chapter information in the "Study the Company" section and the following article: "Why Finding the Right Job Fit Is So Important" posted on America's Job Exchange Web site. Available at **www.americasjobexchange.com/career-advice/right-job-fit**. or group should generate a list of 10 questions to ask an interviewer from the company. The questions should communicate initiative, intelligence, and genuine interest in the company and the job. Have each student or group submit a memo to you that summarizes important facts about the organization and shows the rationale for the selection of the questions. **(Obj. 2 & 3)**

Speak

4. Assign each student to interview a manager, preferably in his or her field, who conducts job interviews regularly. Instruct students to discuss techniques that will improve their interviewing techniques. Students can prepare short presentations to share their findings with the class. Alternatively, you can require them to contribute to a blog related to job interview strategies. **(Obj. 2 & 3)**

Collaborate

5. Divide students into small groups and ask each group to organize an employer panel for a class session on successful interviewing. The following elements should be included in the panel activity:

   a. Contact employers who would be willing to serve on the panel and share their views about successful job interviewing.

   b. In advance of the panel presentation, prepare a list of questions to be asked of the panel.

   c. Select a team member to serve as moderator for the panel discussion.

   d. As part of the panel discussion, solicit questions from the class for response by the guest employers. **(Obj. 1–4)**

DIGGING DEEPER

Ask students to respond to the following discussion questions.

1. How can a job applicant maximize the likelihood of accepting the "right" job?

2. Explain why communication skills are the universal job requirement.

3. How relevant are references when information about an applicant can be easily located through an online search of blogs, social networking sites, and news sources?

Decisions about page format impact the effectiveness of the message. Many companies have policies that dictate the page layout, letter and punctuation style, and other formatting issues. In the absence of company policy, make your format choices from among standard acceptable options illustrated on this style card.

PAGE LAYOUT, PUNCTUATION, AND LETTER STYLE

The default margins set by word processing software typically reflect the standard line length to increase the efficiency of producing business correspondence. Letters are balanced on the page with approximately equal margins on all sides of the letter, a placement often referred to as fitting the letter into a picture frame. Short letters (one or two paragraphs) are centered on the page; all other letters begin 2 inches from the top of the page. Side margins may be adjusted to improve the appearance of extremely short letters.

Current word processing software has increased the default line spacing and space between paragraphs for easier on-screen reading. If you prefer the tighter, traditional spacing, simply adjust the line spacing to 1.0. Also, to conserve space but keep the fresh, open look, try reducing the line spacing in the letter address but retaining the wider line and paragraph spacing in the body of the letter. Another new default is a crisp, open font such as Calibri (replacing the common Times New Roman) designed for easy reading on monitors.

New Document Look

July 24, 2014   **Tap Enter 2 times**

Mr. Bert A. Pittman

1938 South Welch Avenue

Northwood, NE 65432-1938   **Tap Enter 1 time**

Dear Mr. Pittman   **Tap Enter 1 time**

Your recent article, "Are Appraisers Talking to Themselves?" has drawn many favorable comments from local real estate appraisers.
          Tap Enter 1 time

The Southeast Chapter of the Society of Real Estate Appraisers . . .

Traditional Spacing

July 24, 2014   **Tap Enter 4 times (QS)**

Mr. Bert A. Pittman

1938 South Welch Avenue

Northwood, NE 65432-1938   **Tap Enter 2 times (DS)**

Dear Mr. Pittman   **Tap Enter 2 times (DS)**

Your recent article, "Are Appraisers Talking to Themselves?" has drawn many favorable comments from local real estate appraisers.
          Tap Enter 2 times (DS)

The Southeast Chapter of the Society of Real Estate Appraisers . . .

Punctuation Styles. Two punctuation styles are customarily used in business letters: mixed and open. Letters using mixed punctuation style have a colon after the salutation and a comma after the complimentary close. Letters using open punctuation style omit a colon after the salutation and a comma after the complimentary close. Mixed punctuation is the traditional style; however, efficiency-conscious companies are increasingly adopting the open style (and other similar format changes), which is easier to remember.

Letter Styles. Business letters are typically formatted in either block or modified block letter styles. The Sample Letters card has examples of these two styles:

- **Block.** Companies striving to reduce the cost of producing business documents adopt the easy-to-learn, efficient block format. All lines (including paragraphs) begin at the left margin.
- **Modified Block.** Modified block is the traditional letter format still used in many companies. The dateline, complimentary close, and signature block begin at the horizontal center of the page. Paragraphs may be indented one-half inch if the writer prefers or the company policy requires it. However, the indention creates unnecessary keystrokes that increase the production cost. All other lines begin at the left margin.

STANDARD LETTER PARTS

Professional business letters include seven standard parts. Other parts are optional and may be included when necessary.

1

Dateline. When the letterhead shows the company name, address, telephone and/or fax number, and logo, the letter begins with the **dateline.** Use the month-day-year format (September 2, 2014) for most documents prepared for U.S. audiences. When preparing government documents or writing to an international audience, use the day-month-year format (2 September 2014). Company policy may require another format.

2

Letter Address. The **letter address** includes a personal or professional title (e.g., Mr., Ms., or Dr.), the name of the person and company receiving the letter, and the complete address.

3

Salutation. The **salutation** is the greeting that opens a letter. To show courtesy for the receiver, include a personal or professional title (for example, Mr., Ms., Dr., Senator). Refer to the first line of the letter address to determine an appropriate salutation. "Dear Ms. Henson" is an appropriate salutation for a letter addressed to Ms. Donna Henson (first line of letter address). "Ladies and Gentlemen" is an appropriate salutation for a letter addressed to "Wyatt Enterprises," where the company name is keyed as the first line of the letter address.

4

Body. The **body** contains the message of the letter. Because extra space separates the paragraphs, paragraph indention, which requires extra setup time, is not necessary. However, for organizations that require paragraph indention as company policy, the modified block format with indented paragraphs is the appropriate choice.

5

Complimentary Close. The **complimentary close** is a phrase used to close a letter in the same way that you say good-bye at the end of a conversation. To create goodwill, choose a complimentary close that reflects the formality of your relationship with the receiver. Typical examples are "Sincerely," "Cordially," and "Respectfully." Using "yours" in the close has fallen out of popularity (as in "Sincerely yours" and "Very truly yours"). "Sincerely" is considered neutral and is thus appropriate in a majority of business situations. "Cordially" can be used for friendly messages, and "Respectfully" is appropriate when you are submitting information for the approval of another.

6

Signature Block. The *signature block* consists of the writer's name keyed below the complimentary close, allowing space for the writer to sign legibly. A woman may include a courtesy title to indicate her preference (e.g., Miss, Ms., Mrs.), and a woman or man may use a title to distinguish a name used by both men and women (e.g., Shane, Leslie, or Stacy) or initials (E. M. Goodman). A business or professional title may be placed on the same line with the writer's name or directly below it as appropriate to achieve balance.

Title on the Same Line	Title on the Next Line
Ms. Leslie Tatum, President	Ms. E. M. Goodman
Perry Watson, Manager	Assistant Manager
Quality Control Division Head	Richard S. Templeton
	Human Resources Director

7

Reference Initials. The *reference initials* consist of the keyboard operator's initials keyed in lowercase below the signature block. The reference initials and the signature block identify the persons involved in preparing a letter in the event of later questions. Reference initials are frequently omitted when a letter is keyed by the writer. However, company policy may require that the initials of all people involved in preparing a letter be placed in the reference initials line to identify accountability in the case of litigation. For example, the following reference initials show the indicated level of responsibility. The reference line might also include department identification or other information as required by the organization.

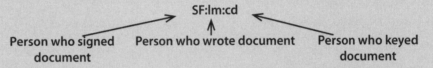

SF:lm:cd

Person who signed document   Person who wrote document   Person who keyed document

OPTIONAL LETTER PARTS

Delivery and Addressee Notations. A *delivery notation* provides a record of how a letter was sent. Examples include Air Mail, Certified Mail, Federal Express, Registered Mail, and Fax Transmission. Addressee notations such as Confidential or Personal give instructions on how a letter should be handled.

Attention Line. An *attention line* is used for directing correspondence to an individual or department within an organization while still officially addressing the letter to the organization. The attention line directs a letter to a specific person (Attention Ms. Laura Ritter), position within a company (Attention Human Resources Director), or department (Attention Purchasing Department). Current practice is to place the attention line in the letter address on the line directly below the company name and use the same format for the envelope address. The appropriate salutation in a letter with an attention line is "Ladies and Gentlemen."

Reference Line. A *reference line* (Re: Contract No. 983–9873) directs the receiver to source documents or to files.

Subject Line. A *subject line* tells the receiver what a letter is about and sets the stage for the receiver to understand the message. For added emphasis, use initial capitals or all capitals, or center the subject line if modified block style is used. Omit the word *subject* because its position above the body clearly identifies its function.

Second-Page Heading. The second and succeeding pages of multiple-page letters and memorandums are keyed on plain paper of the same quality as the letterhead. Identify the second and succeeding pages with a *second-page heading* including the name of the addressee, page number, and the date. Place the heading one inch from the top edge of the paper using either a vertical or horizontal format as illustrated. The horizontal format is more time-consuming to format but looks attractive with the modified block format and may prevent the document from requiring additional pages.

Vertical Format

Communication Systems, Inc.

Page 2

January 19, 2014

Horizontal Format

Communication Systems, Inc.   2   January 19, 2014

Company Name in Signature Block. Some companies prefer to include the *company name* in the signature block, but often it is excluded because it appears in the letterhead. The company name is beneficial when the letter is prepared on plain paper or is more than one page (the second page of the letter is printed on plain paper). Including the company name also may be useful to the writer wishing to emphasize that the document is written on behalf of the company (e.g., a letter establishing an initial customer contact).

Enclosure Notation. An *enclosure notation* indicates that additional items (brochure, price list, résumé) are included in the same envelope. Key the plural form (Enclosures) if more than one item is enclosed. You may identify the number of enclosures (Enclosures: 3) or the specific item enclosed (Enclosure: Bid Proposal). Avoid abbreviations (Enc.) that may give the impression that your work is hurried and careless and may show disrespect for the recipient. Some companies use the word *Attachment* on memorandums when the accompanying items may be stapled or clipped and not placed in an envelope.

Copy Notation. A *copy notation* indicates that a courtesy copy of the document was sent to the person(s) listed. Include the person's personal or professional title and full name after keying "c" for *copy* or "cc" for *courtesy copy*. Key the copy notation below the enclosure notation, reference initials, or signature block (depending on the optional letter parts used).

Postscript. A *postscript*, appearing as the last item in a letter, is commonly used to emphasize information. A postscript in a sales letter, for example, is often used to restate the central selling point; for added emphasis, it may be handwritten or printed in a different color. Often handwritten postscripts of a personal nature are added to personalize the printed document. Postscripts should not be used to add information inadvertently omitted from the letter. Because its position clearly labels this paragraph as a postscript, do not begin with "PS."

Computer File Notation. A *computer file notation* provides the path and file name of the letter. Some companies require this documentation on the file copy to facilitate revision. Place the computer file notation a single space below the last keyed line of the letter.

Block Letter Style with Open Punctuation

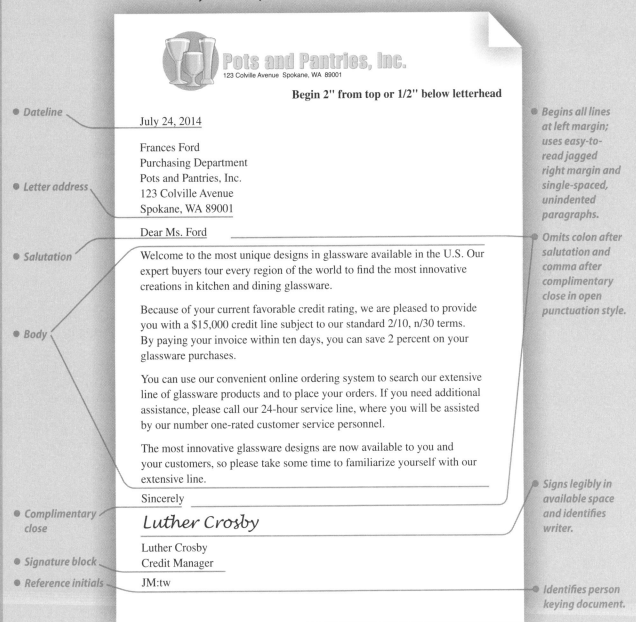

Dateline

• **Begins all lines at left margin; uses easy-to-read jagged right margin and single-spaced, unindented paragraphs.**

Pots and Pantries, Inc.
123 Colville Avenue Spokane, WA 89001

Begin 2" from top or 1/2" below letterhead

July 24, 2014

Letter address

Frances Ford
Purchasing Department
Pots and Pantries, Inc.
123 Colville Avenue
Spokane, WA 89001

Salutation

Dear Ms. Ford

• **Omits colon after salutation and comma after complimentary close in open punctuation style.**

Body

Welcome to the most unique designs in glassware available in the U.S. Our expert buyers tour every region of the world to find the most innovative creations in kitchen and dining glassware.

Because of your current favorable credit rating, we are pleased to provide you with a $15,000 credit line subject to our standard 2/10, n/30 terms. By paying your invoice within ten days, you can save 2 percent on your glassware purchases.

You can use our convenient online ordering system to search our extensive line of glassware products and to place your orders. If you need additional assistance, please call our 24-hour service line, where you will be assisted by our number one-rated customer service personnel.

The most innovative glassware designs are now available to you and your customers, so please take some time to familiarize yourself with our extensive line.

Complimentary close

Sincerely

Luther Crosby

• **Signs legibly in available space and identifies writer.**

Signature block

Luther Crosby
Credit Manager

Reference initials

JM:tw

• **Identifies person keying document.**

The document illustrates contemporary spacing with 1.15 spaces between lines. If using traditional single spacing (1.0), tap Enter 2 times to double-space between paragraphs and 4 times to quadruple space after the dateline and the complimentary close.

Modified Block Letter Style with Mixed Punctuation

Begin 2" from top or 1/2" below letterhead

October 15, 2014   **Tap Enter 2 times**

Mr. Saunders Greyson, Manager

Tropical Importers, Inc.

1240 Coastal Lane

Miami, FL 33140-1000   **Tap Enter 1 time**

Dear Mr. Greyson: **Tap Enter 1 time**

It was a pleasure meeting you at the career fair this morning. The opportunities offered in logistics management identifies your company as being a leader in today's international marketplace.   **Tap Enter 1 time**

My experience and knowledge of logistics management enable me to be a valuable asset to your company:

- Realistic international experience with a delivery company.

- Demonstrated commitment to developing an appreciation for international cultures and business practices.

- Excellent performance evaluations, including special recognition for troubleshooting transportation problems to remote locations.

          Tap Enter 1 time

Please message me so we can discuss my joining Tropical Importers.

          Tap Enter 1 time

          Sincerely,   **Tap Enter 2 times**
                              leaving space for signature

          Brandon Shaw

          Brandon Shaw

Document illustrates contemporary spacing. If using traditional spacing (1.0) between lines, tap Enter 2 times to double space between paragraphs and 4 times to quadruple space after the dateline and the complimentary close.

ENVELOPES

An envelope should be printed on the same quality and color of paper as the letter and generated using the convenient envelope feature of your word processing program. Adjust defaults as needed to adhere to the recommendations of the United States Postal Service (USPS). To increase the efficiency of mail handling, use the two-letter abbreviations for states, territories, and Canadian provinces. USPS official state abbreviations are available at **www.USPS.gov**.

Most companies today do not follow the traditional USPS recommendation to key the letter address in all capital letters with no punctuation. The mixed case format matches the format used in the letter address, looks more professional, and allows the writer to generate the envelope automatically without rekeying text. No mail handling efficiency is lost as today's optical character readers that sort mail can read both upper- and lowercase letters easily. Proper placement of the address on a large and a small envelope generated using an envelope template available with word processing software is shown here:

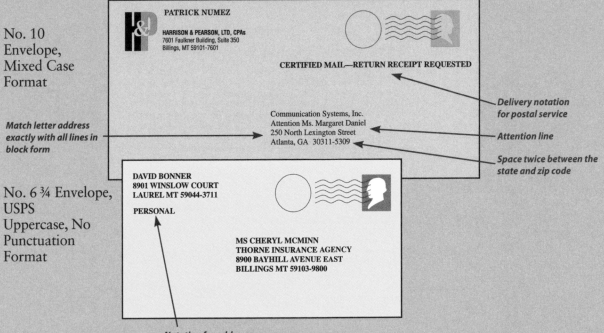

No. 10 Envelope, Mixed Case Format

Match letter address exactly with all lines in block form

PATRICK NUMEZ

HARRISON & PEARSON, LTD, CPAs
7601 Faulkner Building, Suite 350
Billings, MT 59101-7601

CERTIFIED MAIL—RETURN RECEIPT REQUESTED

Communication Systems, Inc.
Attention Ms. Margaret Daniel
250 North Lexington Street
Atlanta, GA 30311-5309

Delivery notation for postal service

Attention line

Space twice between the state and zip code

No. 6 ¾ Envelope, USPS Uppercase, No Punctuation Format

DAVID BONNER
8901 WINSLOW COURT
LAUREL MT 59044-3711

PERSONAL

MS CHERYL MCMINN
THORNE INSURANCE AGENCY
8900 BAYHILL AVENUE EAST
BILLINGS MT 59103-9800

Notation for addressee

Additionally, to create a highly professional image, business communicators should fold letters to produce the fewest number of creases. Here are the proper procedures for folding letters for large (No. 10) and small (6¾) envelopes:

Folding and Inserting Procedures for Large Envelopes

Step 1
With letter face up, fold slightly less than 1/3 of sheet up toward top.

Step 2
Fold down top of sheet to within 1/2 inch of bottom fold.

Step 3
Insert letter into envelope with last crease toward bottom of envelope.

Folding and Inserting Procedures for Small Envelopes

Step 1
With letter face up, fold bottom up to 1/2 inch from top.

Step 2
Fold right third to left.

Step 3
Fold left third to 1/2 inch from last crease.

Step 4
Insert last creased edge first.

MEMORANDUM FORMATS

To increase productivity of memorandums (memos), which are internal messages, companies use formats that are easy to input and that save time. Most companies use customized or standard memo templates found in most word processing software that include the basic headings (TO, FROM, DATE, SUBJECT) to guide the writer in providing the needed transmittal information. Memos may be printed on memo forms, plain paper, or letterhead depending on the preference of the company. Follow the guidelines for formatting a memo illustrated here.

Begin 2" from top of page or 1/2" below letterhead

TO: Sandra Linkletter, President

FROM: Donald Worthy, Sales Manager

DATE: April 1, 2014

SUBJECT: Monthly Sales Report, Appliance Department

Sales for the month remained at about the same level as previous months this year at $23,819. Sales figures for the month by item are as follows:

Item	Quantity Sold	Total Revenue from Sales ($)
Washers	12	5,102
Dryers	11	6,543
Stoves	8	4,276
Refrigerators	10	5,899
Dish Washers	6	1,989

Marketing

This month, we continued to publish a circular, which was distributed each Thursday in the *News Tribune*. The cost of that circular is $2,400 per month. That was our only cost of advertising and marketing. Please see the attached file for a complete breakdown of the departments' costs and sales for the month.

Staffing

We continue to employ two full-time salespeople on the floor and two part-time salespersons to cover the weekend shift. Current staffing levels are sufficient for the current sales volume, but if the home construction sector improves, we expect appliance sales to increase along with that improvement. If this occurs, we will need to hire an additional full-time and part-time sales person to return to our 2008 employment numbers.

Future Plans

We are continuing to look at ways that we might increase our marketing presence in the local community. One suggestion offered by Dale, one of our full-time sales persons, is to have a weekly promotion that runs as a banner on our web page. We could institute this opportunity storewide and have banners for the other departments running randomly with ours throughout the week. The cost of such a promotional program storewide needs to be calculated; perhaps this is something that we might put on our agenda for next week's managers' meetings.

Attachment

STYLECARD FORMAL REPORT

FORMAL REPORT FORMAT

Page arrangement for reports varies somewhat, depending on the documentation style guide followed or individual company preferences. Take advantage of your software's automatic formatting features for efficient formatting and generating report parts. Portions of a sample report are shown below.

Margins. For formal reports, use one-inch side margins. If the report is to be bound, increase the left margin by one-half inch. Use a two-inch top margin for the first page of each report part (table of contents, executive summary) and a one-inch top margin for all other pages. Leave at least a one-inch bottom margin on all pages.

Spacing. While documentation style guides typically specify double spacing of text, company practice is often to single-space reports. Double spacing accommodates editorial comments and changes but results in a higher page count. Even if you choose to double-space the body of a report, you may opt to single-space some elements, such as the entries in your references page and information in tables or other graphic components.

Headings. Several levels of headings can be used throughout the report and are typed in different ways to indicate level of importance. Suggested formatting guidelines for a report divided into three levels are illustrated in the document on the next page. Develop fourth- and fifth-level headings simply by using boldface, underline, and varying fonts.

Formal Report Parts

Title page

Transmittal document

Table of contents

Executive summary

First page of report

Page with graphic

References in APA style

Appendix

Report Format Using Preset Styles

- Capitalizes all letters in report title.

- Places first- and second-level headings at left margin and capitalizes initial letters. Larger font size makes the first level stand out.

- Includes intervening text between first- and second level headings.

- Uses default indentation and decreased spacing between enumerated and bulleted items.

- Places third-level subheadings at left margin and capitalizes first letter.

Format Pointers

This report document illustrates Word 2013 Style Set with style formats applied for the report title, the three heading levels, and the enumerated list. Creating a custom style set allows businesses to create a report style that is consistent with their company image and brand.

The increased spacing after each paragraph eliminates the need for indented paragraphs.

2" top margin

REPORT TITLE Title style (26-point Cambria font)

Tap Enter 1 time

xxx xxxxxx xxxxxxx xxxxx xxxxxxxxx xxxx xxxxx xxxxx xxxxxxx xxxxx xx xxxxxx xxxx x xxxxx xxxxx xxxxxxxxxx xxx xxxx xxxxx xxxxx.

Tap Enter 1 time

First-Level Heading Heading 1 (14-point Cambria font)

Tap Enter 1 time

xxx xxxxxx xxxxxxx xxxxx xxxxxxxxx xxxx xxxxx xxxxx xxxxxxx xxxxx xx xxxxxx xxxx x xxxxx xxxxx xxxxxxxxxx xxx xxxx xxxxx xxxxx.

Tap Enter 1 time

Second-Level Subheading Heading 2 (13-point Cambria font)

Tap Enter 1 time

xxx xxxxxx xxxxxxx xxxxx xxxxxxxxx xxxx xxxxx xxxxx xxxxxxx xxxxx xx xxxxxx xxxx x xxxxx xxxxx xxxxxxxxxx xxx xxxx xxxxx xxxxx.

Tap Enter 1 time

1. xxxx x xxxxxx xx xxxxxx xxxx xxx xxxxxxxxx xx xxxxx xxxxx xx. xx xxxx xxx. Space automatically reduced between enumerated items.

2. xxxx x xxxxxx xx xxxxxx xxxx xxx xxxxxxxxx xx xxxxx xxxxx xx. xx xxxx xxx xxxxx xxxx xx x xxxxxxxxxx.

Tap Enter 1 time

Second-Level Subheading

Tap Enter 1 time

xxx xxxxxx xxxxxxx xxxxx xxxxxxxxx xxxx xxxxx xxxxx xxxxxxx xxxxx xx xxxxxx xxxx x xxxxx xxxxx xxxxxxxxxx xxx xxxx xxxxx xxxxx.

Tap Enter 1 time

Heading 3 (11-point Cambria font)

Third-Level Subheading. xxx xxxxxx xxxxxxx xxxxx xxxxxxxxx xxxx xxxxxx xxxxx xxxxxxx xxxxx xx xxxxxx xxxx x xxxxx xxxxx xxxxxxxxxx xxx xxxx xxxxx xxxxx.

Tap Enter 1 time

Third-Level Subheading. xxx xxxxxx xxxxxxx xxxxx xxxxxxxxx xxxx xxxxxx xxxxx xxxxxxx xxxxx xx xxxxxx xxxx x xxxxx xxxxx xxxxxxxxxx xxx xxxx xxxxx xxxxx.

A number of widely used reference styles are available for documenting the sources of information used in report writing. Two of the more popular style manuals for business writing are as follows:

Publication Manual of the American Psychological Association, 6th ed., Washington, DC: American Psychological Association, 2001.

Joseph Gibaldi, *MLA Handbook for Writers of Research Papers*, 7th ed., New York: Modern Languages Association of America, 2003. The *MLA Handbook* is designed for high school and undergraduate college students; the *MLA Style Manual and Guide to Scholarly Publishing*, 2nd ed. (1998) is designed for graduate students, scholars, and professional writers.

These sources, commonly referred to as the APA and MLA styles, provide general rules for referencing and give examples of the citation formats for various types of source materials. This style card reflects the rules along with examples for the MLA style. Whenever you are not required to use a particular documentation style, choose a recognized one and follow it consistently. Occasionally, you may need to reference something for which no general example applies. Choose the example that is most like your source and follow that format. When in doubt, provide more information, not less. Remember that a major purpose for listing references is to enable readers to retrieve and use the sources. This style card illustrates citation formats for some common types of information sources and refers you to various electronic sites that provide further detailed guidelines for preparing electronic citations.

IN-TEXT PARENTHETICAL CITATIONS

The *MLA Handbook* supports the use of ***in-text citations***. Abbreviated information within parentheses in the text directs the reader to a list of sources at the end of a report. The list of sources at the end contains all bibliographic information on each source cited in a report. This list is arranged alphabetically by the author's last name or, if no author is provided, by the first word of the title.

The in-text citations contain minimal information needed to locate the source in the complete list. The *MLA* style includes the author's last name and the page number for both quotes and paraphrases, but not the date of publication. Note the format of the in-text parenthetical citations shown below.

One author not named in the text, direct quotation

"A recent survey . . . shows that more and more companies plan to publish their annual reports on the Internet" (Prinn 13).

Direct quotation, no page number on source

According to James, "traditional college students have a perspective that is quite different from adult consumers" (par. 2).

Use par. 2 *in place of missing page number only if paragraphs are numbered in original text.*

Multiple authors for sources not named in the text wording

Globalization is becoming a continuous challenge for managers . . . (Tang and Crofford 29).

"For all its difficulty, teamwork is still essential . . . " (Nunamaker et al. 163).

For sources by more than three authors, use et al. *after the last name of the first author or include all last names. Do not underline or italicize* et al.

More than one source documenting the same idea

. . . companies are turning to micromarketing (Heath 48; Roach 54).

More than one source by the same author documenting the same idea

Past research (Taylor, "Performance Appraisal" 6, "Frequent Absenteeism" 89) shows . . .

Reference to author(s) or date in the text wording

Kent Spalding and Brian Price documented the results . . .

In 2006, West concluded . . . (E2).

Omit a page number when citing a one-page article or nonprint source.

No author provided

. . . virtues of teamwork look obvious ("Teams Triumph in Creative Solutions" 61).

Include full title or shortened version of it.

WORKS CITED

The *works cited* page located at the end of your document contains an alphabetized list of the sources used in preparing a report, with each entry containing publication information necessary for locating the source. A researcher often uses sources that provide information but do not result in citations. If you want to acknowledge that you have consulted these works and provide the reader with a comprehensive reading list, include these sources in the list of works cited and refer to list as Works Consulted. Your company guidelines may specify whether to list works cited only or works consulted. If you receive no definitive guidelines, use your own judgment. If in doubt, include all literature cited and read, and label the page with the appropriate title so that the reader clearly understands the nature of the list.

To aid the reader in locating sources in lengthy bibliographies, you may include several subheadings denoting the types of publications documented, for example, books, articles, unpublished documents and papers, government publications, and nonprint media. Check your reference manual to determine if subheadings are allowed.

FORMATS FOR PRINT AND RECORDED REFERENCES

Reference styles for a variety of print and recorded sources prepared using the MLA style are shown in Figure 3. Note that the following rules apply for MLA works cited.

Indention and spacing	Begin first line of each entry at at left margin and indent subsequent lines one-half inch. While the MLA style manual specifies double spacing within and between entries, common practice in preparing reports is to single space each entry and double space between entries.
Author names	List last name first for first author only. Use "and" before final author's name.
Date	Place date at end of citation for books and after periodical title and volume **for articles. Months are abbreviated.**
Capitalization	In titles of books, periodicals, and article titles, capitalize all main words.
Italicizing and quotation marks	Italicize titles of books, journals, and periodicals (or underline if directed). Place titles of articles within quotation marks.
Page notations	Omit the use of *p.* or *pp.* on all citations.

MLA (7th Edition Style)

Writer's Last Name   5

Works Cited

"Best Business Attire." Executive Communications Group. 2003. 30 May 2006 <http://ecglink.com>.

Brody, Mary. "Dress codes: 'Business Conservative' is Making a Comeback." *HR Briefing* 1 Mar. 2003: 7.

Egodigwe, Laura, and Sonya Alleyne. "Here Come the Suits." *Black Enterprise Mar.* 2003: 59–60.

Hudson, Repps. "'Business Casual' on the Wane." *St. Louis Post Dispatch* 15 Apr. 2002. 30 May 2006
    <http://seattlepi.nwsource.com>.

Jones, Clark. "Experts Discuss Ways to Dress in Business Attire for Summer." *Las Vegas Review* 8 June 2003.

Business and Company Resource Center. University of Houston Lib. 29 July 2006 <http:bcrc.college.com/>.

Koestner, Maury. "What Exactly is Business Casual?" *The News-Herald 7* May 2005.

General Businessfile. Texas A & M lib. 31 May 2006 <http://www.epnet.com/>.

Molloy, John T. "Executives Find as Dress Gets Sloppier, Attitudes Slip." *The Houston Chronicle*
    9 December 2005: D2.

White, Ronald. D. "Clashing Dress Styles." *Careerbuilder* 26 Aug. 2001. 12 June 2006
    <http://www.latimes.com>.